YEAR 501

THE CONQUEST CONTINUES

Noam
Chomsky

South End Press ∙ Boston

Text design and layout by the South End Press collective.
Cover design by Birgitta McAlevey

Library of Congress Cataloging-in-Publication Data
Chomsky, Noam
Year 501: the conquest continues/Noam Chomsky
p. cm.
Includes bibliographical references (p.   ) and index.
ISBN 0-89608-445-0 : $30.00. — ISBN 0-89608-444-2 (pbk.) : $16.00
1. United States—Foreign relations—1945-1989. 2. United States-Foreign relations—1989- 3. World politics—1945- 4. Imperialism.
I. Title. II. Title: Year five hundred and one.
E840.C494 1992
327.73—dc20   92-37614
                                                                                          CIP

South End Press, 7 Brookline Street, #1, Cambridge, MA 02139-4146
      06 05 04 03   7 8 9 10 11

Table of Contents

Part I

Old Wine, New Bottles

CHAPTER 1

"THE GREAT WORK OF SUBJUGATION AND CONQUEST"

The year 1992 poses a critical moral and cultural challenge for the more privileged sectors of the world-dominant societies. The challenge is heightened by the fact that within these societies, notably the first European colony liberated from imperial rule, popular struggle over many centuries has achieved a large measure of freedom, opening many opportunities for independent thought and committed action. How this challenge is addressed in the years to come will have fateful consequences.

October 11, 1992 brings to an end the 500th year of the Old World Order, sometimes called the Colombian era of world history, or the Vasco da Gama era, depending on which adventurers bent on plunder got there first. Or "the 500-year Reich," to borrow the title of a commemorative volume that compares the methods and ideology of the Nazis with those of the European invaders who subjugated most of the world.[1] The major theme of this Old World Order was a confrontation between the conquerors and the conquered on a global scale. It has taken various forms, and been given different names: imperialism, neocolonialism, the North-South conflict, core versus periphery, G-7 (the 7 leading state capitalist industrial societies) and their satellites versus the rest. Or, more simply, Europe's conquest of the world.

By the term "Europe," we include the European-settled colonies, one of which now leads the crusade; in accord with South African conventions, the Japanese are admitted as "honorary whites," rich enough to (almost) qualify. Japan was one of the few parts of the South to escape conquest and, perhaps not coincidentally, to join the core, with some of its former colonies in its wake. That there may be more than coincidence in the correlation of independence and development is suggested further by a look at Western Europe, where parts that were colonized followed something like the Third World path. One notable example is Ireland, violently conquered, then barred from development by the "free trade" doctrines selectively applied to ensure subordination of the South—today called "structural adjustment," "neoliberalism," or "our noble ideals," from which we, to be sure, are exempt.[2]

"The discovery of America, and that of a passage to the East Indies by the Cape of Good Hope, are the two greatest and most important events recorded in the history of mankind," Adam Smith wrote in 1776: "What benefits, or what misfortunes to mankind may hereafter result from those great events, no human wisdom can foresee." But it was possible for an honest eye to see what had taken place. "The discovery of America...certainly made a most essential" contribution to the "state of Europe," Smith wrote, "opening up a new and inexhaustible market" that led to vast expansion of "productive powers" and "real revenue and wealth." In theory, the "new set of exchanges...should naturally have proved as advantageous to the new, as it certainly did to the old continent." That was not to be, however.

"The savage injustice of the Europeans rendered an event, which ought to have been beneficial to all, ruinous and destructive to several of those unfortunate countries," Smith wrote, revealing himself to be an early practitioner of the crime of "political correctness," to borrow some rhetoric of contemporary cultural management. "To the natives...both of the East and West Indies," Smith continued, "all the commercial benefits, which can have resulted from those events have been sunk and lost in the dreadful misfortunes which they have occasioned." With "the superiority of force" the Europeans commanded, "they were enabled to commit with impunity every sort of injustice in those remote countries."

Smith does not mention the indigenous inhabitants of North America: "There were but two nations in America, in any respect superior to savages [Peru, Mexico], and these were destroyed almost as soon as discovered. The rest were mere savages"—a convenient idea for the British conquerors, hence one that was to persist, even in scholarship, until the cultural awakening of the 1960s finally opened many eyes.

Over half a century later, Hegel discoursed authoritatively on the same topics in his lectures on philosophy of history, brimming with confidence as we approach the final "phase of World-History," when Spirit reaches "its full maturity and *strength*" in "the *German* world." Speaking from that lofty peak, he relates that native America was "physically and psychically powerless," its culture so limited that it "must expire as soon as Spirit approached it." Hence "the aborigines...gradually vanished at the breath of European activity." "A mild and passionless disposition, want of spirit, and a crouching submissiveness...are the chief characteristics of the native Americans," so "slothful" that, under the kind "authority of the Friars,"

"at midnight a bell had to remind them even of their matrimonial duties."
They were inferior even to the Negro, "the natural man in his completely
wild and untamed state," who is beyond any "thought of reverence and
morality—all that we call feeling"; there is "nothing harmonious with
humanity...in this type of character." "Among the Negroes moral senti-
ments are quite weak, or more strictly speaking non-existent." "Parents sell
their children, and conversely children their parents, as either has the
opportunity," and "The polygamy of the Negroes has frequently for its
object the having many children, to be sold, every one of them, into
slavery." Creatures at the level of "a mere Thing—an object of no value,"
they treat "as enemies" those who seek to abolish slavery, which has "been
the occasion of the increase of human feeling among the Negroes," enabling them to become "participant in a higher morality and the culture
connected with it."

The conquest of the New World set off two vast demographic catastrophes, unparalleled in history: the virtual destruction of the indigenous
population of the Western hemisphere, and the devastation of Africa as the
slave trade rapidly expanded to serve the needs of the conquerors, and the
continent itself was subjugated. Much of Asia too suffered "dreadful misfortunes." While modalities have changed, the fundamental themes of the
conquest retain their vitality and resilience, and will continue to do so until
the reality and causes of the "savage injustice" are honestly addressed.[3]

1. "The Savage Injustice of the Europeans"

The Spanish-Portuguese conquests had their domestic counterpart.
In 1492, the Jewish community of Spain was expelled or forced to convert.
Millions of Moors suffered the same fate. The fall of Granada in 1492, ending
eight centuries of Moorish sovereignty, allowed the Spanish Inquisition to
extend its barbaric sway. The conquerors destroyed priceless books and
manuscripts with their rich record of classical learning, and demolished the
civilization that had flourished under the far more tolerant and cultured
Moorish rule. The stage was set for the decline of Spain, and also for the
racism and savagery of the world conquest—"the curse of Columbus," in
the words of Africa historian Basil Davidson.[4]

Spain and Portugal were soon displaced from their leading role. The
first major competitor was Holland, with more capital than its rivals thanks
in large part to the control of the Baltic trade that it had won in the 16th
century and was able to maintain by force. The Dutch East India Company
(VOC), formed in 1602, was granted virtually the powers of a state,

including the right to make war and treaties. Technically, it was an independent enterprise, but that was an illusion. "The apparent autonomy from metropolitan political control that the VOC enjoyed," M.N. Pearson writes, resulted from the fact that "the VOC was identical with the state," itself controlled by Dutch merchants and financiers. In highly simplified form, we see already something of the structure of the modern political economy, dominated by a network of transnational financial and industrial institutions with internally managed investment and trade, their wealth and influence established and maintained by the state power that they mobilize and largely control.

"The VOC integrated the functions of a sovereign power with the functions of a business partnership," a historian of Dutch capitalism writes: "Political decisions and business decisions were made within the same hierarchy of company managers and officials, and failure or success was always in the last instance measured in terms of profit." The Dutch established positions of strength in Indonesia (to remain a Dutch colony until the 1940s), India, Brazil and the Caribbean, took Sri Lanka from Portugal, and reached to the fringes of Japan and China. The Netherlands, however, fell victim to what was later called "the Dutch disease": inadequate central state power, which left the people "rich perhaps, as individuals; but weak, as a State," as Britain's Lord Sheffield observed in the 18th century, warning the British against the same error.[5]

The Iberian empires suffered further blows as English pirates, marauders and slave traders swept the seas, perhaps the most notorious, Sir Francis Drake. The booty that Drake brought home "may fairly be considered the fountain and origin of British foreign investments," John Maynard Keynes wrote: "Elizabeth paid out of the proceeds the whole of her foreign debt and invested a part of the balance...in the Levant Company; largely out of the profits of the Levant Company there formed the East India Company, the profits of which...were the main foundations of England's foreign connections." In the Atlantic, the entire English operation prior to 1630 was a "predatory drive of armed traders and marauders to win by fair means or foul a share of the Atlantic wealth of the Iberian nations" (Kenneth Andrews). The adventurers who laid the basis for the merchant empires of the 17th-18th centuries "continued a long European tradition of the union of warfare and trade," Thomas Brady adds, as "the European state's growth as a military enterprise" gave rise to "the quintessentially European figure of the warrior-merchant." Later, the newly consolidated English state took over the task of "wars for markets" from "the plunder raids of Elizabethan sea-dogs" (Christopher Hill). The British East India Company was granted its charter in 1600, extended indefinitely in 1609, providing the Company with a monopoly over trade with the East on the authority of the British Crown. There followed brutal wars, frequently conducted with unspeakable barbarism, among the European rivals, drawing in native populations that were often caught up in their own internal struggles. In 1622, Britain drove the Portuguese from the straits of Hormuz, "the key of all India," and ultimately won that great prize. Much of the rest of the world was ultimately parcelled out in a manner that is well known.

Rising state power had enabled England to subdue its own Celtic periphery, then to apply the newly honed techniques with even greater savagery to new victims across the Atlantic. Their contempt for "the dirty, cowkeeping Celts on [England's] fringes" also eased the way for "civilised and prosperous Englishmen" to take a commanding position in the slave trade as "the gradient of contempt...spread its shadow from nearby hearts of darkness to those far over the sea," Thomas Brady writes.

From mid-17th century, England was powerful enough to impose the Navigation Acts (1651, 1662), barring foreign traders from its colonies and giving British shipping "the monopoly of the trade of their own country" (imports), either "by absolute prohibitions" or "heavy burdens" on others (Adam Smith, who reviews these measures with mixed reservations and approval). The "twin goals" of these initiatives were "strategic power and economic wealth through shipping and colonial monopoly," the *Cambridge Economic History of Europe* relates. Britain's goal in the Anglo-Dutch wars from 1652 to 1674 was to restrict or destroy Dutch trade and shipping and gain control over the lucrative slave trade. The focus was the Atlantic, where the colonies of the New World offered enormous riches. The Acts and wars expanded the trading areas dominated by English merchants, who were able to enrich themselves through the slave trade and their "plunder-trade with America, Africa and Asia" (Hill), assisted by "state-sponsored colonial wars" and the various devices of economic management by which state power has forged the way to private wealth and a particular form of development shaped by its requirements.[6]

As Adam Smith observed, European success was a tribute to its mastery of the means and immersion in the culture of violence. "Warfare in India was still a sport," John Keay observes: "in Europe it had become a science." From a European perspective, the global conquests were "small wars," and were so considered by military authorities, Geoffrey Parker writes, pointing out that "Cortés conquered Mexico with perhaps 500 Spaniards; Pizarro overthrew the Inca empire with less than 200; and the entire Portuguese empire [from Japan to southern Africa] was administered and defended by less than 10,000 Europeans." Robert Clive was outnumbered 10 to 1 at the crucial battle of Plassey in 1757, which opened the way to the takeover of Bengal by the East India Company, then to British rule over India. A few years later the British were able to reduce the numerical odds against them by mobilizing native mercenaries, who constituted 90 percent of the British forces that held India and also formed the core of the British armies that invaded China in the mid-19th century. The failure of the North American colonies to provide "military force towards the support of Empire" was one of Adam Smith's main reasons for advocating that Britain should "free herself" from them.

Europeans "fought to kill," and they had the means to satisfy their blood lust. In the American colonies, the natives were astonished by the savagery of the Spanish and British. "Meanwhile, on the other side of the world, the peoples of Indonesia were equally appalled by the all-destructive fury of European warfare," Parker adds. Europeans had put far behind them the days described by a 12th century Spanish pilgrim to Mecca, when "The warriors are engaged in their wars, while the people are at ease." The Europeans may have come to trade, but they stayed to conquer: "trade cannot be maintained without war, nor war without trade," one of the Dutch conquerors of the East Indies wrote in 1614. Only China and Japan were able to keep the West out at the time, because "they already knew the rules of the game." European domination of the world "relied critically upon the constant use of force," Parker writes: "It was thanks to their military superiority, rather than to any social, moral or natural advantage, that the white peoples of the world managed to create and control, however briefly, the first global hegemony in History."[7] The temporal qualification is open to question.

"Twentieth-century historians can agree that it was usually the Europeans who broke violently into Asian trading systems that had been relatively peaceful before their arrival," James Tracy writes, summarizing the scholarly study of merchant empires that he edited. They brought state trading to a region of relatively free markets, "open to all who came in peace, under terms that were widely known and generally accepted." Their violent entry into this world brought a "combination, characteristically if not uniquely European, of state power and trading interest, whether in the form of an arm of the state that conducts trade, or a trading company that behaves like a state." "The principal feature that differentiates European enterprises from indigenous trade networks in various parts of the globe," he concludes, is that the Europeans "organized their major commercial ventures either as an extension of the state...or as autonomous trading companies...which were endowed with many of the characteristics of a state," and were backed by the centralized power of the home country.

Portugal paved the way by extracting a tribute from Asian trade, "first creating a threat of violence to Asian shipping," then selling protection from the threat they posed while providing no further service in return: "in modern terms," Pearson notes, "this was precisely a protection racket." Portugal's more powerful European adversaries took over, with more effective use of violence and more sophisticated measures of management and control. The Portuguese had not "radically altered the structure of [the] traditional system of trade," but it was "smashed to pieces" by the Dutch. The English and Dutch companies "used force in a much more selective, in fact rational way" than their Portuguese predecessors: "it was used only for commercial ends...the bottom line was always the balance sheet." The force at their command, and its domestic base, was far superior as well. The British, not succumbing to the "Dutch disease," largely displaced their major rivals. The leading role of state power and violence is a notable feature in the "essential" contribution of the colonies to "the state of Europe" that Adam Smith described, as in its internal development.[8]

Britain has been considered an exception to the crucial role of state power and violence in economic development; the British liberal tradition held this to be the secret of its success. The assumptions are challenged in a valuable reinterpretation of Britain's rise to power by John Brewer. Britain's emergence "as the military *Wunderkind* of the age" in the late 17th and early 18th centuries, exercising its authority "often brutally and barbarously" over subject peoples in distant lands, he concludes, coincided with an "astonishing transformation in British government, one which put muscle on the bones of the British body politic." Contrary to the liberal tradition, Britain in this period became a "strong state," "a fiscal-military state," thanks to "a radical increase in taxation" and "a sizable public administration devoted to organizing the fiscal and military activities of the state." The state became "the largest single actor in the economy," one of Europe's most powerful states "judged by the criteria of the ability to take pounds out of people's pockets and to put soldiers in the field and sailors on the high seas." "Lobbies, trade organizations, groups of merchants and financiers, fought or combined with one another to take advantage of the protection afforded by the greatest of economic creatures, the state."

During this period, the British tax rate reached a level twice as high as France (traditionally considered the over-centralized all-powerful state), and the discrepancy was widening. Public debt grew rapidly as well. By the end of the 18th century, taxes absorbed almost a quarter of per capita income, rising to over a third during the Napoleonic wars. "Judged both absolutely and comparatively, Britain was heavily taxed." The growth of tax receipts was over five times as high as economic growth in the period when the military *Wunderkind* emerged. Part of the reason was efficiency; to an extent unusual in Europe, tax collection was a central government function. Another factor was the greater legitimacy of the more democratic state. The role of "the largest economic actor in eighteenth-century Britain, namely the state," was not merely to conquer: rather, it acted to promote exports, limit imports, and in general pursue the protectionist import-substitution policies that have opened the way to industrial "take-off" from England to South Korea.[9]

Excessive liberalism apparently contributed to the collapse of the Spanish imperial system. It was too open, permitting "merchants, often non-Spanish, to operate in the entrails of its empire" and allowing "the benefits to pass through and out of Spain." The Dutch, in contrast, kept the benefits "very firmly in the country," while "indigenous merchants were the empire and were the state," Pearson concludes. Britain pursued similar policies of economic nationalism, assigning rights to state-chartered monopolies, first (1581) for Turkey and the entire Middle East, then the rest of Asia and North America. In return for the grant of rights, the quasi-state companies provided regular payments to the Crown, an arrangement that would be replaced by more direct engagement of state power. As British trade and profit rapidly increased in the 18th century, government regulation remained important: "Less restrictions in the nineteenth century were a result of English dominance, not its cause," Pearson observes.

Adam Smith may have eloquently enumerated the harmful impact on the people of England of "the wretched spirit of monopoly," in his bitter condemnations of the East India Company. But his theoretical analysis was not the cause of its decline. The "honorable Company" fell victim to the confidence of British industrialists, particularly the textile manufacturers who had been protected from the "unfair" competition of Indian textiles, but called for deregulation once they convinced themselves that they could win a "fair competition," having undermined their rivals in the colonies by recourse to state power and violence, and used their new wealth and power for mechanization and improved supply of cotton. In contemporary terms, once they had established a "level playing field" to their incontestable advantage, nothing seemed more high-minded than an "open world" with no irrational and arbitrary interference with the honest entrepreneur, seeking the welfare of all.[10]

Those who expect to win the game can be counted on to laud the rules of "free competition"—which, however, they never fail to bend to their interests. To mention only the most obvious lapse, the apostles of economic liberalism have never contemplated permitting the "free circulation of labor...from place to place," one of the foundations of freedom of trade, as Adam Smith stressed.

There is little historical basis for much of the reigning belief on the impact of Adam Smith's doctrines; for example, Chicago economist George Stigler's assertion that Smith "convinced England" from 1850 to 1930 "of the merits of free international trade." What "convinced England"—more accurately, Englishmen who held the reins—was the perception that "free international trade" (within limits) would serve their interests; "it was not until 1846, by which time the British manufacturing interests were sufficiently powerful, that Parliament was prepared for the revolution" of free trade, Richard Morris notes. What convinced England of the contrary by 1930 was the realization that those days had passed. Unable to compete with Japan, Britain effectively barred it from trade with the Commonwealth, including India; the United States followed suit in its lesser empire, as did the Dutch. These were significant factors leading to the Pacific war, as Japan set forth to emulate its powerful predecessors, having naively adopted their liberal doctrines only to discover that they were a fraud, imposed upon the weak, accepted by the strong only when they are useful. So it has always been.[11]

Stigler may well be right, however, that Smith "certainly convinced all subsequent economists." If so, that is a comment on the dangers of illegitimate idealization that isolates some inquiry from factors that crucially affect its subject matter, a problem familiar in the sciences; in this case, separation of abstract inquiry into the wealth of nations from questions of power: Who decides, and for whom? We return to the point as Adam Smith himself understood it.

The wealth of the colonies returned to Britain, creating huge fortunes. By 1700, the East India Company accounted for "above half the trade of the nation," one contemporary critic commented. Through the following half-century, Keay writes, its shares became the "equivalent of a gilt-edged security, much sought after by trustees, charities and foreign investors." The rapid growth of wealth and power set the stage for outright conquest and imperial rule. British officials, merchants, and investors "amassed vast fortunes," gaining "wealth beyond the dreams of avarice" (Parker). That was particularly true in Bengal, which, Keay continues, "was destabilized and impoverished by a disastrous experiment in sponsored government"— one of the many "experiments" in the Third World that have not exactly redounded to the benefit of the experimental subjects. Two English historians of India, Edward Thompson and G.T. Garrett, described the early history of British India as "perhaps the world's high-water mark of graft": "a gold-lust unequalled since the hysteria that took hold of the Spaniards of Cortes' and Pizzaro's age filled the English mind. Bengal in particular was not to know peace again until she has been bled white." It is significant, they remark, that one of the Hindustani words that has become part of the English language is "loot."[12]

The fate of Bengal brings out essential elements of the global conquest. Calcutta and Bangladesh are now the very symbols of misery and despair. In contrast, European warrior-merchants saw Bengal as one of the richest prizes in the world. An early English visitor described it as "a wonderful land, whose richness and abundance neither war, pestilence, nor oppression could destroy." Well before, the Moroccan traveller Ibn Battuta had described Bengal as "a country of great extent, and one in which rice is extremely abundant. Indeed, I have seen no region of the earth in which provisions are so plentiful." In 1757, the same year as Plassey, Clive described the textile center of Dacca as "extensive, populous, and rich as the city of London"; by 1840 its population had fallen from 150,000 to 30,000, Sir Charles Trevelyan testified before the Select Committee of the House of Lords, "and the jungle and malaria are fast encroaching... Dacca, the Manchester of India, has fallen from a very flourishing town to a very poor and small town." It is now the capital of Bangladesh.

Bengal was known for its fine cotton, now extinct, and for the excellence of its textiles, now imported. After the British takeover, British traders, using "every conceivable form of roguery," "acquired the weavers' cloth for a fraction of its value," English merchant William Bolts wrote in 1772: "Various and innumerable are the methods of oppressing the poor weavers...such as by fines, imprisonments, floggings, forcing bonds from them, etc." "The oppression and monopolies" imposed by the English "have been the causes of the decline of trade, the decrease of the revenues, and the present ruinous condition of affairs in Bengal."

Perhaps relying on Bolts, whose book was in his library, Adam Smith wrote four years later that in the underpopulated and "fertile country" of Bengal, "three or four hundred thousand people die of hunger in one year." These are consequences of the "improper regulations" and "injudicious restraints" imposed by the ruling Company upon the rice trade, which turn "dearth into a famine." "It has not been uncommon" for Company officials, "when the chief foresaw that extraordinary profit was likely to be made by opium," to plough up "a rich field of rice or other grain...in order to make room for a plantation of poppies." The miserable state of Bengal "and of some other of the English settlements" is the fault of the policies of "the mercantile company which oppresses and domineers in the East Indies." These should be contrasted, Smith urges, with "the genius of the British constitution which protects and governs North America"—protects, that is, the English colonists, not the "mere savages," he fails to add.

The protection of the English colonists was actually a rather devious instrument. As Smith notes elsewhere, Britain "imposes an absolute prohibition upon the erection of slit-mills in any of her American plantations," and closely regulates internal commerce "of the produce of America; a regulation which effectually prevents the establishment of any manufacture of [hats, wools, woollen goods] for distant sale, and confines the industry of her colonists in this way to such coarse and household manufactures, as a private family commonly makes for its own use" or for its close neighbors. This is "a manifest violation of the most sacred rights of mankind," standard in the colonial domains.

Under Britain's Permanent Settlement of 1793 in India, land was privatized, yielding wealth to local clients and taxes for the British rulers, while "The settlement fashioned with great care and deliberation has to our painful knowledge subjected almost the whole of the lower classes to most grievous oppression," a British enquiry commission concluded in 1832, commenting on yet another facet of the experiment. Three years later, the director of the Company reported that "The misery hardly finds a parallel in the history of commerce. The bones of the cotton-weavers are bleaching the plains of India." The experiment was not a total failure, however. "If security was wanting against extensive popular tumult or revolution," the Governor-General of India, Lord Bentinck, observed, "I should say that the 'Permanent Settlement,' though a failure in many other respects and in most important essentials, has this great advantage, at least, of having created a vast body of rich landed proprietors deeply interested in the continuance of the British Dominion and having complete command over the mass of the people," whose growing misery is therefore less of a problem than it might have been. As local industry declined, Bengal was converted to export agriculture, first indigo, then jute; Bangladesh produced over half the world's crop by 1900, but not a single mill for processing was ever built there under British rule.[13]

While Bengal was despoiled, Britain's textile industry was protected from Indian competition; a matter of importance, because Indian producers enjoyed a comparative advantage in printed cotton textile fabrics for the expanding market in England. A British Royal Industrial Commission of 1916-1918 recalled that Indian industrial development was "not inferior to that of the more advanced European nations" when "merchant adventurers from the West" arrived; it may even be "that the industries of India were far more advanced than those of the West up to the advent of the industrial revolution," Frederick Clairmonte observes," citing British studies. Parliamentary Acts of 1700 and 1720 forbade the import of printed fabrics from India, Persia, and China; all goods seized in contravention of this edict were to be confiscated, sold by auction, and re-exported. Indian calicoes were barred, including "any garment or apparel whatsoever...in or about any bed, chair cushion, window curtain, or any other sort of household stuff or furniture." Later, British taxes also discriminated against local cloth within India, which was forced to take inferior British textiles.

Such measures were unavoidable, Horace Wilson wrote in his *History of British India* in 1826: "Had this not been the case, the mills of Paisley and Manchester would have been stopped in their outset, and could scarcely have been again set in motion, even by the power of steam. They were created by the sacrifice of Indian manufacturers." Economic historian J.H. Clapham concluded that "this restrictive act gave an important, and it may be argued a useful, stimulus to textile printing in Britain," a leading sector of the industrial revolution. By the 19th century, India was financing more than two-fifths of Britain's trade deficit, providing a market for British manufactures as well as troops for its colonial conquests and the opium that was the staple of its trade with China.[14]

"A significant fact which stands out is that those parts of India which have been longest under British rule are the poorest today," Jawaharlal Nehru wrote: "Indeed some kind of chart might be drawn up to indicate the close connection between length of British rule and progressive growth of poverty." In the mid-18th century, India was developed by comparative standards, not only in textiles. "The ship building industry was flourishing and one of the flagships of an English admiral during the Napoleonic wars had been built by an Indian firm in India." Not only textiles, but other well-established industries such as "ship-building, metal working, glass, paper, and many crafts," declined under British rule, as India's development was arrested and the growth of new industry blocked, and India became "an agricultural colony of industrial England." While Europe urbanized, India "became progressively ruralized," with a rapid increase in the proportion of the population dependent on agriculture, "the real, the fundamental cause of the appalling poverty of the Indian people," Nehru writes. In 1840, a British historian testifying before a Parliamentary Inquiry Committee could still say: "India is as much a manufacturing country as an agriculturalist; and he who would seek to reduce her to the position of an agricultural country, seeks to lower her in the scale of civilization," exactly what happened under Britain's "despotic sway," Nehru observes.[15]

Discussing "colonies as mercantile investments," Brazilian economic historian José J. de A. Arruda, concludes that the investments were indeed highly profitable, for some: the Dutch, French, and particularly the British, who also gained the advantages of Portugal's colonial assets; the slave traders, the merchants, the manufacturers; and the New England colonies whose development was spurred by triangular trade with Britain and the sugar colonies of the West Indies. "The colonial world...fulfilled its chief function as a link providing growth for the early accumulation of capital." It promoted "a transfer of colonial riches to the metropoles, which then fought for the appropriation of colonial surplus," contributing substantially to the economic growth of Europe. "THESE COLONIES DID PAY," he concludes. But, he adds, the calculations miss the main point: "profits went to individuals and costs were socialized." The "essence of the system" is "social losses" along with "the possibility of constant advance for capitalism" and for "the private coffers of the mercantilist bourgeoisie." In short, public subsidy, private profit; the expected thrust of policy when its architects are those who can expect to gain the profit.

As for those who lapsed into underdevelopment, Pearson raises but does not pursue the question whether there was "an alternative path to a status that could meet the European challenge," so that China, India, and others subjected to the European conquest might have been able to avoid "being incorporated as peripheries in the world economy, avoid being underdeveloped, avoid suffering as merchant empires turned into much more ominous territorial empires backed by an economically dominant Western Europe."[16]

In his classic condemnation of monopoly power and colonization, Adam Smith has useful commentary on Britain's policies, making some of the same points as Arruda. He describes these policies with some ambivalence, arguing finally that despite the great advantages that England gained from the colonies and its monopoly of their trade, in the long run the practices did not pay, either in Asia or North America. The argument is largely theoretical; adequate data were not available.

But however convincing the argument may be, Smith's discussion also explains why it is not to the point. Abandoning the colonies would be "more advantageous to the great body of the people" of England, he concludes, "though less so to the merchants, than the monopoly which she at present enjoys." The monopoly, "though a very grievous tax upon the colonies, and though it may increase the revenue of a particular order of men in Great Britain, diminishes instead of increasing that of the great body of the people." The military costs alone are a severe burden, apart from the distortions of investment and trade.

For the great body of people of England, the East India monopoly and the North American colonies may indeed have been the "absurdity" Smith claims, and "grievous" as well in their impact on the English colonists.

But for "the contrivers of this whole mercantile system," they were not absurd at all. "Our merchants and manufacturers have been by far the principal architects," and their interests have "been most peculiarly attended to" by the system, though not the interests of consumers and working people. The interests of the owners of the gilt-edged securities of the Company, and others who gained wealth beyond the dreams of avarice, were also "most peculiarly attended to." The costs were socialized, the profits poured into the coffers of the "principal architects." The policies they contrived were reasonable enough in terms of narrow self-interest, however others may have been harmed, including the general population of England.[17]

Smith's conclusion that "Under the present system of management, therefore, Great Britain derives nothing but loss from the dominion which she assumes over her colonies" is highly misleading. From the point of view of policy choices, Great Britain was not an entity. "The wealth of nations" is no concern of the "architects of policy," who, as Smith insists, seek private gain. The fate of the common people is no more their concern than that of the "mere savages" who stand in the way. If an "invisible hand" sometimes provided others with benefits, that is merely incidental. The basic focus on "wealth of nations" and what "Great Britain derives" is faulty from the start, undermined by illegitimate idealization, though at least it is qualified and corrected in Smith's fuller discussion.

The crucial qualifications have commonly been dropped, however, as they enter contemporary ideology in the hands of Smith's latter-day disciples. Thus in introducing the Chicago bicentennial edition of Smith's classic, George Stigler writes that "Americans will find his views on the American colonies especially instructive. He believed that there was, indeed, exploitation—but of the English by the colonists." What he actually believed was that there was exploitation of the English by the "particular order of men" in England who were the architects of policy in their own interest, and a "grievous tax" upon the colonies as well. By removing Smith's emphasis on the basic class conflict, and its crucial impact on policy, we falsify his views, and grossly misrepresent the facts, though constructing a useful instrument to mislead in the service of wealth and power. These are common features of contemporary discussion of international affairs. And of much else: condemnation of the harmful effects of the Pentagon system on the economy, for example, is at best extremely misleading if it does not emphasize that for the architects of policy and the interests they represent (notably, advanced sectors of industry), the effects have hardly been harmful.

Not surprisingly, social policy regularly turns out to be a welfare project for the rich and powerful. Imperial systems, in particular, are one of the many devices by which the poor at home subsidize their masters. And while studies of the cost effectiveness of empire and domination for "the nation" may have academic interest, they are only marginally relevant to the study of policy formation in societies in which the general public is expected to stand aside—that is, all existing societies.

The conclusions, however, are far more general. As indicated by the example of the Pentagon system, the same considerations apply to domestic as to international policy. State power has not only been exercised to enable some to reap wealth beyond the dreams of avarice while devastating subject societies abroad, but has also played a critical role in entrenching private privilege at home. In early modern Holland and England, the government provided the infrastructure for capitalist development, protected vulnerable and crucial production (wool, fisheries) and subjected them to close regulation, and used its monopoly of violence to impose wage labor conditions on formerly independent farmers. Centuries ago, "European societies were also colonized and plundered, less catastrophically than the Americas but more so than most of Asia" (Thomas Brady): "The rapid economic development yielded by the English path proved extremely destructive, both of traditional property rights at home and of institutions and cultures throughout the world." A process of "rural pacification" took place in the developing countries of Europe. "The massive expropriation of the peasantry, which happened in the fullest sense only in England," may well have been the basis for its more rapid economic development as peasants were deprived of property rights they managed to retain in France, and forced into the labor market; "it was precisely the absence of [freedom and property rights] that facilitated the onset of real economic development" in England, Robert Brenner argues in his penetrating inquiry into the origins of European capitalism. The common people had ample reasons to resist "the march of progress," or to seek to deflect it to a different path that sought to preserve and extend other values: "ideas of community, of togetherness, of the whole superseding the parts, and of the common good that transcends ever particular good" (Brady).

Such ideas animated the "vast communal movements" of pre-capitalist Europe, Brady writes, and "brought elements of self-government into the hands of the Common Man," arousing "contempt and sometimes fear in the traditional elites." The common people who sought freedom and the common good were "craftsmen of shit," "rabble" ("canaille") who should "die of starvation." They were condemned by the Emperor Maximilian as "wicked, crude, stupid peasants, in whom there is neither virtue, noble blood, nor proper moderation, but only immoderate display, disloyalty, and hatred for the German nation"—the "anti-Americans" of their day. The democratic upsurge in 17th century England evoked harsh denunciation of the "rascal multitude," "beasts in men's shapes," "depraved and corrupt." Twentieth century democratic theorists advise that "The public must be put in its place," so that the "responsible men" may "live free of the trampling and the roar of a bewildered herd," "ignorant and meddlesome outsiders" whose "function" is to be "interested spectators of action," not participants, lending their weight periodically to one or another member of the leadership class (elections), then returning to their private concerns (Walter Lippmann). The great mass of the population, "ignorant and mentally deficient," must be kept in their place for the common good, fed with "necessary illusion" and "emotionally potent oversimplifications" (Wilson's Secretary of State Robert Lansing, Reinhold Niebuhr). Their "conservative" counterparts are only more extreme in their adulation of the Wise Men who are the rightful rulers—in the service of the rich and powerful, a minor footnote regularly forgotten.[18]

The rabble must be instructed in the values of subordination and a narrow quest for personal gain within the parameters set by the institutions of the masters; meaningful democracy, with popular association and action, is a threat to be overcome. These too are persistent themes, that only take new forms.

Adam Smith's nuanced interpretation of state interference with international trade extended to the domestic scene as well. The praise in his opening remarks for "the division of labor" is well-known: it is the source of "the greatest improvement in the productive powers of labour, and the greater part of the skill, dexterity, and judgment with which it is any where directed, or applied," and the foundation of "the wealth of nations." The great merit of free trade, he argued, is that it contributes to these tendencies. Less familiar is his denunciation of the inhuman consequences of the division of labor as it approaches its natural limits. "The understandings of the greater part of men are necessarily formed by their ordinary employments," he wrote. That being so, "the man whose life is spent in performing a few simple operations, of which the effects too are, perhaps, always the same, or very nearly the same, has no occasion to exert his understanding...and generally becomes as stupid and ignorant as it is possible for a human creature to be... But in every improved and civilized society this is the state into which the labouring poor, that is, the great body of the people, must necessarily fall, unless government takes some pains to prevent it." Society must find some way to overcome the devilish impact of the "invisible hand."

Other major contributors to the classical liberal canon go much further. Wilhelm von Humboldt, who inspired John Stuart Mill, described the "leading principle" of his thought as "the absolute and essential importance of human development in its richest diversity," a principle that is not only undermined by the narrow search for efficiency through division of labor, but by wage labor itself: "Whatever does not spring from a man's free choice, or is only the result of instruction and guidance, does not enter into his very nature; he does not perform it with truly human energies, but merely with mechanical exactness"; when the laborer works under external control, "we may admire what he does, but we despise what he is."[19]

Smith's admiration for individual enterprise was tempered still further by his contempt for "the vile maxim of the masters of mankind": "All for ourselves, and nothing for other people." While the "mean" and "sordid" pursuits of the masters might yield incidental benefit, faith in this consequence is mere mysticism, quite apart from the more fundamental failure to comprehend the "leading principle" of classical liberal thought that Humboldt stressed. What survives of these doctrines in contemporary ideology is an ugly and distorted image, contrived in the interests of the masters.[20]

Centralized state power dedicated to private privilege and authority, and the rational and organized use of savage violence, are two of the enduring features of the European conquest. Others are the domestic colonization by which the poor subsidize the rich, and the contempt for democracy and freedom. Yet another enduring theme is the self-righteousness in which plunder, slaughter, and oppression are clothed.

A leading liberal figure lecturing at Oxford in 1840, with the spectacle of Bengal and the rest of India before him, lauded the "British policy of colonial enlightenment," which "stands in contrast to that of our ancestors," who kept their colonies "in subjection in order to derive certain supposed commercial advantages from them," whereas we "give them commercial advantages, and tax ourselves for their benefit, in order to given them an interest in remaining under our supremacy, that we may have the pleasure of governing them." We "govern them by sheer weight of character and without use of force," the virtual ruler of Egypt from 1883 to 1906, Lord Cromer, explained: this we can do because the British "possess in a very high degree the power of acquiring the sympathy and confidence of any primitive races with which they are brought into contact." His colleague Lord Curzon, Viceroy of India, proclaimed that "In the Empire we have found not merely the key to glory and wealth, but the call to duty, and the means of service to mankind." The early Dutch conquerors were sure that traders of all nations would flock to the VOC because "the good old free manner of our nation is highly praised." The Seal of the Governor and Company of Massachusetts Bay in 1629 depicts an Indian pleading "Come over and help us." The record to this day is replete with appeals to the divine will, civilizing missions, partnerships in beneficence, noble causes, and the like. Heaven must be full to overflowing, if the masters of self-adulation are to be taken at their word.[21]

Their labors are not unavailing. Among the educated classes, fairy tales of righteous mission and benevolence have long risen to the level of doctrinal truths, and much of the general public seems to believe them as well. In 1989, half the US public believed that foreign aid is the largest element in the federal budget of the country that had, by then, sunk to last place among the industrial countries, with foreign aid barely detectable in the budget and a niggardly 0.21 percent of GNP. Those who harken to their tutors may even believe that the next highest item is Cadillacs for welfare mothers.[22]

The subject peoples find odd ways to express their gratitude. To the leading figure of modern Indian nationalism, "the only possible parallel" to the Viceroy "would be that of Hitler." The ideology of British rule "was that of the herrenvolk and the master race," an idea "inherent in imperialism" that "was proclaimed in unambiguous language by those in authority" and manifested in practice, as Indians "were subjected to insult, humiliation, and contemptuous treatment." Writing from a British prison in 1944, Nehru was not unmindful of the benevolent intent of the rulers:

> The solicitude which British industrialists and economists have shown for the Indian peasant has been truly gratifying. In view of this, as well as of the tender care lavished upon him by the British Government in India, one can only conclude that some all-powerful and malign fate, some supernatural agency, has countered their intentions and measures and made that peasant one of the poorest and most miserable beings on earth.[23]

Nehru was something of an Anglophile. Others have been less genteel about the matter, though Western culture, having the guns and wealth, remains largely immune.

It would not be fair to charge that atrocities pass unmentioned. One of the most notorious slaughterers was King Leopold of Belgium, responsible for the death of perhaps 10 million people in the Congo. His contributions and defects were duly recorded in the *Encyclopaedia Britannica,* which describes the "enormous fortune" that he gained by "exploitation of this vast territory." The last line of the lengthy entry reads: "but he had a hard heart towards the natives of his distant possession." Half a century later, Alfred Cobban, in his *History of Modern France,* castigates Louis XVI for failing to protect France's interests in the West Indies. The slave trade on which these interests rested merits a parenthetical comment: "its morality as yet is barely the subject of discussion." True enough.[24]

Illustrations are not hard to find.

2. "Felling Trees and Indians"

The English colonists in North America pursued the course laid out by their forerunners in the home country. From the earliest days of colonization, Virginia was a center of piracy and pillage, a base to raid Spanish commerce and plunder French settlements on the coast of Maine—and to exterminate the "devil worshippers" and "cruel beasts" whose generosity had enabled the colonists to survive, hunting them down with savage dogs, massacring women and children, destroying crops, spreading smallpox with infected blankets, and other measures that readily came to the minds of barbarians fresh from their Irish exploits. North American pirates reached as far as the Arabian sea in the late 17th century. By then "New York had become a thieve's market where pirates disposed of loot taken on the high seas," Nathan Miller observes, while "corruption...was the lubricant that greased the wheels of the nation's administrative machinery"; "graft and corruption played a vital role in the development of modern American society and in the creation of the complex, interlocking machinery of government and business that presently determines the course of our affairs," Miller writes, ridiculing the great shock expressed at Watergate.[25]

As state power consolidated, private-sector violence was suppressed in favor of the more organized state form, though the US would not permit American citizens apprehended for slave trading to be judged by foreign courts. That was no small matter; the British navy was refused permission to search any American slaver, "and American naval vessels were almost never there to search her, with the result that most of the slave ships, in the 1850s, not only flew the American flag but were owned by American citizens." The US would not accept the standards proposed by Muammar Qaddafi, who urged in 1992 that charges concerning Libya's alleged terrorism be brought to the World Court or some other neutral tribunal, a proposal dismissed with disdain by Washington and the press, which have little use for instruments that might lapse into excessive independence.[26]

After the colonies gained their independence in the course of the great international conflict that pitted England against France, Spain, and Holland, state power was used to protect domestic industry, foster agricultural production, manipulate trade, monopolize raw materials, and take the land from its inhabitants. Americans "concentrated on the task of felling trees and Indians and of rounding out their natural boundaries," as diplomatic historian Thomas Bailey described the project in 1969.[27]

These tasks, and the rhetorical accompaniment, have been eminently reasonable by reigning standards of Political Correctness; the challenge to them in the past few years has, not surprisingly, elicited much outrage among guardians of doctrinal purity. Hugo Grotius, a leading 17th century humanist and the founder of modern international law, determined that the "most just war is against savage beasts, the next against men who are like beasts." George Washington wrote in 1783 that "the gradual extension of our settlements will as certainly cause the savage, as the wolf, to retire; both being beasts of prey, tho' they differ in shape." What is called in official PC rhetoric "a pragmatist," Washington regarded purchase of Indian lands (typically, by fraud and threat) as a more cost-effective tactic than violence. Thomas Jefferson predicted to John Adams that the "backward" tribes at the borders "will relapse into barbarism and misery, lose numbers by war and want, and we shall be obliged to drive them, with the beasts of the forests into the Stony mountains"; the same would be true of Canada after the conquest he envisioned, while all blacks would be removed to Africa or the Caribbean, leaving the country without "blot or mixture." A year after the Monroe Doctrine, the President called for helping the Indians "to surmount all their prejudices in favor of the soil of their nativity," so that "we become in reality their benefactors" by transferring them West. When consent was not given, they were forcibly removed. Consciences were eased further by the legal doctrine devised by Chief Justice John Marshall: "discovery gave an exclusive right to extinguish the Indian right of occupancy, either by purchase or by conquest"; "that law which regulates, and ought to regulate in general, the relations between the conqueror and conquered was incapable of application to…the tribes of Indians, …fierce savages whose occupation was war, and whose subsistence was drawn chiefly from the forest."

The colonists, to be sure, knew better. Their survival depended on the agricultural sophistication and generosity of the "fierce savages," and they were familiar with the prevailing norms of violence on all sides. Observing the Narragansett-Pequot wars, Roger Williams remarked that their fighting was "farre less bloudy and devouring than the cruell Warres of Europe," from which the colonists had learned their trade. John Underhill sneered at the "feeble Manner" of the Indian warriors, which "did hardly deserve the Name of fighting," and their laughable protests against the "furious" style of the English that "slays too many men"—not to speak of women and children in undefended villages, a European tactic that had to be taught to the backward natives. These were common features of the world conquest, as noted earlier.

The useful doctrines of Justice Marshall and others remained in place through modern scholarship. The highly regarded authority A.L. Kroeber attributed to the East Coast Indians a kind of "warfare that was insane, unending," inexplicable "from our point of view" and so "dominantly emphasized within [their culture] that escape was well-nigh impossible," for any group that would depart from these hideous norms "was almost certainly doomed to early extinction"—a "harsh indictment [that] would carry more weight," Francis Jennings observes, "if its rhetoric were supported by either example or reference," in this influential scholarly study. The Indians were hardly pacifists, but they had to learn the techniques of "total war" and true savagery from the European conquerors, with their ample experience in the Celtic regions and elsewhere.[28]

Respected statesmen continued to uphold the same values. To Theodore Roosevelt, the hero of George Bush and the liberal commentators who gushed over Bush's sense of "righteous mission" during the 1991 Gulf slaughter, "the most ultimately righteous of all wars is a war with savages," establishing the rule of "the dominant world races." The hideous and cowardly Sand Creek massacre in Colorado in 1864, Nazi-like in its bestiality, was "as righteous and beneficial a deed as ever took place on the frontier." This "noble minded missionary," as contemporary ideologues term him, did not limit his vision to the "beasts of prey" who were being swept from their lairs within the "natural boundaries" of the American nation. The ranks of savages included the "dagos" to the south, and the "Malay bandits" and "Chinese halfbreeds" who were resisting the American conquest of the Philippines, all "savages, barbarians, a wild and ignorant people, Apaches, Sioux, Chinese boxers," as their resistance amply demonstrated. Winston Churchill felt that poison gas was just right for use against "uncivilized tribes" (Kurds and Afghans, particularly). Noting approvingly that British diplomacy had prevented the 1932 disarmament convention from banning bombardment of civilians, the equally respected statesman Lloyd George observed that "we insisted on reserving the right to bomb niggers," capturing the basic point succinctly. The metaphors of "Indian fighting" were carried right through the Indochina wars. The conventions retain their vibrancy, as we saw in early 1991 and may again, before too long.[29]

The extraordinary potential of the United States was evident from the earliest days, and of no small concern to the guardians of established order. The Czar and his diplomats were concerned over "the contagion of revolutionary principles," which "is arrested by neither distance nor physical obstacles," the "vicious principles" of republicanism and popular self-rule already established in a part of North America. Metternich too warned of the "flood of evil doctrines and pernicious examples" that might "lend new strength to the apostles of sedition," asking "what would become of our religious institutions, of the moral force of our governments, and of that conservative system which has saved Europe from complete dissolution" if the flood is not stemmed. The rot might spread, to adopt the rhetoric of their heirs as they switched roles and took over the leadership of the conservative system in the mid-20th century.[30]

Flawed as they were, these doctrines and examples constituted a dramatic advance in the endless struggle for freedom and justice; the Wise Men of the time were right to fear their spread. Their 18th century advocates, however, were hardly apostles of sedition and did not delay in imposing their vision of "a political democracy manipulated by an elite" (Richard Morris), the old aristocracy and, in later years, the rising business classes: a "solid and responsible leadership seized the helm," as Morris puts it approvingly. The most dread fears were therefore quickly put to rest. The ex-revolutionaries were also not lacking in ambition. And like Metternich and the Czar, they feared the "pernicious examples" at their borders. Florida was conquered to remove the threat of "mingled hordes of lawless Indians and negroes," John Quincy Adams wrote with the enthusiastic approval of Thomas Jefferson, referring to runaway slaves and indigenous people who sought freedom from the tyrants and conquerors, setting a bad example. Jefferson and others advocated the conquest of Canada to cut off support for the native population by "base Canadian fiends," as the president of Yale University called them. Expansion to north and south was blocked by British power, but the annexation of the West proceeded inexorably, as its inhabitants were destroyed, cynically cheated, and expelled.[31]

"The task of felling trees and Indians and of rounding out their natural boundaries" required that the New World be rid of alien interlopers. The main enemy was England, a powerful deterrent, and the target of frenzied hatred in broad circles. The War for Independence itself had been a fierce civil war enmeshed in an international conflict; relative to population, it was not greatly different from the Civil War almost a century later, and it caused a huge exodus of refugees fleeing from the richest country in the world to escape the retribution of the victors. US-British conflict continued, including war in 1812. In 1837, after some Americans supported a rebellion in Canada, British forces crossed the border and set fire to the US vessel *Caroline,* eliciting from Secretary of State Daniel Webster a doctrine that has become the bedrock of modern international law: "respect for the inviolable character of the territory of independent states is the most essential foundation of civilization," and force may be used only in self-defense, when the necessity "is instant, overwhelming and leaving no other choice of means, and no moment of deliberation." The doctrine was invoked at the Nuremberg tribunal, for example, in rejecting the claim of the Nazi leaders that their invasion of Norway was justified to forestall Allied moves. We need waste no words on how the US has observed the principle since 1837.[32]

The US-British conflict was based on real interests: for the US, its desire to expand on the continent and in the Caribbean; for the dominant world power of the day, concern that the maverick across the seas was a threat to its wealth and power.

Though there was considerable sympathy in England for the rebel cause, the leaders of the newly independent country tended to see a different picture. Great Britain "hated and despised us beyond every earthly object," Thomas Jefferson wrote to Monroe in 1816, giving Americans "more reason to hate her than any nation on earth." Britain was not only an enemy of the United States, but "truly hostis humani generis," an enemy of the human race, he wrote to John Adams a few weeks later. "Taught from the cradles to scorn, insult and abuse us," Adams responded, "Britain will never be our friend till we are her master." Jefferson had proposed a different solution to Abigail Adams in 1785: "I fancy it must be the quantity of animal food eaten by the English," he speculated, "which renders their character insusceptible to civilization. I suspect it is in their kitchens and not their churches that their reformation must be worked." Ten years later, he expressed his fervent hope that French armies would liberate Great Britain, improving both its character and cuisine.[33]

The dislike was reciprocated, interlaced with no little contempt. In 1865 a progressive English gentleman offered to endow a lectureship at Cambridge University for American studies, to be filled every other year by a visitor from Harvard. Cambridge dons protested against what one called, with admirable literary flair, "a biennial flash of Transatlantic darkness." Some found the concerns exaggerated, recognizing that the lecturers would come from the class that felt itself "increasingly in danger of being swamped by the lower elements of a vast democracy." But most feared that the lectures would spread "discontent and dangerous ideas" among defenseless students. The threat was beaten back in a show of the kind of political correctness that continues to predominate in the academic world, as wary as ever of the lower elements and their strange ideas.[34]

Recognizing that England's military force was too powerful to confront, Jacksonian Democrats called for annexation of Texas to gain a world monopoly of cotton. The US would then be able to paralyze England and intimidate Europe. "By securing the virtual monopoly of the cotton plant" the US had acquired "a greater influence over the affairs of the world than would be found in armies however strong, or navies however numerous," President Tyler observed after the annexation and the conquest of a third of Mexico. "That monopoly, now secured, places all other nations at our feet," he wrote: "An embargo of a singlè year would produce in Europe a greater amount of suffering than a fifty years' war. I doubt whether Great Britain could avoid convulsions." The same monopoly power neutralized British opposition to the conquest of the Oregon territory.

The editor of the *New York Herald*, the country's largest-selling newspaper, exulted that Britain was "completely bound and manacled with the cotton cords" of the United States, "a lever with which we can success-fully control" this dangerous rival. Thanks to the conquests that provided a monopoly of the most important commodity in world trade, the Polk Administration boasted, the US could now "control the commerce of the world and secure thereby to the American Union inappreciable political and commercial advantages." "Fifty years will not elapse ere the destinies of the human race will be in our hands," a Louisiana congressman pro-claimed, as he and others looked to "mastery of the Pacific" and control over the resources on which Europe was dependent. Polk's Secretary of Treasury reported to Congress that the conquests of the Democrats would guarantee "the command of the trade of the world."

The national poet, Walt Whitman, wrote that our conquests "take off the shackles that prevent men the even chance of being happy and good." Mexico's lands were taken over for the good of mankind: "What has miserable, inefficient Mexico...to do with the great mission of peopling the New World with a noble race?" Others recognized the difficulty of taking Mexico's resources without burdening themselves with its "imbecile" pop-ulation, "degraded" by "the amalgamation of races," though the New York press was hopeful that their fate would be "similar to that of the Indians of this country—the race, before a century rolls over us, will become extinct." Articulating the common themes of manifest destiny, Ralph Waldo Emerson had written that the annexation of Texas was simply a matter of course: "It is very certain that the strong British race which has now overrun much of this continent, must also overrun that trace, and Mexico and Oregon also, and it will in the course of ages be of small import by what particular occasions and methods it was done." In 1829, Minister to Mexico Joel Poinsett, later Secretary of War responsible for driving the Cherokees to death and destruction on their Trail of Tears, had informed Mexico that "the United States are in a state of progressive aggrandizement, which has no example in the history of the world"; and rightly so, the slave-owner from

South Carolina explained, because "the mass of its population is better educated, and more elevated in its moral and intellectual character, than that of any other. If such is its political condition, is it possible that its progress can be retarded, or its aggrandizement curtailed, by the rising prosperity of Mexico?"

The concerns of the expansionists went beyond their fear that an independent Texas would break the US resource monopoly and become a rival; it might also abolish slavery, igniting dangerous sparks of egalitarianism. Andrew Jackson thought that an independent Texas, with a mixture of Indians and fleeing slaves, might be manipulated by Britain to "throw the whole west into flames." Once again, the British might launch "mingled hordes of lawless Indians and negroes" in a "savage war" against the "peaceful inhabitants" of the United States. In 1827, Poinsett had reported to Washington that the "half-breed" Cherokee chief Richard Fields and the "notorious" John Hunter had "hoisted a red and white banner," seeking to establish a "union of whites and Indians" in Texas; Hunter was a white man raised by the Indians who returned to the West to try to prevent genocide. The British also noted with interest their "Republic of Fredonia." Stephen Austin, head of a nearby white colony, warned Hunter that his plans were folly; if the Republic were established, Mexico and the US would join in "annihilating so dangerous and troublesome a neighbor," and would be satisfied with "*nothing short of extermination or expulsion.*" "The U.S. would soon sweep the country of Indians and drive them as they always have driven them to ruin and extermination." Washington would, in short, continue in its policies of genocide (in contemporary terminology), putting an end to "this madness" of a free Red-White society. Austin had successfully cleared out the "natives of the forest" from his own colony before moving on to put down the uprising, with Hunter and Fields assassinated.[35]

The logic of the annexation of Texas was essentially that attributed to Saddam Hussein by US propaganda after his conquest of Kuwait. But the comparisons should not be pressed too far. Unlike his 19th century American precursors, Saddam Hussein is not known to have feared that slavery in Iraq would be threatened by independent states nearby, or to have publicly called for their "imbecile" inhabitants to "become extinct" so that the "great mission of peopling the Middle East with a noble race" of Iraqis might be carried forward, placing "the destinies of the human race in the hands" of the conquerors. And even the wildest fantasies did not accord Saddam potential control over oil of the kind the American expansionists of the 1840s sought over the major resource of the day. There are many interesting lessons to learn from the history so extolled by enraptured intellectuals.

3. Showers of Benevolence

After the mid-19th century conquests, New York editors proudly observed that the US was "the only power which has never sought and never seeks to acquire a foot of territory by force of arms"; "Of all the vast domains of our great confederacy over which the star spangled banner waves, not one foot of it is the acquirement of force or bloodshed"; the remnants of the native population, among others, were not asked to confirm this judgment. The US is unique among nations in that "By its own merits it extends itself." That is only natural, since "all other races...must bow and fade" before "the great work of subjugation and conquest to be achieved by the Anglo-Saxon race," conquest without force. Leading contemporary historians accept this flattering self-image. Samuel Flagg Bemis wrote in 1965 that "American expansion across a practically empty continent despoiled no nation unjustly"; no one could think it unjust if Indians were "felled" along with trees. Arthur M. Schlesinger had earlier described Polk as "undeservedly one of the forgotten men of American history": "By carrying the flag to the Pacific he gave America her continental breadth and ensured her future significance in the world," a realistic assessment, if not, perhaps, exactly in the intended sense.[36]

Such doctrine could not easily survive the cultural awakening of the 1960s, at least outside the intellectual class, where we are regularly regaled by orations on how "for 200 years the United States has preserved almost unsullied the original ideals of the Enlightenment...and, above all, the universality of these values" (Michael Howard, among many others). "Although we are reaching for the stars and have showered less favored peoples with our benevolence in unmatched flow, our motives are profoundly misunderstood and our military intentions widely mistrusted," another distinguished historian, Richard Morris, wrote in 1967, contemplating the "unhappy" fact that others fail to understand the nobility of our cause in Vietnam, a country "beset by internal subversion and foreign aggression" (by Vietnamese, that is). Writing in 1992 on "the self-image of Americans," *New York Times* correspondent Richard Bernstein notes with alarm that "many who came of age during the 1960s protest years have never regained the confidence in the essential goodness of America and the American government that prevailed in earlier periods," a matter of much concern to cultural managers since.[37]

The basic patterns established in the early conquest persist to the current era. As the slaughter of the indigenous population by the Guatemalan military approached virtual genocide, Ronald Reagan and his officials, while lauding the assassins as forward-looking democrats, informed Congress that the US would provide arms "to reinforce the improvement in the human rights situation following the 1982 coup" that installed Ríos Montt, perhaps the greatest killer of them all. The primary means by which Guatemala obtained US military equipment, however, was commercial sales licensed by the Department of Commerce, the General Accounting Office of Congress observed, putting aside the international network that is always ready to exterminate the beasts of the field and forest if there are profits to be made. The Reaganites were also instrumental in maintaining slaughter and terror from Mozambique to Angola, while gaining much respect in left-liberal circles by the "quiet diplomacy" that helped their South African friends cause over $60 billion in damage and 1.5 million deaths from 1980 to 1988 in the neighboring states. The most devastating effects of the general catastrophe of capitalism through the 1980s were in the same two continents: Africa and Latin America.[38]

One of the grandest of the Guatemalan killers, General Héctor Gramajo, was rewarded for his contributions to genocide in the highlands with a fellowship to Harvard's John F. Kennedy School of Government—not unreasonably, given Kennedy's decisive contributions to the vocation of counterinsurgency (one of the technical terms for international terrorism conducted by the powerful). Cambridge dons will be relieved to learn that Harvard is no longer a dangerous center of subversion.

While earning his degree at Harvard, Gramajo gave an interview to the *Harvard International Review* in which he offered a more nuanced view of his own role. He took personal credit for the "70 percent-30 percent civil affairs program, used by the Guatemalan government during the 1980s to control people or organizations who disagreed with the government," outlining the doctrinal innovations he had introduced: "We have created a more humanitarian, less costly strategy, to be more compatible with the democratic system. We instituted civil affairs [in 1982] which provides development for 70 percent of the population, while we kill 30 percent. Before, the strategy was to kill 100 percent." This is a "more sophisticated means" than the previous crude assumption that you must "kill everyone to complete the job" of controlling dissent, he explained.

It is unfair, then, for journalist Alan Nairn, who had exposed the US origins of the Central American death squads, to describe Gramajo as "one of the most significant mass-murderers in the Western Hemisphere" as Gramajo was sued for horrendous crimes. We can also now appreciate why former CIA director William Colby, who had some firsthand experience with such matters in Vietnam, sent Gramajo a copy of his memoirs with the inscription: "To a colleague in the effort to find a strategy of counterinsurgency with decency and democracy," Washington-style.

Given his understanding of humanitarianism, decency, and democracy, it is not surprising that Gramajo appears to be the State Department's choice for the 1995 elections, according to the Guatemala *Central America Report,* citing Americas Watch on the Harvard fellowship as "the State Department's way of grooming Gramajo" for the job, and quoting a US Senate staffer who says: "He's definitely their boy down there." A "senior commander in the early 1980s, when the Guatemalan military was blamed for the deaths of tens of thousands of people, largely civilians," Gramajo "is seen as a moderate by the U.S. Embassy," Kenneth Freed reports, quoting a Western diplomat, and assuring us of Washington's "repugnance" at the actions of the security forces it supports and applauds. The *Washington Post* reports that many Guatemalan politicians expect Gramajo to win the elections, not an unlikely prospect if he's the State Department's boy down there. Gramajo's image is also being prettified. He offered the *Post* a sanitized version of his interview on the 70 percent-30 percent program: "The effort of the government was to be 70 percent in development and 30 percent in the war effort. I was not referring to the people, just the effort." Too bad he expressed himself so badly—or better, so honestly—before the Harvard grooming took effect.[39]

It is not unlikely that the rulers of the world, meeting in G-7 conferences, have written off large parts of Africa and Latin America, superfluous people who have no place in the New World Order, to be joined by many others, in the home societies as well.

Diplomacy has perceived Latin America and Africa in a similar light. Planning documents stress that the role of Latin America is to provide resources and a favorable business and investment climate. If that can be achieved with formal elections under conditions that safeguard business interests, well and good. If it requires state terror "to destroy permanently a perceived threat to the existing structure of socioeconomic privilege by eliminating the political participation of the numerical majority...," that's too bad, but preferable to the alternative of independence; the words are those of Latin Americanist Lars Schoultz, describing the goals pursued by the National Security States that had their roots in Kennedy Administration policies. As for Africa, State Department Policy Planning chief George Kennan, assigning to each part of the South its special function in the New World Order of the post-World War II era, recommended that it be "exploited" for the reconstruction of Europe, adding that the opportunity to exploit Africa should afford the Europeans "that tangible objective for which everyone has been rather unsuccessfully groping...," a badly needed psychological lift, in their difficult postwar straits. Such recommendations are too uncontroversial to elicit comment, or even notice.[40]

The genocidal episodes of the Colombian-Vasco da Gama era are by no means limited to the conquered regions of the South, as is sufficiently attested by the exploits of the leading center of Western civilization 50 years ago. Throughout the era, there have been savage conflicts among the core societies of the North, sometimes spreading far beyond, particularly in this terrible century. For most of the world's population, these are much like shoot-outs between rival drug gangs or mafia dons. The only question is who will gain the right to rob and kill. In the post-World War II era, the US has been the global enforcer, guaranteeing the interests of privilege. It has, therefore, compiled an impressive record of aggression, international terrorism, slaughter, torture, chemical and bacteriological warfare, human rights abuses of every imaginable variety. That is not surprising; it goes with the turf. Nor is it surprising that the occasional documentation of these facts far from the mainstream elicits tantrums among the commissars.

One might note that there are few novelties here either. From Biblical days, there has rarely been a welcome mat for the bearers of unwanted messages; the "responsible men" are the false prophets, who tell more comforting tales. Las Casas's eyewitness description of "the Destruction of the Indies" has been available, in theory, since 1552. It has hardly been a literary staple since. In 1880, Helen Jackson wrote a remarkable account of "A Century of Dishonor," a "sad revelation of broken faith, of violated treaties, and of inhuman acts of violence [that] will bring a flush of shame to the cheeks of those who love their country," Bishop H.B. Whipple of Minnesota wrote in his preface. Flushes of shame were few, even when it was reprinted in 1964 ("Limited to 2,000 copies"). The abolitionists are honored mostly in retrospect. They were "despised and ostracised, and insulted," Mark Twain wrote—"by the 'patriots'": "None but the dead are permitted to speak truth." His own anti-imperialist essays are scarcely known. The first collection appeared in 1992; its editor notes that his prominent role in the Anti-Imperialist League, a major preoccupation in the last ten years of his life, "seems to have remained unmentioned in all biographies." The murder of six Jesuit intellectuals by the US-trained Atlacatl Brigade in November 1989 elicited much outrage. They were murdered, John Hassett and Hugh Lacey write in introducing their work, "because of the role they played *as intellectuals, researchers, writers, and teachers* in expressing their solidarity with the poor" (their emphasis). There is no surer way to annihilate them forever than to suppress their words—virtually unknown, unmentioned, though problems they addressed are at the heart of the major foreign policy issue of the decade framed by their murder and the assassination of Archbishop Romero, also ignored and forgotten. Soviet dissidents may have been honored in the

West, but at home it was those who upheld official verities and berated the "apologists for imperialism" who were the respectable moderates.

True, such figures as Las Casas may be trotted out occasionally to prove our essential goodness. Explaining that "the demographic catastrophe which befell early Latin America was...caused not by wickedness but by human failing and by a form of fate: the grinding wheels of long-term historical change," the London *Economist* writes that "Where cruelties and atrocities occurred, historians know of them precisely because of the 16th century Spanish passion for justice, for they were condemned by moralists or recorded and punished in the courts." Most important, the conquerors "meant well, sincerely believing" they were offering their victims "a divinely approved order" as they slaughtered, tortured, and enslaved them, which shows the silliness of the "politically correct" loonies who rant about "the savage injustice of the Europeans" (Adam Smith). Columbus himself wanted nothing more than "to care for the Indians and let no harm or hurt be done to them"—his own words, settling the issue. What better proof could there be of the nobility of our cultural heritage than Columbus's tender solicitude and the Spanish passion for justice?

How curious that the leading chronicler, Las Casas, should have written at the end of his life, in his will: "I believe that because of these impious, criminal and ignominious deeds perpetrated so unjustly, tyrannically and barbarously, God will vent upon Spain His wrath and His fury, for nearly all of Spain has shared in the bloody wealth usurped at the cost of so much ruin and slaughter."[41]

The horrifying record of what actually occurred, if noticed at all, is considered insignificant, even a proof of our nobility. Again, that goes with the turf. The most powerful mafia don is also likely to dominate the doctrinal system. One of the great advantages of being rich and powerful is that you never have to say: "I'm sorry." It is here that the moral and cultural challenge arises, at the end of the first 500 years.

CHAPTER 2

THE CONTOURS OF WORLD ORDER

1. The Logic of North-South Relations

"Rounding out their natural boundaries" was the task of the colonists in their home territory, which, by the end of the 19th century, extended to the mid-Pacific. But the "natural boundaries" of the South also have to be defended. Hence the dedicated efforts to ensure that no sector of the South goes a separate way, and the trepidations, often near-hysteria, if some deviation is detected. All must be properly integrated into the global economy dominated by the state capitalist industrial societies.

The South is assigned a service role: to provide resources, cheap labor, markets, opportunities for investment and, lately, export of pollution. For the past half-century, the US has shouldered the responsibility for protecting the interests of the "satisfied nations" whose power places them "above the rest," the "rich men dwelling at peace within their habitations" to whom "the government of the world must be entrusted," as Winston Churchill put the matter after World War II.

US interests are therefore understood in global terms. The primary threat to these interests is depicted in high-level planning documents as "radical and nationalistic regimes" that are responsive to popular pressures for "immediate improvement in the low living standards of the masses" and development for domestic needs. These tendencies conflict with the demand for "a political and economic climate conducive to private investment," with adequate repatriation of profits (NSC 5432/1, 1954) and "protection of our raw materials" (George Kennan). For such reasons, as was recognized in 1948 by the clear-sighted head of the State Department Policy Planning staff, "We should cease to talk about vague and...unreal objectives such as human rights, the raising of the living standards, and democratization," and must "deal in straight power concepts," not "hampered by idealistic slogans" about "altruism and world-benefaction," if we are to maintain the "position of disparity" that separates our enormous wealth from the poverty of others (Kennan).

The profoundly anti-democratic thrust of US policy in the Third World, with the recurrent resort to terror to eliminate "the political participation of the numerical majority," is readily understandable. It follows at once from the opposition to "economic nationalism," which is, quite commonly, an outgrowth of popular pressures and organization. Such heresies must therefore be extirpated. Entirely independent of the Cold War, these have been salient features of policy; notoriously, the savage and destructive policies of the past decade, which are, accordingly, hailed for bringing democracy and a new respect for human rights to the world, exactly as one would expect in a well-behaved intellectual culture.

The domestic analogue is apparent, though other devices are needed to tame the "bewildered herd" at home.[1]

As discussed earlier, "free trade" is highly regarded by those who expect to win the competition, though honored in the breach when interests so dictate. Correspondingly, opposition to economic nationalism (for others) is virtually a reflex among global planners. It became a primary theme of US policy after its own resort to protectionism, import substitution, and other such "ultranationalist" methods enabled the US to play the game successfully. By the mid-1940s, US dominance had reached extraordinary levels. The virtues of economic liberalism were therefore extolled with much fervor, in tandem with calls for extending the huge state subsidies for domestic enterprise. The only problem was how to help backward minds appreciate the merits of policies that would serve US interests so splendidly.

At the Chapultepec (Mexico) hemispheric conference in February 1945, the US called for "An Economic Charter of the Americas" that would eliminate economic nationalism "in all its forms." This policy stood in sharp conflict with the Latin American stand, which a State Department officer described as "The philosophy of the New Nationalism [that] embraces policies designed to bring about a broader distribution of wealth and to raise the standard of living of the masses." State Department Political Adviser Laurence Duggan wrote that "Economic nationalism is the common denominator of the new aspirations for industrialization. Latin Americans are convinced that the first beneficiaries of the development of a country's resources should be the people of that country." The US position, in contrast, was that the "first beneficiaries" should be US investors, while Latin America fulfills its service function. It should not undergo "excessive industrial development" that infringes on US interests, the Truman and Eisenhower Administrations held.[2]

Given the power relations, the US position prevailed.

With regard to Asia, the principles were first given a definitive form in an August 1949 draft of NSC 48, Bruce Cumings observes. The basic principle it enunciated was "reciprocal exchange and mutual advantage." A corollary, again, is opposition to independent development: "none of [the Asian countries] alone has adequate resources as a base for general industrialization." India, China, and Japan may "approximate that condition," but no more. Japan's prospects were regarded as quite limited: it might produce "knick-knacks" and other products for the underdeveloped world, a US survey mission concluded in 1950, but nothing more. Though doubtless infused by racism, such conclusions were not entirely unrealistic before the Korean war revived Japan's stagnating economy. "General industrialization in individual countries could be achieved only at a high cost as a result of sacrificing production in fields of comparative advantage," the draft continued. The US must find ways of "exerting economic pressures" on countries that do not accept their role as suppliers of "strategic commodities and other basic materials," the germ of later policies of economic warfare, Cumings observes.

Prospects for development in Africa were never taken seriously, White Africa aside. For the Middle East, the major concern was that the energy system be in US hands, operating in the manner designed by the British: local management would be delegated to an "Arab Façade," with "absorption" of the colonies "veiled by constitutional fictions as a protectorate, a sphere of influence, a buffer State, and so on," a device more cost-effective than direct rule (Lord Curzon and the Eastern Committee, 1917-1918). But we must never run the risk of "losing control," as John Foster Dulles warned. The Façade would therefore consist of family dictatorships that keep pretty much to what they are told, and ensure the flow of profits to the US, its British client, and their energy corporations. They are to be protected by regional enforcers, preferably non-Arab (Turkey, Israel, Iran under the Shah, Pakistan), with British and US muscle in reserve. The system has operated with reasonable efficiency over a considerable period, and has new prospects today with secular nationalist forces in the Arab world in utter disarray, and the Soviet deterrent removed.[3]

The basic themes of internal planning sometimes reach the public, as when the editors of the *New York Times,* applauding the overthrow of the parliamentary Mossadegh regime in Iran, observed that "Underdeveloped countries with rich resources now have an object lesson in the heavy cost that must be paid by one of their number which goes berserk with fanatical nationalism." The service areas must be protected from "Bolshevism" or "Communism," technical terms that refer to social transformation "in ways that reduce their willingness and ability to complement the industrial economies of the West," in the words of an important scholarly study of the 1950s. Most important, the historical record conforms very well to this commonly articulated understanding of the role of the South.[4]

"Radical and nationalistic regimes" are intolerable in themselves, even more so if they appear to be succeeding in terms that might be meaningful to oppressed and suffering people. In that case they become a "virus" that might "infect" others, a "rotten apple" that might "spoil the barrel." For the public, they are "dominoes" that will topple others by aggression and conquest; internally, the absurdity of this picture is often (not always) conceded, and the threat is recognized to be what Oxfam once called "the threat of a good example," referring to Nicaragua. When Henry Kissinger warned that the "contagious example" of Allende's Chile would "infect" not only Latin America but also southern Europe, sending to Italian voters the message that democratic social reform was a possible option, he did not anticipate that Allende's hordes would descend upon Rome. Although the Sandinista "Revolution without Borders" was a spectacularly successful government-media fraud, the propaganda images reflected an authentic concern: from the perspective of a hegemonic power and its intellectual servants, declaration of an intent to provide a model that will inspire others—the actual source of the imagery—amounts to aggression.[5]

When a virus is detected, it must be destroyed, and potential victims immunized. The Cuban virus called forth invasion, terror, and economic warfare, and a rash of National Security States to prevent the rot from spreading. The story was the same in Southeast Asia in the same years. The standard approach to the virus itself is a two-track policy, as in the case of Allende's Chile. The hard line called for a military coup, finally achieved. The soft line was explained by Ambassador Edward Korry, a Kennedy liberal: to "do all within our power to condemn Chile and the Chileans to utmost deprivation and poverty, a policy designed for a long time to come to accelerate the hard features of a Communist society in Chile." Hence even if the hard line did not succeed in introducing fascist killers to exterminate the virus, the vision of "utmost deprivation" would suffice to keep the rot from spreading, and ultimately demoralize the patient itself. And crucially, it would provide ample grist for the mill of the cultural managers, who can produce cries of anguish at "the hard features of a Communist society," pouring scorn on those "apologists" who describe what is happening. The point was made clearly by Bertrand Russell in his bitterly critical account of Bolshevik Russia in its early days:

Every failure of industry, every tyrannous regulation brought about by the desperate situation, is used by the Entente as a justification of its policy. If a man is deprived of food and drink, he will grow weak, lose his reason, and finally die. This is not usually considered a good reason for inflicting death by starvation. But where nations are concerned, the weakness and struggles are regarded as morally culpable, and are held to justify further punishment.

There is, evidently, much satisfaction to be gained by careful inspection of those who are writhing under our boot, to see if they are behaving properly; when they are not, as is often the case, indignation is unconstrained. Far worse atrocities of our own, or of our "moderate" and "improving" clients, are merely an aberration, soon to be overcome.[6]

To introduce further technical terminology, "rotten apples" constitute a threat to "stability." As Washington prepared to overthrow the first democratic government in Guatemala in 1954, a State Department official warned that Guatemala "has become an increasing threat to the stability of Honduras and El Salvador. Its agrarian reform is a powerful propaganda weapon; its broad social program of aiding the workers and peasants in a victorious struggle against the upper classes and large foreign enterprises has a strong appeal to the populations of Central American neighbors where similar conditions prevail." "Stability" means security for "the upper classes and large foreign enterprises," and it must naturally be preserved. It is understandable, then, that Eisenhower and Dulles should have felt that the "self-defense and self-preservation" of the United States might be at stake when they were advised that "a strike situation" in Honduras might "have had inspiration and support from the Guatemalan side of the border."[7]

So important is "stability" that "desirable reforms" must not be implemented. In December 1967, Freedom House issued a statement by 14 noted scholars who declared themselves to be "the moderate segment of the academic community," praising US policies in Asia as "remarkably good," particularly in Indochina, where our courageous defense of freedom contributed greatly to "political equilibrium in Asia," improving "the morale—and the policies—of our Asian allies and the neutrals." The point is illustrated by what they cite as our greatest triumph, the "dramatic changes" that took place in Indonesia in 1965, when the army, encouraged by our stand in Indochina, took matters in hand and slaughtered several hundred thousand people, mostly landless peasants (see chapter 5). Quite generally, the moderate scholars explain, "many types of reform increase instability, however desirable and essential they may be in long-range terms. For people under siege, there is no substitute for security." The terms "people," "stability," etc., have their usual PC meanings.

Many noted scholars agreed with MIT political scientist Ithiel Pool that throughout the Third World, "it is clear that order depends on somehow compelling newly mobilized strata to return to a measure of passivity and defeatism." The same lessons were soon to be drawn by the Trilateral Commission for the population of the West, who were undermining "democracy" by attempting to enter the arena of democratic politics instead of keeping to their "function" as "spectators," as their betters run the show.[8]

Such thinking is pervasive, and understandable. It will persist, as long as threats to order and stability remain. The continuities are apparent, and quite independent of the Cold War. After the Gulf War, when the Cold War was lost as a pretext beyond hope of resurrection, George Bush returned to support for his old friend and ally Saddam Hussein as he crushed the Shi'ites in the South and then the Kurds in the North. Western ideologues explained that although these atrocities offend our delicate sensibilities, we must nevertheless accept them in the name of "stability." The chief diplomatic correspondent of the *New York Times,* Thomas Friedman, outlined Bush Administration reasoning: Washington seeks "the best of all worlds: an iron-fisted Iraqi junta without Saddam Hussein," a return to the days when Saddam's "iron fist held Iraq together, much to the satisfaction of the American allies Turkey and Saudi Arabia," not to speak of the boss in Washington. Saddam Hussein committed his first serious crime on August 2, 1990, when he disobeyed orders. Therefore he must be destroyed, but some clone must be found to ensure "stability." In accord with the same doctrines, the Iraqi democratic opposition was barred from contact with Washington, hence from the mainstream US media, throughout the crisis (and, indeed, before and after). It was not until summer 1992, in the context of electoral concerns, that the Bush Administration opened limited contacts with Iraqi democrats.[9]

These are leading features of the New World Order, as of the old, well-documented in the internal record, regularly illustrated in historical practice, bound to persist as contingencies change.

Official PC rhetoric includes a variety of other terms. Thus the aspiring intellectual must master the term "security threat," referring to anything that might infringe upon the rights of US investors. Another is "pragmatism," a term which, for us, means "doing what we want." For others, the meaning is: "doing what we want." In the case of the Arab-Israel conflict, for example, the US has stood virtually alone for many years in blocking any peace process that accords national rights to Palestinians, but of the two brands of Israeli rejectionism (Labor and Likud), it has preferred the former. Accordingly, Likud's Yitzhak Shamir was "ideological" but Labor's Yitzhak Rabin is "pragmatic." "Mr. Rabin's pragmatic, non-ideological approach fits in well with the Bush team," *Times* State Department spokesman Thomas Friedman writes, recognizing that the Bush team is pragmatic by definition, agreeing with itself. Jerusalem correspondent Clyde Haberman applauds Rabin's election in June 1992 as a victory for "pragmatism." Similarly, Palestinians are "pragmatic" if they accept the fact that the US sets the rules: they have no national rights, because the US has so decreed. They must therefore accept "the autonomy of a POW camp" described by Israeli journalist Danny Rubinstein, an "autonomy" in which they will be free to collect their garbage in designated areas not taken over by Israel—as long as the garbage cans do not display the colors of the Palestinian flag, a leading Israeli civil libertarian adds. The term "peace process" is another of those to be mastered: in PC rhetoric, it refers to whatever the US happens to be doing, perhaps blocking the peace process, as in this and many other cases.[10]

There are other skills to be learned, to some of which we return; but the task is not too onerous, as demonstrated by the ease with which they are mastered.

The "Communist" danger to "stability" is further enhanced by their unfair advantages. The Communists are able to "appeal directly to the masses," President Eisenhower complained. Our plans for "the masses" preclude any such appeal. Secretary of State John Foster Dulles, in private conversation with his brother Allen, who headed the CIA, deplored the Communist "ability to get control of mass movements," "something we have no capacity to duplicate." "The poor people are the ones they appeal to and they have always wanted to plunder the rich."[11] The same concerns extend to "the preferential option for the poor" of the Latin American Church and other commitments to independent development or democracy—and also to such friends as Mussolini, Trujillo, Noriega, and Saddam Hussein when they forget their assigned role.

2. After Colonialism

The United States had become the world's major industrial economy by the turn of the century, and its leading creditor by World War I, a position maintained until the Reaganites took command, quickly converting the US into the world's leading debtor. During World War II, quasi-totalitarian measures at last overcame the effects of the Great Depression, more than tripling US industrial production and teaching valuable lessons to the corporate managers who ran the wartime economy. There has been no serious challenge since to their conclusion that private wealth and power, which were nurtured by large-scale state intervention in the first place, can be sustained and enhanced only through the same means; only in rhetorical flourishes, or on the remote margins, is capitalism regarded as a viable system. With much of the world in ruins, the US had attained a historically unparalleled peak of economic and military dominance. State and corporate planners were well aware of their unprecedented power, and intent on using it to construct a global order to benefit the interests they serve.

The highest priority was to ensure that the industrial heartland, German-based Europe and Japan, would be firmly within the US-dominated world order, controlled by domestic financial-industrial sectors linked to US state-corporate power. The first order of business, then, was to undermine the antifascist resistance with its popular base in the "rascal multitude," to weaken labor, and to restore traditional conservative rule, often including fascist collaborators. This task was undertaken on a global scale in the late 1940s, with considerable violence when that proved necessary, notably in Greece and South Korea.

In this New World Order, North-South relations were reconstructed, though not in any fundamental way. The US sought a generally open world based on the principles of liberal internationalism, expecting to prevail in a competition that was "free and fair." These considerations led to a measure of support for the rising anti-colonial forces. But within limits. A 1948 CIA memorandum observed that a balance must be struck between "supporting local nationalist aspirations and maintaining the colonial economic interests of countries to whom aid has been pledged in Western Europe"; there could be little doubt as to the relative weights when serious US interests are at stake. Similarly, the imperial system that Japan had sought to construct had to be restored to it, under over-arching US control. These considerations led to tactical decisions to favor traditional colonial preference systems for rival/allies; temporarily, in the context of postwar reconstruction and reestablishment of trade patterns with the industrial powers on which the US economy relied.

Intending to organize the Far East pretty much on its own, Washington barred its allies from any role in determining the fate of Japan. The goal was "to guarantee U.S. security by insuring long-term American domination of Japan" and "to exclude the influence of all foreign governments" (Melvyn Leffler, expressing a scholarly consensus; "security" having its usual meaning). Given US power, that goal was easily attained, irrespective of wartime agreements. In the Middle East and Latin America, the ideological system confers on the United States the right to pursue its "needs" and "wants," respectively. The plan, therefore, was to restrict foreign interference, apart from an occasional subordinate role assigned to client powers, notably Britain in the Middle East. Britain serves as "our lieutenant (the fashionable word is partner)," as a senior Kennedy adviser put it; the British are to hear only the fashionable word.[12]

The character of planning is well-illustrated by the case of Italy. Like Greece, its importance extended to the Middle East. "U.S. strategic interests" required control over "the line of communications to the Near East outlets of the Saudi-Arabian oil fields" through the Mediterranean, a September 1945 interagency review observed. These interests would be threatened if Italy were to fall into "the hands of any great power"—in translation: if it were to escape from the hands of the proper great power. Italy "could be used to guarantee—or, in the wrong hands, impair—oil supplies from the Near East," Rhodri Jeffrey-Jones observes.

It was expected that the Communist Party, with its strong labor support and the prestige conferred by its role in the struggle against Fascism and the Nazi occupiers, would win the 1948 elections. That result could have a "demoralizing effect throughout Western Europe, the Mediterranean, and the Middle East," US policymakers warned. It would be the "first instance in history of a communist accession to power by popular suffrage and legal procedure," and "so unprecedented and portentous an event must produce a profound psychological effect in those countries threatened by the Soviets and...striving to retain their freedom." To translate again to English, it might influence popular movements that sought to pursue an independent and often radical democratic course, thus undermining the US policy of restoring the traditional order dominated by conservative business and often pro-fascist sectors ("freedom"). In short, Italy might become a "virus infecting others." The US planned military intervention if the election could not be controlled by other means. A combination of force, threats, control over desperately needed food, and other measures succeeded in overcoming the threat of a free election. Substantial US efforts to subvert Italian democracy continued at least to the mid-1970s. In later years, as noted, it was feared that Chile might be a "virus infecting" Italy.[13]

For similar reasons, after Washington failed to disrupt the 1984 election in Nicaragua by terror, its doctrinal system effaced the terrible event from history; the media rigorously excluded the approval voiced by international observers including hostile ones, US Latin American scholars who studied the election in depth, and the leading figure of Central American democracy, José Figueres.

The life of those responsible for world order is never easy, as Metternich and the Czar had recognized in their day.

Apart from subversion, policymakers sought other ways "to stabilize Italy," Sallie Pisani writes in her study of the early days of the CIA. Subversion to achieve stability is standard procedure, quite intelligible to those who have mastered PC rhetoric; it is even possible to "destabilize a freely elected Marxist government in Chile" because "we were determined to seek stability" (James Chace). One idea for Italy was to thin the disruptive population by inducing emigration. Marshall Plan money was used to rebuild the Italian merchant marine to "double the number of Italian emigrants who can be carried overseas each year," the chief of the ECA (Marshall Plan) mission for Italy reported. It was also used to retrain workers, "thereby making them more acceptable to other countries," he added. Europe had unemployment problems, and more "wops" was the last thing wanted in the US. Congress therefore authorized funds for the "purpose of transporting emigrants from Italy to parts of the world other than the United States." The ECA decided upon South America, with its "relatively less developed areas." It funded an emigration survey "to locate specific lands suitable for Italian settlement" in South America, and to help prepare the ground. The first recipient of such aid was Brazil, in 1950.

The project was considered highly sensitive, and concealed from Italians completely. "Propaganda to stabilize the remaining Italians was equally important," Pisani writes, and a "sophisticated campaign" was conducted in Italy, as in France, another potential "virus." A problem in France, the ECA mission noted, was that "The French are allergic to propaganda. They often confuse what we call information with what they call propaganda." Washington policymakers agreed that "overt American propaganda" would not be a good idea for Europeans, because of their experiences with the Nazis. The ECA therefore adopted the concept of "indirection," defined as the ability to "get across the ECA and U.S. Government foreign policy point of view, without either ECA or the U.S. Government being identified as the source of the material." At home, where the population is better trained, "information" suffices.[14]

In the Western hemisphere, the US had largely displaced its European rivals by World War II, and therefore rejected the principles of the new world order for "our little region over here which never has bothered anybody," as Secretary of War Henry Stimson described the hemisphere when explaining why all regional systems must be dismantled apart from our own, which are to be extended. The US insisted that hemispheric affairs be handled by regional organizations, which it is sure to dominate; very much the principle for which Saddam Hussein was roundly condemned in

1990, when he proposed that the problems of the Gulf be dealt with by the Arab League. But here too there are limits. If the Latin Americans "attempt irresponsible use of their numerical strength in the O.A.S.," John Dreier explains in his study of the organization, "if they carry to extremes the doctrine of nonintervention, if they leave the United States no alternative but to act unilaterally to protect itself, they will have destroyed not only the basis of hemispheric cooperation for progress but all hope of a secure future for themselves." The guardians of world order must be ever alert for signs of irresponsibility.

The same had been true of Roosevelt's Good Neighbor Policy, which carried an "implicit obligation of reciprocity," State Department Latin America official Robert Woodward pointed out: "the admittance into an American government of an alien ideology" would "compel the United States to take defensive measures," unilaterally. Others, needless to say, have no such right, in particular, no right to defend themselves from the US and its "ideology," which are not "alien": indeed, the US has no ideology, apart from "pragmatism," in the technical sense. The general point was clarified by Carter's Latin America adviser Robert Pastor, at the critical extreme: the US wants other nations "to act independently, *except* when doing so would affect U.S. interests adversely"; the US has never wanted "to control them," as long as developments do not "get out of control." Others can be quite free, as long as they are "pragmatic."[15]

To assist "countries striving to retain their freedom," the US has been forced regularly to launch terrorist attacks against them or invade them outright, and to use its unparalleled capacities for economic warfare and subversion. The mission requires a cooperative class of intellectuals to shape "information" properly for the rascal multitude, rarely a problem.

After World War II, the importance of the traditional service role of the South was enhanced by "the realization that the food and fuel of Eastern Europe were no longer available to Western Europe at prewar levels" (Leffler). Each region was assigned its status and "function" by the planners. The US would take charge of Latin America and the Middle East, in the latter, with the help of its lieutenant. Africa was to be "exploited" for the reconstruction of Europe, while Southeast Asia would "fulfill its major function as a source of raw materials for Japan and Western Europe" (George Kennan and his State Department Policy Planning Staff, 1948-1949). The US too would purchase raw materials from the former colonies, thus reconstructing the triangular trade patterns whereby the industrial societies purchase US manufacturing exports by earning dollars from raw materials exports by their traditional colonies. The "dollar gap" that impeded export of US manufactures to Europe was considered an extremely serious problem by Dean Acheson and other top planners; overcoming it was taken to be a critical necessity for the US economy, which, it was assumed, would otherwise sink back into deep depression or face state intervention of the kind that would interfere with corporate prerogatives rather than enhancing them. By this reasoning, sophisticated and extensively articulated, former colonies could be granted nominal self-government, but often little more.[16]

The framework of postwar global planning entailed that colonial relations must be reestablished in new forms and "ultranationalist" tendencies suppressed, particularly if they threaten "stability" elsewhere; the destiny of the South remains much as before. Both the industrial core and its subservient periphery were to be guarded against association with the "Sino-Soviet bloc" (or its components, when the bitter antagonism internal to the "bloc" could no longer be denied). The latter "bloc," a huge segment of the former Third World that had departed from its traditional role, had to be "contained" or, if possible, restored to the service function by "rollback." A significant factor in the Cold War was the imposition of Soviet rule over traditional service areas, separating them from the US-dominated state capitalist world, and the threat that Soviet power might contribute to the breakaway of other areas, even influencing popular sectors within the industrial core itself, a threat considered particularly severe in the early postwar period.

North-South relations vary somewhat over the years, but rarely beyond these basic limits. The realities are described in a 1990 report by the South Commission, chaired by Julius Nyerere and consisting of leading Third World economists, government planners, religious leaders, and others. The Commission observes that there were some gestures to Third World concerns in the 1970s, "undoubtedly spurred" by concern over "the newly found assertiveness of the South after the rise in oil prices in 1973"—incidentally, not entirely unwelcome to the US and UK. As the threat of Southern assertiveness abated, the report continues, the industrial societies lost interest and turned to "a new form of neo-colonialism," monopolizing control over the world economy, undermining the more democratic elements of the United Nations, and in general proceeding to institutionalize "the South's second class status" through the 1980s.

The pattern is consistent; it would be remarkable if it were otherwise.

Reviewing the miserable state of the traditional Western domains, the South Commission called for a "new world order" that will respond to "the South's plea for justice, equity, and democracy in the global society." The prospects for this plea are revealed by the attention granted it; the study was ignored, as are Third World voices generally. They are of slight interest to the rich men to whom "the government of the world must be entrusted."[17]

Several months later, George Bush appropriated the phrase "New World Order" as a cover for his war in the Gulf. In this case, word got out, and Bush-Baker rhetoric inspired much elevated discourse about the prospects opening before us. In the South, in contrast, the "New World Order" imposed by the powerful is perceived, not unrealistically, as a bitter international class war, with the advanced state capitalist economies and their transnational corporations monopolizing the means of violence and controlling investment, capital, technology, and planning and management decisions, at the expense of the huge mass of the population. Local elites in the Southern dependencies can share in the spoils. The US and UK, which wield the whip, may well continue their decline toward societies with notable Third World characteristics, dramatically obvious in the inner cities and rural areas; it is likely that continental Europe will not lag far behind, despite the impediment of a labor movement that has not yet been entirely restored to its proper place.

3. The Rich Men's Club

The US-designed global system required that order must reign within the rich men's club as well. Its lesser members are to pursue their "regional interests" within the "overall framework of order" managed by the United States, the only power with "global interests and responsibilities," Kissinger informed Europe in 1973 ("the Year of Europe"). In the early postwar years, a European third force could not be tolerated. The formation of NATO was in large part motivated by the need "to integrate Western Europe and England into an orbit amenable to American leadership," Leffler observes: "Neither an integrated Europe nor a united Germany nor an independent Japan must be permitted to emerge as a third force or a neutral bloc." Neutralism would be "a shortcut to suicide," Secretary of State Dean Acheson stated. The same was true outside the core industrial societies. While recognizing that the Russians were not responsible for conflicts in the Third World, Acheson warned in 1952 that the Russians might exploit such conflicts in an effort to "force the maximum number of non-Communist countries to pursue a neutral policy and to deny their resources to the principal Western powers"—that is, to deny them on the terms the West demanded. General Omar Bradley also warned of "the suicide of neutralism," with Japan in mind.[18]

Western planners "did not expect and were not worried about Soviet aggression," Leffler writes, summarizing a well-established scholarly consensus: "The Truman administration supported the Atlantic alliance primarily because it was indispensable to the promotion of European stability through German integration." This was the basic motivation for the North Atlantic treaty signed in Washington in April 1949, which led to the establishment of NATO, and in response, the Warsaw Pact. Preparing for the April meeting, US policymakers "became convinced that the Soviets might really be interested in striking a deal, unifying Germany, and ending the division of Europe." This was regarded not as an opportunity, but as a threat to the "primary national security goal": "to harness Germany's economic and military potential for the Atlantic community"—and to block "the suicide of neutralism."[19]

Note that "national security" is used here in its technical sense, unrelated to the security of the nation, which could only be endangered by these conscious steps toward superpower confrontation. Similarly, the phrase "Atlantic community" refers to its ruling elements, not its populations, whose interests are readily sacrificed if power and profits so dictate; by shifting production overseas to labor that is kept docile and cheap by state violence, for example.

"The real issue," the CIA concluded in 1949, "is not the settlement of Germany," which, it was believed—and feared—might be reached by an accord with the Kremlin. Rather, it is "the long-term control of German power." This "great workshop" must be controlled by the US and its clients, with no participation from the Soviet Union, despite the well-understood security interests of the country that had just been virtually destroyed by Germany for the second time in 30 years, and had borne the brunt of the war against the Nazis; and in violation of the wartime agreements on the Soviet role in Germany, which the US had already violated by March 1946, Leffler observes. The withdrawal of Soviet troops from Germany might be a desirable goal, Acheson held, but "the withdrawal of American and British troops from Germany would be too high a price." The "trend of our thinking," George Kennan recognized, "means...that we do not really want to see Germany reunified at this time, and that there are *no* conditions on which we would really find such a solution satisfactory." Unification of Germany might be a long-term desideratum, but "only if the circumstances are right," the State Department emphasized. US troops would therefore remain in Germany even if the Soviets proposed a mutual withdrawal; Germany would be integrated as a subsidiary part of the US-dominated global economy; and the Russians would have no significant voice in the outcome, would not receive reparations, and would not influence German industrial (or military) development.[20]

That outcome would serve two crucial goals: weakening the Soviet rival, and reinforcing US dominance over its allies. Moves to end the Cold

War, in contrast, would serve neither of these goals, and hence were never a serious option.

A third reason for opposing unification, Leffler observes, was concern over the "appeal of the left," reinforced by "the more vigorous recovery and political activism in the Soviet zone," including the space allowed for works councils with some managerial authority in denazified enterprises, and trade union organization. Washington feared that a unified labor movement and other popular organizations might interfere with US plans to restore traditional business rule. The British Foreign Office also feared "economic and ideological infiltration" from the East, which it perceived as "something very like aggression"; political successes by the wrong people are commonly described as "aggression" in the internal record. In a united Germany, the British Foreign Office warned, "the balance of advantage seems to lie with the Russians," who could exercise "the stronger pull." Division of Germany was therefore to be preferred, with the Soviet Union excluded from any voice over the heartland of German industry in the wealthy Ruhr/Rhine industrial complex.[21]

For many reasons, confrontation seemed preferable to accommodation. Whether that might have been possible is a matter for speculation. Throughout, a major concern was integration of the core industrial societies in a world order dominated by the US state-corporate nexus.

A decade later, Europe had substantially recovered, thanks in large measure to the policies of "international military Keynesianism" undertaken by Washington from shortly before the Korean war—which served as a pretext on the assumption, too convenient to require evidence, that the Russians were setting forth on world conquest. As recovery proceeded, fears of European independence and neutralist tendencies increased. Kennedy's Ambassador to London, David Bruce, saw "dangers" if Europe "struck off on its own, seeking to play a role independent of the US"; like others, he wanted "partnership—with the United States in a superior position," Frank Costigliola comments. Kennedy's "Grand Design" was an effort to manage the allies, but with mixed results. France was a particular annoyance. Kennedy feared that President Charles de Gaulle might make a deal with the Russians that "would be acceptable to the Germans," and was "extremely concerned" about intelligence reports suggesting a Franco-Russian deal to shut the US out of Europe, close associates recalled. Another concern was the gold drain, taken to be French-inspired. A still further irritant was de Gaulle's position on Indochina. His advocacy of diplomacy and neutralization was completely unacceptable to the Kennedy Administration, which was committed to military victory and, at the time, was struggling to undermine and deflect Vietnamese initiatives on all sides to settle that conflict without a major international war. In Indochina, as in Europe and throughout the Third World, neutralism was anathema to US planners, "a shortcut to suicide."[22]

Mounting difficulties in controlling the allies led to Kissinger's 1973 admonitions. The "major problem" in the Western alliance, he felt, was "the domestic evolution in many European countries," which might lead to an independent course. The development of Eurocommunism aroused new concerns—which Kissinger shared with Brezhnev, who also was not pleased by the call for a "democratic path to socialism" that opposed "all foreign intervention." Kissinger cited post-fascist Portugal and Italy as situations that, "while not the result of détente or of Soviet policy," posed political problems for the US: "We cannot encourage dialogue with Communist parties within NATO nations," he informed US Embassies, whether or not they follow "the Moscow line": "The impact of an Italian Communist Party that seemed to be governing effectively would be devastating—on France, and on NATO, too." Consequently, the US must oppose the rise of the Communist party in Portugal after the collapse of the fascist dictatorship (which had posed no problem), even if it were to follow the Italian Eurocommunist model. "It was feared that Eurocommunism would make Western communist parties more palatable and attractive to the publics of Western countries," Raymond Garthoff writes in his comprehensive study of the period: the US "gave a higher priority to...protecting the Western alliance and American influence in it" than to "weakening Soviet influence in the East."[23]

Again, we see the dual problem: the combination of democratic developments that escape corporate control, and decline of US power. Neither is acceptable; jointly, they pose a grave danger to "security" and "stability."

By the 1970s, the problems were becoming unmanageable, and a sharply different course was initiated, to which we return in the next section. They persist into the 1990s. An illustration is the controversy over a secret February 1992 Pentagon draft of Defense Planning Guidance, leaked to the press, which describes itself as "definitive guidance from the Secretary of Defense" for budgetary policy to the year 2000. The draft develops standard reasoning. The US must hold "global power" and a monopoly of force. It will then "protect" the "new order" while allowing others to pursue "their legitimate interests," as Washington defines them. The US "must account sufficiently for the interests of the advanced industrial nations to discourage them from challenging our leadership or seeking to overturn the established political and economic order," or even "aspiring to a larger regional or global role." There must be no independent European security system; rather, US-dominated NATO must remain the "primary instrument of Western defense and security, as well as the channel for U.S. influence and participation in European security affairs." "We will retain the pre-eminent responsibility for addressing selectively those wrongs which threaten not only our interests, but also those of our allies or friends"; the United States alone will determine what are "wrongs" and when they are to be selectively "righted." As in the past, the Middle East is a particular concern. Here "our overall objective is to remain the predominant outside power in the region and preserve U.S. and Western access to the region's oil" while deterring aggression (selectively), maintaining strategic control and "regional stability" (in the technical sense), and protecting "U.S. nationals and property." In Latin America, the primary threat is Cuban "military provocation against the U.S. or an American ally," the standard Orwellian reference to the escalating US war against Cuban independence.

"Western European and third world diplomats here were sharply critical of some of the language in the document," Patrick Tyler reported from Washington. "Senior White House and State Department officials have harshly criticized" it as well, claiming that it "in no way or shape represents U.S. policy." The Pentagon spokesman "pointedly disavowed some of the central policy statements" of the document, noting, however, that "its basic thrust mirrors the public statements and testimony of Defense Secretary Dick Cheney." This constitutes a "tactical withdrawal" by the Pentagon, Tyler suggests, prompted by the "reaction in Congress and from senior Administration officials." Quite possibly Administration criticisms also reflect concerns over the alarms that the document set off in many capitals, and their harsh criticism too is a tactical withdrawal. Cheney and Undersecretary for Policy Paul Wolfowitz "endorsed [the] principal views" of the document, senior officials acknowledged. There was also criticism in the press, notably from *Times* foreign policy specialist Leslie Gelb, who objected to the "daydreaming about being the world's policeman" and one "disturbing omission": "the document seems to be silent about any American role in insuring Israeli security."[24]

To what extent the other members of the club will accept the suzerainty of the enforcer who pledges to "account sufficiently for their interests" is an unsettled question. In the present case, protests and concerns over cost led the Administration to revise the plan a few months later, replacing traditional themes by tepid clichés—at least for public consumption. Meanwhile France and Germany moved to implement a Franco-German military corps independent of NATO, over intense US opposition. France also blocked US efforts to extend the NATO alliance (including the related North Atlantic Cooperation Council) to include Hungary, Poland, and Czechoslovakia. US officials allege that "the French don't want an American-led NATO to take on further responsibilities in Eastern Europe" and perpetuate the alliance, the *Wall Street Journal* reported.[25]

The debates reflect a real foreign policy dilemma. With its economy in relative decline and its social base in serious disrepair, particularly after a decade of Reaganite borrow-and-spend abandon, is the US in a position to maintain the hegemonic role it has played for half a century? And will others accept a subordinate role? Will they be willing to pay the costs, as the US exploits its comparative advantage in military force to maintain the particular version of global order demanded by the domestic power interests, costs that the US is no longer in a position to sustain itself? It is not clear that the other rich men will agree to employ the US as their "Hessians," as widely advocated in the business press during the build-up to the Gulf war, perhaps along with its British lieutenant. The latter is also in social and economic decline but "well qualified, motivated, and likely to have a high military profile as the mercenary of the international community," the military correspondent of the London *Independent* comments—again, a regular theme during the Gulf war, accompanied by much triumphant breast-beating among British jingoists, dreaming of the good old days when they had "the right to bomb niggers" with no whining from the left-fascists.[26]

To understand the discussion, it is necessary to decode the conventional euphemisms in which it is framed ("responsibility," "security," "defense," etc.). The code words disguise a basic question: Who is going to run the show?

4. The End of the Affluent Alliance

The basic framework of policy formation tends to remain in place as long as the institutions of power and domination are stable, with the capacity to deflect challenges and accommodate or displace competing forces. That has been true of the United States in the postwar period, indeed long before. Nevertheless, policies have to be adapted to changing contingencies.

A change in world order of lasting importance was recognized officially in August 1971, when Richard Nixon announced his "New Economic Policy," dismantling the international economic order established after World War II (the Bretton Woods system), in which the US served, in effect, as international banker, with the dollar as the world's sole international currency, convertible to gold at $35 an ounce. By that time, "the affluent alliance had come to the end of the road" and "the disorder was getting too serious for aspirins," international economist Susan Strange observed. German-led Europe and Japan had recovered from wartime destruction, and the US was facing the unanticipated costs of the Vietnam war. The world economy was entering an era of "tripolarity"—and also, crucially, of stagnation and declining profitability of capital.[27]

The predictable reaction was a rapid intensification of the class war that is waged with unceasing dedication by the corporate sector, its political agents, and ideological servants. The years that followed saw an attack on real wages, social services, and unions—indeed any kind of functioning democratic structure—so as to overcome the troublesome "crisis of democracy" brought about by the illegitimate efforts of the public to bring their interests into the political arena. The ideological component of the offensive sought to strengthen authority and habits of obedience, to diminish social consciousness and such human frailties as concern for others, and to instruct young people that they are confirmed narcissists. Another objective has been to establish a de facto world government insulated from popular awareness or interference, devoted to the task of ensuring that the world's human and material resources are freely available to the transnational corporations (TNCs) and international banks that are to control the global system.

The US remains the largest single economy, though declining relative to its major rivals, which are not without their own problems. Those faced by the US are also too serious for aspirins, though little more is available thanks to doctrinal and policy triumphs that have diminished the capacity for constructive social action directed to the needs of the irrelevant majority, one happy consequence of Reaganite debt-creation.

Nixon's response to the decline of US economic hegemony was forthright: "when you're losing, change the rules of the game," economist Richard Du Boff observes. Nixon suspended the convertibility of the dollar to gold, overturning the international monetary system, imposed temporary wage-price controls and a general import surcharge, and initiated fiscal measures that directed state power, beyond the previous norm, to welfare for the rich: reduction of federal taxes and domestic expenditures, apart from the required subsidies to the corporate sector. These have been the guiding policies since. They were accelerated during the Reagan years, largely following Carter Administration prescriptions that were reshaped by the more doctrinaire Reaganites to bring about a huge growth in debt at every level (federal, state, local, household, corporate), with little to show in the way of productive investment. One crucial element is the incalculable debt of unmet social needs, a mounting burden imposed upon the large majority of the population and future generations.

Nixon's initiatives constituted "a sort of mercantilist revolution in domestic and foreign policy," political economist David Calleo observed a few years later. The international system grew more disorderly, "with rules eroded and power more significant." There was less "rational control over national economic life," hence great advantages to internationalist business and banking, freed from capital controls and official restraint and secure in the expectation of a state-organized public bail-out if something goes wrong. International capital markets rapidly expanded as a consequence of the decline of regulation and control, the huge flow of petrodollars after the 1973-1974 oil price rise, and the information-telecommunications revolution, which greatly facilitated capital transfers. Vigorous bank initiatives to stimulate new borrowing contributed to the Third World debt crisis and the current instability of the banks themselves.[28]

The rise in oil prices (preceded by a comparable increase in price of US coal, uranium, and agricultural exports) yielded temporary advantages for the US and British economies, providing windfall profits for the energy corporations, primarily US and British, and inducing them to bring into production high-cost oil (Alaska, North Sea) that had been withheld from the market. For the US, rising energy costs were substantially offset by military and other exports to the Middle East oil producers and huge construction projects for them. Their profits also flowed to Treasury securities and investment; support for the economies of the US and UK has long been the primary responsibility of the Arab Facade of local managers.[29]

The same years saw the stagnation and collapse of the Soviet empire, which had interfered with the planned global order in crucial ways (chapter 3). The power of the state capitalist industrial societies was enhanced further by the economic catastrophe that swept through most of their domains in the 1980s. The sense of foreboding throughout the Third World is readily understandable.

Japan and continental Europe recovered from the recession of the early 1980s, though without resuming earlier growth rates. US recovery involved massive borrowing and state stimulation of the economy, mainly through the Pentagon-based public subsidy to high technology industry, along with a sharp increase in protectionist measures and a rise in interest rates. This contributed to the crisis of the South as interest payments on the debt rose while investment and aid declined, and the wealthy classes invested their riches in the West. There was a huge capital flow from South to North, with effects that were generally disastrous, apart from the NICs (newly industrialized countries) of East Asia, where the state is powerful enough to control capital flight and direct the economy efficiently. The catastrophe of capitalism in the 1980s also had an impact on Eastern Europe, contributing to the disintegration of the Soviet empire and the virtual disappearance of Russia from the world scene.[30]

In earlier years, the nonaligned countries had sought to gain some control over their fate. Initiatives were taken through UNCTAD (the UN Conference on Trade and Development) to create a "new international economic order" with support and stabilization programs for primary commodities, in the hope of stemming the deterioration in terms of trade and controlling the sharp price fluctuations that have a devastating impact on economies that rely on few primary exports. UNESCO undertook parallel efforts to provide Third World countries with access to international communications, a virtual monopoly of the advanced industrial societies.

These initiatives naturally elicited enormous hostility on the part of the world rulers, and were turned back decisively in the 1980s. The US led a fierce attack on the United Nations that effectively eliminated it as an independent force in world affairs. UNESCO inspired particular hatred, because of its Third World orientation and the threat to ideological domination. The demolition operation and the return of the UN to US control have been lauded here as a restoration of the ideals of the founders, not without justice. Extraordinary deceit has been required to conceal the fact that it has been primarily the US, secondarily Britain, that have vetoed Security Council resolutions and generally undermined the UN for over 20 years, and to sustain the standard pretense that "Soviet obstructionism" and "shrill Third World anti-Americanism" are what rendered the UN ineffective. The no less extraordinary levels of deceit that accompanied the government-media campaign to eliminate UNESCO heresies are documented in an important study, which, needless to say, had no effect whatsoever on the flow of necessary lies.[31]

The hysteria about "political correctness" is an interesting domestic analogue. Its extent is truly something to behold, including a stream of best-sellers with anecdotes, many concocted, about alleged horrors in the universities, angry speeches, and a flood of articles from the news columns to the sports pages and journals of opinion that gushed forth suddenly, as if on command; a study of one six-month period found over a mention per day in the Los Angeles Times. The outrage has a basis in reality. There really are a great many people who oppose racist and sexist oppression, have respect for other cultures, and do not look kindly upon atrocities in a "good cause," and the abuses that so horrify the faithful are not entirely fanciful; even the clumsiest propaganda usually takes off from something real. But as in the case of official enemies abroad, the real abuses, whatever they may be, have little relation to the drama constructed around them.

The phenomenon did not emerge from nowhere. One crucial component of the post-affluence class war has been a far-reaching takeover of the ideological system by the right, with a proliferation of right-wing think tanks, a campaign to extend conservative control still further over ideologically significant sectors of the colleges and universities, now replete with professorships of free enterprise, lavishly funded far-right student journals, and so on; and an array of other devices to restrict the framework of discussion and thought, as much as possible, to the reactionary end of the already narrow spectrum. Things actually reached such a point that a respected liberal foreign policy analyst could describe the statist-conservative *New York Times,* without irony, as the "establishment left" (Charles Maynes). In the political system, "liberal" joined "socialist" as a scare word; by 1992, the Democratic Party scarcely needed to make a gesture to popular constituencies it had once professed to represent. Gore Vidal hardly exaggerates when he describes US politics as a one-party system with two right wings. One aspect of this ideological triumph has been the deeper implantation of Orwellian rhetoric and standards of Political Correctness to which one must adhere to join respectable discussion, a number of examples already illustrated. Departure from these conventions of belief and rhetoric is virtually unthinkable, in the mainstream.[32]

The next chapter comes as no surprise to students of cultural management. After a period of intense and one-sided ideological struggle, in which business interests and the right-wing have won a remarkable victory in the doctrinal and political institutions, what could be more natural than a propaganda campaign claiming that it is left-fascists who have taken the commanding heights and control the entire culture, imposing their harsh standards everywhere? The situation is even more dire than 25 years ago, when calls for destroying the university "rang across every campus in the United States, and libraries were burned, and universities wrecked" and "it was impossible to imagine anything more slimy, sickly and stifling than the moral climate" in universities where black students were "a curse" until at last "the pus" was "squeezed out of the university," to quote some of the imagery that entrances the British right.[33] We hear heartfelt pleas for succor for the fading remnants who still resist the relentless left-wing onslaught, courageously upholding the banner of historical truth and Western culture in some embattled newspaper or isolated state college in central Idaho. What could be better designed to suppress the serious questions about doctrinal control, or a look at the hand that firmly holds the rod?

The complaints of those who continue to maintain their iron control with little challenge are not without their comic aspects. For every 100 articles berating the left-fascists who control everything, there might be one responding weakly that the takeover is not so complete as claimed, and none telling the truth—which is obvious enough, if only from the distribution of views allowed to surface. But restricting thought is a serious matter, and respected figures do not crack a smile as they march in the parade, bewailing the fact that they may have lost some comparative literature department (perhaps to a right-wing "deconstructionist" or liberal "relativist" denounced as left-fascists).

To the totalitarian mentality, even the slightest deviation is an awesome tragedy, and evokes the most impressive frenzy. And the spectacle makes a useful contribution to entrenching further the ideological controls that prevent the rascal multitude from attending to what is happening around them.

5. The "Vile Maxim of the Masters"

The world economy has not returned to the growth rates of the Bretton Woods era. The decline of the South was particularly severe in Africa and Latin America, where it was accompanied by rampant state terror. It was accelerated by the neoliberal economic doctrines dictated by the world rulers. The UN Economic Commission for Africa found that countries pursuing the recommended IMF programs had lower growth rates than those that relied on the public sector for basic human needs. The disastrous impact of neoliberal policies in Latin America was particularly striking.[34]

On occasion, developed societies take their own rhetoric semi-seriously and fail to protect themselves from the destructive impact of unregulated markets. The consequences are much the same as in the traditional colonial domains, if not so lethal. Australia in the 1980s is a case in point. Free market experiments carried by the Labor government succeeded in reducing national income by over 5 percent a year by the end of the decade. Real wages declined, Australian enterprises fell under foreign control, and the country advanced towards the status of a resource base for the Japan-centered state capitalist region, which maintained its dynamic growth thanks to the radical departures from neoliberal dogma that had spurred development in the first place. In Britain after a decade of Thatcherism, "prospects remain bleak because of insufficient reinvestment in the physical UK economy," the director of a US investment firm observes, echoing a Japanese counterpart who says, "We think it will take a long time for the UK economy to recover."[35]

As noted, the rich industrial societies themselves are taking on something of a Third World cast, with islands of extreme wealth and privilege amidst a rising sea of poverty and despair. This is particularly true of the US and Britain, subjected to Reagan-Thatcher discipline. Continental Europe is not too far behind, despite the residual power of labor and the social contract it has defended, and Europe's ability to export its slums through the device of "guest workers." The collapse of the Soviet empire offers new means to establish the North-South divide more firmly within the rich societies. During the May 1992 strike of public workers in Germany, the chairman of Daimler-Benz warned that the corporation might respond to strikes by transferring manufacturing facilities for its Mercedes cars elsewhere, perhaps to Russia, with its ample supply of trained, educated, healthy and (it is hoped) docile workers. The chairman of General Motors can wield similar threats with regard to Mexico and other sectors of the Third World. And East Europe. While GM plans to close 21 plants in the US and Canada, it has opened a $690 million assembly plant in East Germany with great expectations, heightened by the fact that, thanks to 43 percent unofficial unemployment, workers are willing to "work longer hours than their pampered colleagues in western Germany" at 40 percent of the wage and with few benefits, the *Financial Times* reports. Capital can readily move; people cannot, or are not permitted to by those who applaud Adam Smith's doctrines when it suits their needs.

It is not that Daimler-Benz is greatly suffering from the labor costs that management deplores. Two weeks after issuing the threat to move Mercedes production to Russia, the same chief executive, Edzard Reuter, announced the "excellent result" of an exceptionally strong first-quarter performance for 1992, with a profit rise of 14 percent and a 17 percent increase in sales, largely abroad; German workers are not quite the intended market for the Mercedes division, the chief profit earner for this huge conglomerate, which will slash up to 10,000 jobs in 1992, Reuter added, with another 10,000 to follow. Such facts, however, do not impress the US press, where the news columns bitterly assailed striking German workers for their "soft life," long vacations, and general lack of understanding of their proper place as tools of production for the rich and powerful. They should learn the lessons taught to American workers by the Caterpillar corporation at the same time: profits and productivity up, wages down, the right to strike effectively eliminated by the free resort to scabs ("permanent replacement workers").[36]

These are the fruits of the fierce corporate campaign undertaken as soon as American workers finally won the right to organize in the mid-1930s, after long years of bitter struggle and violent repression unmatched in the industrial world. Perhaps we may even return to the days when the admired philanthropist Andrew Carnegie could preach the virtues of "honest, industrious, self-denying poverty" to the victims of the great depression of 1896, shortly after he had brutally crushed the steel workers union at Homestead, while announcing that the defeated workers had sent him a wire saying, "Kind master, tell us what you wish us to do and we will do it for you." It was because he knew "how sweet and happy and pure the home of honest poverty is" that Carnegie sympathized with the rich, he explained, meanwhile sharing their grim fate in his lavishly appointed mansions.[37]

So a well-ordered society should run, according to the "vile maxim of the masters."

It is therefore only natural that when the battered unions finally recognize the reality of the ceaseless class war waged against them by the highly class-conscious corporate sector, the business press should react with wonder at the fact that some *unions* still cling to outdated "class-warfare ideology" and the "battered Marxist view" that "workers form a class of citizens with shared interests separate from those who own and control business"; and even exhibit such "quirks" as low pay for union leaders, who are treated like other members. The masters, in contrast, keep firmly to this "battered Marxist view," often expressing it in vulgar Marxist rhetoric—with values reversed, of course.[38]

Under existing conditions of social organization and concentration of power, (selective) free trade is hardly likely to increase the general welfare, as it could under other social arrangements. Those who declare their allegiance to Adam Smith are careful not to attend to his words: the principles of economic liberalism can have favorable consequences when implemented with appreciation for fundamental human rights. When shaped by "the savage injustice of the Europeans" and blind obedience to "the vile maxim," the consequences may favor "the architects" of policy, but others only by accident.

The experience of the US-Canada free trade agreement illustrates the process. In two years, Canada lost hundreds of thousands of jobs, many to industrialized regions of the US where government regulations virtually bar unions (the Orwellian term is "right to work," meaning "effectively illegal to organize"). These government policies, natural in a business-run society with the public largely marginalized, leave workers unprotected and much easier to exploit than in Canada, with its more vigorous union movement and its cultural climate of solidarity. The agreement has also been used to require Canada to abandon measures to protect the Pacific salmon, to bring pesticide regulations in line with more lax US standards, to refrain from steps to reduce emissions from lead, zinc and copper smelters, to end subsidies for replanting of forests after logging, and to bar a single-payer auto insurance plan in Ontario modeled on Canada's health insurance system, which would cost US insurance companies hundreds of millions of dollars in profits, if enacted. All such practices have been judged illegal barriers to free trade. By similar reasoning, the US objects to a GATT provision that allows countries to restrict food exports in times of need, demanding that US agribusiness must control raw materials no matter what the human cost.

At the same time, Canada, an asbestos exporter, is bringing charges against the US for imposing EPA standards on asbestos use in violation of trade commitments and the "international scientific evidence" about health risks of asbestos: the EPA has improperly gone beyond the "least burden-some requirements" for the corporations, Canada claims. At the GATT negotiations, the US is backing corporate proposals to restrict environmental and consumer protection to cases supported by "scientific evidence," to be judged by an agency made up of government officials and executives from chemical and food corporations.[39]

Perhaps the most dramatic current examples of the cynical pursuit of the "vile maxim" in international trade are Washington pressures to force Third World countries to accept US exports of tobacco, the world champion killer among lethal narcotics by a substantial margin. The Bush Administration launched its hypocritical "drug war" (timed nicely to produce the proper mood for the invasion of Panama) simultaneously with steps to force Third World countries to import this leading killer, and to allow advertising aimed at new markets, women and children particularly. GATT backed these efforts. The media, while climbing aboard the "drug war" bandwagon with appropriate fanfare, obliged the Administration further by completely suppressing the major drug story of the day. There were no headlines reading "US Demands to be World's Leading Narcotrafficker," or even a line in the back pages (statistically insignificant dissidents aside).

With Eastern Europe rejoining the Third World, drug pushers are leading the way in investment. "Cigarette makers flock to E. Europe," an upbeat front-page story is headlined in the *Boston Globe* : "While many American companies have been criticized for not being aggressive in investing in Eastern Europe, American cigarette companies have been trail-blazers." A tobacco executive explains: "There is little awareness of health and environmental problems in Hungary. We have about 10 years of an open playing field"—ten years of profits, before PC left-fascists begin to interfere with lucrative mass murder. "Of 30 developed countries," the news report reads, "life expectancy is shortest in Eastern Europe." US corporations will try to improve the statistics further, "trail-blazers for capitalism," basking in applause.

Note that Romania, Bulgaria, Russia, the former Yugoslavia, etc., are "developed countries," to be compared with Western Europe so as to demonstrate the evils of Communism—but not with Brazil, Guatemala, the Philippines, and other quasi-colonial domains that they resembled before they separated from the traditional Third World. That practice is an ineradicable feature of contemporary ideology. Honesty on this crucial issue is strictly *verboten*.[40]

Another story in the same issue illustrates how flexible an instrument economic doctrine can be. It celebrates the achievements of New Hampshire in dealing with its fiscal problems. The method was to encourage a successful enterprise that has become "the largest retail volume outlet for wine and liquor in the world, according to state officials," with $62 million in profits from sales of over $200 million in 1991, a $5 million increase in profit in a year. The increase is attributed in part to doubling of the advertising budget for alcohol, which ranks second to tobacco as a killer. The enterprise is a state monopoly. Hence its profits allow the most conservative state in the union to keep to the free market doctrines its leaders revere and to avoid taxes that would rob the wealthy to enrich welfare mothers. Another free market triumph, unnoticed.[41]

In theory, free trade arrangements should lower wages in high-wage countries and raise them in the poorer areas to which capital shifts, increasing global equity. But under prevailing conditions, a different outcome is likely. The senior economist at the Environment Department of the World Bank, Herman Daly, points out that the vast and growing supply of underemployed people in the Third World will "keep the supply of labor very large, and will make it impossible for wages worldwide to be bid up very much." Repression and terror lend their assistance. The outcome will be huge profits and chipping away at high wages and social gains, including laws against child labor, limits on working hours, and protection of the environment. "Anything that raises costs [is] going to tend to be competed down to the lowest common denominator in free international trade," Daly predicts—precisely as intended.[42]

Under current conditions of power and control, selective free trade will tend to drive the level of existence to the lowest grade for people who are spectators, not participants in the decisions that affect their lives. The basic thrust is well-described by Andrew Reding: "Unable to impose its agenda on a 'gridlocked' Congress that, however imperfectly, still responds to civil society ('special interest groups'), the Bush administration is linking up with like-minded elites abroad in an effort to legislate from without, ...constructing what amounts to international government, though a peculiar form thereof in which only business and trade representatives have any voice"; "Under cover of free trade, foreign governments and businesses are gaining an effective veto over national, state, and provincial legislation that elevates human welfare." There is, however, nothing in the least "peculiar" about this pursuit of the vile maxim of the masters, adapted to the current age.[43]

The maxim requires a slight amendment: "all for themselves *now*." The longer term is as irrelevant as other people. Thus in a lead news story, the *Wall Street Journal* hails George Bush's "extraordinary coup" in compelling the entire world to abandon plans for a meaningful agreement on greenhouse gases at the June 1992 Rio conference. Someone more clever than I could pen a wonderful story or cartoon on the final edition of the *Journal*, going to press with a passionate editorial demonstrating that global warming is a left-wing fraud just as the rising sea level engulfs the corporate headquarters.[44]

Overall, the 1980s accelerated a global rift between a small sector enjoying great privilege, and a growing mass of people suffering deprivation and misery. Though superfluous for wealth production or consumption, the only human functions recognized in the dominant institutions and their ideology, these people must be dealt with somehow. Current social policy in the US is to coop them up in urban centers where they can prey upon one another; or to lock them in jail, a useful concomitant of the drug war (see chapter 4.3).

The internationalization of capital that has accelerated since 1971 gives a somewhat new character to competition among national states. To cite one indication, while the US share in world exports of manufactures declined 3.5 percent from 1966 to 1984, the share of US-based TNCs slightly increased. And international trade patterns yield a very different picture if imports from overseas subsidiaries are counted as domestic production. Foreign affiliates increased their share of total exports of manufactures by US-based firms from under 18 percent in 1957 to 41 percent in 1984. "If such foreign production could be brought back to the United States," Richard Du Boff observes, "the nation's exports would double, according to some Commerce Department projections." A 1992 World Bank study reports that "intra-firm trade within the largest 350 [TNCs] contributed about 40% of total trade. More than a third of U.S. trade is between foreign affiliates and their U.S.-based parents." Over half of Malaysia's exports to the US were from US affiliates, Taiwan's five leading electronics exporters are US firms, 47 percent of Singapore's exports in 1982 were by US-owned firms. "Similarly, exports of electrical goods by Japanese producers in Korea had much to do with the rise of Korea in world electronics." "So all the textbook trade theory about comparative advantage and the virtues of frictionless open trading systems is nonsense," Doug Henwood observes, noting that the current estimates are probably higher than these figures, from the early 1980s: "Several hundred economically and politically powerful corporations with global networks dominate trade largely on their own terms, and then serve as their governments' advisors on trade strategy."

Commercial products reflect these tendencies; to take one example, almost a third of the market price of a GM Pontiac LeMans goes to producers in South Korea, over a sixth to Japan, about the same to a combination of Germany, Singapore, Britain, Barbados, and others. As a social entity, the country and most of its population may decline; the corporate empires are playing a different game, based on the theological doctrine that the masters have the right to make investment decisions, unencumbered by concerns of their servants in workplace and community. With somewhere between one-quarter and one-half of world trade already conducted within North-based TNCs, these are factors of growing importance as we look towards Year 501.[45]

6. The New Imperial Age

The realities are often presented with admirable frankness by the rulers and their ideologists. The London *Financial Times* features a lead article by the economic correspondent of the BBC World Service, James Morgan, under the heading: "The fall of the Soviet bloc has left the IMF and G7 to rule the world and create a new imperial age." We can, at last, approach the fulfillment of Churchill's vision, no longer troubled by the "hungry nations" who "seek more" and thus endanger the tranquility of the rich men who rule by right.

In the current version, "The construction of a new global system is orchestrated by the Group of Seven, the IMF, the World Bank and the General Agreement on Tariffs and Trade (GATT)," in "a system of indirect rule that has involved the integration of leaders of developing countries into the network of the new ruling class"—who, not surprisingly, turn out to be the old ruling class. Local managers can share the wealth, as long as they properly serve the rulers.

Morgan takes note of "the hypocrisy of the rich nations in demanding open markets in the Third World while closing their own." He might have added the World Bank report that the protectionist measures of the industrial countries reduce national income in the South by about twice the amount provided by official aid, largely export-promotion, most of it to the richer sectors of the "developing countries" (less needy, but better consumers). Or the UNCTAD estimate that *non-tariff* barriers (NTBs) of the industrial countries reduce Third World exports by almost 20 percent in affected categories, which include textiles, steel, seafood, animal feed and other agricultural products, with billions of dollars a year in losses. Or the World Bank estimate that 31 percent of the South's manufacturing exports are subject to NTBs as compared with the North's 18 percent. Or the 1992 report of the UN Human Development Program, reviewing the increasing gap between the rich and the poor (by now, 83 percent of the world's wealth in the hands of the richest billion, with 1.4 percent for the billion at the bottom of the heap); the doubling of the gap since 1960 is attributed to policies of the IMF and World Bank, and the fact that 20 of 24 industrial countries are more protectionist today than they were a decade ago, including the US, which celebrated the Reagan revolution by doubling the proportion of imports subject to restrictive measures. "And the upshot of decades of lending for development is that poor countries have lately been transferring more than $21 billion a year into the coffers of the rich," the *Economist* observes, summarizing the gloomy picture.

Individual cases fill out the details: for example, the quotas imposed by the US, UK, and France on their commercial rival Bangladesh, on grounds that its textiles threatened local industry; as the *Financial Times* puts it, "The Bangladesh government has been particularly stung by a US decision to impose anti-dumping duties of up to 42 percent on shop towels," imports that "amounted to a princely $2.46 [million]" from "one of the poorest of nations." Or the dumping of highly subsidized US and EC wheat and beef surpluses in Mali, Burkina Faso, and Togo, undermining native producers in such powerful competitors as the Sahel. Or US concerns over the threat to the US steel industry posed by imports from Trinidad-Tobago.[46]

"Third world [finance] ministers who have painfully dragged their own budgets out of persistent deficit have been particularly galled by the failure of industrial nations" to observe the rules, the *Financial Times* reports. "Echoing the gloom felt " in the South, World Bank president Lewis Preston deplored the practices of the industrial societies, who demand that the Third World "bear the burden of [structural] adjustment in the rich countries as well as in their own" and repeatedly fail to live up to their promises to reduce protection and provide aid. After a meeting of high-level officials of the donor countries, "World Bank officials say openly" that "they will back away from" their promises once again. Even "once-generous donors such as Sweden" are cutting back, while "less generous countries, such as the UK and US, ...are expected to cut still further" their minuscule contributions. A meeting of non-governmental organizations (NGOs) meanwhile concluded that "Structural adjustment imposed by the World

Bank and [IMF] have brought disaster to the working poor of as many as 100 countries," forced "to open their markets to a flood of cheap imports" while the rich refuse "to abandon their subsidies, quotas and high tariffs." The result is "'brutal' suppression of wages and living standards" and elimination of social programs, the effects increasing as the programs are implemented over the past decade or more.[47]

The institutions of "the new ruling class," which now "run large parts of the developing world and eastern Europe," "encourage" their clients to follow "the right kind of reform policy," Morgan continues. They must scrupulously avoid the policies that have led to successful development from 17th century England to East Asia's "little dragons" today, keeping to "the right kind" that have been highly beneficial to the international ruling class, if to few others. And when economic controls do not suffice to "encourage" proper behavior, we can resort once again to the security forces.

The simmering economic crisis does not, of course, leave the rulers unburdened. But they can call upon state power to come to the rescue. When Continental Illinois Bank and Trust faced collapse in 1984, the government was expected to respond, and did, with "the largest nationalization in American history" (Howard Wachtel). The director who presided over the financial disaster, Roger Anderson, was punished by appointment to the Federal Advisory Council, where he became an official adviser to director Paul Volker of the Federal Reserve, which had refused to use its disciplinary and control authority as it observed the growing crisis. If the collapse of the Olympia and York real estate empire indeed causes the $3 billion of losses that the banks initially feared, taxpayers will again be called upon to render the proper services. Austerity may be the right remedy for Latin American peasants, Polish workers, and the forgotten people of South-Central Los Angeles; but not for the people who count.[48]

The government also has the duty of raising protectionist barriers when needed: for example, to allow the US steel industry, which arose in the first place behind protectionist walls, to recapitalize by effectively restricting steel imports to 20 percent of the market since 1982. At the same time, it has the parallel responsibility of undermining unions, so that new "low-cost, non-union producers" can pay their labor force between one-half and one-third of what steel workers had gained after a century of bloody struggle, and thus become "exemplars of the lean and mean" in the admiring words of the London *Economist*, echoed by the *New York Times*, which also lauds the success of the "decade of protection from imported steel" and the resort to "nonunion work forces" for lowering costs.[49]

One important achievement of the new imperial age is that it further marginalizes the general population, clearing the way to uplifting rhetoric about our democratic ideals without fear that the wrong people might take it seriously. The global rulers can now operate with fewer constraints, more coordination and central management, and less interference from the rabble, who not only have no influence over the decisions of the rulers (the basic principle of capitalist autocracy), but also lack any awareness of them. Who follows the crucial decisions of the GATT negotiators or the IMF, with their enormous impact on global society? Or of the TNCs and international banks and investment firms that dominate production, commerce, and the conditions of life worldwide? The North American Free Trade Agreement (NAFTA) will have large-scale consequences (a bonanza for investors, very likely a disaster for workers and the environment). Its contents are unknown. The text was withheld even from the Labor Advisory Committee, which is required by law to review such measures, until one day before its report was due. Congress abdicated responsibility. Citizens know nothing[50]

For the past several hundred years, elite democratic theory has tended to range within a narrow spectrum. At one extreme, we have the libertarian thinker John Locke, who held that citizens have no right to discuss public affairs, though they may know about them; the modern variant is a bit more forthcoming (see p.18). At the other extreme we have statist reactionaries of the Reaganite variety ("conservatives"), who reject the right of the public even to know what their leaders are doing and therefore establish illegal state propaganda agencies, favor large-scale clandestine operations, block release of information about the government even from the distant past, and in other ways protect state power from scrutiny. Reagan-era censorship reached unprecedented heights, including suppression of the documentary record so extreme that the chairman of the academic advisory board for the State Department resigned in protest. The new imperial age marks a further move towards the authoritarian extreme of formal democratic practice.[51]

The public is not unaware of what is happening, though with the success of the policies of isolation and breakdown of organizational structure, the response is erratic and self-destructive: faith in ridiculous billionaire saviors, myths of past innocence and noble leaders, religious and jingoist fanaticism, conspiracy cults, unfocused skepticism and disillusionment—a mixture that has not had happy consequences in the past.

CHAPTER 3

NORTH-SOUTH/EAST-WEST

1. An Oversize "Rotten Apple"

In the broader framework just reviewed, the Cold War can be understood, in large measure, as an interlude in the North-South conflict of the Columbian era, unique in scale but similar to other episodes in significant respects.

Even in the pre-Columbian era, Eastern and Western Europe were diverging, with a fault line dividing Germany, East and West. "From the middle of the fifteenth century," Robert Brenner writes, "in much of western Europe, the conditions for crisis finally receded, and there was a new period of economic upturn." The "long-established and better-organized" peasant communities of Western Europe, "with established traditions of (often successful) struggle for their rights" and "an impressive network of village institutions for economic regulation and political self-government," were able to "break feudal controls over their mobility and to win full freedom," while in the East, "serfdom rose with a vengeance," opening the way to the "development of underdevelopment." In Poland, for example, national output appears to have reached a mid-16th century peak that was not attained again for 200 years. "The relative absence of village solidarity in the east...appears to have been connected with the entire evolution of the region as a colonial society," under "the leadership of the landlords."

The Third World, Leften Stavrianos observes, "made its first appearance in Eastern Europe," which began to provide raw materials for the growing textile and metal industries of England and Holland as far back as the 14th century, and then followed the (now familiar) path towards underdevelopment as trade and investment patterns took their natural course, superimposed on the divergent social patterns. The process soon left "the East as perhaps Europe's first colonial territories, a Third World of the 16th century providing raw materials for the industrialists back west, a testing ground for bankers and financiers to practice what they would later perfect in more distant lands" (John Feffer). Russia itself was so vast and militarily powerful that its subordination to the economy of the West was delayed, but by the 19th century it was well on the way towards the fate of the South, with deep and widespread impoverishment and foreign control of key sectors of the economy.

A late 19th century Czech traveller to Russia described the fading of Europe as one travels East, narrowing finally down to the railway and a few hotels: "The aristocratic landowner would furnish his country house in the European way; similarly, the continuously multiplying factories in the countryside are European oases. All technical and practical equipment is European: railways, factories, and banks...; the army, the navy and partly the bureaucracy as well." Foreign capital participation in Russian railways reached 93 percent by 1907, capital for development was mostly foreign, largely French, and debt was rising rapidly, as Russia settled into the typical Third World pattern. By 1914, Russia was "becoming a semi-colonial possession of European capital" (Teodor Shanin).

"Many Russians, whatever their political beliefs, resented the semi-colonial status accorded to their country in the West," Z.A.B. Zeman writes: "The Bolshevik revolution was, in a critical sense, the reaction of a developing, essentially agrarian society against the West: against its political self-absorption, economic selfishness and military wastefulness. The present North-South divide between the rich and the poor countries, and the tensions it has created in the twentieth century, had its European, East-West antecedents." Beyond Russia itself, "contrasts between the East and the West of Europe...became sharper than they had ever been" in the 19th and early 20th centuries, he adds, remaining so for much of Eastern Europe through the interwar period.[1]

The Bolshevik takeover in October 1917, which quickly aborted incipient socialist tendencies and destroyed any semblance of working-class or other popular organization, extricated the USSR from the Western-dominated periphery, setting off the inevitable reaction, beginning with immediate military intervention by Britain, France, Japan, and the US. These were, from the outset, basic elements of the Cold War.

The logic was not fundamentally different from the case of Grenada or Guatemala, though the scale of the problem surely was. Bolshevik Russia was "radical nationalist." It was "Communist" in the technical sense, unwilling "to complement the industrial economies of the West"; in contrast, it was not in the least "Communist" or "socialist" in the literal sense of these terms, socialist elements of the pre-revolutionary period having been quickly demolished. Furthermore, though no conceivable military threat, the Bolshevik example had undeniable appeal elsewhere in the Third World. Its "very existence...constituted a nightmare" to US policymakers, Melvyn Leffler observes: "Here was a totalitarian country with a revolutionary ideology that had great appeal to Third World peoples bent on throwing off Western rule and making rapid economic progress." US and British officials feared that the appeal extended to the core industrial countries, as discussed earlier.

The Soviet Union was, in short, a gigantic "rotten apple." Adopting the basic logic and rhetoric of the North-South conflict, one may therefore justify the Western invasion after the revolution as a defensive action "in response to a profound and *potentially far-reaching intervention* by the new Soviet government in the internal affairs, not just of the West, but of virtually every country in the world," namely, "the Revolution's challenge...to the very survival of the capitalist order." "The security of the United States" was "in danger" already in 1917, not just in 1950, and intervention was therefore entirely warranted in defense against the change of the social order in Russia and the announcement of revolutionary intentions (diplomatic historian John Lewis Gaddis; my emphasis).[2]

The "rapid economic growth" aroused particular attention in the South—and corresponding concerns among Western policymakers. In his 1952 study of late development, Alexander Gerschenkron describes the "approximate sixfold increase in the volume of industrial output" as "the greatest and the longest [spurt of industrialization] in the history of the country's industrial development," though this "great industrial transformation engineered by the Soviet government" had "a remote, if any" relation to "Marxian ideology, or any socialist ideology for that matter"; and was, of course, carried out at extraordinary human cost. In his studies 10 years later of long-term trends in economic development, Simon Kuznets listed Russia among the countries with the highest rate of growth of per capita product, along with Japan and Sweden, with the US—having started from a far higher peak—in the middle range over a century, slightly above England.[3]

The ultranationalist threat was greatly enhanced after Russia's leading role in defeating Hitler left it in control of Eastern and parts of Central Europe, separating these regions too from the domains of Western control. The rotten apple was so huge—and after World War II, so militarily powerful as well—and the virus it was spreading so dangerous, that this particular facet of the North-South conflict took on a life of its own from the outset. Long before Lenin and Trotsky took power, the threat of "Communism" and "anarchism" had regularly been invoked by the business-government-press complex to justify the violent suppression of attempts by working people to organize and to gain elementary rights. The Wilson Administration was able to extend these techniques, exploiting the Bolshevik takeover as an opportunity to crush the labor movement and independent thought, with the backing of the press and business community; the pattern has been standard since. The October revolution also provided the framework for Third World intervention, which became "defense against Communist aggression," whatever the facts might be. Avid US support for Mussolini from his 1922 March on Rome, later support for Hitler, was based on the doctrine that Fascism and Nazism were understandable, if sometimes extreme, reactions to the far more deadly Bolshevik threat—a threat that was internal, of course; no one thought the Red Army was on the march. Similarly, the US had to invade Nicaragua to protect it from Bolshevik Mexico, and 50 years later, to attack Nicaragua to protect Mexico from Nicaraguan Bolshevism. The supple character of ideology is a wonder to behold.

Facts are commonly reshaped to establish that some intended target of attack is an outpost of the Kremlin (later, Peiping). On deciding in 1950 to support France's effort to quell the threat of independent nationalism in Vietnam, Washington assigned to the intelligence services the task of demonstrating that Ho Chi Minh was a puppet of Moscow or Peiping (either would do). Despite diligent efforts, evidence of "Kremlin-directed conspiracy" could be found "in virtually all countries except Vietnam," which appeared to be "an anomaly." Nor could links with China be detected. The natural conclusion was that Moscow considers the Viet Minh "sufficiently loyal to be trusted to determine their day-to-day policy without supervision." Lack of contact therefore proves the enormity of the designs of the Evil Empire. There are numerous other examples.

A variant is illustrated by the case of Guatemala. As the US prepared to overthrow its government, an Embassy officer advised that a planned OAS resolution to bar arms and Communist agents would "enable us to stop ships including our own to such an extent that it will disrupt Guatemala's economy," thus leading to a pro-US coup or increased Communist influence, which would in turn "justify...the U.S. to take strong measures," unilaterally if necessary. In accord with such reasoning, a routine foreign policy procedure is to use embargo, terror, and the threat of greater violence to compel the target to turn to the Russians for support, thus revealing itself to be a tentacle of the Soviet conspiracy, reaching out to strangle us. The technique was used against Guatemala and Nicaragua with extreme clumsiness, but great success in a highly conformist intellectual culture.[4]

2. "Logical Illogicality"

As Russia absorbed the major blows of Nazi force, Stalin became an ally, the admired "Uncle Joe"; but with ambivalence. Roosevelt's wartime strategy, he confided to his son in private, was for the US to be the "reserves," waiting for the Russians to exhaust themselves in the combat against the Nazis, after which the Americans would move in for the kill. One of the preeminent Roosevelt scholars, Warren Kimball, concludes that "aid to the Soviet Union became a presidential priority" on the assumption that Red Army victories would allow the President to keep US soldiers out of a land war in Europe. Truman went much further. When Germany attacked the Soviet Union in June 1941, he commented that "If we see that Germany is winning we ought to help Russia and if Russia is winning we ought to help Germany and that way let them kill as many as possible." By 1943, the US began to reinstate Fascist collaborators and sympathizers in Italy, a pattern that extended through the world as territories were liberated, reinstating the tolerance for fascism as a barrier to radical social change. Recall that Soviet aggression was not an issue prewar, nor anticipated postwar.[5]

The problem of the enormous rotten apple led to some odd contortions in policymaking. In an important study of July 1945, transmitted by Secretary of War Stimson to the Secretary of State, military planners tried to put a satisfactory gloss on the US intention to take control of the world and surround Russia with military force, while denying the adversary any rights beyond its borders. "To argue that it is necessary to preserve a unilateral military control by the U.S. or Britain over Panama or Gibraltar and yet deny a similar control to Russia at the Dardanelles may seem open to the criticism of being illogical," they worried, particularly since the Dardanelles provided Russia with its only warm water access and was, in fact, to be kept firmly under unilateral US-British control. But the criticism is only superficially plausible, the planners concluded: the US design is "a logical illogicality." By no "stretch of the imagination" could the US and Britain be thought to have "expansionist or aggressive ambition." But Russia

> has not as yet proven that she is entirely without expansionist ambitions... She is inextricably, almost mystically, related to the ideology of Communism which superficially at least can be associated with a rising tide all over the world wherein the common man aspires to higher and wider horizons. Russia must be sorely tempted to combine her strength with her ideology to expand her influence over the earth. Her actions in the past few years give us no assured bases for supposing she has not flirted with the thought.

In short, the burden is upon the Russians to prove that they have no intention of associating with the rascal multitude who "aspire to higher and wider horizons," with the "poor who have always wanted to plunder the rich" (Dulles). Until they do so convincingly, it is only logical for responsible men who do not consort with criminal elements bent on plunder, and flirt with no such subversive thoughts as higher aspirations, to establish their unilateral control over the world. Russia must demonstrate that it is not a potential threat to "the very survival of the capitalist order" (Gaddis). Once it has clearly accepted the principle that Churchill's rich men must have their way everywhere, it may be allowed to enter the servants' quarters.

The notion of "logical illogicality" is another useful tool in the ideological kit, which merits wider use.

The severity of the danger had been underscored a month earlier by William Donovan, director of the OSS (the precursor of the CIA). In a Europe "racked by war and suffering widespread misery," he warned, the Soviets have "a strong drawing card in the proletarian philosophy of Communism." The US and its allies have "no political or social philosophy equally dynamic or alluring." As noted, the same problem was deplored by Eisenhower and Dulles ten years later, and regularly by the US in Indochina.[6]

The reasoning outlined in 1945 prevailed throughout the Cold War period, and follows naturally from the general logic of the North-South conflict. The same reasoning has often been applied at home, for example, after World War I, when "there could be no nice distinctions drawn between the theoretical ideals of the radicals and their actual violations of our national laws" and "no time to waste on hairsplitting over infringement of liberty" (Attorney-General Palmer and the *Washington Post,* during Wilson's Red Scare). The same doctrine was invoked to justify the bombing of Libyan cities in 1986 in "self-defense against future attack," as the government announced to much acclaim among devoted advocates of international law.[7]

"Clear and present dangers" cannot be tolerated, however clouded the clarity and remote the present.

The logic is simple: the rich men rule by right the world they own, and cannot be expected to tolerate potential criminal action that might interfere with "stability." The threat has to be cut off at the pass. And if it takes form, we are entitled to do what we must to set things right.

It was not Stalin's crimes that troubled Western leaders. Truman noted in his diary, "I can deal with Stalin," who is "honest—but smart as hell." Others agreed, among them Eisenhower, Leahy, Harriman, and Byrnes. What went on in Russia was not his concern, Truman declared. Stalin's death would be a "real catastrophe," he felt. But cooperation was contingent on the US getting its way 85 percent of the time, Truman made clear. Melvyn Leffler—who has examined the record in close detail and has much respect for the achievements and foresight of the early postwar leadership—remarks that "Truman liked" Stalin. He comments on the lack of any "sense of real compassion and/or moral fervor" in the documentary record. "These men were concerned primarily with power and self-interest, not with real people facing real problems in the world that had just gone through fifteen years of economic strife, Stalinist terror, and Nazi genocide."[8]

The animating concern was not Stalin's awesome crimes, but the apparent successes in development with their broad appeal, and the possibility that the Russians might be "flirting with the thought" of lending support to "aspirations of the common man" in the West, and subjugated and oppressed people everywhere. The failure of East Europe to resume its traditional role as a supplier of food and raw materials to the West compounded these concerns. The problem is not crimes, but insubordination, a fact illustrated by a host of gangsters from Mussolini, Hitler, and Stalin to Saddam Hussein.

Though US planners did not expect a Soviet attack on the West, they were concerned about Soviet military power, for two fundamental reasons. First, they feared that the USSR might respond to the US takeover of the world, not recognizing the "logic" in our "illogicality." Particularly ominous from the Soviet point of view was the reconstruction and rearmament of Germany and Japan, two powerful traditional enemies, and their incorporation within the US system of power, which was intent on exterminating the Soviet virus. That these developments posed a major threat to Soviet security was well-understood by US planners, who therefore feared a possible reaction.

Second, Soviet power served to deter US violence, impeding US actions to ensure that the "periphery" fulfills its service function. What is more, for its own cynical reasons the Kremlin often lent support to targets of US attack and subversion, and sought to gain advantage where it could. The very existence of Soviet power provided a certain space for maneuver in the South. As a counterweight to US power, it opened the way toward nonalignment, which, US planners feared, would deprive the West of control over the domains required to maintain traditional privilege and power. Exploiting these openings, Third World leaders sought to carve out an independent role in world affairs. By the 1960s, the UN, previously a docile instrument and hence much admired, fell under "the tyranny of the majority." The growing influence of undeserving elements set off intensive US efforts to destroy the errant organization, which continue under a different guise with the UN, at last, safely back under control.[9]

In short, the USSR was not only guilty of ultranationalism and under-mining "stability" through the rotten apple effect. It was committing yet another crime: interfering with US designs and helping the victims resist, an intolerable affront that few in the South could match, though Cuba did as it blocked US-backed South African aggression in Angola. Accordingly, there could be no accommodation, no détente. Even as the Soviet Union collapsed through the 1980s, the test of Gorbachev's "New Thinking" put forth in the liberal press was his willingness to allow US violence to proceed without impediment; failing that criterion, his gestures are meaningless, more Communist aggressiveness.[10]

For such reasons, the US had no serious interest in resolving the Cold War conflict except on terms of Soviet submission. Though we lack Soviet records, and therefore can only speculate on what internal thinking may have been, what is available suggests that Stalin and his successors would have been willing to accept the role of junior managers in the US-dominated world system, running their own dungeon without external interference, and cooperating in joint efforts to maintain global "stability," much as they did in the 1930s, when Communist armies spearheaded the onslaught against the popular social revolution in Spain.

The view from Washington was spelled out clearly by Secretary of State Dean Acheson to an executive session of the Senate Foreign Relations Committee, where he explained the US negotiating position on Germany for the forthcoming May 1949 meeting of foreign ministers. Acheson's stance was "so uncompromising," Leffler writes, that members of the Committee "were stunned." In response to Arthur Vandenberg's concern that the US position would institutionalize a permanent Cold War, Acheson responded that the goal was not to avoid Cold War but to consolidate Western power, under US control of course. "When Senator Claude Pepper urged Acheson to consider the possibility of treating the Soviets fairly," Acheson "scorned the idea," informing the Committee that "he aimed to integrate west German strength into Western Europe and establish a flourishing Western community that would serve as a magnet to the Kremlin's eastern satellites": the result would be not only to undermine Soviet power but also to restore quasi-colonial relations with the East. When the foreign ministers meeting broke down in a predictable stalemate, "Acheson was elated," Leffler continues. The Soviets "are back on the defensive," Acheson declared: "They are visibly concerned and afraid of the fact that they have lost Germany."[11]

As discussed, apparent Soviet interest in a peaceful European settle-ment in 1949 was regarded not as an opportunity but as a threat to "national security," overcome by the establishment of NATO. On similar grounds, the

US never even considered Stalin's proposals for a unified and demilitarized Germany with free elections in 1952, and did not pursue Khrushchev's call for reciprocal moves after his radical cutbacks in Soviet military forces and armaments in 1961-1963 (well-known to the Kennedy Administration, but dismissed). On the eve of his election, Kennedy had written that Russia was attempting to conquer Europe "by the indirect route of winning the vast outlying raw materials region," the conventional reference to Soviet support for nonalignment and neutralism. Gorbachev's efforts to reduce Cold War confrontation in the mid-1980s (including unilateral force reductions and proposals to ban nuclear weapons tests, abolish the military pacts, and remove naval fleets from the Mediterranean) were ignored. Reduction of tension is of little value, short of the return of the miscreants to their service role.[12]

The Soviet Union reached the peak of its power by the late 1950s, always far behind the West. A 1980 study of the Center for Defense Information (CDI), tracing Russian influence on a country-by-country basis since World War II, concluded reasonably that Soviet power had declined from that peak to the point where by 1979, "the Soviets were influencing only 6 percent of the world's population and 5 percent of the world's GNP, exclusive of the Soviet Union." By the mid-1960s, the Soviet economy was stagnating or even declining; there was an accompanying decline in housing, commerce, and life expectancy, while infant mortality increased by a third from 1970 to 1975.[13]

The Cuban missile crisis of 1962, revealing extreme Soviet vulnerability, led to a huge increase in military spending, levelling off by the late 1970s. The economy was then visibly stagnating and the autocracy unable to control rising dissidence. The command economy had carried out basic industrial development but was unable to proceed to more advanced stages, and also suffered from the global recession that devastated much of the South. By the 1980s, the system collapsed, and the core countries, always far richer and more powerful, "won the Cold War." Much of the Soviet empire will probably return to its traditional Third World status, with the old CP privileged class (the *Nomenklatura*) taking on the role of the Third World elites linked to international business and financial interests.[14]

A 1990 World Bank report describes the outcome in these terms: "The Soviet Union and the People's Republic of China have until recently been among the most prominent examples of relatively successful countries that deliberately turned from the global economy," relying on their "vast size" to make "inward-looking development more feasible than it would be for most countries," but "they eventually decided to shift policies and take a more active part in the global economy." A more accurate rendition would be that their "vast size" made it possible for them to withstand the refusal of the West to allow them to take part in the global economy on terms other than traditional subordination, the "active part in the global economy" dictated to the South by the world rulers.[15]

Throughout the period, great efforts have been undertaken to present the Soviet Union as larger than life, about to overwhelm us. The most important Cold War document, NSC 68 of April 1950, sought to conceal the Soviet weakness that was unmistakably revealed by analysis, so as to convey the required image of the "slave state" pursuing its "implacable purpose" of gaining "absolute authority" over the world, its way barred only by the United States, with its almost unimaginable nobility and perfection. So awesome was the threat that Americans must come to accept "the necessity for just suppression" as a crucial feature of "the democratic way." They must accept "a large measure of sacrifice and discipline," including thought control and a shift of government spending from social programs to "defense and foreign assistance" (in translation: subsidy for advanced industry and export promotion). In a 1948 book, liberal activist Cord Meyer, an influential figure in the CIA, wrote that the right to strike must be "denied" if it is not voluntarily restricted, given "the urgency of [the] defense plans" required. And "citizens of the United States will have to accustom themselves to the ubiquitous presence of the powerful secret police needed for protection against sabotage and espionage." As under Wilson, fascist methods are needed to guard against the threat to "stability."

By 1980, no one with eyes open could fail to perceive the "loss of hegemony and relative economic decline" of both superpowers "as the bipolar system of the postwar years has gradually evolved to something more complex," and the corresponding decline of "the Cold War system that proved so useful for both superpowers as a device for controlling their allies and mobilizing domestic support for the ugly and often costly measures required to impose the desired form of order and stability on their respective domains." Nor was there any doubt as to their relative strength and influence, as the CDI and other sane analysts were aware. Nevertheless, the period was marked by rising hysteria about the gargantuan Soviet system, leaping from strength to strength, straddling the globe, challenging the US and even threatening its survival, establishing positions of strength in Cambodia, Nicaragua, Mozambique, and other such crucial centers of strategic power.[16]

These delusionary efforts were accompanied by much fantasy about Soviet military spending. Again, no little ingenuity was required, if only because the Pentagon's own figures in 1982 showed that NATO (including the US, facing no foreign threat) outspent the Warsaw Pact (including the

USSR, deploying much of its force on the border with its Chinese enemy) by $250 billion from 1971 to 1980. But these figures, as economist Franklyn Holzman has been demonstrating for some years, are inaccurate, much overstating Soviet strength. When corrected, they reveal a total gap in NATO's favor of about $700 billion for the decade of the 1970s. The Carter military build-up, extended under Reagan, and pressures on the NATO powers to do the same, were "justified in part by the false claims of a steady increase in the Soviet rate of military spending," Raymond Garthoff observes: "The 'relentless Soviet buildup' to an important extent reflected an American error in estimating Soviet outlays, rather than being a 'disquieting index of Soviet intentions'," as claimed during the late Carter years, and "the American lead in absolute numbers of strategic bombs and warheads actually widened between 1970 and 1980." Holzman makes a strong case that the errors involved "deliberate [CIA] distortion" from the late 1970s, under intense political pressure.[17]

Exaggeration of the enemy's power is a characteristic feature of the North-South conflict; at the outer limits, one hears that Sandinistas were about to march on Texas, even that *Grenada* was a menace, "strategically located" to threaten US oil supplies, as "the Cubans surely appreciate" (Robert Leiken). The procedure was not invented with the Cold War. "A review of alarmist scenarios from the past might well begin with the threat from Chile posited in the 1880s by advocates of a new navy," John Thompson observes, reviewing the "tradition" of "exaggeration of American vulnerability." Recall as well the "mingled hordes of lawless Indians and negroes" who compelled us to conquer Florida in self-defense, and on back to colonial days.[18]

The purpose is transparent. The cultural managers must have at hand the tools to do their work. And apart from the most cynical, planners must convince themselves of the justice of the actions, often monstrous, that they plan and implement. There are only two pretexts: self-defense and benevolence. It need not be assumed that use of the tools is mere deception or careerism, though sometimes it is. Nothing is easier than to convince oneself of the merits of actions and policies that serve self-interest. Expressions of benevolent intent, in particular, must be regarded with much caution: they can be taken seriously when the policies advocated happen to be harmful to self-interest, a historical category that is vanishingly small.

In the Cold War case, there is another factor that may have helped extend the delusional system beyond its normal practitioners: the Russians had their own reasons for depicting themselves as an awesome superpower marching on towards a still grander future. When the world's two major propaganda systems agree on some doctrine, however fanciful, it is not easy to escape its grip.

A striking example is the delusion that the Cold War was a struggle between socialism and capitalism. The Soviet Union, from 1917, has been even more remote from socialism than the US and its allies have been from capitalism, but again, both major propaganda systems have had a longstanding interest in claiming otherwise: the West, so as to defame socialism by associating it with Leninist tyranny, and the USSR, so as to gain what prestige it could by associating itself with socialist ideals—ideals whose force was powerful and wide-ranging. "I believe that socialism is the grandest theory ever presented, and I am sure some day it will rule the world," Andrew Carnegie told the *New York Times,* and when it does, "we will have attained the millennium." To this day, almost half the population find the phrase "from each according to his ability, to each according to his need" to be such an obvious truth that they attribute it to the US Constitution, a text largely unknown but taken to be akin to Holy Writ. The absurd association of Bolshevik tyranny with socialist freedom was doubtless reinforced by the accord between the two major doctrinal systems, though for intellectuals, the appeal of Lenin's authoritarian deviation from the socialist tradition has deeper roots.[19]

By the early 1980s it was becoming impossible to sustain the illusion of Soviet power, and a few years later, it was laid to rest.

3. Return to Normalcy

If early modern Eastern Europe was "a testing ground for bankers and financiers to practice what they would later perfect in more distant lands" (Feffer), then by the 1980s the shoe was on the other foot: it was to be a "testing ground" for the doctrines of laissez-faire economic development that had been avoided by every successful developed country, and applied under Western tutelage in the South with destructive effects. A symbolic illustration of the reversal is the role of Harvard economist Jeffrey Sachs, who "in the 1980s had devastated the Bolivian economy in the name of monetary stability," Feffer accurately observes, and then moved on to Poland to offer the harsh medicine conventionally prescribed for the service areas.

Following the rules, Poland has seen "the creation of many profitable private businesses," the knowledgeable analyst Abraham Brumberg observes, along with "a drop of nearly 40 percent in production, enormous hardships and social turmoil," and "the collapse of two governments." In

1991, gross domestic product (GDP) declined 8-10 percent with an 8 percent fall in investment and a near doubling of unemployment, reaching 11 percent of the workforce in early 1992, after an official GDP decline of 20 percent in two years. A 1992 World Bank report on the Polish economy, discussed by Anthony Robinson in the *Financial Times,* concluded that "The fiscal situation has worsened to the point where hyperinflation is an immediate danger. Unemployment has reached a level that cannot be tolerated for long. Investment in infrastructure and human resource development has shrunk to levels that, if maintained, will undermine the prospects for sustained growth." It warned that "None of the long-term supply side reforms" that the Bank advocates "stands any chance of success if Poland slides back into hyperinflation, or if its economy continues to decline as dramatically as it has in the last two years." "Private savings were virtually eliminated by hyperinflation and the 1990 economic stabilisation programme," Robinson adds, while problems were exacerbated by capital flight of several tens of millions of dollars a month. While the decline will "bottom out," prospects appear dim for much of the population.

Russia has been going the same way. "On some estimates," Michael Haynes observes, "capital flight from the USSR was somewhere between $14-19 billion in 1991," some of it short-term, some for longer-term structural reasons. Production declined in 1991. Economic and finance minister Yegor Gaidar warned of a further drop of 20 percent in early 1992, with the "worst period" still ahead. Light industrial production fell by 15-30 percent in the first 19 days of January 1992 while deliveries of meat, cereals, and milk fell by a third or more. From early 1989 through mid-1992, according to IMF and World Bank statistics, industrial output fell by 45 percent and prices rose 40-fold in Poland and real wages were almost halved; figures for the rest of Eastern Europe were not much better.

Western ideologists are impressed with what has been achieved, but concerned that economic irrationality might impede further progress. Under the heading "Factory Dinosaurs Imperil Poland's Economic Gain," *New York Times* correspondent Stephen Engelberg looks at "a worst-case instance of how the industrial legacies of the Communist system threaten to drag down economic reform plans in Poland and other Eastern European nations": the city of Rzeszow, dependent on an aircraft manufacturer for employment, tax revenues, even heat from industrial by-products. The free market policies have "brought cities like Warsaw or Cracow alive with commerce," Engelberg notes, doubling the number of private businesses (though the people too impoverished to buy even basic goods do not reach the threshold). But this welcome progress is threatened by calls for government intervention to meet minimal human needs and rescue enterprises suffering

from loss of markets and supplies and unpaid debts after the collapse of
the USSR.

No less ominous, Engelberg observes, is "social unrest from the
workers," who now have a measure of control in factories and even go on
strike to prevent closure of plants that might be rescued by "Government-
guaranteed loans to rebuild foundries." The Solidarity Union calls on the
Government "to forgive overdue taxes and place big new airplane orders
for the Polish army." A Solidarity leader says that "the Government has to
make a decision whether or not it needs an aircraft industry or whether it
has to be restructured or whether one-half should produce aviation and the
rest something else." But Western analysts understand that such decisions
are not for the Poles to make: they are to be made by the "free market"—or
more accurately, the powerful institutions that dominate it. And no embarrassing questions are raised about the fate of the US aircraft industry, or
advanced industry in general, without the huge public subsidy to create
and maintain it; and so on through the functioning parts of the economy.
Or about the Chrysler bail-out or Reagan's rescue of Continental Illinois
Bank; or the hundreds of billions of taxpayer dollars to pay off S&L
managers and investors, freed from both regulation and risk by the genius
of Reaganomics. We put aside the question of how "economic irrationality"
of the kind denied to the Third World created an economy in which
Americans no longer pursue their comparative advantage in exporting furs.

The problem of uppity workers is also noted by *Financial Times*
correspondent Anthony Robinson. He writes that many communities de-
pend upon "large plants where workers' councils exert strong influence on
management unversed in the ways of the market." This unwarranted
influence of working people undermines the lessons of economic rationality and democracy that we are patiently trying to impart. Economic rationality requires that the tools of production overcome their reluctance to see
their communities and families destroyed. "It is not for the commodity to
decide where it should be offered for sale, to what purpose it should be
used, at what price it should be allowed to change hands, and in what
manner it should be consumed or destroyed," as Karl Polanyi commented
in his classic study of the laissez-faire experiment in 19th century England,
quickly terminated as it came to be understood by the business classes that
their interests would be harmed by the free market, which "could not exist
for any length of time without annihilating the human and natural substance
of society; it would have physically destroyed man and transformed his
surroundings into a wilderness."

As for democracy, in the approved sense it allows no room for any
popular interference in the totalitarian structure of the corporate economy,

with all that follows in other spheres of life. The role of the public is to follow orders, not to interfere.

Gabrielle Glaser reports one of the results of "Poland's opening to Western market forces" in the *New York Times* under the heading: "Booming Polish Market: Blond, Blue-Eyed Babies." An "unexpected side effect" of the free market, she writes, is "a booming traffic" in this commodity, as "young mothers are being pressed to sign away the rights to their children." The numbers may reach tens of thousands. "I hate to say it," the director of a state adoption agency comments, "but it seems to me that Poland has one of the most serious markets of white babies." Polish journals tend to shy away from the role of the Church, Glaser reports, but one inquiry reported that the Mother Superior of one adoption home receives $15,000 for each baby girl and up to $25,000 for each baby boy. Asked about the report, she replied: "I cannot give you any information. Good-bye." She did, however, display her papal award for "defending life," "an honor Pope John Paul II bestows on anti-abortion crusaders in his native Poland," Glaser comments.

Why this side effect is "unexpected," Glaser does not explain. Indeed, as she notes, such reports "are not new in Eastern Europe or the third world: Romania became notorious for the practice after its 1989 revolution." Post-1989 Romania is a curious choice. The phenomenon is a well-known concomitant of the integration of the South into the world order in the service role; reports of sale of children are, in fact, some of the more benign that are familiar to those who do not choose to shield themselves from the wrong kind of facts. The "side effects" of the subjection of the South to market forces are not in the least unexpected, except to the laser-like vision of the trained ideologue.

"Unexpected side effects" of the invisible hand have also been found in Russia, again eliciting much surprise. A front-page *New York Times* headline reads: "The Russians' New Code: If It Pays, Anything Goes." "It is not just a matter of crime, corruption, prostitution, smuggling, and drug and alcohol abuse," all on the rise: "There is also a widespread view that...people are out for themselves and anything goes"—unlike the United States, where pursuit of "the vile maxim of the masters" is unknown, or the Third World domains that have been subject to our helping hand. "Swindles and bribes are hardly a new phenomenon in Russia," correspondent Celestine Bohlen observes, and were familiar in the "old Communist system"—again, unlike the US and its clients.

During the same days, the *Times* was reporting the saga of President Fernando Collor of Brazil, the fair-haired boy of Washington and the business community, who broke new records in corruption in a richly-endowed country that has been a "testing area" for US experts for half a century (see chapter 7). One may recall a few domestic examples of corruption as well, from the days of the Founding Fathers, no slouches in this game, and on to the Reaganites and Wall Street in the 1980s. Corruption is an intrinsic feature of "the old Communist system," the ideological institutions (correctly) proclaim: under "capitalist democracy," it is an aberration, quickly corrected.

The new "ostentatious wealth sets most citizens' nerves on edge," Bohlen continues, describing the standard consequences of neoliberal remedies. "Crime has soared in Russia after the collapse of Communism, as it did in Eastern Europe," including white-collar crimes, which have "taken off." But "the levels of crime are still well below New York's standards." There is still room for progress towards the capitalist ideal.

The economies of Eastern Europe stagnated or declined through the eighties, but went into free fall as the IMF regimen was adopted with the end of the Cold War in 1989. By the fourth quarter of 1990, Bulgaria's industrial output (which had previously remained steady) had dropped 17 percent, Hungary's 12 percent, Poland's over 23 percent, Romania's 30 percent. The UN Economic Commission for Europe reported in late 1991 that the region's output had declined 1 percent in 1989, 10 percent in 1990, and 15 percent in 1991, predicting a further decline of 20 percent for 1991, with the same or worse likely in 1992. One result has been a general disillusionment with the democratic opening, even some growing support for the former Communist parties. In Russia, the economic collapse has led to much suffering and deprivation, as well as "weariness, cynicism, and anger, directed at all politicians, from Yeltsin down," Brumberg reports, and particularly at the ex-*Nomenklatura* who, as predicted, are coming to be the typical Third World elite serving the interests of the foreign masters. In public opinion polls, half the respondents considered the August 1991 *Putsch* illegal, one-fourth approved, and the rest had no opinion.

Support for democratic forces is limited, not because of opposition to democracy, but because of what it becomes under Western rules. It will either have the very special meaning dictated by the needs of the rich men, or it will be the target of destabilization, subversion, strangulation, and violence until proper behavior is restored. Exceptions are rare.[20]

Loss of faith in democracy is of small concern in the West, though the "bureaucratic capitalism" that might be introduced by Communists-turned-yuppies is a potential problem. In the Western doctrinal system, democratic forms are meritorious as long as they do not challenge business control. But they are secondary: the real priority is integration into the global economy with the opportunities this provides for exploitation and plunder.

With IMF backing, the European Community (EC) has provided a clear test of good behavior for Eastern Europe. In the old days, the Russians had to prove that they were not "flirting with the thought" of supporting the aspirations of "the common man." Today, East Europe must demonstrate that "economic liberalization with a view to introducing market economies" is irreversible. There can be no attempts at a "Third Way" with unacceptable social democratic features, let alone more substantive steps towards democracy and freedom, such as workers' control. The chief economic adviser to the EC, Richard Portes, defined acceptable "regime change" not in terms of democratic forms, but as "a definitive exit from the socialist planned economy—and its irreversibility." One recent IMF report, Peter Gowan notes, "concentrates overwhelmingly on the Soviet Union's role as a producer of energy, raw materials, and agricultural products, giving very little scope for the republics of the former Soviet Union to play a major role as industrial powers in the world market." Transfer of ownership to employees, he notes, "has commanded strong popular support in both Poland and Czechoslovakia," but is unacceptable to the Western overseers, conflicting with the free market capitalism to which the South must be subjected.

The South, that is. Conforming to traditional practice, the EC has raised barriers to protect its own industry and agriculture, thereby closing off the export market that might enable the East bloc to reconstruct its economies. When Poland removed all import barriers, the EC refused to reciprocate, continuing to discriminate against half of Polish exports. The EC steel lobby called for "restructuring" of the East European industry in a way that would incorporate it within the Western industrial system; the European chemical industry warned that construction of free market economies in the former Soviet empire "must not be at the expense of the long-term viability of Western Europe's own chemical industry." And as noted, none of the state capitalist societies accept the principle of free movement of labor, a *sine qua non* of free market theory. Eastern Europe, or at least large parts of it, is to return to the Third World service role.[21]

The situation is reminiscent of Japan in the 1930s, or of the Reagan-Bush Caribbean Basin Initiative, which encourages open export-oriented economies in the region while keeping US protectionist barriers intact, undermining possible benefits of free trade for the targeted societies.[22] The patterns are as pervasive as they are understandable.

The US has watched developments in Eastern Europe with some discomfort. Through the 1980s, it sought to impede East-West trade relations and the dissolution of the Soviet empire. In August 1991, George Bush advised Ukraine not to secede just before it proceeded to do so. One reason is that after Reagan's wild party for the rich, the US is not well-placed to join German-led Europe and Japan in taking advantage of the newly opened sectors of the South. Liberal Democrats urge that "foreign aid" be diverted from Central America to the USSR, warning that without the traditional export-promotion devices, the EC and Japan will exploit "the vast trade and investment potential of Eastern Europe" while "We debate how to clear up two foreign policy debacles" (Senator Patrick Leahy); no serious person would be so rude as to suggest that we might at least help wash away some of the rivers of blood we have spilled. In 1992, President Bush proposed his Freedom Support Act to remedy the problem. A "stream of high-ranking US officials and big-business leaders" lobbied for the measure, Amy Kaslow reports. Ambassador Robert Strauss urged rapid action "lest US firms lose out to competitors...in the huge consumer market of the former Soviet Union." The Act will provide "new opportunities" for US "farmers [agribusiness] and manufacturers," and "help pave the way for US corporations to explore vast new markets." There is no confusion about just whose "Freedom" is being "Supported."[23]

4. Some Free Market Successes

It would only be fair to add that the IMF-World Bank recipe now being imposed upon the former Soviet empire has its successes. Bolivia is a highly-touted triumph, its economy rescued from disaster by the 1985 New Economic Policy prescribed by the expert advisers now plying their craft in Eastern Europe. Public employment was sharply cut, the national mining company was sold off leading to massive unemployment of miners, real wages dropped, rural teachers quit in droves, regressive taxes were introduced, the economy shrank along with productive investment, while inequality increased. In the capital, Melvin Burke writes, "street vendors and beggars contrast with the fancy boutiques, posh hotels and Mercedes-Benzes." Real per capita GNP is three-fourths what it was in 1980, and foreign debt absorbs 30 percent of export earnings. As a reward for this economic miracle, the IMF, Interamerican Development Bank, and the G-7 Paris Club offered Bolivia extensive financial assistance, including secret payments to government ministers.

The miracle that is so admired is that prices stabilized and exports are booming. About two-thirds of export earnings are now derived from coca production and trade, Burke estimates. The drug money explains the stabilization of currency and price levels, he concludes. About 80 percent of the $3 billion in annual drug profits is spent and banked abroad, mainly in the US, providing a lift to the US economy as well. This profitable export business "obviously serves the interests of the new illegitimate bourgeoisie and the 'narco-generals' of Bolivia," Burke continues, and "also apparently serves the United States national interest, inasmuch as money laundering has not only been tolerated by the United States but has, in fact, been encouraged." It is "the poor peasant coca growers" who "struggle to survive against the combined armed might of the United States and the Bolivian military," Burke writes. There are always plenty more to ensure that the economic miracle will continue, eliciting much praise.

Confirming these figures, Waltrad Morales estimates that about 20 percent of the labor force depends for a livelihood on coca/cocaine production and trade, which amounts to about half of Bolivia's GDP. The export miracle has disrupted land prices and agricultural development, "and as a consequence Bolivians can no longer feed themselves." Malnutrition for children under 5 is over 50 percent higher than the (awful) regional average. A third of the country's food must be imported. "This 'national food crisis'—further aggravated by the neoliberal economic model—has contributed to the marginalisation of the peasantry, which has forced many of them to grow coca leaf in order to survive," in a downward cycle.[24]

On to Poland.

Achievements have also been recorded elsewhere, thanks to timely US intervention and expert management. Take Grenada. After its liberation in 1983—following several years of US economic warfare and intimidation that have been effectively barred from history—it became the largest per capita recipient of US aid (after Israel, a special case). The Reagan Administration proceeded to make it a "showcase for capitalism," the conventional formula as a country is rescued from its population and set on the right course by its benefactors; Guatemala in 1954 is another announced "showcase" that should be famous (see chapter 7.7). The reform programs, which brought the usual social and economic disaster, are condemned even by the private sector they were designed to benefit. Furthermore, "the invasion has had the long-term effect of neutering the island's political life," Carter Special Assistant Peter Bourne reports from Grenada where he is teaching at the Medical School whose students were "rescued": "No creative vision aimed at plans for solving Grenada's social and economic ills has emerged from the lackluster and pliantly pro-American leaders" as the island suffers from record levels of alcoholism and drug abuse, and "crippling social malaise," while much of the population can only "flee their beautiful country."

There is, however, one bright spot, Ron Suskind reports in a front-page *Wall Street Journal* article headlined "Made Safe by Marines, Grenada Now is Haven for Offshore Banks." The economy may be "in terrible economic shape," as the head of a local investment firm and member of Parliament observes—thanks to USAID-run structural adjustment programs, the *Journal* fails to add. But the capital "has become the Casablanca of the Caribbean, a fast-growing haven for money laundering, tax evasion and assorted financial fraud," with 118 offshore banks, one for every 64 residents. Lawyers, accountants, and some businessmen are doing well; as, doubtless, are the foreign bankers, money launderers, and drug lords, safe from the clutches of the carefully crafted "drug war."[25]

The US liberation of Panama recorded a similar triumph. The poverty level has increased from 40 percent to 54 percent since the 1989 invasion. Guillermo Endara, sworn in as President at a US military base on the day of the invasion, would receive 2.4 percent of the vote if an election were held, according to 1992 polls. His government designated the second anniversary of the US invasion a "national day of reflection." Thousands of Panamanians "marked the day with a 'black march' through the streets of this capital to denounce the US invasion and the Endara economic policies," the French press agency reported. Marchers claimed that US troops had killed 3000 people and buried many corpses in mass graves or thrown them into the sea. The economy has not recovered from the battering it received from the US embargo and the invasion. A leader of the Civic Crusade, which led the middle-class opposition to Noriega, told *Chicago Tribune* reporter Nathaniel Sheppard that "Economic sanctions imposed by the U.S. against our will in 1987 to oust Noriega did nothing to hurt him but ruined our economy. Now we believe the sanctions may have been part of a plan to destroy our economy in such a way that we would not have strong ground to demand dignity and better treatment from the US." George Bush's June 1992 visit, which ended quickly in a well-publicized fiasco, "focused attention on long-simmering animosity toward Bush" for the invasion, Sheppard reported; the "rifle-toting American troops" in residential neighborhoods are a particular irritant, and the mood was not improved when security forces accompanied by "about eight American personnel" invaded the home of a National Assembly member, rifling through papers, taking passports, firing shots, and intimidating his wife, who was home alone, he alleged.

A post-invasion report on Panama presented to the UN Committee of Economic, Social and Cultural Rights by Mexican Ambassador Javier Wimer reports that the economy has collapsed, with "catastrophic effects in the areas of food, housing, and basic services such as health, education, and culture." Human rights violations are on the rise as a result of the invasion and subsequent efforts to "liquidate the vestiges of the former nationalism," with labor rights under particular attack along with any institutions that might be "nuclei of civic protest and political opposition." The governments of Panama and the US are jointly responsible for "serious and systematic" human rights violations, his report concluded. According to the respected *Central America Report* (Guatemala, *CAR*), the US drug war may be providing a cover for attacks on community activists by the security forces and other human rights abuses.

But some indicators are up. The General Accounting Office of Congress reported that drug trafficking "may have doubled" since the invasion while money laundering has "flourished," as was predicted at once by everyone who paid attention to the tiny European elite whom the US restored to their traditional rule. A study financed by USAID reported that narcotics use in Panama is the heaviest in Latin America, up by 400 percent since the invasion. The executive-secretary of the Center of Latin American Studies, which participated in the study, says that US troops "constitute a very lucrative market for drugs," contributing to the crisis. The increase is "unprecedented, ... especially among the poor and the young," the *Christian Science Monitor* reports.[26]

Another triumph of free market democracy was recorded in Nicaragua, where the Chamorro government and US Ambassador Harry Shlaudeman signed accords opening the way for the US Drug Enforcement Agency (DEA) to operate there "in an attempt to control the growing drug trafficking problem," *CAR* reports. The DEA agent in Costa Rica declared that Nicaragua is now "being used as a corridor for transferring Colombian cocaine to the United States," and a Department of Justice prosecutor added that the Nicaraguan financial system is laundering drug money. There is also a growing drug epidemic within Nicaragua, fueled by the high level of drug use by recent returnees from Miami as well as the continued economic decline and the new avenues for drug trafficking since the US regained control. "Since the installation of the Chamorro government and the massive return of Nicaraguans from Miami," *CAR* reports, "drug consumption has increased substantially in a country long free from drug usage." Miskito leader Steadman Fagoth accused two members of the Chamorro cabinet, his former contra associate Brooklyn Rivera and the minister of fishing for the Atlantic Coast, of working for the Colombian cartels. The Nicaraguan delegate to the Ninth International Conference on the Control of Drug Trafficking in April 1991 alleged that Nicaragua "has now become a leading link in cocaine shipments to the US and Europe." In Managua, the number of street children is rapidly increasing, as is drug addiction, which had been virtually eliminated by 1984. Ten-year-old children sniff glue on the street, saying that "it takes away hunger."

In fairness, we should mention a sign of economic progress now that the US has regained control: marketing of shoe cement to fill the children's bottles, imported through a multinational supplier, has become a lucrative business.[27]

A conference attended by government officials and NGOs in Managua in August 1991 concluded that the country now has 250,000 addicts and is becoming an international bridge for drug transport, (in comparison 400,000 addicts are reported in Costa Rica, 450,000 in Guatemala, 500,000 in El Salvador). Addiction is increasing particularly among young people. A conference organizer commented that "In 1986 there wasn't one reported case of hard drugs consumption" while "in 1990, there were at least 12,000 cases." 118 drug dealing operations were identified in Managua alone, though it is the Atlantic Coast that has become the international transit point for hard drugs, leading to increased addiction. US journalist Nancy Nusser reports from Managua that cocaine has become "readily available only since president Violeta Chamorro took office in April 1990," according to dealers. "There wasn't any coke during the Sandinistas' time, just marijuana," one dealer said. Minister of Government Carlos Hurtado said that "the phenomenon of cocaine trafficking existed before, but at a low level." Now it is burgeoning, primarily through the Atlantic Coast according to "a ranking Western diplomat with knowledge of drug trafficking" (probably from the US Embassy), who describes the Coast now as "a no man's land." In the *Miami Herald*, Tim Johnson reports that El Salvador too "is finding itself afflicted by a new scourge: drug trafficking." It is now outranked only by Panama and Guatemala as a corridor for cocaine shipments to the US.[28]

Drugs are becoming "the newest growth industry in Central America," *CAR* reports, as a result of the "severe economic conditions in which 85 percent of the Central American population live in poverty" and the lack of jobs, conditions exacerbated by the neoliberal onslaught. But the problem has not reached the level of Colombia, where security forces armed and trained by the US are continuing their rampage of terror, torture, and disappearances, targeting political opposition figures, community activists, trade union leaders, human rights workers, and the peasant communities generally while US aid "is furthering the corruption of the Colombian security forces and strengthening the alliance of blood between right-wing politicians, military officers and ruthless narcotics traffickers," according to human rights activist Jorge Gómez Lizarazo, a former judge. The situation in Peru is still worse.[29]

These are only symptoms of much deeper malaise, to which we return in Part III.

5. After the Cold War

There is little reason to expect that "the great work of subjugation and conquest" will change in any fundamental way with the passing of the Cold War phase of the North-South conflict. But as always, stable policies must be adapted to changing contingencies, as they were when a New World Order was established in 1945, and again when Richard Nixon announced his "New Economic Policy" in 1971, in both cases, reflecting real changes in the distribution of power. The Soviet decline that accelerated from the late 1970s yields a situation that is also new in a number of respects, though major tendencies persist, including the internationalization of production and finance, the disorders of the affluent alliance, the relative weakening of the still-dominant US economy, and the marginalization of much of the domestic public of the world-dominant societies.

One consequence of the Soviet collapse is the project of imposing the neoliberal mode of subordination on large parts of the region. A second is that new pretexts are needed for intervention. Despite much bombast, the problem of the vanishing pretext was recognized through the 1980s. The population was therefore regaled with international terrorists, Hispanic narcotraffickers, Islamic fundamentalists, crazed Arabs, and other useful constructions, as attempts were made to adapt the standard formula for diverting and subduing the public: fear of some Great Satan, followed by awe as our Grand Leaders heroically overcome him and march on to new triumphs. Regular confrontations were manufactured with the convenient Libyan punching bag; Grenada was about to cut off sea lines and bomb us from a Cuban-built airbase; Sandinistas were spreading their "revolution without borders" and advancing on Texas; Noriega (after he was fired) was leading the Colombian cartel to poison our children; Saddam Hussein stepped out of line and became the Beast of Baghdad, etc. But in general, as the variety of targets illustrates, the formula is not available as routinely as before. President Bush has been criticized for his failure to formulate grand designs in the manner of his predecessors, but that is unfair, given the disappearance of the "monolithic and ruthless conspiracy" to which JFK could appeal, and its variants. The standard formula may lose its effectiveness for other reasons too, as conditions of life decline for the superfluous population.

Other consequences were pointed out forthrightly by rational analysts. In a 1988 end-of-year analysis of the Cold War in the *New York Times*, Dimitri Simes wrote that the impending disappearance of the Soviet enemy offers the US three advantages: first, we can shift NATO costs to European competitors; second, we can end "the manipulation of America by third world nations," "resist unwarranted third world demands for assistance," and strike a harder bargain with "defiant third world debtors"; and third, military power can be used more freely "as a United States foreign policy instrument...against those who contemplate challenging important American interests," with no fear of "triggering counterintervention," the deterrent having been removed. In brief, the US can regain some power within the rich men's club, tighten the screws on the Third World, and resort more freely to violence against defenseless victims. The senior associate of the Carnegie Endowment for International Peace was right on target.[30]

The fall of the Berlin wall in November 1989 can be taken as the symbolic end of the Cold War. After that, it took real dedication to conjure up the Soviet threat, though habits die slowly. Thus, in early 1990, much excitement was generated by a document published anonymously by University of California Sovietologist Martin Malia, railing about how Brezhnev had "intervened at will throughout the Third World" and "Russia bestrode the world" while "the liberal-to-radical mainstream of Anglo-American Sovietology" regarded Stalinism as having "a democratic cast," indulging in "blatant fantasies...about democratic Stalinism" and "puerile fetishization of Lenin," along with a host of similar insights apparently picked up in some Paris café. But in the 1990s, only the most disciplined minds can handle this kind of fare with appropriate gravity.[31]

Much can be learned about the Cold War era by observing what happened after the Berlin wall fell. The case of Cuba is instructive. For 170 years, the US has sought to prevent Cuban independence. From 1959, the pretext for invasion, terror, and economic warfare was the security threat posed by this outpost of the Kremlin. With the threat gone, the reaction was uniform: we must step up the attack. The banner is now democracy and human rights, upheld by political leaders and moralists who have demonstrated their commitment to these values with such integrity over the years, for example, during the murderous US crusade against the Church and others who dared organize the undeserving public in Central America through the 1980s. It would not be easy to invent a clearer demonstration of the fraudulence of the Cold War pretext; being doctrinally unacceptable, the conclusions remain invisible (see chapter 6).

US opposition to Haitian independence for two centuries also continued, quite independently of the Cold War. Events of the 1980s, notably after the fall of the Berlin wall, also illustrate with much clarity traditional US distaste for democracy and indifference to human rights. We return to details (chapter 8).

Another instructive example is Saddam Hussein, a favored friend and trading partner of the West right through his worst atrocities. As the Berlin wall was tottering in October 1989, the White House intervened directly, in a highly secret meeting, to ensure that Iraq would receive another $1 billion in loan guarantees, overcoming Treasury and Commerce department objections that Iraq was not creditworthy. The reason, the State Department explained, was that Iraq was "very important to US interests in the Middle East"; it was "influential in the peace process" and was "a key to maintaining stability in the region, offering great trade opportunities for US companies." As is the norm, Saddam Hussein's crimes were of no account until he committed the crime of disobedience. And the West soon returned to tacit support for him against an even greater enemy, freedom and democracy in the Third World, as already discussed.[32]

Again the lesson is clear: the priorities are profits and power; democracy in more than form is a threat to be overcome; human rights are of instrumental value for propaganda purposes, nothing more.

As Simes had observed, one consequence of the Soviet collapse is that overt intervention became a more feasible option. It comes as small surprise, then, that Bush should inaugurate the post-Cold War era by invading Panama to save us from the arch-demon Noriega, after a carefully designed propaganda campaign to which the press lent its considerable talents, even suppressing the fact that the invasion was accompanied by the announcement of new aid for Bush's friends in Beijing and Baghdad, who made Noriega look like a choir boy in comparison. Real interests again were served: US business partners were placed back in power, the security forces were returned to US control, and the Washington was able to direct the fate of the Panama Canal. The meaning of the Cold War is once again dramatically illustrated, though the doctrinal system remains immune.[33]

The second act of post-Cold War aggression was Iraq's invasion of Kuwait on August 2, 1990, shifting Saddam Hussein overnight from moderate-who-is-improving to reincarnation of Attila the Hun. The US-UK alliance moved quickly to bar the diplomatic track for fear that peaceful means might "defuse the crisis" with "a few token gains" for their former friend, as the Administration position was outlined by *Times* diplomatic correspondent Thomas Friedman in late August. Had these fears been realized, the invasion would have resembled the US invasion of Panama, an unacceptable outcome of course. The *Times* and its colleagues dutifully suppressed the opportunities for a negotiated Iraqi withdrawal that opened from mid-August, according to high-ranking US officials. On the eve of the January 15, 1991 bombing, the US population, by about 2 to 1, favored a diplomatic settlement along the lines of an Iraqi proposal that had been released by US officials, but were unaware of the existence of this proposal, and the instant US rejection of it, thanks to media discipline. The rascal multitude, once again, was kept in its proper place. At no time was the Administration called upon to present an argument for war rather than diplomacy—at least one that could not be refuted instantly by a literate teenager. The doctrinal institutions succeeded brilliantly in excluding every fundamental question that would have arisen in a functioning democracy.

The war policy was also strongly opposed by the population in the region. The Iraqi democratic opposition, always rebuffed by Washington (hence the press), opposed US policy throughout: the pre-August 1990 support for the Iraqi dictator, the refusal to explore peaceful means, and finally the tacit support for Saddam Hussein as he crushed the Shi'ite and Kurdish rebellions. One leading spokesman, banker Ahmad Chalabi, who described the outcome of the war as "the worst of all possible worlds" for the Iraqi people, attributed the US stand to its traditional policy of "supporting dictatorships to maintain stability." In Egypt, the one Arab ally with a degree of internal freedom, the semi-official press wrote that the outcome demonstrated that the United States only wanted to cut Iraq down to size and thus to establish its own unchallenged hegemony, in "collusion with Saddam himself" if necessary, agreeing with the "savage beast" on the need to "block any progress and abort all hopes, however dim, for freedom or equality and for progress towards democracy" (April 9). The media suppressed the basic facts throughout with their usual discipline. Thus, immediately after Egypt denounced the US for colluding with Saddam, *Times* correspondent Alan Cowell informed the public of the "strikingly unanimous view" among the Arab allies in support of the US position that "whatever the sins of the Iraqi leader, he offered the West and the region a better hope for his country's stability than did those who have suffered his repression" (April 11). The *Times* does deserve credit, however, for Friedman's lucid explanation of why we must seek some clone of Saddam Hussein to rule with an "iron fist" rather than face the threat of freedom for the people of Iraq ("instability").

The United Nations suffered further blows. The invasion of Kuwait was unusual in that the US and UK opposed an act of international violence, and thus did not pursue their usual resort to the veto or other means to block UN efforts to reverse the crime. But under US pressure, the Security Council was compelled to wash its hands of the matter, radically violating the UN Charter by leaving individual states free to act as they chose. Further

US pressures prevented the Council from responding to the call of member states for meetings, as stipulated by council rules that the United States had vigorously upheld when they served its interests. That Washington has little use for diplomatic means or institutions of world order, unless they can be used as instruments of its own power, has been dramatically illustrated in Southeast Asia, the Middle East, Central America, and elsewhere. Nothing is likely to change in this regard, including the efficiency with which the facts are concealed.[34]

In the case of Iraq, the disappearance of the Soviet deterrent was a crucial factor in the US-UK decision for war, as widely discussed. It might have been a factor in the invasion of Panama, as claimed by Reagan Latin America hand Elliott Abrams, who exulted that the US was now free to use force without fear of a Russian reaction.

Hostility to functioning democracy in Central America continued without any change. As the Berlin Wall fell, elections were held in Honduras in "an inspiring example of the democratic promise that today is spreading throughout the Americas," in George Bush's words. The candidates represented large landowners and wealthy industrialists, with close ties to the military, the effective rulers, under US control. Their political programs were virtually identical, and the campaign was largely restricted to insults and entertainment. Human rights abuses by the security forces escalated before the election. Starvation and misery were rampant, having increased during the "decade of democracy," along with capital flight and the debt burden. But there was no major threat to order, or to investors.

At the same time, the electoral campaign opened in Nicaragua. Its 1984 elections do not exist in US commentary. They could not be controlled, and therefore are not an inspiring example of democracy. Taking no chances with the long-scheduled 1990 elections, Bush announced as the campaign opened in November that the embargo would be lifted if his candidate won. The White House and Congress renewed their support for the contra forces in defiance of the Central American presidents, the World Court, and the United Nations, rendered irrelevant by the US veto. The media went along, continuing to suppress the US subversion of the peace process with the diligence required on important affairs of state. Nicaraguans were thus informed that only a vote for the US candidate would end the terror and illegal economic warfare. In Latin America, the electoral results were generally interpreted as a victory for George Bush, even by those who celebrated the outcome. In the United States, in contrast, the outcome was hailed as a "Victory for U.S. Fair Play," with "Americans United in Joy," Albanian-style, as *New York Times* headlines put it.

It is not that the celebrants were unaware of how the US victory was achieved. Rather, there was unconcealed joy at the grand success in subverting democracy. *Time* magazine, for example, was quite frank about the means employed to bring about the latest of the "happy series of democratic surprises" as "democracy burst forth" in Nicaragua. The method was to "wreck the economy and prosecute a long and deadly proxy war until the exhausted natives overthrow the unwanted government themselves," with a cost to us that is "minimal," leaving the victim "with wrecked bridges, sabotaged power stations, and ruined farms," and thus providing the U.S. candidate with "a winning issue": ending the "impoverishment of the people of Nicaragua." To appreciate the character of the political culture, it is only necessary to imagine the same story appearing in Stalinist Russia with a few names changed, an intellectual exercise far beyond the capacity of Western commissars.[35]

The frankness is refreshing, and reveals with exactitude just what is meant by the "Americans United in Joy" who proclaim their dedication to "democracy."

Washington has employed similar methods to bring "democracy" to Angola; here too the country has been devastated, with a death toll reaching hundreds of thousands. From 1975, Angola was under attack by South Africa and the terrorist forces of Jonas Savimbi's UNITA, operating from Namibia and then Zaire with US support. Virtually alone, the US refused to recognize the MPLA government and subjected it to economic warfare. South Africa finally withdrew after a military defeat by the Cuban forces that had resisted its aggression since 1975, and a peace agreement was signed (May 1991) calling for elections. As in Central America, the US moved at once to subvert it, continuing its support for UNITA terror. The results are described by South African journalist Phillip van Niekerk: peasants "don't like UNITA," "But most of the people are afraid that if UNITA loses the elections, the war will go on" (quoting a Dutch development worker in the countryside).

People who are "aware of the atrocities committed by UNITA" may be "appalled" at the prospects, van Niekerk continues, but continuation of the war is more than the population can bear. The ruling MPLA "sacrificed a generation to repel the years of South African aggression and US-funded destabilization by Unita," Victoria Brittain writes. It lost any early credibility; what it might have done without the US-South African attack is anyone's guess. A "new wave of white settlers" is "re-colonizing" Angola, van Niekerk reports, now Afrikaners, later perhaps Portuguese returning to reclaim their lands. "The only optimism," Brittain concludes, "comes from the South African businessmen who occupy the lobbies of the newly refurbished hotels" in Luanda, where cynics say that "If Unita wins they'll have the country handed to them on a plate, if the MPLA wins they'll still have the country, for a handful of rands."[36]

It is, again, only natural that at the dissident extreme, Anthony Lewis should laud the "consistent American policy" from the 1970s "to help negotiate an end to the brutal civil war" in Angola, and the successful pursuit by the Bush Administration of "a peaceful policy" aiming at "a political solution in Nicaragua."[37]

The traditional attitude toward democracy was reiterated by a Latin America Strategy Development Workshop at the Pentagon in September 1990. It concluded that current relations with the Mexican dictatorship are "extraordinarily positive," untroubled by stolen elections, death squads, endemic torture, scandalous treatment of workers and peasants, and so forth. But "a 'democracy opening' in Mexico could test the special relationship by bringing into office a government more interested in challenging the U.S. on economic and nationalist grounds," the fundamental concern over many years.[38]

Each year, the White House sends to Congress a report explaining that the military threat we face requires vast expenditures—which, accidentally, sustain high-tech industry at home and repression abroad. The first post-Cold War edition was in March 1990. The Russians having disappeared from the scene, the report at last recognized frankly that the enemy is the Third World. US military power must target the Third World, it concluded, primarily the Middle East, where the "threats to our interests...could not be laid at the Kremlin's door," a fact that can now be acknowledged, the Soviet pretext having disappeared. For the same reason, the threat now becomes "the growing technological sophistication of Third World conflicts." The US must therefore strengthen its "defense industrial base," with incentives "to invest in new facilities and equipment as well as in research and development," and develop further forward basing and counterinsurgency and low-intensity conflict capacities.[39]

In brief, the prime concerns continue to be power within the rich men's club, control of the service areas, and state-organized public subsidy for advanced industry at home. Democracy must be opposed with vigor, except in the PC sense of unhampered business rule. Human rights retain their usual irrelevance. Policies remain stable, adapted to new contingencies, with parallel adjustments by the cultural managers. The points are so glaringly obvious, and made with such manic consistency, that it takes real talent to miss them.

6. The Soft Line

With the end of the Cold War, the US is more free to use force to control the South, but several factors are likely to inhibit the resort to these traditional methods. Among them are the successes of the past years in crushing popular nationalist and reform tendencies, the elimination of the "Communist" appeal to those who hope to "plunder the rich," and the economic catastrophes of the last decade. In light of these achievements, limited forms of diversity and independence can be tolerated with less concern that they will lead to a challenge to ruling business interests. Control can be exercised by economic measures: the IMF regimen, selective resort to free trade measures, and so forth. Democratic forms are tolerable, even preferable, as long as "stability" is ensured. If this dominant value is threatened, the iron fist must strike.

Another inhibiting factor is that the domestic base for foreign adventures has eroded. An early Bush Administration National Security Policy Review concluded that "much weaker enemies" (meaning any acceptable target) must be defeated "decisively and rapidly," because domestic "political support" is so thin.[40] Another problem is that other centers of economic power have their own interests, though the Defense Planning study cited earlier is correct in noting that basic interests are shared, notably, the concern that the Third World fulfill its service function. And the increasing internationalization of the economy gives a somewhat new cast to interstate competition, as already discussed. These are factors of growing importance.

The use of force to control the Third World is a last resort. Economic weapons are more efficient, when feasible. Some of the newer mechanisms can be seen in the GATT negotiations. Western powers call for liberalization when that is in their interest, and for enhanced protection when *that* is in their interest. One major US concern is the "new themes": guarantees for "intellectual property rights," such as patents and software, that will enable TNCs to monopolize new technology; and removal of constraints on services and investment, which will undermine national development programs in the Third World and effectively place economic and social policy decisions in the hands of TNCs and the financial institutions of the North. These are "issues of greater magnitude" than the more publicized conflict over agricultural subsidies, according to William Brock, head of the Multilateral Trade Negotiations Coalition of major US corporations.[41]

In general, each of the wealthy industrial powers advocates a mixture of liberalization and protection (the Multifiber Arrangement and its extensions, the US-Japan semiconductor agreement, Voluntary Export Arrangements, etc.), designed for the interests of dominant domestic forces, and particularly for the TNCs that are to run the world economy. The effects would be to restrict Third World governments to a police function to control their working classes and superfluous population, while TNCs gain free access to their resources and monopolize new technology and global investment and production—and of course are granted the central planning, allocation, production, and distribution functions denied to governments, unacceptable agents because they might fall under the influence of popular pressures reflecting domestic needs. The outcome may be called "free trade" for doctrinal reasons, but it might more accurately be described as "a system of world economic governance with parameters defined by the unregulated market and rules administered by supranational banks and corporations" (Howard Wachtel), a system of "corporate mercantilism" (Peter Phillips), with managed commercial interactions within and among huge corporate groupings, and regular state intervention in the three major Northern blocs to subsidize and protect domestically-based international corporations and financial institutions.[42]

The facts have not been lost on Third World commentators, who have been protesting eloquently. But their voices are as welcome as those of Iraqi democrats.

Meanwhile, the US is establishing a regional bloc that will enable it to compete more effectively with the Japan-led region and the EC. Canada's role is to provide resources and some services and skilled labor, as it is absorbed more fully into the US economy with reduction of the welfare system, labor rights, and cultural independence. The Canadian Labour Congress reported the loss of over 225,000 jobs in the first two years of the Free Trade Agreement, along with a wave of takeovers of Canadian-based companies (see chapter 2.5). Mexico, Central America, and the Caribbean are to supply cheap labor for assembly plants, as in the maquiladora industries of northern Mexico, where harsh working conditions, low wages, and the absence of environmental controls offer highly profitable conditions for investors. Internal repression and structural adjustment will ensure ample cheap and docile labor. These regions are also to provide export crops and markets for US agribusiness. Mexico and Venezuela are also to provide oil, with US corporations granted the right to take part in production, reversing efforts at domestic control of natural resources. The press failed to give Bush sufficient credit for his achievements in his Fall 1990 tour of Latin America. Mexico was induced to allow US oil companies new access to its resources, a policy goal of a half-century. US companies will now be able "to help Mexico's nationalized oil company," as the *Wall Street Journal* prefers to construe the matter. Our fondest wish for many years has been to help our little brown brothers, and at last the ignorant peons will allow us to cater to their needs.[43]

Such policies are to be extended to appropriate sectors of South America. And, crucially, the United States will attempt to maintain its dominant influence over Gulf oil production and the profits that derive from it. Other economic powers, of course, have their own ideas, and potential sources of conflict abound.

There are many familiar reasons why wealth and power tend to reproduce. It should, then, come as little surprise that the Third World continues to fall behind the North. UN statistics indicate that as a percent of developed countries, Africa's GDP per capita (minus South Africa) declined by about 50 percent from 1960 to 1987. The decline was almost as great in Latin America.[44]

For similar reasons, within the rich societies themselves, large sectors of the population are becoming superfluous by the reigning values and must be marginalized or suppressed, increasingly so in the past 20-year period of economic stagnation and pressures on corporate profit. As noted earlier, societies of the North—notably the United States—are taking on certain Third World aspects. The distribution of privilege and despair in a society with the enormous advantages of ours is not, of course, what one finds in Brazil or Mexico. But the tendencies are not hard to see.

In general, prospects for the overwhelming majority at home and abroad are not auspicious, in the "new imperial age."

Part II
High Principles

CHAPTER 4

DEMOCRACY AND THE MARKET

---

1. The Freedom that Counts

Among global planners, few captured the essence of policy more clearly than George Kennan when he advised in 1948 that if we are to maintain the "disparity" between our wealth and the poverty of others we must put aside "idealistic slogans" and keep to "straight power concepts." Deviation from these guidelines is rare. Such ideals as democracy and the market are well and good, as long as the tilt of the playing field guarantees that the right folks win. If the rascal multitude try to raise their heads, they must be beaten into submission in one or another way: in the Third World, outright violence often suffices. If market forces interfere with domestic privilege, free trade is quickly cast to the flames.

The truth of the matter was well articulated by a US banker in Venezuela under the murderous Pérez Jiménez dictatorship: "You have the freedom here to do what you want to do with your money, and to me, that is worth all the political freedom in the world." That about sums it up.[1]

These doctrines are too deeply-rooted in institutional structures to be seriously challenged within the ruling state-corporate nexus. It can, on occasion, produce someone who will deliver moral lessons on human rights. But when some real interest is at stake, the rhetoric is quickly shelved: say, when it is necessary to support virtual genocide in Timor, to protect Somoza's National Guard while it is slaughtering thousands of civilians, or to tilt towards China and Pol Pot, to select a few examples from the period of an unusual deviation toward High Principle.

The consistent practice is illustrated over a broad range throughout this discussion and in sources cited. To select another case that brings out fundamental principles sharply, consider the response when General Chun's military dictatorship in South Korea crushed the democracy movement in Kwangju in May 1980. Paratroopers "carried out three days of barbarity with the zeal of Nazi storm troopers," an Asia Watch investigative mission reported, "beating, stabbing and mutilating unarmed civilians, including children, young girls, and aged grandmothers." Two thousand people were killed in this rampage, they estimate. The US received two requests for assistance: the citizens committee that had called for democracy requested help in negotiations; General Chun requested the release of 20,000 troops under US command to join the storm troopers. The latter request was honored, and US naval and air units were deployed in a further show of US support.

"Koreans who had expected help from Carter were dumbfounded," Tim Shorrock writes, as "the news of direct support from the US was broadcast to the people of Kwangju from helicopters and proclaimed throughout the nation in blazing newspaper headlines." A few days later, Carter sent the head of the Export-Import Bank to Seoul to assure the military junta of US economic support, approving a $600 million loan. As Chun took over the presidency by force, Carter said that while we would prefer democracy, "The Koreans are not ready for that, according to their own judgment, and I don't know how to explain it any better."

Chun arrested thousands of "subversives" calling for democracy, sending them to military-run "purification" camps. Hundreds of labor leaders were purged; new legislation severely weakened unions, leading to a 30 percent drop in membership. Censorship became even more harsh. Gratified with this progress, the Reagan Administration honored Chun by selecting him as the first head of state to visit after the inauguration. Visiting Korea in 1986, Secretary of State George Shultz praised the "terrific job being done in security" and in the economy, and the "impressive movement" towards democracy. He expressed his strong support for General Chun. He harshly criticized the democratic opposition, refusing to meet with its leaders Kim Dae Jung and Kim Young Sam, and explaining that "how [countries] design things can vary and you can still call it democracy."

To show how much has changed with the Cold War over, President Bush chose the amiable Mobutu of Zaire as the first African leader to be received at the White House, hailing him as "one of our most valued friends" and making no reference to human rights violations. Among others rewarded for their contributions to democracy and human rights were Bush's friends in Baghdad and Beijing, and Romania's mad dictator Ceausescu.[2]

2. The Flight of the Bumble Bee

In the current phase of intellectual corruption, it must be stressed that, like democracy and human rights, the economic doctrines preached by the rulers are instruments of power, intended for others, so that they can be more efficiently robbed and exploited. No wealthy society accepts these conditions for itself, unless they happen to confer temporary advantage; and their history reveals that sharp departure from these doctrines was a large factor in development.

At least since the work of Alexander Gerschenkron in the 1950s, it has been widely recognized by economic historians that "late development" has been critically dependent on state intervention. Japan and the Newly Industrialized Countries (NICs) on its periphery are standard contemporary examples. In a major study, 24 leading Japanese economists review the decision by the Ministry of International Trade and Industry (MITI) after World War II to disregard prevailing economic theory and to assign a "predominant role in the formation of industry policy" to the state bureaucracy, "in a system that is rather similar to the organisation of the industrial bureaucracy in socialist countries." Each sector of industry has its section of the government bureaucracy, which works "in close co-operation" with an industry association. Heavy protection, subsidies and tax concessions, financial controls, and a variety of other devices were employed to overcome market deficiencies that would have prevented development. Rejecting standard doctrine, MITI determined that "long-term self-reliance for Japan would be delayed or even undermined by following its apparent comparative advantage into labour intensive sectors." The radical defiance of economic precepts set the stage for the Japanese miracle, the economists conclude. Western specialists do not disagree. Chalmers Johnson notes that Japan could be described as "the only communist nation that works."

Some have suggested—only half in jest—that Japan's support for the Brookings Institution and other advocates of standard doctrine is intended to reinforce belief in the classical theory, to the detriment of its commercial rivals.[3]

The same has been true of the NICs in Japan's periphery. In her important work on South Korean economic progress, Alice Amsden cites such factors as land distribution and wage-salary differentials that are equitable by Western standards, state intervention on the Japanese model to "get prices 'wrong' in order to stimulate investment and trade," and high discipline of labor, but more strikingly, of capital, which is controlled by "price ceilings, controls on capital flight, and incentives that made diversification into new industries contingent on performing well in old ones." Much the same has been true throughout East Asia, she notes. Case by case, the record of export-led growth refutes the doctrines of the neoliberal "New Orthodoxy," economist Stephen Smith points out. Success was based "on activist trade and industrial policies" that deliberately alter market incentives to place "long-run development goals over short-run comparative advantage." The most extensive comparative study concludes that "periods of significant export expansion are almost always preceded by periods of strong import substitution"—measures of state intervention in violation of the market (Chenery, et al.). The comparison of Brazil and the East Asian NICs is telling. Until 1980, they developed in parallel, with "active industrial and export policies" and import substitution. But the debt crisis compelled Brazil to adopt IMF-World Bank New Orthodoxy, elevating "trade liberalization over domestic growth objectives" and turning to the export of primary products, with grim consequences. The NICs, with much more powerful state controls, prevented the market disaster, barring capital flight and directing capital to investment.[4]

Meanwhile China, the one "Communist" country that has kept the Western experts at arms length, remains the only one with rapid economic development (along with vigorous repression and no pretense of democracy). "One phenomenal success has been 'township and village enterprises', for the most part factories owned by rural farmers," which "now account for close to 20 percent of China's GNP, employing more than 100 million people," financial correspondent David Francis writes, quoting a World Bank spokesman who predicts that they "will most assuredly be the single most dynamic form of enterprise on the Chinese scene."

The German economic miracle also relied on its departures from standard precepts, from the 19th century. The post-World War II system involves elements of "corporatism," defined as the "broad concertation between employer and employee representatives across industries, which is usually established and sometimes continually supervised under state auspices" (Charles Meier), though this conception underplays the role of central financial institutions, "a particularly significant actor in the German political economy," Michael Huelshoff writes. "The Reagan nightmare of supply side economics and military Keynesianism" and its "fiscal recklessness and monetary astringency" have received particularly harsh criticism in Germany (James Sperling). The smaller successful economies adopt similar means. Thus Holland relied on cartels coordinated through the Ministry of Economic Affairs for its postwar economic reconstruction, regulating production, sales, supplies, prices, etc. Not all of the more than 400 still operating in 1992 will survive the EC, but the government announced that a "green light" will be given to "positive cartels" that offer protection for companies launching new technologies.

"A strict free-marketeer would declare the German economy, like the bumble-bee, theoretically incapable of flight," the *Economist* observes with puzzlement, reviewing such departures from orthodoxy as "well-trained and well-paid workers, who sit on oversight boards," "giant, bank-owned industries unbothered by shareholders, secure from predators and heedless of profit," high taxes, "cradle-to-grave welfare," and other sins: "the German economy's riposte to this ancient caricature is to fly." The theory remains in force, however.

Low wages do not appear to have been a major factor in late development, however attractive they may be to TNCs. "Neither Germany nor the United States industrialized by competing against Britain on the basis of low wages," Amsden points out, and the same was true of Japan, which undercut British textiles in the 1920s by modern production facilities more than low wages. In Germany and other successful economies, labor conditions and benefits are high, by comparative standards. A study of industrial productivity by MIT specialists notes further that Germany, Japan, and other countries that maintained the "craft tradition" with more "direct participation of skilled workers in production decisions" have been more successful in modern industry than the United States, with its tradition of deskilling and marginalizing workers in the "mass-production model"; lessened hierarchy, responsibility in the hands of production workers, and training in new technologies has also improved results in the US, they conclude. Economist David Felix makes a similar point in comparing Latin America and East Asia. Asians who were less subordinated to Europe and the US than Latin American elites did not assign such high status to foreign-made consumption goods, "allowing much larger segments of the craft sector to survive, accumulate, and modernize the technology," while also easing balance-of-payments pressures. Amsden attributes South Korea's success in part to reliance on workers' initiative on the shop floor in preference to managerial hierarchies.[5]

It is, however, not only "late development" that is crucially dependent on departures from doctrinal orthodoxy. The same was true of the "early development" of England, as already discussed. The United States as well. High tariffs and other forms of state intervention may have raised costs to American consumers, but they allowed domestic industry to develop, from textiles to steel to computers, barring cheaper British products in earlier years, providing a state-guaranteed market and public subsidy for research and development in advanced sectors, creating and maintaining capital-intensive agribusiness, and so on. Elimination of tariffs in the 1830s would have bankrupted "about half the industrial sector of New England," economic historian Mark Bils concludes.

There were experiments with unconstrained markets in 19th century England, quickly abandoned. Free trade was (selectively) introduced and dropped as domestic power interests dictated. In the US, business regularly turned to the state to overcome its problems, initiating government bureaucracies from the 1880s and demanding protection and subsidy. By the

1930s, faith that capitalism might be viable had virtually disappeared, as the advanced countries moved towards one or another form of state-integrated economic system. It should be a virtual truism that "Since World War II, military spending had become the backbone of our goods production. It could be, and was, managed to sustain the level of aggregate demand and unemployment, adjusted periodically as the business cycle might require, and used to help meet the growth targets..." (Richard Bartel). Military spending in World War II convinced corporate executives of the validity of the Keynesian model of state intervention, and they have taken for granted since that the state must intervene actively to protect and subsidize the wealthy and privileged, notoriously during the Reagan years.[6]

The crucial role in industrial development of the "visible hand"—planning and coordination of production, marketing and R&D—is well-known from the studies of business enterprise by Alfred Chandler over the past 30 years. Summarizing and extending work by Chandler, David Landes, and other historians of development, William Lazonick argues that industrial capitalism has passed through three major phases: the "proprietary capitalism" of 19th century England, with family-owned firms and a substantial degree of market coordination; the "managerial capitalism" of the United States, with "administrative coordination" for planning and organization; and the "collective capitalism" of the Japanese model, which allows still more efficent long-term planning and coordination. In each case, private enterprise has relied extensively on the state power that it largely controls, though in different ways. The TNCs extend these internally coordinated, state-supported systems worldwide.[7]

"Import substitution [through state intervention] is about the only way anybody's ever figured out to industrialize," development economist Lance Taylor observes: "In the long run, there are no laissez-faire transitions to modern economic growth. The state has always intervened to create a capitalist class, and then it has to regulate the capitalist class, and then the state has to worry about being taken over by the capitalist class, but the state has always been there." Furthermore, state power has regularly been invoked by investors and entrepreneurs to protect then from destructive market forces, to secure resources, markets, and opportunities for investment, and in general to safeguard and extend their profits and power.[8]

With the conventional pretext gone, Washington sought new ways to maintain the subsidy to advanced industry. One method is foreign arms sales, which also help alleviate the balance-of-payments crisis. As the Cold War came to a definitive end, the Bush Administration created a Center for Defense Trade to stimulate arms sales while proposing government guarantees of up to $1 billion in loans for purchase of US arms. The Defense

Security Assistance Agency was reported to have sent more than 900 officers to some 50 countries to promote US weapons sales. Pentagon officials trace the policy to a July 1990 order that Embassy officials should expand their assistance to US arms exporters; the Gulf war was then prominently featured as a sales promotion device. At a Pentagon-industry conference in May 1991, industry officials asked the government to pick up the costs of US military equipment and personnel sent to contractor trade shows around the world for sales promotion. The Pentagon agreed, reversing a 25-year policy. The first taxpayer-funded display was at the June 1991 Paris Air Show.

Lawrence Korb of the Brookings Institution, formerly Assistant Secretary of Defense in charge of logistics, observed that the promise of arms sales had kept stocks of military producers high despite the end of the Cold War, with arms sales rising from $12 billion in 1989 to almost $40 billion in 1991. Moderate declines in purchases by the US military were more than offset by other arms sales by US companies. Since "President Bush called last May [1991] for restraint in weapons sales to the Middle East," AP correspondent Barry Schweid reported in early 1992, "the United States has transferred roughly $6 billion in arms to the region," part of the $19 billion in US weapons sent to the Middle East since Iraq's invasion of Kuwait. From 1989 through 1991, US arms exports to the Third World increased by 138 percent, making the US far and away the leading arms exporter. The sales since May 1991 are "fully consistent with the president's initiative and the guidelines" in his call for restraint, State Department spokesman Richard Boucher announced—quite accurately, given the actual intent.

Bush Administration calls for restraint were timed for the triumphal celebration of the Gulf war, as part of the PR campaign on the new era of peace and tranquility that we are entering, thanks to the valor of our grand leader. On February 6, 1991, Secretary of State James Baker told the House Foreign Committee that the time had come for concrete steps to stem the flow of armaments to the Middle East, "an area that is already over-militarized." On March 6, in his triumphant address to a cheering joint session of Congress, the President announced that control of arms sales would be one of his major postwar goals: "it would be tragic," he said, "if the nations of the Middle East and Persian Gulf were now, in the wake of war, to embark on a new arms race."

In recognition of the scale of the tragedy, the Administration, a few days earlier, had provided the Senate Foreign Relations Committee with a confidential listing of planned sales reaching to record levels, more than half for the Middle East; and informed Congress of a $1.6 billion sale of advanced fighter aircraft to Egypt. A week after the speech, Congress was informed of a $760 million deal for Apache helicopters to the United Arab Emirates. The Pentagon then used the Paris Air Show for an unprecedented sales pitch, displaying with pride (and hope) the goods that had so magnificently destroyed a defenseless Third World country. Secretary of Defense Cheney announced new arms transfers to Israel and plans to stockpile $200 million worth of US weapons there; another $7 billion in weapon sales, mainly to the Middle East, was announced in July. The UK followed the same path. China was the only weapons exporter to call for concrete limits on arms sales to the Middle East, a proposal quickly dismissed by the US and its allies.[9]

Military Keynesian initiatives have not been limited to the taxpayer subsidy (R&D) and a state-guaranteed market. While the US "lags far behind nations like Japan and Germany in per-capita spending on foreign economic aid," William Hartung points out, about one-third of its foreign aid budget "is devoted to direct grants or loans to foreign governments for the purchase of U.S. military equipment"; other programs are shaped to the same ends.

Such considerations, however, should not obscure the more fundamental role of the Pentagon system (including NASA and DOE) in maintaining high-tech industry generally, just as state intervention plays a crucial role in supporting biotechnology, pharmaceuticals, agribusiness, and most competitive segments of the economy. The Reagan Administration sharply increased protectionist measures along with steps to support failing banks and industries, and generally to assist US corporate power.

By IMF standards, the United States, after a decade of Reaganite folly, is a prime candidate for severe austerity measures. But it is far too powerful to submit to the rules, intended for the weak.

As noted, the World Bank now estimates that protectionist measures of the industrial countries—keeping pace with free market bombast—reduce the national income of the South by twice the amount of the official "development assistance." The latter may help or harm the recipients, but that is incidental. Typically, it is a form of export promotion. One notable example is the Food for Peace program, designed to subsidize US agribusiness and induce others to "become dependent on us for food" (Senator Hubert Humphrey), and to promote the global security network that keeps order in the Third World by requiring that local governments use counterpart funds for armaments (thus also subsidizing US military producers).

A more significant case is the Marshall Plan. Its goal was "to avert 'economic, social and political' chaos in Europe, contain Communism (meaning not Soviet intervention but the success of the indigenous Communist parties), prevent the collapse of America's export trade, and achieve the goal of multilateralism," and provide a crucial economic stimulus for "individual initiative and private enterprise both on the Continent and in the United States," undercutting the fear of "experiments with socialist enterprise and government controls," which would "jeopardize private enterprise" in the United States as well (Michael Hogan, in the major scholarly study). The Marshall Plan also "set the stage for large amounts of private U.S. direct investment in Europe," Reagan's Commerce Department observed in 1984, establishing the basis for the modern TNCs, which "prospered and expanded on overseas orders, ...fueled initially by the dollars of the Marshall Plan" and protected from "negative developments" by "the umbrella of American power," *Business Week* observed in 1975, lamenting that this golden age of state intervention might be fading away. Aid to Israel, Egypt, and Turkey, the leading recipients in recent years, is motivated by their role in maintaining US dominance of the Middle East, with its enormous oil energy reserves.[10]

So it goes case by case.

The utility of free trade as a weapon against the poor is illustrated by a World Bank study on global warming, designed to "forge a consensus among economists" (of the rich men's club) in advance of the June 1992 Rio conference on global warming, *New York Times* business correspondent Silvia Nasar reported under the headline "Can Capitalism Save the Ozone?" (the implication being: "Yes"). Harvard economist Lawrence Summers, chief economist of the World Bank, explained that the world's environmental problems are largely "the consequence of policies that are misguided on narrow economic grounds," particularly the policies of the poor countries that "have been practically giving away oil, coal and natural gas to domestic buyers in hopes of fostering industry and keeping living costs low for urban workers" (Nasar). If the poor countries would only have the courage to resist the "extreme pressure to improve the performance of their economies" and to protect their population from starvation, then environmental problems would abate. "Creating free markets in Russia and other poor countries may do more to slow global warming than any measures that rich countries are likely to adopt in the 1990's," the World Bank concludes—correctly, since the rich are hardly likely to pursue policies detrimental to their interests. In the small print, the consensus economists also recognize that "more effective government regulation" reduces pollution, but grinding down the poor has obvious advantages.

The same page of the *Times* business section carries an item on a confidential memo of the World Bank leaked to the *Economist*. Its author is the same Lawrence Summers. He writes: "Just between you and me, shouldn't the World Bank be encouraging *more* migration of the dirty industries to the [Third World]?" This makes good sense, Summers explains:

for example, a cancer-producing agent will have larger effects "in a country where people survive to get prostate cancer than in a country where under-5 mortality is 200 per thousand." Poor countries are "*under*-polluted," and it is only reasonable to encourage "dirty industries" to move to them. "The economic logic behind dumping a load of toxic waste in the lowest-wage country is impeccable and we should face up to that." To be sure, there are "arguments against all of these proposals" for exporting pollution to the Third World: "intrinsic rights to certain goods, moral reasons, social concerns, lack of adequate markets, etc." But these arguments have a fatal flaw: they "could be turned around and used more or less effectively against every Bank proposal for liberalisation."

"Mr Summers is asking questions that the World Bank would rather ignore," the *Economist* observes, but "on the economics, his points are hard to answer." Quite true. We have the choice of taking them to be a *reductio ad absurdum* argument and thus abandoning the ideology, or accepting the conclusions: on grounds of economic rationality, the rich countries should export pollution to the Third World, which should cut back on its "misguided" efforts to promote economic development and protect the population from disaster. That way, capitalism can overcome the environmental crisis. Free market capitalism is, indeed, a wondrous instrument. Surely there should be two Nobel prizes awarded annually, not just one.

Confronted with the memo, Summers said that it was only "intended to provoke debate"—elsewhere, that it was a "sarcastic response" to another World Bank draft. Perhaps the same is true of the World Bank "consensus" study. In fact, it is often hard to determine when the intellectual productions of the experts are intended seriously, or are a perverse form of sarcasm. The huge numbers of people subjected to these doctrines do not have the luxury to ponder this intriguing question.[11]

Though not intended for us, "free trade does, however, have its uses," Arthur MacEwan observes in a review of the uniform record of industrial and agricultural development through protectionism and other measures of state intervention: "Highly developed nations can use free trade to extend their power and their control of the world's wealth, and businesses can use it as a weapon against labor. Most important, free trade can limit efforts to redistribute income more equally, undermine progressive social programs, and keep people from democratically controlling their economic lives." It is hardly surprising that the "New Evangelists" of neoliberal theology have won an overwhelming victory within the doctrinal system. The evidence about successful development and the actual consequences of neoliberal doctrine is dismissed with the contempt that irrelevant nuisance so richly deserves. "The carrying out of [God's] plan...is the History of the world," Hegel explained: "That which does not accord with it, is negative, worthless existence."[12]

3. The Good News

In the post-affluence period, the ideological institutions have dedicated themselves with renewed vigor to convincing the intended victims of the great benefits of the Higher Truths designed for subject peoples. The wonderful news about the marvels of free market economies is broadcast to the people of the South who have been devastated by these doctrines for years, and East Europeans are invited to share in the good fortune as well. Elites in the targeted countries are quite supportive, anticipating that they will benefit, whatever happens to the lesser orders.

One aspect of the internationalization of the economy is the extension of the two-tiered Third World model to the core countries. Market doctrine thus becomes an essential ideological weapon at home as well, its highly selective application safely obscured by the doctrinal system. Wealth and power are increasingly concentrated among investors and professionals who benefit from internationalization of capital flow and communication. Services for the general public—education, health, transportation, libraries, etc.—become as superfluous as those they serve, and can therefore be limited or dispensed with entirely. Some, it is true, are still needed, notably prisons, a service that must in fact be extended, to deal with useless people. As care for the mentally ill declines, prisons become "surrogate mental hospitals," a study of the National Alliance for the Mentally Ill and Ralph Nader's *Public Citizen* observes. The psychiatrist who led the research observes that "there were far fewer psychotic people in jail 100 years ago than we have today," as we revert to practices reformed in the 19th century. Almost 30 percent of jails detain mentally ill people without criminal charges. The drug war has also made a major contribution to this technique of social control. The dramatic increase in the prison population in the late 1980s is largely attributable not to criminal acts, but to cocaine dealing and possession, as well as the harsher sentencing favored by "conservatives." The US has by far the highest rate of imprisonment in the world, "largely because of drug-related crimes" (Mathea Falco). How fortunate we are not to be in China, where the "lingering police-state mentality leaves little room for the kinds of creative solutions the West favors in addressing social maladies such as drug addiction," the *Wall Street Journal* explains.

Prisons also offer a Keynesian stimulus to the economy, both the construction business and white collar employment; the fastest growing profession is reported to be security personnel. They also offer a method of economic conversion that does not infringe on corporate prerogatives and hence is acceptable. "Fort Devens top pick for US prison," a front-page *Boston Globe* headline happily proclaims; the new federal prison may overcome the harm to the local economy when the army base closes.[13]

High on the list of targets for the New Evangelists is public education, dispensable, since the rich can buy what they want in the "education market" and the thought that one might be concerned about the larger society has been relegated to the ashcan of history along with other ancient prejudices. An upbeat story in the liberal *Boston Globe* describes an experiment in the "desperate city" of Baltimore, where schools are collapsing. Several schools are being handed over to a for-profit company that will introduce the "entrepreneurial spirit": "private-sector efficiency and a new educational model...means, for example, hiring nonunion custodians and placing special education students into mainstream classrooms." The former special education teachers, and the union custodians with their higher benefits, will be picked up by the schools that remain public. Another achievement of the "entrepreneurial spirit" is to replace high-cost teachers with low-wage interns and volunteers (parents). These miracles of capitalism should "provide valuable lessons as America seeks ways to improve its education system."[14]

A central feature of the recent ideological offensive has been the attack on "big government" and pleas for relief for the poor taxpayer—undertaxed (with the least progressive taxes, by a good margin) in comparison with other developed countries,[15] a major reason for the steady deterioration of education, health, highways, indeed anything that might benefit the irrelevant public. At the same time, protectionist devices, subsidy, bail-outs, and other familiar elements of the welfare state for the rich are quietly extended, while praise for the free market resounds to the skies. The combination is a major achievement of the state-corporate-media alliance.

4. Reshaping Industrial Policy

The world is complicated; even the most successful plans carry hidden costs. "The Reagan nightmare of supply side economics and military Keynesianism" had no more enthusiastic champion than the *Wall Street Journal*, which now complains about the predictable effects as they impinge on wealth and power. "Public higher education—one of the few areas where America still ranks supreme—is being pounded by state spending cuts," the *Journal* reports, echoing the concerns of businesses that "rely heavily on a steady stream of graduates." This is one of the long-predicted consequences of the cutback of federal services for all but the wealthy and powerful, which devastated states and local communities. Class war is not easy to fine tune.

The economic managers of the 1980s not only left the US with a legacy of unprecedented public and private debt, but also with the lowest rate of net private investment of any major industrial economy. Net new investment in the 1980s fell to its lowest level (as a share of national income) since World War II. In 1989-1990, the US fell behind Japan in absolute level of industrial investment, with a population twice as large. The US position in high-tech industry also declined. Another legacy of "the nightmare" is a decline of spending for research and development—like health and education, "investment" for the future. R&D has fallen to "perilous" levels, the policymaking arm of the National Science Foundation (National Science Board) reported in a 1992 study. Corporate spending, which had risen steadily before, virtually levelled (in constant dollars) from 1985. These trends, if continued, would be "fatal to the technological competitiveness of the US," the co-chairman said. Blaming bad management practices and corporate debt, the NSB reports that the US falls below its major trade competitors in total R&D, and 25 percent below in non-military industrial R&D. Corporate debt reached such levels that "by the time the recession began in July 1990, corporate interest rates were absorbing 44 percent of pretax profits, more than double the average for the 1960s and 1970s," economist Robert Pollin writes. Borrowing was used for consumption and financial speculation, including $1 trillion spent on mergers and acquisitions, with no indication of economic rationalization but ample evidence of a heavy debt burden, and a decline of 5 percent in corporate R&D as compared to a 5 percent increase for companies not involved in these practices, the NSF reported (for 1986-1987).[16]

For 40 years, US industrial policy has been based on the Pentagon system, with its regular stimulus to high-tech industry and state-guaranteed market to cushion management decisions. When a government stimulus was needed, a threat to our existence could readily be concocted: the Korean War in 1950, Kennedy's "missile gap," the impending Russian takeover of the world and the "window of vulnerability" in the late Carter-early Reagan years. The fakery was evident in each case, but Soviet power and tyranny were real enough, and that sufficed. Massive state intervention in the economy provided the US with a comfortable lead in advanced sectors of technology. It served as "an important pillar of the economy," ideologists and business leaders now concede as they lament the passing of the Soviet threat, which could always be invoked to keep the government crutch in place. In the post-World War II period, military spending has led the way out of recession, a senior economist at the Boston Federal Reserve Bank observes, and "There has never been a time when a rise in defense spending would mean more for the economy than now." Many economists consider the major factor in the Bush recession to be the cutback in military procurement—orders placed with factories, which have not only accounted for a healthy segment of the output of goods and services but have had a substantial multiplier effect, creating jobs in companies that produce consumer goods for the relatively high-paid workers in companies that are profitable thanks to the taxpayer subsidy. "The impact is bigger than you can see by just looking at the numbers," conservative economist Herbert Stein of the American Enterprise Institute notes. "The abrupt dissolution of the Soviet Union" has undermined the device instituted to maintain the economy after World War II, *Times* economics correspondent Louis Uchitelle reports, and "leading military companies" like General Electric are in trouble, as is high-tech industry generally.[17]

The old pretexts are gone, and it is no longer so simple to hail the virtues of free market capitalism while feeding at the public trough. New methods are needed.

At the same time, the cutting edge is shifting towards other areas, notably biotechnology. Like other competitive sectors of the economy, the pharmaceutical and health industries and agribusiness have always benefitted from a state-organized subsidy for research, development, and marketing. These areas are now gaining a greater role in planning for the years ahead. In the early postwar years, research would "spin off" electronics and computer firms. Today, biotech firms are springing up around the same research institutions, by rather similar mechanisms.

The US National Institutes of Health are engaged in what the *Wall Street Journal* calls "the biggest race for property since the great land rush of 1889," in this case, "staking U.S. patent claims to thousands of pieces of genetic material—DNA—that NIH scientists are certain are fragments of unknown genes." The purpose, the NIH explains, is to ensure that US corporations dominate the biotechnology business, which the government expects "to be generating annual revenue of $50 billion by the year 2000," and vastly more beyond. A patent for a basic human blood cell could allow a California company to "corner the market for a broad array of life-saving technologies," to cite merely one example. The biotech business took off after a 1980 Supreme Court decision granting a patent for an oil-dissolving microorganism developed through genetic engineering, the *Journal* observes. Medical procedures such as bone-marrow transplants and gene-based therapies will also be protected by patent. The same could be true of engineered animals and seeds.

We are now speaking of control of the essentials of life. By comparison, electronics deals with mere conveniences.

Foreign governments that are able to intend to retaliate. The scientific community at home and abroad has also expressed its opposition to these efforts. One cynical researcher remarked that as government-industry efforts are proceeding, some day parents might have to pay royalties for having children. A meeting at the National Academy of Sciences sent "a strong message that the U.S. and international genetics community is still vehemently opposed to NIH's moves," *Science* magazine reports. Representatives of leading US and European scientific organizations "argued that if the NIH is allowed to go ahead, it will start a patent stampede that will destroy international collaboration and hinder product development." The first South-North Human Genome Conference passed a unanimous resolution saying that "intellectual property should be based on the uses of sequences rather than the sequences themselves," and leading European scientists called for an international treaty to block patenting of gene sequences as such. A representative of the (US) Industrial Biotechnology Association noted that industry has reservations too, but the organization "believes that NIH had no choice but to file the applications," and NIH Director Bernardine Healy said that NIH will proceed in order "to protect its options—and those of the taxpayer," the latter phrase being one of the euphemisms for those who stand to profit, and for whom social policy is regularly designed in state capitalist welfare states (for the rich).

In March 1992, Senator Mark Hatfield introduced legislation calling for a moratorium on patenting of genetically-related organisms, but withdrew it after "it drew widespread industry opposition and in particular sparked an all-out lobbying effort by the Industrial Biotechnology Association," the newsletter of the health research industry reported. Administration officials also lobbied against the amendment, as did the Congressional Biotechnology Caucus. A moratorium "would lead us to forfeit our lead in biotechnology, where patent rights are a key to the large [private] investment needed for product development," the Secretary of Health and Human Services asserted. Meanwhile, a study of the National Academy of Sciences and Engineering proposed a $5 billion quasi-governmental company "to channel federal money into private applied research": publicly-funded research that will yield private profit. Another report, entitled *The Government Role in Civilian Technology: Building a New Alliance,* calls for new efforts to extend "the close and longstanding" government-industry relationship that has "helped to establish the commercial biotechnology industry." It recommends a government-funded "Civilian Technology Corporation" to assist US industry to commercialize technology by encouraging "cooperative R&D ventures in pre-commercial areas." The ventures will be "cooperative"—with the public paying the costs—up to the point of product development. At that point costs change to profits, and the public hands the enterprise over to private industry.[18]

The "vile maxim of the masters" has a corollary in the state capitalist societies: public subsidy, private profit.

A few weeks after these reports appeared, the head of the NIH project resigned along with virtually his entire staff to set up a private laboratory, with a stake of $70 million from a group of venture capitalists. The chairman of the funding corporation "said he had suddenly realized that there was an international race to lock up the human genome," and that the NIH lacked the funds to win; "I suddenly said to myself, 'My God—if this thing doesn't get done in a substantive way in the United States, that is the end of biotechnology in the U.S.'" There may also be a buck or two for the benefactors attempting to save the US economy, who will keep the rights to any product developed. Scientists "are aghast at the possibility that the human genome could be locked up and owned by private investors," also noting that the technique used to isolate the gene leaves the scientific work—discovering the function of the already patented gene—to be done by others. Scientists generally are calling for an international agreement to prohibit such patents. For now, the race to lock up the future biotech industry continues.[19]

These developments give new urgency to the US demand for increased protection for "intellectual property"—including patents—at the ongoing GATT negotiations. "America's interest in intellectual property is by no means altruistic," the *Economist* observes. "From movies to microchips, America ran a healthy $12 billion surplus on its trade in ideas in 1990," while most other developed countries ran a loss, and the Third World is not even in the game. The new protectionist measures are intended to ensure that US corporations dominate the health and agricultural industries, thus controlling the essentials for human life; and to guarantee to US pharmaceutical corporations huge profits. Prices of the 20 most used prescription drugs rose at four times the inflation rate from 1984 to 1991, a 1992 study revealed, yielding skyrocketing profits for the drug companies; nearly half the 10 percent annual increase was devoted to marketing, profits, and administrative expenses.

"Basic biomedical research has long been heavily subsidized by United States taxpayers," the *New York Times* business pages observe, and "high-tech pharmaceuticals owe their origin largely to these investments and to Government scientists," funded by billions of taxpayer dollars. But drugs created with a public subsidy are priced beyond the reach of those who pay for their development, let alone the bulk of the world's population. Protection of "intellectual property" is designed to guarantee monopoly profits to the publicly-subsidized corporations, not to benefit those who pay; and the South must be denied the right to produce drugs, seeds, and other necessities at a fraction of the cost.

On similar grounds, the US refused to sign the a treaty on preserving the world's biological species. The Assistant Secretary of State for the Environment, Curtis Bohlen, said that the treaty "fails to give adequate patent protection to American companies that transfer biotechnology to developing companies," and "tries to regulate genetically engineered materials, a competitive area in which the United States leads," the *Times* reports.[20]

The US International Trade Commission estimates that US companies stand to gain $61 billion a year from the Third World if "intellectual property" rights are protected in accord with US demands, a cost to the South of somewhere between $100-300 billion when extrapolated to the other industrial countries, dwarfing the debt service flow of capital from South to North. The same US demands will require poor farmers to pay royalties to TNCs for seeds, denying them the traditional right to re-use seeds from their harvests. Cloned varieties of commercial crops exported by the South (palm oil, cotton, rubber, etc.) will also be commercial property, subject to increased royalties. "The main beneficiaries will be the core group of less than a dozen seeds and pharmaceuticals companies which control over 70 percent of world seeds trade," and agribusiness generally, Kevin Watkins observes.[21]

While the US seeks to ensure monopoly control for the future, the drug companies it protects are cheerfully exploiting the accumulated knowledge of indigenous cultures for products that bring in some $100 billion profits annually, offering virtually nothing in return to the native people who lead researchers to the medicines, seeds, and other products they have developed and refined over thousands of years. "The annual world market value for medicines derived from medicinal plants discovered from indigenous peoples is US $43 billion," ethnobotanist Darrell Posey estimates. "Less than 0.001 percent of the profits from drugs that originated from traditional medicine have ever gone to the indigenous people who led researchers to them." Profits of at least the same scale derive from natural insecticides, insect repellents, and plant genetic materials, he believes. The international seed industry alone accounts for some $15 billion a year, based in large measure on genetic materials from crop varieties "selected, nurtured, improved and developed by innovative Third World farmers for hundreds, even thousands of years," Maria Elena Hurtado adds.[22]

Only the knowledge of the rich and powerful merits protection.

The director of India's Working Group on Patent Laws comments that "the levels of contradiction and hypocrisy are breathtaking." The rich "call for competitiveness, but what they want is monopoly. It is blackmail. They are seeking to do through economic rules what formerly the powerful did through armies of invasion and occupation." The manager of a Bombay drug company adds that the West "protected their own infant industries, and they pirated the world to create wealth; and they now preach to other countries to practice what they never did themselves." The developed countries "only permitted product patents after their domestic industry and infrastructure were well established. Germany allowed product patents in pharmaceuticals only in 1966, Japan in 1976, Italy in 1982." The effect of the new economic rules will be to prevent such countries as India from manufacturing life-saving drugs at a fraction of the cost charged by the state-subsidized corporations of the rich countries.

Like other developed countries, the US did not abide by the rules it now seeks to impose. In the 19th century, the US rejected foreign claims to intellectual property rights on grounds that they would hamper its economic development. Japan followed the same course. And today, the concept of "intellectual property rights" is finely crafted to suit the needs of the powerful. Exactly as in the case of "free trade," Churchill's disruptive "hungry nations" with their indecent clamor are to be denied the methods that were used by the "rich men dwelling at peace within their habitations."[23]

The array of plans of the rulers is viewed from the South as "an act of unbridled piracy," Watkins observes, given that the genetic materials used by the Western corporations to create their patented and protected products are derived from Third World crops and wild plants, cultivated, refined, and identified over countless generations. The seed and pharmaceutical companies thus "reap monopoly profits, while the genius of the Third World farmers, past and present, in selecting and developing individual seed strains goes unrewarded." The New World Order as a whole is described by Egypt's leading newspaper, *al-Ahram*, as "codified international piracy," referring in this case to Bush Administration maneuvers to set up a confrontation with Qaddafi for domestic political purposes in the routine manner. The terminology is apt enough.[24]

The unbridled piracy takes on increased urgency as indigenous agriculture and knowledge are undermined by pressures on the South to abandon production for domestic needs in favor of ecologically unsustainable agroexport in the interests of the TNCs. One consequence is that the world's biological resources—mostly in the South—are in decline, raising the danger of disease and blight to potentially quite serious levels. To whatever extent biotechnology may provide a remedy, the effect again will be to transfer power and wealth to the world rulers, if the demands of the corporations for increased protection are implemented. That they will be is almost a foregone conclusion, given the distribution of power and the insulation of decision-making from public interference in the new imperial age of Year 501.

CHAPTER 5

HUMAN RIGHTS: THE PRAGMATIC CRITERION

1. Reality and its Abuse

Prominent among the high principles to which we are dedicated, alongside of Democracy and the Market, stands Human Rights, which became "the Soul of our foreign policy," fortuitously, just at the moment when popular revulsion over monstrous crimes had become difficult to contain.

It is recognized, to be sure, that our service to the cause of humanity is not entirely without flaw. By "granting idealism a near exclusive hold on our foreign policy," we go too far, press thinkers warn, quoting high-ranking officials. This nobility puts us at a disadvantage in dealing with the "fierce savages" of whom Justice Marshall warned, a problem that has bedeviled Europe throughout its history of "encounters." The Korean war raised "serious questions as to how the soft, humanitarian West could compete with such people" as the "ruthless" Asian leaders, top Kennedy adviser Maxwell Taylor wrote. Taylor's "uncomfortable thoughts about the future of the West in Asia" were echoed by leading liberal critics of the Vietnam war as it spiraled out of control. The "Asian poor" used "the strategy of the weak," inviting us to carry our "strategic logic to its conclusion, which is genocide," but we are unwilling to "destroy ourselves...by contradicting our own value system." Soft humanitarians, we feel that "genocide is a terrible burden to bear" (William Pfaff, Townsend Hoopes). Strategic analyst Albert Wohlstetter explains that "the Vietnamese were able to bear the costs imposed on their subjects more easily than we could impose them." We are simply too noble for this cruel world.

The dilemma we face has engaged the deepest thinkers. Hegel pondered "the contempt of humanity displayed by the Negroes" of Africa, "who allow themselves to be shot down by thousands in war with Europeans. Life has a value only when it has something valuable as its object," a thought beyond the grasp of these "mere things." Unable to comprehend our lofty values, the savages confound us in our quest for justice and virtue.[1]

The burdens of the righteous are not easy to bear.

There are ways to test the theses that are confidently proclaimed. Thus one might look into the correlation between US aid and the human rights climate. That was done by the leading academic scholar on human rights in Latin America, Lars Schoultz, who found that US aid "has tended to flow disproportionately to Latin American governments which torture their citizens, ...to the hemisphere's relatively egregious violators of fundamental human rights." The flow of aid includes military aid, is not correlated with need, and runs through the Carter period, when at least some attention was given to human rights concerns. A broader study by Edward Herman found the same correlation worldwide. Herman carried out another study that directs us to the reasons. Aid is closely correlated with improvement in the investment climate, a result commonly achieved by murdering priests and union leaders, massacring peasants trying to organize, blowing up the independent press, and so on. We therefore find the secondary correlation between aid and egregious violation of human rights. These studies precede the Reagan years, when the questions are not even worth posing.

Another approach is to investigate the relation between the source of atrocities and the reaction to them. There is extensive work on that topic, again with sharp and consistent results: the atrocities of official enemies arouse great anguish and indignation, vast coverage, and often shameless lying to portray them as even worse than they are; the treatment is the opposite in all respects when responsibility lies closer to home. (Atrocities that do not bear on domestic power interests are generally ignored.) Without comparable inquiry, we know that exactly the same was true of Stalinist Russia and Nazi Germany. The importance of the finding is greatly heightened by the fact, which commissars on all sides labor to obscure, that on elementary moral grounds, abuses cry out for attention insofar as we can do something about them; primarily our own, and those of our clients.

There have also been numerous case studies of the close match between policy and Kennan's advice on "unreal objectives such as human rights" when wealth and power are at stake.[2]

None of the facts have the slightest impact on the Higher Truths. But that makes sense too. As in the case of Democracy and the Market, the factual record merely deals with Hegel's "negative, worthless existence," not "God's plan" and "the pure light of this divine Idea." The point has sometimes been made explicit by contemporary scholars, notably Hans Morgenthau, a founder of the realist school, who urged that to adduce the factual record is "to confound the abuse of reality with reality itself." Reality itself is the "transcendent purpose" of the nation, which is indeed noble; the abuse of reality is the irrelevant factual record.[3]

The record is misleading if it keeps to the support for horrendous atrocities and fails to reveal the welcome accorded them when they are seen to be in a good cause, a leading feature of the 500-year conquest. The reaction to the US-directed atrocities in Central America in the past decade is one well-studied example. To illustrate how firmly this pillar of the traditional culture is in place, it would only be fitting to consider the earliest Asian outpost of European colonialism, the Dutch East Indies, during the era of US global management.

2. Securing the Anchor

"The problem of Indonesia" is "the most crucial issue of the moment in our struggle with the Kremlin," Kennan wrote in 1948. "Indonesia is the anchor in that chain of islands stretching from Hokkaido to Sumatra which we should develop as a politico-economic counter-force to communism" and a "base area" for possible military action beyond. A Communist Indonesia, he warned, would be an "infection" that "would sweep westward" through all of South Asia. Resource-rich Indonesia was also designated to be a critical part of the "Empire toward the South" that the US intended to recreate for Japan, now within the US-dominated system.

In accord with standard reasoning, "ultra-nationalism" in Indonesia would prevent Southeast Asia from "fulfilling its main function" as a service area for the core industrial powers. Accordingly, the US urged the former Dutch rulers to grant independence, but under Dutch tutelage, an outcome critical to "Western Europe's economic rehabilitation, and to America's strategic well-being," Leffler observes, and to Japan's reconstruction as well. The principled antagonism to independent nationalism that animates US foreign policy took on particular significance in this case.[4]

After its liberation from the Dutch, Indonesia was ruled by the nationalist leader Sukarno. At first, the United States was willing to tolerate this arrangement, particularly after Sukarno and the army suppressed a land reform movement supported by the Indonesian Communist Party [PKI] in the Madiun region in 1948, virtually destroying the party's leadership and jailing 36,000 people. But Sukarno's nationalist and neutralist commitments soon proved entirely unacceptable.

The two major power centers in Indonesia were the army and the PKI, the only mass-based political force. Internal politics were dominated by Sukarno's balancing of these two forces. Western aims were largely shared by the army, who therefore qualified as moderates. To achieve these aims, it was necessary somehow to overcome the anti-American extremists. Other methods having failed, mass extermination remained as a last resort.

In the early 1950s, the CIA tried covert support of right-wing parties, and in 1957-1958 the US backed and participated in armed insurrection against Sukarno, possibly including assassination attempts. After the rebellions were put down, the US turned to a program of military aid and training coupled with a cutback of economic aid, a classic mode of pre-coup planning, followed in Chile a few years later, and attempted in Iran with the dispatch of arms via Israel from shortly after the Khomeini takeover—one of the many crucial elements of the Iran-contra affair suppressed in the subsequent cover-up.[5] Universities and corporations also lent their willing hands.

In a RAND study published by Princeton University in 1962, Guy Pauker, closely involved with US policy-making through RAND and the CIA, urged his contacts in the Indonesian military to take "full responsibility" for their country, "fulfill a mission," and "strike, sweep their house clean." In 1963, former CIA staff officer William Kintner, then at a CIA-subsidized research institute at the University of Pennsylvania, warned that "If the PKI is able to maintain its legal existence and Soviet influence continues to grow, it is possible that Indonesia may be the first Southeast Asia country to be taken over by a popularly based, legally elected communist government... In the meantime, with Western help, free Asian political leaders—together with the military—must not only hold on and manage, but reform and advance while liquidating the enemy's political and guerrilla armies." The prospects for liquidation of the popularly based political forces were regarded as uncertain, however. In a 1964 RAND memorandum, Pauker expressed his concern that the groups backed by the US "would probably lack the ruthlessness that made it possible for the Nazis to suppress the Communist Party of Germany... [These right-wing and military elements] are weaker than the Nazis, not only in numbers and in mass support, but also in unity, discipline, and leadership."

Pauker's pessimism proved unfounded. After an alleged Communist coup attempt on September 30, 1965, and the murder of six Indonesian generals, pro-American General Suharto took charge and launched a bloodbath in which hundreds of thousands of people, mostly landless peasants, were slaughtered. Reflecting on the matter in 1969, Pauker noted that the assassination of the generals "elicited the ruthlessness that I had not anticipated a year earlier and resulted in the death of large numbers of Communist cadres."

The scale of the massacre is unknown. The CIA estimates 250,000 killed. The head of the Indonesia state security system later estimated the toll at over half a million; Amnesty International gave the figure of "many more than one million." Whatever the numbers, no one doubts that there was incredible butchery. Seven-hundred-fifty-thousand more were arrested, according to official figures, many of them kept for years under miserable conditions without trial. President Sukarno was overthrown and the military ruled unchallenged. Meanwhile the country was opened to Western exploitation, hindered only by the rapacity of the rulers.

The US role in these events is uncertain, one reason being the gaps in the documentary record. Gabriel Kolko observes that "U.S. documents for the three months preceding September 30, 1965, and dealing with the convoluted background and intrigues, much less the embassy's and the CIA's roles, have been withheld from public scrutiny. Given the detailed materials available before and after July-September 1965, one can only assume that the release of these papers would embarrass the U.S. government." Ex-CIA officer Ralph McGehee reports that he is familiar with a highly classified CIA report on the agency's role in provoking the destruction of the PKI, and attributes the slaughter to the "C.I.A. [one word deleted] operation." The deletion was imposed by CIA censorship. Peter Dale Scott, who has carried out the most careful attempt to reconstruct the events, suggests that the deleted word is "deception," referring to CIA propaganda that "creates the appropriate situations," in McGehee's uncensored words, for this and other mass murder operations (citing also Chile). McGehee referred specifically to atrocity fabrication by the CIA to lay the basis for violence against the PKI.[6]

There is no doubt that Washington was aware of the slaughter, and approved. Secretary of State Dean Rusk cabled to Ambassador Marshall Green on October 29 that the "campaign against PKI" must continue and that the military, who were orchestrating it, "are [the] only force capable of creating order in Indonesia" and must continue to do so with US help for a "major military campaign against PKI." The US moved quickly to provide aid to the army, but details have not been made public. Cables from the Jakarta Embassy on October 30 and November 4 indicate that deliveries of communications equipment to the Indonesian army were accelerated and the sale of US aircraft approved, while the Deputy Chief of Mission noted that "The embassy and the USG were generally sympathetic with and admiring of what the army was doing."[7]

For clarity, we must distinguish several issues. On the one hand, there are questions of historical fact: What took place in Indonesia and Washington in 1965-1966? There are also questions of cultural history: How did the US government, and articulate sectors at home, react to what they took to be the facts? The political history is murky. On the matter of cultural history, however, the public record provides ample evidence. The cultural history is by far the more informative with regard to the implications for the longer term. It is from the reactions that we draw lessons for the future.

There is no serious controversy about Washington's sympathy for "what the army was doing." An analysis by H.W. Brands is of particular interest in this connection.[8] Of the more careful studies of the events themselves, his is the most skeptical concerning the US role, which he regards as basically that of a confused observer, with "only a marginal ability to change a very dangerous situation for the better." But he leaves no doubt about Washington's enthusiasm about the turn "for the better" as the slaughter proceeded.

According to Brands's reconstruction of events, by early 1964 the US was engaged in "quiet efforts to encourage action by the army against the PKI," ensuring that when the expected conflict broke out, "the army [would know] it had friends in Washington." The goal of the continuing civic action and military training programs, Secretary of State Dean Rusk commented, was "strengthening anti-Communist elements in Indonesia in the continuing and coming struggle with the PKI." Chief of Staff Nasution, regarded by US Ambassador Howard Jones as "the strongest man in the country," informed Jones in March 1964 that "Madiun would be mild compared with an army crackdown today," referring to the bloody repression of 1948.

Through 1965, the main question in Washington was how to encourage army action against the PKI. US emissary Ellsworth Bunker felt that Washington should keep a low profile so that the generals could proceed "without the incubus of being attacked as defenders of the neo-colonialists and imperialists." The State Department agreed. Prospects, however, remained uncertain, and September 1965 ended, Brands continues, "with American officials anticipating little good news soon."

The September 30 strike against the army leadership came as a surprise to Washington, Brands concludes, and the CIA knew little about it. Ambassador Green, who had replaced Jones, told Washington he could not establish any PKI role, though the official story then and since is that it was a "Communist coup attempt."

The "good news" was not long in coming. "American officials soon recognized that the situation in Indonesia was changing drastically and, from their perspective, for the better," Brands continues. "As information arrived from the countryside indicating that a purge of the PKI was beginning, the principal worry of American officials in Jakarta and in Washington was that the army would fail to take advantage of its opportunity," and when the army seemed to hesitate, Washington sought ways "to encourage the officers" to proceed. Green recommended covert efforts to "spread the story of the PKI's guilt, treachery, and brutality," though he knew of no PKI role. Such efforts were undertaken to good effect, according to McGehee's account of the internal CIA record. George Ball, the leading Administration dove, recommended that the US stay in the background because "the generals were doing quite well on their own" (Brands's paraphrase), and the military aid and training programs "should have established clearly in the minds of the army leaders that the US stands behind them if they should need help" (Ball). Ball instructed the Jakarta embassy to exercise "extreme caution lest our well-meaning efforts to offer assistance or steel their resolve may in fact play into the hands of Sukarno and [his political associate] Subandrio." Dean Rusk added that "If the army's willingness to follow through against the PKI is in anyway contingent on or subject to influence by the United States, we do not want to miss the opportunity to consider U.S. action."

Brands concludes that US covert aid "may have facilitated the liquidation of the PKI," but "at most it speeded what probably would have happened more slowly." "Whatever the American role in these developments," he continues, "the administration found the overall trend encouraging. In mid-December Ball reported with satisfaction that the army's campaign to destroy the PKI was 'moving fairly swiftly and smoothly.' At about the same time Green cabled from Jakarta: 'The elimination of the communists continues apace'." By early February 1966, President Johnson was informed that about 100,000 had been massacred. Shortly before, the CIA reported that Sukarno was finished, and "The army has virtually destroyed the PKI."

Nevertheless, Brands continues, "Despite that good news the administration remained reluctant to commit itself publicly to Suharto," fearing that the outcome was still uncertain. But doubts soon faded. Johnson's new National Security Adviser Walt Rostow "found Suharto's 'New Order' encouraging," US aid began to flow openly, and Washington officials began to take credit for the great success.

According to this skeptical view, then, "The United States did not overthrow Sukarno, and it was not responsible for the hundreds of thousands of deaths involved in the liquidation of the PKI," though it did what it could to encourage the army to liquidate the only mass popular organization in Indonesia, hesitated to become more directly involved only because it feared that these efforts would be counterproductive, greeted the "good news" with enthusiasm as the slaughter mounted, and turned enthusiastically to assisting the "New Order" that arose from the bloodshed as the moderates triumphed.

4. Celebration

The public Western reaction was one of relief and pride. Deputy Undersecretary of State Alexis Johnson celebrated "The reversal of the Communist tide in the great country of Indonesia" as "an event that will probably rank along with the Vietnamese war as perhaps the most historic turning point of Asia in this decade" (October 1966). Appearing before a Senate Committee, Secretary of Defense Robert McNamara was asked whether US military aid during the pre-coup period had "paid dividends." He agreed that it had, and was therefore justified—the major dividend being a huge pile of corpses. In a private communication to President Johnson in March 1967, McNamara went further, saying that US military assistance to the Indonesian army had "encouraged it to move against the PKI when the opportunity was presented." Particularly valuable, he said, was the program bringing Indonesian military personnel to the United States for training at universities, where they learned the lessons they put to use so well. These were "very significant factors in determining the favorable orientation of the new Indonesian political elite" (the army), McNamara argued. A congressional report also held that training and continued communication with military officers paid "enormous dividends." The same reasoning has long been standard with regard to Latin America, with similar results.[9]

Across a broad spectrum, commentators credited the US intervention in Vietnam with having encouraged these welcome developments, providing a sign of American commitment to the anti-Communist cause and a "shield" behind which the generals could act without undue concern about Sukarno's Chinese ally. A Freedom House statement in November 1966 signed by "145 distinguished Americans" justified the US war in Vietnam for having "provided a shield for the sharp reversal of Indonesia's shift toward Communism," with no reservations concerning the means employed. Speaking to US troops in November 1966, President Johnson told them that their exploits in Indochina were the reason why "In Indonesia there are 100 million people that enjoy a measure of freedom today that they didn't enjoy yesterday." These reactions reflect the logic of the US war in Indochina.[10]

In line with his general skepticism, Brands believes these claims to be exaggerated. McNamara's "attempts to appropriate responsibility for the general's rise to power," he thinks, were a reaction to President Johnson's "enthusiasm for the Suharto regime." US assurances to the Indonesian military "certainly had *some* effect on Suharto's assessment of his prospects," but not much, because they "merely reiterated the obvious fact that the United States prefers rightists to leftists"—including rightists who conduct a huge slaughter and install a terrorist "New Order." As for the war in Vietnam, the CIA doubted that "the US display of determination in Vietnam directly influenced the outcome of the Indonesian crisis in any significant way," CIA director Helms wrote to Walt Rostow in 1966. As Brands himself puts it, the Johnson administration had been concerned that Indonesia might suffer "the fate from which the United States was then attempting to rescue South Vietnam." Fortunately, Indonesia rescued itself.

There was no condemnation of the slaughter on the floor of Congress, and no major US relief agency offered aid. The World Bank restored Indonesia to favor, soon making it the third largest borrower. Western governments and corporations followed along.

Those close at hand may have drawn further lessons about peasant massacre. Ambassador Green went on to the State Department, where he presided over the bombing of rural Cambodia, among other achievements. As the bombing was stepped up to historically unprecedented levels in 1973, slaughtering tens of thousands of peasants, Green testified before Congress that the massacre should continue because of our desire for peace: our experience with "these characters in Hanoi" teaches that only the rivers of blood of Cambodian peasants might bring them to the negotiating table. The "experience" to which he referred was the 1972 Christmas bombings of Hanoi, undertaken to force those characters in Hanoi to modify the agreements reached with the Nixon Administration in October but rejected by Washington, then restored without change after the US stopped the bombing because it proved too costly. The events and their remarkable aftermath having been concealed by the Free Press, Green could be confident that there would be no exposure of his colossal fabrications in the interest of continued mass murder.[11]

Returning to Indonesia, the media were pleased, even euphoric. As the army moved to take control, *Times* correspondent Max Frankel described the delight of Johnson Administration officials over the "dramatic new opportunity" in Indonesia. The "military showed power," so that "Indonesia can now be saved from what had appeared to be an inevitable drift towards a peaceful takeover from within"—an unthinkable disaster, since internal politics was not under US control. US officials "believe the army will cripple and perhaps destroy the Communists as a significant political force," leading to "the elimination of Communist influences at all levels of Indonesian society." Consequently, there is now "hope where only two weeks ago there was despair."[12]

Not everyone was so enthusiastic about the opportunity to destroy the one popular political force in the country. Japan's leading newspaper, *Asahi Shimbun,* urged caution: "In view of the fact that the Communist influence is deeply entrenched among the Indonesian grassroots, it would cause further deterioration in the confused national state of affairs if a firm crackdown were carried out against them."[13] But such more somber reflections were rare.

In mid-1966, well after the results were known, *U.S. News & World Report* headlined a long and enthusiastic story "Indonesia: 'HOPE...WHERE ONCE THERE WAS NONE.'" "Indonesians these days can talk and argue freely, no longer fearful of being denounced and imprisoned," the journal reported, describing an emerging totalitarian terror state with hundreds of thousands in prison and the blood still flowing. In a cover story, *Time* magazine celebrated "The West's best news for years in Asia" under the heading "Vengeance with a Smile," devoting 5 pages of text and 6 more of pictures to the "boiling bloodbath that almost unnoticed took 400,000 lives." The new army regime is "scrupulously constitutional," *Time* happily announced, "based on law not on mere power," in the words of its "quietly determined" leader Suharto with his "almost innocent face." The elimination of the 3 million-member PKI by its "only possible rival," the army, and the removal from power of the "genuine folk hero" Sukarno, may virtually be considered a triumph of democracy.[14]

The leading political thinker of the *New York Times*, James Reston, chimed in under the heading "A Gleam of Light in Asia." The regular channel for the State Department, Reston admonished Americans not to let the bad news in Vietnam displace "the more hopeful developments in Asia," primary among them being "the savage transformation of Indonesia from a pro-Chinese policy under Sukarno to a defiantly anti-Communist policy under General Suharto":

> Washington is being careful not to claim any credit for this change in the sixth most populous and one of the richest nations in the world, but this does not mean that Washington had nothing to do with it. There was a great deal more contact between the anti-Communist forces in that country and at least one very high official in Washington before and during the Indonesian massacre than is generally realized. General Suharto's forces, at times severely short of food and munitions, have been getting aid from here through various third countries, and it is doubtful if the coup would ever have been attempted without the American show of strength in Vietnam or been sustained without the clandestine aid it has received indirectly from here.

The news story on Indonesia the same day carried more glad tidings. Headlined "Indonesians View U.S. Films Again," it described "the biggest public social event in the Indonesian capital these days," the showing of

American films to "smartly dressed Indonesians" who "alight from expensive limousines," "one sign of the country's rejection of the anti-American pro-Communist policy of the Indonesian Government" before the gleam of light broke through the clouds.[15]

Recall that according to the skeptical view of Brands and others, Reston's proud claim that the US government could fairly claim credit for the massacre and the establishment of the "New Order" was exaggerated, though understandable.

Editorial reaction to the bloodbath was judicious. The *Times* was pleased that the Indonesian army had "de-fused the country's political time-bomb, the powerful Indonesian Communist party," and praised Washington for having "wisely stayed in the background during the recent upheavals" instead of assisting openly and trumpeting its glee; the idea that Washington, or anyone, should have protested and sought to abort the useful slaughter was beyond the pale. Washington should continue this wise course, the editors urged, supporting international aid to the "Indonesian moderates" who had conducted the massacre. A February 1966 editorial outlined the likely advantages for the United States now that the Indonesian military had taken power and "proceeded to dismantle the entire P.K.I. apparatus." A follow-up in August recognized that there had been a "staggering mass slaughter of Communists and pro-Communists," with hundreds of thousands killed. This "situation...raises critical questions for the United States," which, fortunately, have been correctly answered: Washington "wisely has not intruded into the Indonesian turmoil" by "embrac[ing] the country's new rulers publicly," which "could well hurt them"—the only "critical question" that comes to mind. A month later the editors described the relief in Washington over the fact that "Indonesia was lost and has been found again." The successes of the "moderates" had been rewarded "with generous pledges of rice, cotton and machinery" and preparations to resume the economic aid that was held back before the "staggering mass slaughter" set matters right. The US "has adequate reasons of state to come to terms with the new regime," not to speak of more than adequate reasons of profit.[16]

Within a few years, a complete role reversal had been achieved. George McArthur of the *Los Angeles Times,* a respected Asia hand, wrote in 1977 that the PKI had "attempted to seize power and subjected the country to a bloodbath," placing their necks under the knife in a major Communist atrocity.[17]

By then, the Indonesian generals, in addition to compiling one of the worst human rights records in the world at home, had escalated their 1975 attack on the former Portuguese colony of East Timor to near-genocidal levels, with another "staggering mass slaughter," which bears comparison to the atrocities of Pol Pot in the same years. In this case, the deed was done with the crucial support of the Human Rights Administration and its allies. They understand "reasons of state" as well as the *Times* editors, who, with their North American and European colleagues, did what they could to facilitate the slaughter by suppressing the readily available facts in favor of (occasional) fairy tales told by Indonesian generals and the State Department. US-Canadian reporting on Timor, which had been substantial before the invasion in the context of Western concerns over the collapse of the Portuguese empire, reduced to zero in 1978 as atrocities peaked along with the flow of US arms.[18]

    Times editors were not alone in extolling the moderates who had stirred up the "boiling bloodbath." "Many in the West were keen to cultivate Jakarta's new moderate leader, Suharto," the *Christian Science Monitor* later reported. *Times* Southeast Asia correspondent Philip Shenon adds, more cautiously, that Suharto's human rights record is "checkered." The London *Economist* described this great mass murderer and torturer as "at heart benign," doubtless thinking of his compassion for TNCs. Unfortunately, there are those who try to impugn his benign nature: "propagandists for the guerrillas" in East Timor and West Papua (Irian Jaya) "talk of the army's savagery and use of torture"—including the Bishop and other church sources, thousands of refugees in Australia and Portugal, Western diplomats and journalists who have chosen to see, Amnesty International and other human rights organizations. They are all "propagandists," rather than intrepid champions of human rights, because they have quite the wrong story to tell.[19]

    In the *Wall Street Journal*, Barry Wain, editor of its Asia affiliate, described how General Suharto "moved boldly in defeating the coup makers and consolidating his power," using "strength and finesse" to take total control. "By most standards, he has done well," though there have been a few problems, specifically, government involvement in the killing of several thousand alleged criminals from 1982 to 1985. Some lingering questions about earlier years aside, a few weeks before Wain's laudatory column, *Asiaweek* reported another massacre in Sumatra, where armed troops burnt a village of 300 people to the ground, killing dozens of civilians, part of an operation to quell unrest in the province. Suharto is "a Figure of Stability," a *Wall Street Journal* headline reads, using the term in the PC sense already discussed. The upbeat story does not overlook the events of 1965. One sentence reads: Suharto "took command of the effort to crush the coup attempt, and succeeded."[20]

When the victims are classified as less than human—wild beasts in the shape of men, Communists, terrorists, or whatever may be the contemporary term of art—their extermination raises no moral qualms. And the agents of extermination are praiseworthy moderates—our Nazis, to translate from Newspeak. The practice is standard. Recall the "moderate" General Gramajo, to mention someone who might aspire to Suharto's league.

5. Closing the Books

In 1990-1991, several events elicited some uncharacteristic concern over US-backed Indonesian atrocities. In May 1990, States News Service released a study in Washington by Kathy Kadane, which found that

> The U.S. government played a significant role by supplying the names of thousands of Communist Party leaders to the Indonesian army, which hunted down the leftists and killed them, former U.S. diplomats say... As many as 5000 names were furnished to the Indonesian army, and the Americans later checked off the names of those who had been killed or captured, according to U.S. officials... The lists were a detailed who's-who of the leadership of the party of 3 million members, [foreign service officer Robert] Martens said. They included names of provincial, city and other local PKI committee members, and leaders of the "mass organizations," such as the PKI national labor federation, women's and youth groups.

The names were passed on to the military, which used them as a "shooting list," according to Joseph Lazarsky, deputy CIA station chief in Jakarta at the time, who adds that some were kept for interrogation or "kangaroo courts" because the Indonesians "didn't have enough goon squads to zap them all." Kadane reports that top US Embassy officials acknowledged in interviews that they had approved of the release of the names. William Colby compared the operation to his Phoenix program in Vietnam, in exculpation of his own campaign of political assassination (which Phoenix clearly was, though he denies it).

"No one cared as long as they were Communists, that they were being butchered," said Howard Federspiel, then Indonesia expert for State Department intelligence; "No one was getting very worked up about it." "It really was a big help to the army," Martens said. "They probably killed a lot of people, and I probably have a lot of blood on my hands, but that's not all bad." "There's a time when you have to strike hard at a decisive moment."

The story was picked up by a few newspapers, though no one got worked up about it. Just more business as usual; after all, the US Embassy had done much the same in Guatemala a decade earlier, as another useful slaughter was getting underway.[21]

While ruffling some feathers briefly, the report was soon consigned to oblivion. The Newspaper of Record (the *New York Times*) waited almost two months to take notice, long enough to marshal the required denials. Reporter Michael Wines repeats every government propaganda cliché about the events themselves, however tenuous, as unquestioned fact. Ambassador Green dismisses the Kadane report as "garbage." He and others claim that the US had nothing to do with the list of names, which were of no significance anyway. Wines cites a Martens letter to the *Washington Post* saying that the names were publicly available in the Indonesian press, but not his amplification of this remark, in which he stressed the importance of handing over the list of names; Martens wrote that he "saw nothing wrong with helping out," and still doesn't, because "the pro-Communist terror leading to the final coup...against the non-Communist army leaders...had prevented systematic collection of data on the Communists" (a fanciful tale, but no matter). Wines says nothing about the *Times* celebration of the slaughter, or the pride of their leading political commentator on the US role in expediting it.[22]

Stephen Rosenfeld of the *Washington Post* was one of the few in the national press to be troubled by the Kadane revelations. His reaction too is instructive.

After the Kadane story appeared, the *Post* carried a letter by Indonesian human rights activist Carmel Budiardjo, who pointed out that direct US complicity in the massacre was already known from the cable traffic between the US Embassy in Jakarta and the State Department published by Gabriel Kolko, specifically, the Green-Rusk interchange cited earlier. A month later, Rosenfeld expressed some concern, adding that "in the one account I read"—namely, Kolko's book—some doubts are raised about Communist complicity in the alleged coup attempt that served as the pretext for the massacres (note the evasion of the crucial issues, a deft stroke). But, Rosenfeld continued, Kolko's "typical revisionist blame-America-first point of view makes me distrust his conclusions." He expressed the hope that "someone whose politics are more mainstream would sift through the material and provide an independent account." His plea for rescue appears under the heading, "Indonesia 1965: Year of Living Cynically?"

Fortunately, relief was soon on its way. A week later, under the heading "Indonesia 1965: Year of U.S. Irrelevance," Rosenfeld wrote that he had received in the mail an "independent account" by a historian "without political bias"—that is, one who could assure him that the state he loves had done no wrong. This antidote was "full of delights and surprises," concluding that the US had no responsibility for the deaths or the overthrow of Sukarno. It "clears Americans of the damaging lingering suspicion of responsibility for the Indonesian coup and massacre," Rosenfeld concludes happily: "For me, the question of the American role in Indonesia is closed."[23]

How easy is the life of the true believer.

The article that closed the books, to Rosenfeld's immense relief, was the Brands study reviewed earlier. That Brands is an "independent" commentator "without political bias" is demonstrated throughout: The US war in Vietnam was an attempt "to rescue South Vietnam"; the information reaching Washington that "The army has virtually destroyed the PKI" in a huge massacre was "good news"; "the most serious deficiency of covert warfare" is "its inevitable tendency to poison the well of public opinion," that is, to tar the US with "bum raps" elsewhere; etc. Much more significant are the "delights and surprises" that put any lingering doubts to rest. Since the study closes all questions for good, we may now rest easy in the knowledge that Washington did all it could to encourage the greatest massacre since the days of Hitler and Stalin, welcomed the outcome with enthusiasm, and immediately turned to the task of supporting Suharto's aptly named "New Order." Thankfully, there is nothing to trouble the liberal conscience.

One interesting non-reaction to the Kadane report appeared in the lead article in the *New York Review of Books* by Senator Daniel Moynihan. He fears that "we are poisoning the wells of our historical memory," suppressing unpleasant features of our past. He contrasts these failures with the "extraordinary period of exhuming the worst crimes of its hideous history" now underway in the Soviet Union. Of course, "the United States has no such history. To the contrary." Our history is quite pure. There are no crimes to "exhume" against the indigenous population or Africans in the 70 years following *our* revolution, or against Filipinos, Central Americans, Indochinese, and others later on. Still, even we are not perfect: "not everything we have done in this country has been done in the open," Moynihan observes, though "not everything could be. Or should have been." But we conceal too much, the gravest crime of our history.[24]

It is hard to believe that as he was writing these words, the Senator did not have the recent revelations about Indonesia in mind. He, after all, has a special personal relation to Indonesian atrocities. He was UN Ambassador at the time of the Indonesian invasion of East Timor, and takes pride, in his memoirs, in having forestalled any international reaction to the aggression and massacre. "The United States wished things to turn out as they did," he writes, "and worked to bring this about. The Department of

State desired that the United Nations prove utterly ineffective in whatever measures it undertook. This task was given to me, and I carried it
forward with no inconsiderable success." Moynihan was well aware of
how things turned out, noting that within a few weeks some 60,000
people had been killed, "10 percent of the population, almost the
proportion of casualties experienced by the Soviet Union during the
Second World War." Thus he took credit for achievements that he
compares to those of the Nazis. And he is surely familiar with the
subsequent US government role in escalating the slaughter, and the
contribution of the media and political class in concealing it. But the
newly released information about the US role in mass slaughter did not
stir his historical memory, or suggest some reflections on our practices,
apart from our single blemish: insufficient candor.

Moynihan's successes at the UN have entered history in the conventional manner. Measures taken against Iraq and Libya "show again
how the collapse of Communism has given the Security Council the
cohesion needed to enforce its orders," *Times* UN correspondent Paul
Lewis explains in a front-page story: "That was impossible in earlier
cases like...Indonesia's annexation of East Timor."[25]

There was also a flicker of concern about Indonesia after Iraq invaded
Kuwait in August 1990. It was hard not to notice the similarity to Indonesia's
(vastly more murderous) aggression and annexation. A decade earlier,
when glimmerings of what had happened finally began to break through,
there had been occasional notice of the comparison between Suharto's
exploits in Timor and the simultaneous Pol Pot slaughters. As in 1990, the
US and its allies were charged at most with "ignoring" Indonesian atrocities.
The truth was well concealed throughout: Indonesia was given critical
military and diplomatic support for its monstrous war crimes; and crucially,
unlike the case of Pol Pot and Saddam, these could readily have been
halted, simply by withdrawal of Western aid and breaking the silence.

Ingenious efforts have been made to explain away the radically
different response to Suharto, on the one hand, and Pol Pot and Saddam, on
the other, and to avoid the obvious explanation in terms of interest, which
of course covers a vastly wider range. William Shawcross offered a "more
structurally serious explanation" for the Timor-Cambodia case: "a comparative lack of sources" and lack of access to refugees, Lisbon and Australia
being so inaccessible in comparison with the Thai-Cambodian border.
Gérard Chaliand dismissed France's active support for the Indonesian
slaughter in the midst of a great show of anguish about Pol Pot on grounds
that the Timorese are "geographically and historically marginal." The
difference between Kuwait and Timor, according to Fred Halliday, is

that Kuwait "has been up and running as an independent state since 1961";
to evaluate the proposal, recall that the US prevented the UN from interfering with Israel's invasion of Lebanon or following through on its condemnation of Israel's (virtual) annexation of the Syrian Golan Heights, and that,
unlike Suharto in Timor, Saddam had offered to withdraw from Kuwait,
how seriously we do not know, since the US rejected the offers instantly
out of fear that they might "defuse the crisis." A common stance is that
"American influence on [Indonesia's decision to invade] may easily be
exaggerated," though the US "averted its eyes from East Timor" and "could
have done far more than it did to distance itself from the carnage" (James
Fallows). The fault, then, is failure to act, not the decisive contribution to
the ongoing carnage by increasing the flow of arms as atrocities mounted
and by rendering the UN "utterly ineffective" because "The United States
wished things to turn out as they did" (Ambassador Moynihan), while the
intellectual community preferred to denounce the crimes of official enemies. Others tried different techniques to evade the obvious, adding further
footnotes to the inglorious story.[26]

The Australian government was more forthright. "There is no binding
legal obligation not to recognize the acquisition of territory that was
acquired by force," Foreign Minister Gareth Evans explained, adding that
"The world is a pretty unfair place, littered with examples of acquisition by
force..." (in the same breath, following the US-UK lead, he banned all
official contacts with the PLO with proper indignation because of its
"consistently defending and associating itself with Iraq's invasion of Kuwait"). Prime Minister Hawke declared that "big countries cannot invade
small neighbors and get away with it" (referring to Iraq and Kuwait),
proclaiming that in the "new order" established by the virtuous Anglo-
Americans, "would-be aggressors will think twice before invading smaller
neighbours." The weak will "feel more secure because they know that they
will not stand alone if they are threatened," now that, at last, "all nations
should know that the rule of law must prevail over the rule of force in
international relations."

Australia has a special relation to Timor; tens of thousands of Timorese were killed during World War II protecting a few Australian guerrillas
fighting in Timor to deter an impending Japanese invasion of Australia.
Australia has been the most outspoken defender of the Indonesian invasion. One reason, known early on, is the rich natural gas and oil reserves
in the Timor Gap, "a cold, hard, sobering reality that must be addressed,"
Foreign Minister Bill Hayden explained frankly in April 1984. In December
1989, Evans signed a treaty with the Indonesian conquerors dividing up
Timor's wealth; through 1990, Australia received $Aus. 31 million from sales

of permits to oil companies for exploration. Evans's remarks, quoted above, were made in explanation of Australia's rejection of a protest against the treaty brought to the World Court by Portugal, generally regarded as the responsible authority.[27]

While British political figures and intellectuals lectured with due gravity on the values of their traditional culture, now at last to be imposed by the righteous in the "new world order" (referring to Iraq-Kuwait), British Aerospace entered into new arrangements to sell Indonesia jet fighters and enter into co-production arrangements, "what could turn out to be one of the largest arms packages any company has sold to an Asian country," the *Far Eastern Economic Review* reported. Britain had become "one of Indonesia's major arms suppliers, selling £290 million worth of equipment in the 1986-1990 period alone," Oxford historian Peter Carey writes.[28]

The public has been protected from such undesirable facts, kept in the shadows along with a Fall 1990 Indonesian military offensive in Timor under the cover of the Gulf crisis, and the Western-backed Indonesian operations that may wipe out a million tribal people in West Papua, with thousands of victims of chemical weapons among the dead according to human rights activists and the few observers. Solemn discourse on international law, the crime of aggression, and our perhaps too-fervent idealism can therefore proceed, untroubled. The attention of the civilized West is to be focused, laser-like, on the crimes of official enemies, not on those it could readily mitigate or bring to an end.[29]

The Timor-Kuwait embarrassment, such as it was, quickly subsided; reasonably, since it is only one of a host of similar examples that demonstrate the utter cynicism of the posturing during the Gulf War. But problems arose again in November 1991, when Indonesia made a foolish error, carrying out a massacre in the capital city of Dili in front of TV cameras and severely beating two US reporters, Alan Nairn and Amy Goodman. That is bad form, and requires the conventional remedy: an inquiry to whitewash the atrocity, a tap on the wrist for the authorities, mild punishment of subordinates, and applause from the rich men's club over this impressive proof that our moderate client is making still further progress. The script, familiar to the point of boredom, was followed routinely. Meanwhile Timorese were harshly punished and the atmosphere of terror deepened.

Business proceeded as usual. A few weeks after the Dili massacre, the Indonesia-Australia joint authority signed six contracts for oil exploration in the Timor Gap, with four more in January. Eleven contracts with 55 companies were reported by mid-1992, including Australian, British, Japanese, Dutch, and US. The naive might ask what the reaction would have been had 55 western companies joined with Iraq in exploiting Kuwaiti oil, though the analogy is imprecise, since Suharto's atrocities in Timor were a hundred times as great. Britain stepped up its arms sales, announcing plans in January to sell Indonesia a naval vessel. As Indonesian courts sentenced Timorese "subversives" to 15-year terms for having allegedly instigated the Dili massacre, British Aerospace and Rolls-Royce negotiated a multi-million pound deal for 40 Hawk fighter-trainers, adding to the 15 already in service, some used in crushing the Timorese. Meanwhile Indonesia was targeted for a new sales campaign by British firms because of its prospects for aerospace industries. As the slight tremor subsided, others followed suit.[30]

The "Gleam of Light in Asia" in 1965-1966 and the glow it has left until today illuminate the traditional attitudes towards human rights and democracy, the reasons for them, and the critical role of the educated classes. They reveal with equal brilliance the reach of the pragmatic criterion that effectively dismisses any human values in the culture of respectability.

Part III

Persistent Themes

CHAPTER 6

A "RIPE FRUIT"

When new bottles replace the old, the taste of the wine may change, though for victims of the "savage injustice" of the conquerors, it rarely loses its bitterness. Nor does it matter much, for the most part, whose hand wields the rod. Sometimes it does. During the American revolution, Francis Jennings writes, most of the indigenous population "were eventually driven by events to fight for their 'ancient protector and friend' the king of England," recognizing what lay ahead if the rebels won. Much the same was true of the black population, their awareness heightened by the British emancipation proclamation of 1775 offering to free "all indentured servants, Negroes or others...able and willing to bear arms," while condemnation of the slave trade was deleted from the Declaration of Independence "in complaisance to South Carolina and Georgia" (Thomas Jefferson). Even employees were considered chattel by the rebels. Local committees opposed granting them permission to enlist in George Washington's army because "all Apprentices and servants are the Property of their masters and mistresses, and every mode of depriving such masters and mistresses of their Property is a Violation of the Rights of mankind, contrary to the...Continental Congress, and an offence against the Peace of the good People of this State" (Pennsylvania); an indication of "how Patriot employers may have felt about the Revolutionary fervor of their employees," Richard Morris observes.

As well as Samuel Johnson, enslaved people could notice that "we hear the loudest *yelps* for liberty among the drivers of negroes," including those who urged their slaves to "be content with their situation, and expect a better condition in the next world," Federal Judge Leon Higginbotham comments. Among the huge mass of refugees fleeing rebel terror, including many "boat people" whose misery has never entered standard history, were thousands of blacks who fled "to freedom in Great Britain, the West Indies, Canada, and, eventually, Africa" (Ira Berlin). The indigenous population well understood what Alexander Hamilton had in mind when he wrote, in the *Federalist Papers,* that "the savage tribes on our Western frontier ought to be regarded as our natural enemies," and the natural allies of the

Europeans, "because they have most to fear from us, and most to hope from them." Their worst fears were soon to be confirmed.[1]

Latin America provides the richest evidence of the persistence of dominant foreign policy themes, which fall within the broader framework of the world conquest. One of the most grave of Latin America's many problems since the overthrow of Spanish rule was foreseen by the Liberator, Simón Bolívar, in 1822: "There is at the head of this great continent a very powerful country, very rich, very warlike, and capable of anything." "In England," Piero Gleijeses observes, "Bolívar saw a protector; in the United States, a menace." Naturally so, given the geopolitical realities.[2]

Britain had its own reasons for containing the aggressive upstart across the seas. With regard to the Caribbean, Foreign Minister George Canning pointed out in 1822 that "the possession by the United States of both shores of the channel through which our Jamaica trade must pass, would...amount to a suspension of that trade, and to a consequent total ruin." As discussed earlier, the Jacksonian Democrats intended not only to strangle and control England, but far more: to "place all other nations at our feet" and "control the commerce of the world."[3]

The United States did not look forward to the independence of the Spanish colonies. "In the Congressional debates of the period," Gleijeses notes, "there was much more enthusiasm for the cause of the Greeks than that of the Spanish Americans." One reason was that Latin Americans "were of dubious whiteness," at best "from degraded Spanish stock," unlike the Greeks, who were assigned a special role as the Aryan giants who created civilization in the version of history constructed by European racist scholarship.[4] Yet another reason was that, unlike the Founding Fathers, Bolívar freed his slaves, revealing himself to be a rotten apple that might spoil the barrel.

A broader issue was brought forth by the major intellectual reviews of the day. They concluded that "South America will be to North America...what Asia and Africa are to Europe"—*our* Third World. This perception retains its vitality through the 20th century. Commenting on Secretary of State James Baker's efforts to enhance "regional problem-sharing," *Times* correspondent Barbara Crossette notes "the realization in the United States and throughout the hemisphere that European and Asian trading blocs can be best tackled by a large free-trade area in this part of the world"—the "realization" by sectors that count, by *Times* standards; others have their reservations about the design constructed in the interests of the masters. The World Bank is also less sanguine about the prospects. A 1992 report concludes that the US will gain more from free trade agreements than Latin America, apart from Mexico and Brazil—meaning, those elements in Mexico and Brazil linked to international capital; and that the region would do better with a customs union on the model of the European Community with a common external tariff, excluding the US, something definitely not in the cards.[5]

In the 19th century, the British deterrent prevented US dominance of the hemisphere. But the conception of "our confederacy" as "the nest, from which all America, North and South, is to be peopled" (Thomas Jefferson) was firmly implanted, along with his corollary that it is best for Spain to rule until "our population can be sufficiently advanced to gain it from them piece by piece."[6]

There were internal conflicts over the matter. American merchants "were eager to contribute to the cause of freedom—as long as the rebels were able to pay, preferably cash," Gleijeses notes. And the well-established tradition of piracy provided a reservoir of American ship owners and seamen (British too) who were happy to offer their services as privateers to attack Spanish shipping, though extension of their terrorist vocation to American vessels led to much moral outrage and a government crackdown. Apart from England, liberated Haiti also provided assistance to the cause of independence, but on the condition that slaves be freed. Haiti too was a dangerous rotten apple, punished for independence in a manner to which we return in chapter 8.

The concept of Panamericanism advanced by Bolívar was diametrically opposed to that of the Monroe Doctrine at the same time. A British official wrote in 1916 that while Bolívar originated the idea of Panamericanism, he "did not contemplate the consummation of his policy under the aegis of the United States." In the end, it was "Monroe's victory and Bolívar's defeat," Gleijeses comments.

The status of Cuba was of particular significance, a striking illustration of the resilience of traditional themes. The US was firmly opposed to the independence of Cuba, "strategically situated and rich in sugar and slaves" (Gleijeses). Jefferson advised President Madison to offer Napoleon a free hand in Spanish America in return for the gift of Cuba to the United States. The US should not go to war for Cuba, he wrote to President Monroe in 1823, "but the first war on other accounts will give it to us, or the Island will give itself to us, when able to do so." Secretary of State John Quincy Adams described Cuba as "an object of transcendent importance to the commercial and political interests of our Union." He too urged Spanish sovereignty until Cuba would fall into US hands by "the laws of political...gravitation," a "ripe fruit" for harvest. Support for Spanish rule was near universal in the Executive branch and Congress; European powers, Colombia, and Mexico were approached for assistance in the endeavor of blocking the liberation of Cuba. A prime concern was the democratic tendencies in the Cuban independence movement, which advocated abolition of slavery and equal rights for all. There was again a threat that "the rot would spread," even to our own shores.[7]

By the end of the 19th century, the US was powerful enough to ignore the British deterrent and conquer Cuba, just in time to prevent the success of the indigenous liberation struggle. Standard doctrines justified relegating Cuba to virtual colonial status. Cubans were "ignorant niggers, half-breeds, and dagoes," the New York press observed; "a lot of degenerates...no more capable of self-government than the savages of Africa," the military command added. The US imposed the rule of the white propertied classes, who had no weird notions about democracy, freedom, and equal rights, and were thus not degenerates. The "ripe fruit" was converted to a US plantation, terminating the prospects for successful independent development.[8]

With US economic and political domination of the region well established a generation later, President Franklin Delano Roosevelt initiated his "Good Neighbor Policy"; market forces are the most efficient device of control, if they suffice. First, however, it was necessary to overturn the government of Dr. Ramón Grau San Martín, which would be a threat to US "commercial and export interests in Cuba," Ambassador Sumner Welles advised. The ranking expert on Latin America, Welles was particularly disturbed that workers had taken over sugar mills and set up what he called a "soviet government" in them. There can be "no confidence either in the policies nor stability of this regime," he informed Secretary of State Cordell Hull, who told the press that the US would "welcome any government representing the will of the people of the Republic and capable of maintaining law and order throughout the island"—not the Grau government. Welles conceded that law and order were being maintained, but this appearance of stability was only "the quiet of panic," he explained. It was a situation of "passive anarchy," State Department adviser Adolf Berle added, another term that perhaps finds its place alongside of "logical illogicality."

FDR told the press that Grau was backed only by "his local army" of 1500 men "and a bunch of students," a government lacking any legitimacy. Welles's replacement, Jefferson Caffery, testified later as to the "unpopularity with all the better classes in the country of the de facto [Grau] government," which was "supported only by the army and ignorant masses." When the US-backed Mendieta government that replaced Grau had problems subduing the population, Caffery explained further that "in numbers, the ignorant masses of Cuba reach a very high figure."

Roosevelt's refusal to recognize the Grau government "meant in effect an economic strangulation of the island," David Green points out, "since the United States would not negotiate a new sugar purchase agreement with a government it did not recognize," and the dependent economy could not survive without one. Army Chief of Staff Fulgencio Batista understood the message, and threw his support to opposition leader Carlos Mendieta, who replaced Grau and was immediately recognized by Washington. Relations were readjusted, with the result that Cuba became more fully incorporated "within the protective system of the United States," a member of the US Tariff Commission noted. The US retained effective control over Cuban affairs, keeping its highly stratified and repressive internal social system intact along with the dominant role of foreign enterprise.[9]

The Batista dictatorship that took over a few years later served US "commercial and export interests in Cuba" admirably, thus enjoying full support.

Castro's overthrow of the dictatorship in January 1959 soon elicited US hostility, and a return to the traditional path. By late 1959, the CIA and the State Department concluded that Castro had to be overthrown. One reason, State Department liberals explained, was that "our business interests in Cuba have been seriously affected." A second was the rotten apple effect: "The United States cannot hope to encourage and support sound economic policies in other Latin American countries and promote necessary private investments in Latin America if it is or appears to be simultaneously cooperating with the Castro program," the State Department concluded in November 1959. But one condition was added: "in view of Castro's strong though diminishing support in Cuba, it is of great importance, however, that the United States government not openly take actions which would cause the United States to be blamed for his failure or downfall."

As for Castro's support, public opinion studies provided to the White House (April 1960) concluded that most Cubans were optimistic about the future and supported Castro, while only 7 percent expressed concern about Communism and only 2 percent about failure to hold elections. Soviet presence was nil. In the United States, Jules Benjamin observes, "The liberals, like the conservatives, saw Castro as a threat to the hemisphere, but without the world communist conspiracy component."

By October 1959, planes based in Florida were carrying out strafing and bombing attacks against Cuban territory. In December, CIA subversion was stepped up, including supply of arms to guerrilla bands and sabotage of sugar mills and other economic targets. In March 1960, the Eisenhower Administration formally adopted a plan to overthrow Castro in favor of a regime "more devoted to the true interests of the Cuban people and more acceptable to the U.S."—the two conditions being equivalent—emphasizing again that this must be done "in such a manner as to avoid any appearance of U.S. intervention."

Sabotage, terror, and aggression were escalated further by the Kennedy Administration, along with the kind of economic warfare that no small country can long endure. Cuban reliance on the US as an export market and for imports had, of course, been overwhelming, and could hardly be replaced without great cost. The New Frontiersmen were obsessed with Cuba from the first moments. During the presidential campaign of 1960, Kennedy had accused Eisenhower and Nixon of threatening US security by allowing "the Iron Curtain...90 miles off the coast of the United States." "We were hysterical about Castro at the time of the Bay of Pigs [April 1961] and thereafter," Defense Secretary Robert McNamara later testified to the Church Committee. A few days before the decision to invade Cuba, Arthur Schlesinger advised the President that "the game would be up through a good deal of Latin America" if the US were to tolerate "another Cuba"; or this one, JFK determined. Much of Kennedy's Latin American policy was inspired by the fear that the virus would infect others and limit US hegemony in the region.

At the first cabinet meeting after the failed Bay of Pigs invasion, the atmosphere was "almost savage," Chester Bowles noted privately: "there was an almost frantic reaction for an action program." The President's public posture was no less militant: "the complacent, the self-indulgent, the soft societies are about to be swept away with the debris of history. Only the strong...can possibly survive," he told the country. Kennedy broke all diplomatic, commercial, and financial ties with Cuba, a terrible blow to the Cuban economy, given the dependency that had been established under US suzerainty. He succeeded in isolating Cuba diplomatically, but efforts to organize collective action against it in 1961 were unsuccessful, perhaps because of a problem noted by a Mexican diplomat: "If we publicly declare that Cuba is a threat to our security, forty million Mexicans will die laughing." Fortunately, the educated classes in the United States were capable of a more sober evaluation of the threat posed to the survival of the Free World.[10]

Theoretically, medicines and some food were exempt from the embargo, but food and medical aid were denied after Cyclone Flora caused death and destruction in October 1963. Standard procedure, incidentally. Consider Carter's refusal to allow aid to any West Indian country struck by the August 1980 hurricane unless Grenada was excluded (West Indians refused, and received no aid). Or the US reaction when Nicaragua was fortuitously devastated by a hurricane in October 1988. Washington could scarcely conceal its glee over the welcome prospects of widespread starvation and vast ecological damage, and naturally refused aid, even to the demolished Atlantic Coast area with longstanding links to the US and deep resentment against the Sandinistas; its people too must starve in the ruins of their shacks, to satisfy our blood-lust. US allies timidly followed orders, justifying their cowardice with the usual hypocrisy. To demonstrate that its malice is truly bipartisan, Washington reacted in much the same way when a tidal wave wiped out fishing villages leaving hundreds dead and missing in September 1992. The *New York Times* headline reads: "U.S. Sends Nicaragua Aid As Sea's Toll Rises to 116." "Foreign governments, including the United States, responded with immediate help today for the survivors," the *Times* excuse for a reporter wrote, while Washington announced "that it was making $5 million available immediately as a result of the disaster." Such nobility. Only in the small print at the end do we discover that the $5 million is being diverted from scheduled aid that had been withheld—but not, Congress was assured, from the over $100 million aid package that the Administration had suspended because the Nicaraguan government is not yet sufficiently subservient to its wishes. The humanitarian donation amounts to an impressive $25,000.[11]

Any weapon, however cruel, may be used against the perpetrators of the crime of independence. And, crucially, the awed self-adulation must never falter. "It was a narrow escape," Mark Twain wrote: "If the sheep had been created first, man would have been a plagiarism."[12]

The Kennedy Administration also sought to impose a cultural quarantine to block the free flow of ideas and information to the Latin American countries, fearing the rotten apple effect. In March 1963, JFK met with seven Central American presidents who agreed "To develop and put into immediate effect common measures to restrict the movement of subversive nationals to and from Cuba, and the flow of materials, propaganda and funds from that country." The unwillingness of Latin American governments to emulate US controls on travel and cultural interchange always greatly troubled the Kennedy liberals, as did their legal systems, requiring evidence for crimes by alleged "subversives," and their excessive liberalism generally.[13]

Immediately after the Bay of Pigs failure, Kennedy initiated a program of international terrorism to overthrow the regime, reaching quite remarkable dimensions. These atrocities are largely dismissed in the West, apart from some notice of the assassination attempts, one of them implemented on the very day of the Kennedy assassination. The terrorist operations were formally called off by Lyndon Johnson. They continued, however, and were escalated by Nixon. Subsequent actions are attributed to renegades beyond CIA control, whether accurately or not, we do not know; one high-level Pentagon official of the Kennedy-Johnson Administrations, Roswell Gilpatric, has expressed his doubts. The Carter Administration, with the support of US courts, condoned hijacking of Cuban ships in violation of the anti-hijacking convention that Castro was respecting. The Reaganites rejected Cuban initiatives for diplomatic settlement and imposed new sanctions on the most outlandish pretexts, often lying outright, a record reviewed by Wayne Smith, who resigned as head of the US Interests Section in Havana in protest.[14]

From the Cuban perspective, the Kennedy terror seemed to be a prelude to invasion. The CIA concluded in September 1962—before Russian missiles were detected in mid-October—that "the main purpose of the present [Soviet] military buildup in Cuba is to strengthen the Communist regime there against what the Cubans and Soviets conceive to be a danger that the US may attempt by one means or another to overthrow it." In early October, the State Department confirmed this judgment, as did a later State Department study. How realistic these fears were, we may only speculate.

Of interest, in this connection, is Robert McNamara's reaction to the late Andrei Gromyko's allegation that Soviet missiles were sent to Cuba "to strengthen the defensive capability of Cuba—that is all." In response, McNamara acknowledged that "If I had been a Cuban or Soviet official, I believe I would have shared the judgment you expressed that a U.S. invasion was probable" (a judgment that he says was inaccurate). The probability of nuclear war after a US invasion was "99 percent," McNamara added. Such an invasion was frighteningly close after JFK dismissed Khrushchev's offer of mutual withdrawal of missiles from Cuba and Turkey (the latter obsolete, already ordered withdrawn). Indeed, Cuba itself might have initiated nuclear war when a US terrorist (Mongoose) team blew up a factory, killing 400 people according to Castro, at one of the most tense moments of the crisis, when the Cubans may have had their fingers on the button.[15]

The March 1960 plan to overthrow Castro in favor of a regime "more devoted to the true interests of the Cuban people and more acceptable to the U.S." remains in force in 1992 as the US pursues its venerable task of preventing Cuban independence, with 170 years of experience behind it. Also in force is the Eisenhower directive that the crime should be perpetrated "in such a manner as to avoid any appearance of U.S. intervention." Accordingly, the ideological institutions must suppress the record of aggression, campaigns of terror, economic strangulation, and the other devices employed by the Lord of the hemisphere in its dedication to "the true interests of the Cuban people."

That dictate has been followed with loyalty perhaps beyond the norm. In respected scholarship, US terrorism against Cuba has been excised from the record in a display of servility that would impress the most dedicated totalitarian. In the media, Cuba's plight is regularly attributed to the demon Castro and "Cuban socialism" alone. Castro bears full responsibility for the "poverty, isolation and humbling dependence" on the USSR, the *New York Times* editors inform us, concluding triumphantly that "the Cuban dictator has painted himself into his own corner," without any help from us. That is true by virtue of doctrinal necessity, the ultimate authority. The editors conclude that we should not intervene directly as some "U.S. cold warriors" propose: "Fidel Castro's reign deserves to end in home-grown failure, not martyrdom." Taking their stand at the dovish extreme, the editors advise that we should continue to stand aside, watching in silence as we have been doing for 30 years, so the naive reader would learn from this (quite typical) version of history, crafted to satisfy the demands of authority.

News reports commonly observe the same conventions. Cuba is a basket case, *Times* Caribbean correspondent Howard French reports, "a Communist oddity in an increasingly free-market world," "a Communist dead end" struggling vainly against "economic realities." These "realities," we are to understand, are the failures of sterile Communist doctrine, unaffected by US terror and economic warfare. The former is passed over in silence. The latter is mentioned, but only as posing a tactical question: we must decide whether the embargo should be tightened, or simply maintained on the assumption that the "economic realities" alone will work "inexorably to bring about a dramatic transformation." Any opinion outside this spectrum is another "oddity," not to be sampled by a responsible journalist operating in the free market of ideas.

Boston Globe Latin America specialist Pamela Constable adopts the same conventions. Reviewing *Miami Herald* correspondent Andres Oppenheimer's *Castro's Final Hour,* she opens by explaining that he "is far from a rabid anticommunist, but his credentials as a seasoned journalistic observer of Latin America make his [book], a relentless exposure of the cynical, obsessive workings of Fidel Castro's aging socialist regime, all the more persuasive." He portrays Cuba "as a classic, decaying dictatorship, ruled by a man whose ideals have long succumbed to the hard logic of power," "clinging to a failed system with determined but fatal defiance." In "hilarious and tragic detail," Oppenheimer shows how "life for average Cubans has become a gantlet of woes and absurdities," which she recounts with much amusement. "Oppenheimer leaves little room for doubt that

like other messianic tyrants, Castro has sown the seeds of his own destruction."
The words "United States" do not appear; there is no hint of any US contribution
to the "hilarious" trials of the average Cubans, or to the "failed system" or
Castro's mad course of self-destruction. The "hard logic of power" is simply a
fact of nature, evoking none of the passion aroused by Castro's evil nature. The
norms are universal; Cuba is just a special case. Surveying the terrible decline
of Nicaragua after the US-backed government took over, Constable writes that
"Two problems underlie the disaster gripping this poor, tropical nation":
"lingering hostility" between the Sandinistas and the right, and corruption.
Could the rampages of a terrorist superpower have had some marginal effect
on the "collapsed socialist economy" and US efforts to recreate the glories that
preceded? The idea cannot be expressed, probably even thought, at the
dissident extreme of the commissar culture.

The same book is reviewed in the *New York Times* by Clifford Krauss.
Again, Cuba's plight is attributed to the crimes and lunacies of the demon alone.
The US does receive an oblique mention, in one phrase: Castro (not Cuba)
"has survived a host of calamities: the missile crisis, the trade embargo, the
Mariel exodus, repeated harvest shortfalls and endless rationing." That concludes the US role. Oppenheimer is praised for describing Cuba's travail "with
insight and wit"—odd, how amusing it is to watch our victims suffer—but more
importantly, for having unearthed hitherto undreamt-of iniquity. Insatiable in
his quest for power and love of violence, Castro sent "experienced officers" to
train Nicaraguans to resist the terrorist army the US dispatched from its
Honduran bases with orders to attack "soft targets" such as health clinics and
agricultural cooperatives (with explicit approval of the State Department and
left-liberal opinion, in the latter case). The monster even considered retaliation
"in case the United States under Ronald Reagan invaded Nicaragua," and he
was "far more involved than we knew" in supplying the army of Panama "in
anticipation of the United States invasion."

But for those who believe that there are limits to what the criminal mind
might contemplate, there is still more. "With Cuban soldiers in Angola to
support the Marxist Government, Mr. Castro made himself an obstacle to a
negotiated settlement of that country's civil war in the 1980's." Connoisseurs
who miss *Pravda* in the good old days will recognize this as the *Times* spin
on Cuba's support for the government recognized by virtually everyone apart
from the US, and its success in repelling US-backed South African aggression,
thus setting the stage for a negotiated settlement, which Washington at once
disrupted by continuing its support for its terrorist clients to ensure that the
war, which had already cost hundreds of thousands of lives and destroyed
the country, will leave the remains in the hands of South Africa and
Western investors.[16]

Whatever one may think of Cuba, such performances provide an enlightening "exposure of the cynical, obsessive workings" of a propaganda system of mechanical predictability, run by an intellectual class of truly awe-inspiring moral cowardice. Matters have changed little since the days when the *New York Times* editors, 60 years ago, hailed our magnificent record in the Caribbean region, where we were acting with "the best motives in the world" as Marines pursued the "elusive bandit Sandino" with the cheers of Nicaraguans ringing in their ears, contrary to the whining of the "professional 'liberals'"—though it was unfortunate, the editors felt, that the clash "comes just at a time when the Department of State is breathing grace, mercy and peace for the whole world." In Cuba, we were able "to save the Cubans from themselves and instruct them in self-government," granting them "independence qualified only by the protective Platt amendment"—which "protected" US corporations and their local allies. "Cuba is very near at hand," the editors proceed, "to refute" the charge of "the menace of American imperialism." We were "summoned" by the Cuban people who have, finally, "mastered the secret of stability" under our kind tutelage. And while "our commercial interests have not suffered in the island," "we have prospered together with a free Cuban people," so "no one speaks of American imperialism in Cuba."[17]

Commentators affect great anguish over Castro's crimes and abuses. Would that it were believable. Demonstrably, for most it is utterly cynical pretense. The conclusion is established conclusively by comparison of the hysterical outrage over Castro's human rights violations and the evasion or outright suppression of vastly worse atrocities right next door, at the very same time, by US clients, acting with US advice and support. History has been kind enough to provide some dramatic test cases to prove the point.[18]

The professed concern for "the true interests of the Cuban people" and for "democracy" need not detain us. Concern for the "true interests" of US business, in contrast, is real enough. The same is true of the concerns over public opinion in Cuba and Latin America. Kennedy knew what he was doing when he sought to block travel and communication. The fears are understandable in the light of the Cuban public opinion polls cited earlier, or the reaction to its Agrarian Reform Law of May 1959, acclaimed by one UN organization as "an example to follow" in all Latin America. Or by the conclusion of the World Health Organization's representative in Cuba in 1980 that "there is no question that Cuba has the best health statistics in Latin America," with the health organization "of a very much developed country" despite its poverty. Or by a UNICEF report on the "State of the World's Children 1990," reviewed in a Peruvian Church journal, which lists a series of Latin American countries as among those with the highest infant

mortality rates in the world, though Costa Rica and Chile have low rates for
the region, and "Cuba is the only country on a par with developed nations."
Or by the interest in Brazil and other Latin American countries in Cuban
biotechnology, unusual if not unique for a small and poor country. Or by
the kind of discussion we can read in the Australian press, safely remote,
reviewing the efforts to achieve the "historic strategic objective" of restoring
Cuba "to Washington's sphere of influence":

> That Cuba has survived at all under these circumstances is an achieve-
> ment in itself. That it registered the highest per capita increase in gross
> social product (wages and social benefits) of any economy in Latin
> America—and almost double that of the next highest country—over the
> period 1981-1990 is quite remarkable. Moreover, despite the economic
> difficulties, the average Cuban is still better fed, housed, educated and
> provided for medically than other Latin Americans, and—again atypi-
> cally—the Cuban Government has sought to spread the burden of the
> new austerity measures equally among its people.

Worse yet, such perceptions are hardly unusual in the region itself, a
product of direct experience and relative freedom from the rigid doctrinal requirements that constrain US orthodoxy and its European
camp-followers. They are commonly articulated by leading figures. To
select one poignant example, Father Ignacio Ellacuría, the rector of the
Jesuit university of El Salvador (UCA), wrote in a Latin American Church
journal in November 1989 that for all its abuses, "the Cuban model has
achieved the best satisfaction of basic needs in all of Latin America in a
relatively short time," while "Latin America's actual situation points out
prophetically the capitalist system's intrinsic malice and the ideological
falsehood of the semblance of democracy that accompanies, legitimates,
and cloaks it."

It was for expressing such thoughts that he was assassinated by
US-trained elite troops as the article appeared, and buried deep beneath
shrouds of silence by those who feigned great indignation here.[19]

As in numerous other cases, it is not Castro's crimes that disturb the
rulers of the hemisphere, who cheerfully support the Suhartos and Saddam
Husseins and Gramajos, or look the other way, as long as they "fulfill their
main function." Rather, it is the elements of success that arouse fear and
anger and the call for vengeance, a fact that must be suppressed by
ideologists—not an easy task, given the overwhelming evidence confirming this elementary principle of the intellectual culture.

In the 1980s, the US extended its economic warfare, barring industrial
products containing any Cuban nickel, a major Cuban export. Those not

affected by political Alzheimer's might recall the US Treasury Department order of April 1988 barring import of Nicaraguan coffee processed in a third country if it is not "sufficiently transformed to lose its Nicaraguan identity"— recalling the language of the Third Reich, a *Boston Globe* editor observed. The US prohibited a Swedish medical supply company from providing equipment to Cuba because one component is manufactured in the US. Aid to the former Soviet Union was conditioned on its suspension of aid to Cuba. Gorbachev's announcement that such aid would be canceled was greeted with banner headlines: "Baker Hails Move," "Soviets Remove Obstacle to U.S. Economic Aid," "The Cuban-Soviet Connection: 31-Year Irritant to the U.S." At last, the grievous injury to us may be relieved.

In early 1991, the US resumed Caribbean military maneuvers, including rehearsal of a Cuba invasion, a standard technique of intimidation. In mid-1991, the embargo was tightened further, cutting remittances from Cuban-Americans, among other measures. In April 1992, gearing up for the election, President Bush barred ships that go to Cuba from US ports. New laws proposed by congressional liberals, cynically entitled the Cuban Democracy Act, would extend the embargo to US subsidiaries abroad, allowing seizure of cargo of ships that had landed in Cuba if they enter US territorial waters. The ferocity of the hatred for Cuban independence is extreme, and scarcely wavers across the narrow mainstream spectrum.[20]

There has never been any effort to conceal the fact that the disappearance of the Soviet deterrent (like the removal of the British deterrent a century earlier) and the decline of East bloc economic relations with Cuba merely facilitates Washington's efforts to achieve its longstanding aims through economic warfare or other means. Candor is entirely in order: only the most devilish anti-American, after all, could question our right to act as suits our fancy. If, say, we choose to invade some defenseless country to capture one of our agents who no longer follows orders, and then try him for crimes committed while on our payroll, who could question the majesty of our system of justice? True, the UN did, but our veto took care of that childish tantrum. Even the Supreme Court has since accorded the US the right to kidnap alleged criminals abroad to bring them to justice here. Not for us the qualms of Adolf Hitler, who returned a German emigré abducted by Himmler's gangsters from Switzerland in 1937 after the Swiss government protested, appealing to basic principles of international law.[21]

In a typical commentary on Cuba's happy plight, the editors of the *Washington Post* urged that the US seize the opportunity to crush Castro: "For his great antagonist, the United States, to give relief and legitimacy to this used-up relic at this late hour would be to break faith with the Cuban people—and with all the other democrats in the hemisphere." Pursuing the same logic, the editors, through the 1980s, called upon the US to coerce Nicaragua until it was restored to the "Central American mode" of the Guatemalan and Salvadoran terror states, observing their admirable "regional standards"; and scoffed at Gorbachev's "New Thinking" because he had not yet offered the US a free hand to achieve its objectives by the means condemned by the World Court (in a judgment that discredited the Court, the press and liberal commentators concluded). The *Post* speaks for the people of Cuba just as the State Department did in the Eisenhower-Kennedy years; as William McKinley spoke for "the vast majority of the population" of the Philippines who "welcome our sovereignty" and whom he was "protecting...against the designing minority" while slaughtering them by the hundreds of thousands; and as his proconsul Leonard Wood spoke for the decent (i.e., wealthy European) people of Cuba who favored US domination or annexation and had to be protected from the "degenerates."[22] The US has never been short of good will for the suffering people of the world who have to be protected from the machinations of evil-doers. As for the *Post's* love of democracy, charity dictates silence. Its peers scarcely differ.

The Cuban record demonstrates with great clarity that the Cold War framework has been scarcely more than a pretext to conceal the standard refusal to tolerate Third World independence, whatever its political coloration. Traditional policies remain beyond serious challenge within the mainstream. The most obvious questions are ruled illegitimate, if not unthinkable. We can anticipate, then, efforts of the usual kind to ensure that the "ripe fruit" drops into the hands of its rightful owners, or is plucked more vigorously from the tree.

A cautious policy would be to tighten the stranglehold, resorting to economic and ideological warfare to punish the population while intimidating others to refrain from interfering. As suffering increases, it can be assumed, so will protest, repression, more unrest, etc., in the predictable cycle. At some stage, internal collapse will reach the point where the Marines can be sent in cost-free to "liberate" the island once again, restoring the old order while the faithful chant odes to our grand leaders and their righteousness. Transitory tactical concerns might accelerate the process, if a need is felt to arouse jingoist passions. But it is unlikely that Washington will veer far from the policies outlined in the Bush Administration National Security Policy Review already cited (p. 94).

Chapter 7

World Orders Old and New: Latin America

1. "The Colossus of the South"

"When the resources of that vast country are taken into account," the editors of the *Washington Post* wrote in 1929, "it becomes evident that within a few years Brazil will become one of the leading powers of the world." "The United States rejoices in the rise of this great republic in South America," which "has found the road to permanent prosperity and peace." The euphoric predictions seemed not unreasonable. "Brazil is notable for its tremendously favorable combination of large size, low population density, and rich endowment of natural resources," Peter Evans observes, and it had nothing to fear from external enemies. In the second half of the 19th century, real per capita income rose more rapidly in Brazil than in the United States. Its leading export, coffee, was under control of local capital (Brazil provided over 80 percent of world output by the turn of the century). Some weaknesses were showing: the economy relied so heavily on exporting primary products that this rich agricultural country had to import even food staples. Nevertheless, the "colossus of the South," as the *New York Herald Tribune* termed it in 1926, appeared to be a true counterpart to the Colossus of the North, well-placed to rise to prosperity and power. It seemed, indeed, "a mighty realm of limitless potentialities," "a nation which staggers the imagination," as other US journals described it.

The *Wall Street Journal,* in 1924, offered a more caustic glimpse of the future: "No territory in the world is better worth exploitation than Brazil's." Five years later, "American businessmen boasted a larger share of the export market than their British rivals" and "New York had replaced London as the major source of new capital investment" (Joseph Smith). US investment grew tenfold from 1913 to 1930; trade more than doubled, while that of Britain declined by nearly 20 percent. The picture was much the same throughout the region. Direct US investment in Latin American enterprises almost doubled to $3.5 billion in the 1920s, while portfolio investment (bonds and securities) more than quadrupled to over $1.7

billion. Venezuelan oil under the Gómez dictatorship, mines in Bolivia, Chile and elsewhere, and the riches of Cuba were among the favored targets. From 1925-1929, US capital inflow to Latin America was about $200 million a year, while the annual outflow to US investors was about $300 million.[1]

Serious US interest in Brazil dates from 1889, when the monarchy was overthrown and a republic established, and a Pan-American conference was held in Washington "as part of a wider strategy designed to oust European competition and thereby secure American commercial ascendancy in Latin American markets," Smith writes. The US was hesitant to recognize the republican government, in part because "the conservative instincts of American politicians were alarmed at the overthrow of a symbol of authority and stability by military violence." But as incoming Secretary of State James Blaine recognized, "Brazil holds in the South much the same relationship to the other countries that the United States does in the North," and commercial opportunities were vast. Hesitations were soon overcome.

Recognized to offer "incalculable" commercial opportunities, Brazil was chosen as the site of the third (1906) Pan-American conference, where Secretary of State Elihu Root declared that the US and Brazil, "acting together, would form a single and eternal guarantee for the integrity of America." From 1900 to 1910, US trade and investment with Latin America more than doubled, growing at the fastest rate in the world. As global power shifted toward the United States with World War I, Washington was able to implement the Monroe Doctrine beyond its Caribbean sphere. The already substantial US economic and political influence throughout the hemisphere increased, giving rise to the euphoria of the 1920s.[2]

US dominance of the Brazilian market peaked after World War II, when the US supplied half of Brazil's imports and bought over 40 percent of its exports. By then, the vision of Washington planners was so expansive that Latin America had come to play only a minor part, though it was not forgotten. "Latin America's role in the new world order," Stephen Rabe observes, was "to sell its raw materials" and "to absorb surplus U.S. capital." In short, it was to "fulfill its major function" and be "exploited" for the benefit of the core industrial countries, along with the rest of the South.[3]

Rabe's description of the New World Order of 1945 is no less apt today; the same is true of Bolívar's concerns about the "very powerful country, very rich, very warlike, and capable of anything" that stands "at the head of this great continent." The major theme of the Colombian era—the service role assigned to the South—persists as we advance to a "new imperial age."

2. "The Welfare of the World Capitalist System"

The New World Order of 1945 is sometimes described with considerable candor in mainstream scholarship. A highly-regarded study of US-Brazilian relations by the senior historian of the CIA, Gerald Haines, opens frankly: "Following World War II the United States assumed, out of self-interest, responsibility for the welfare of the world capitalist system." He could have gone on to quote the 1948 CIA memorandum on "the colonial economic interests" of our Western European allies, or George Kennan's call for reopening Japan's "Empire toward the South," among other analyses reflecting real interests.[4]

"American leaders tried to reshape the world to fit U.S. needs and standards," Haines continues. It was to be an "open world"—open to exploitation by the rich, but not completely open even to them. The US desired a "closed hemispheric system in an open world," Haines explains, following Latin Americanist David Green, who had described the system "formalized" after World War II as "A closed hemisphere in an open world." It was to be a world closed to others in regions already controlled by the US or held to be of critical importance (Latin America and the Middle East), and open where US dominance had not been established. Haines's phrase captures the vaunted principle of the Open Door in its doctrinally approved sense: What we have (if it is important enough), we keep; elsewhere, open access to all. The operative principle was articulated by the State Department in 1944 in a memorandum called "Petroleum Policy of the United States." The US then dominated Western Hemisphere production, which was to remain the largest in the world for another quarter century. That system must remain closed, the memorandum declared, while the rest of the world must be open. US policy "would involve the preservation of the absolute position presently obtaining, and therefore vigilant protection of existing concessions in United States hands coupled with insistence upon the Open Door principle of equal opportunity for United States companies in new areas."[5]

That Latin America would be ours is an expectation that goes back to the earliest days of the Republic, given an early form in the Monroe Doctrine. The intentions were articulated plainly and illustrated consistently in action. It is hard to improve upon the formulation by Woodrow Wilson's Secretary of State, Robert Lansing, which the President found "unanswerable" though "impolitic" to state openly:

In its advocacy of the Monroe Doctrine the United States considers its own interests. The integrity of other American nations is an incident, not an end. While this may seem based on selfishness alone, the author of the Doctrine had no higher or more generous motive in its declaration.

With some reason, Bismarck had described the Monroe Doctrine in 1898 as a "species of arrogance, peculiarly American and inexcusable."

Wilson's predecessor, President Taft, had foreseen that "the day is not far distant" when "the whole hemisphere will be ours in fact as, by virtue of our superiority of race, it already is ours morally." Given the awesome power that the US had achieved by the mid-1940s, Washington saw no reason to tolerate any interference in "our little region over here" (Stimson).[6]

In the global order of 1945, Haines continues, the goal was "to eliminate all foreign competition" from Latin America. The US undertook to displace its French, British, and Canadian rivals so as "to maintain the area as an important market for U.S. surplus industrial production and private investments, to exploit its vast reserves of raw materials, and to keep international communism out." Here the term "communist" is to be understood in its usual technical sense: those who appeal to "the poor people [who] have always wanted to plunder the rich," in John Foster Dulles's phrase. Plans were similar for the Middle East, to which the US extended the Monroe Doctrine after World War II, with enormous consequences for southern Europe, North Africa, and the region itself.

Though Haines happens to be concentrating on the richest and most important country of Latin America, the conclusions generalize. In Brazil, he writes, the US worked to prevent economic nationalism and what the Truman and Eisenhower Administrations called "excessive industrial development"—that is, development that might compete with US corporations; competition with. foreign capital was not "excessive," therefore allowed. That US demand had been imposed on the hemisphere generally by February 1945, as already discussed (chapter 2.1).

What was new in these priorities was the scale, not the character. The intent of the prewar Good Neighbor programs, David Green writes, was "to stimulate a certain diversification of Latin American production in the expectation that the Latin Americans would find ready markets in the hemisphere; [but] such diversification was to be limited to products not competitive with existing lines of production in already established Western Hemisphere markets," meaning in practice US lines of production. The proposals of the Inter-American Advisory Commission called for the US to absorb Latin American imports so as to enhance "the development of Latin America's capacity for *purchasing more United States manufactures*" (Green's emphasis). The earliest projects of the US-dominated inter-American agencies "were all of a consumer-goods rather than a producer goods variety." The purpose "was certainly not to cut into the United States' 'share' of exports to Latin America," specifically "machinery and heavy industry exports."

The occasional exceptions highlighted the point. Washington agreed to finance a Brazilian steel project, but as government economist Simon Hanson pointed out, that meant only a "shift in the type" of American steel exports to Brazil, not a loss in total volume or value: the Brazilian plant would produce "the simpler manufactured products," which in turn would "require import of more complex materials" requiring more advanced technology; that "is where we come in," keeping US export markets safe. An analysis concluded that "the countries who will lose most of the Brazil business which will ultimately be handled by this plant are England and Germany."[7]

Quite generally, Haines observes, US leaders "opposed major industrialization plans of the Third World nations and rejected foreign aid programs based on public loans to promote economic growth." They preferred a "mercantilist approach," with Third World economies integrated "into their U.S.-dominated free trade system"; the concept of "mercantilist free trade" captures nicely the doctrinal framework. The US "tried to guide and control Brazilian industrial development for the benefit of private U.S. corporations and to fit Brazil into its regional economic plans." The humanitarian Point Four program, which was to be "a model for all Latin America," was designed "to develop larger and more efficient sources of supply for the American economy, as well as create expanded markets for U.S. exports and expanded opportunities for the investment of American capital."

What US planners "envisioned, but seldom stated, was a neocolonial relationship, with Brazil furnishing the raw materials for American industry and the United States supplying Brazil with manufactured goods." They pursued a "neocolonial, neomercantilist policy"—which is, somehow, "a classic liberal approach to development," showing again how flexible an instrument economic theory can be. Industrial development was tolerable only if it was "complementary to U.S. industry." The basic concept was "that Brazilian development was all right as long as it did not interfere with American profits and dominance," and ample profit remittance was guaranteed. Agricultural development was also promoted, as long as it avoided "destabilizing" programs like land reform, relied on US farm equipment, fostered "commodities that complemented US production, such as coffee, cacao, rubber, and jute," and created "new markets for U.S. agricultural commodities" such as dairy products and wheat.

"Brazilian desires were secondary," Haines observes, though it was useful "to pat them a little bit and make them think that you are fond of them," in Dulles's words.

The Cold War framework was in place at once. By 1946, Soviet machinations in Brazil were of much concern to Ambassador Adolf Berle, a leading liberal statesman from the New Deal through Kennedy's New Frontier. The Russians are like the Nazis, he warned: "Horribly, cynically, and terribly, they exploit any center of thought or action which may make trouble for the United States"; they are so unlike us, in this regard. Intelligence could detect no Soviet trouble-making in Brazil apart from economic missions and other common practices. But as usual, that conclusion was not considered relevant, and Berle's position was endorsed. As Haines summarizes an intelligence report a few months later, "the Soviet Union might conceivably find it to its advantage in the future to fish in troubled inter-American waters," so no chances could be taken, another illustration of the "logical illogicality" that governed global policy planning. The potential Communists must be eliminated before they have a chance to interfere with our pursuit of our goals.

US leaders used Brazil as a "testing area for modern scientific methods of industrial development," Haines observes. US experts provided instructions on all sorts of topics. For example, they encouraged Brazilians to open the Amazon to development and to follow the US model of railroad operation—the latter a touch of black humor, perhaps. But crucially, they provided Brazil with sincere advice on how to benefit US corporations.

Throughout, Haines's account is interlarded with such phrases as "the best of intentions," "sincerely believed," etc. By lucky accident, what was "sincerely believed" conformed nicely to the interests of US investors, however ruinous it might be to our wards. Again, Haines strikes traditional chords, including the faith in the benign intent that so miraculously serves self-interest.

3. Protecting Democracy

Haines focuses on the early years, but he gives a foretaste of what was to come when he refers to the goal of "cultivating the Brazilian military," which US officials "promoted...as the protector of democracy." This far-sighted program to achieve our democratic vision came to fruition as the generals took command in 1964, terminating Brazil's postwar parliamentary interlude and instituting a neo-Nazi National Security State with ample torture and repression, inspiring their counterparts throughout the hemisphere to do the same in a notable illustration of the "domino theory" which, for some reason, is rarely discussed under this rubric. Following approved neoliberal doctrine under continued US tutelage, the Generals proceeded to create an "economic miracle" that was much admired, though with some reservations about the sadistic violence by which it was instituted.

The military-run National Security States were a direct outcome of US policy and doctrine. From World War II, US planners sought to integrate the Latin American military within the US command structure. During the war, they had laid the basis for a permanent coordinated supply system, with standardized US weapons for the continent. These measures, it was assumed, would "prove very profitable" to the booming US military industries (General "Hap" Arnold, referring, in this case, to the postwar aviation industry); and control over military supplies would provide economic and political leverage as well, enabling the US to deter nationalist tendencies and to counter "subversion." A corollary would be a takeover of training missions, displacing European rivals. Truman's Inter-American Military Cooperation Act of 1946 sought to secure a US monopoly of supply and training in a "militarily closed hemisphere under United States domination" (Green). The need to replace European rivals was stressed in internal documents in later years, and soon accomplished.

The problem of combating "subversion" had come to the fore in 1943, when Bolivian mine owners called on government troops to suppress striking tin miners, killing hundreds of them in the "Catavi massacre." There was no US reaction until the nationalist, anti-oligarchic, pro-labor National Revolutionary Movement (MNR) deposed the dictatorship a year later. The US denounced the new regime as "pro-fascist" (on flimsy pretexts) and as opposed to "Anglo-Yankee imperialism" (accurately, in this case), demanded that all MNR members be excluded from positions of power, and quickly secured its overthrow in favor of a military government. A State Department memo identified one decisive theme: the mine owners, it observed, are afraid of the MNR's "announced intention to interest itself in the betterment of the workers, fearing this can only be done at the expense of the mining interests." The broader fear was radical nationalism (chapter 2.1).

The Kennedy Administration moved the process forward, shifting the mission of the Latin American military from "hemispheric defense" to "internal security," meaning war against the population. Academic experts explained soberly that the military are a "modernizing" force, when guided by their US tutors.

The basic reasoning was explained in a secret 1965 study by Robert McNamara's Defense Department, which found that "U.S. policies toward the Latin American military have, on the whole, been effective in attaining the goals set for them": "improving internal security capabilities" and "establishing predominant U.S. military influence." The military now understands their tasks and are equipped to pursue them, thanks to the substantial increase in training and supply carried out by the Kennedy Administration in 1961-1962. These tasks include the overthrow of civilian governments "whenever, in the judgment of the military, the conduct of these leaders is injurious to the welfare of the nation"; this is a necessity in "the Latin American cultural environment," the Kennedy liberals explained, sure to be carried out properly now that the judgment of the military is based upon "the understanding of, and orientation toward, U.S. objectives." Proceeding along these lines, we can assure the proper outcome to the "revolutionary struggle for power among major groups which constitute the present class structure" in Latin America, and can guarantee "private U.S. investment" and trade, the "economic root" that is the strongest of the roots of "U.S. political interest in Latin America."[8]

The vulgar Marxist rhetoric affected by the Kennedy-Johnson planners is common in internal documents, as in the business press.

Returning to Brazil, plans for a military coup were initiated shortly after João Goulart became President in August 1961. The military were wary of his populist rhetoric and appeal, and angered by his efforts to raise minimum wages of civilian laborers. Concerns of the US business community were enhanced when the Chamber of Deputies passed a bill placing conditions on foreign investment and limiting remittance of profits on the grounds that they were "bleeding the Brazilian economy." Though Goulart, a faithful member of the Brazilian elite, was anti-Communist, US labor leaders and Embassy officials were alarmed at his involvement with labor and peasant organizations and appointment of Brazilian Communists to staff positions; "an openly Communist course," the CIA warned. The appropriate Cold War context had been spelled out by JFK, shortly before assuming office (see p. 73).

By early 1962, Brazilian military commanders had notified Kennedy's Ambassador, Lincoln Gordon, that they were organizing a coup. At JFK's personal initiative, the US began to lend clandestine and overt support to right-wing political candidates. The President's feeling, in agreement with Gordon and the US business community, was that "the military probably represented the key to the future," Ruth Leacock concludes. Robert Kennedy was dispatched to Brazil in December 1962 to influence Goulart to "confront the communist problem," as the US Embassy put it. RFK informed Goulart that the President was seriously concerned about the infiltration of "Communists and anti-American nationalist leftists" into the government, the military, the unions, and student groups, and about the "ill treatment [of] American and other foreign private investors." If Goulart wanted US aid, Kennedy said, he must see to it that "personnel in key Brazilian positions" were pro-American, and impose economic measures that the US recommended.

Relations remained tense, particularly over the austerity plan that the Kennedy Administration demanded as a condition for aid, and its admonitions about left-wing influence. In March 1963, the CIA again reported plans for a military coup; US corporate executives were, by then, privately urging a total US aid cutoff to expedite the coup plans. In August, US Defense Attaché Vernon Walters warned the Pentagon that Goulart was promoting "ultranationalist officers" in preference to "pro-democratic pro-US officers" (the two terms presumably being synonymous). Relations harshened further under the Johnson Administration. Senator Albert Gore informed the Senate Foreign Relations Committee, then considering US aid, that he had heard that "all of the members of the Brazilian Congress who advocated the kind of reforms which we have made a prerequisite for Alliance for Progress aid are now in prison." Ambassador Gordon cabled Washington that the US should increase military aid for Brazil because the military was essential in the "strategy for restraining left wing excesses of Goulart government." Meanwhile the CIA was "financing the mass urban demonstrations against the Goulart government, proving the old themes of God, country, family, and liberty to be as effective as ever," Philip Agee noted in his Diary.

Recall that aid to the military is standard operating procedure for overthrowing a civilian government. The device was also used effectively in Indonesia and Chile, and tried in Iran in the early 1980s, the first stage in what later became (suitably recrafted) the Iran-contra affair.[9]

On March 31, the generals took over, with US support and plans for further action if necessary "to assure success of takeover." The Generals had carried out a "democratic rebellion," Gordon cabled Washington. The revolution was "a great victory for the free world," which prevented a "total loss to the West of all South American Republics" and should "create a greatly improved climate for private investments." "The principal purpose for the Brazilian revolution," he testified before Congress two years later, "was to preserve and not destroy Brazil's democracy." This democratic revolution was "the single most decisive victory of freedom in the mid-twentieth century," Gordon held, "one of the major turning points in world history" in this period. Adolf Berle agreed that Goulart was a Castro clone who had to be removed. Secretary of State Dean Rusk justified US recognition for the coup regime on the grounds that "the succession there occurred as foreseen by the Constitution," a statement that was not "entirely accurate," Thomas Skidmore judiciously observes.

US labor leaders demanded their proper share of the credit for the violent overthrow of the parliamentary regime, while the new government proceeded to crush the labor movement and to subordinate poor and working people to the overriding needs of business interests, primarily foreign, reducing real wages by 25 percent within 3 years and redistributing income "toward upper-income groups who were destined to be the great consumers of the Brazilian miracle" (Sylvia Ann Hewlett, who sees the brutal repression and attack on living standards as "an essential prerequisite for a new cycle of capitalist growth within the Brazilian domestic economy"). Washington and the investment community were naturally delighted. As the relics of constitutional rule faded away and the investment climate improved, the World Bank offered its first loans in 15 years and US aid rapidly increased along with torture, murder, starvation, disease, infant mortality—and profits.[10]

4. Securing the Victory

The United States was the "regime's most reliable ally," Thomas Skidmore observes in the most comprehensive scholarly study of what came next. US aid "saved the day" for the ruling Generals; the process also "turned the U.S. into a kind of unilateral IMF, overseeing *every* aspect of Brazilian economic policy." "In almost every Brazilian office involved in administering unpopular tax, wage, or price decisions, there was the ubiquitous American adviser," the new US Ambassador discovered in 1966. Once again, the US was well-positioned to use Brazil as a "testing area for modern scientific methods of industrial development" (Haines), and therefore has every right to take credit for what ensued. Under US guidance, Brazil pursued orthodox neoliberal policies, "doing everything right" by monetarist criteria, and "strengthening the market economy" (Skidmore). The "economic miracle" proceeded in parallel with the entrenchment of the fascist National Security State, not accidentally; a regime that could not wield the knout could hardly have carried out measures with such a deleterious impact on the population.

The neoliberal reforms did not exactly succeed in "building Brazilian capitalism," Skidmore continues (though they did help build foreign corporations). They provoked a severe industrial recession, driving many businesses to ruin. To counter these effects and to prevent still further foreign takeover of the economy, the government turned to the public sector, strengthening the despised state corporations.

In 1967, economic policy was taken over by technocrats led by the highly respected conservative economist Antonio Delfim Neto, an enthusiastic supporter of "the Revolution of March 31," which he saw as a "huge demonstration by society" and "the product of a collective consensus" (among those who qualify as "society"). Declaring its devotion to the principles of economic liberalism, the government instituted indefinite wage controls. "Worker protests, up to now infrequent and small, were handily suppressed," Skidmore notes, as fascist rule hardened further over the whole society, with harsh censorship, elimination of judicial independence, removal of many faculty, and revised curricula to promote patriotism. The new compulsory course in "Moral and Civic Education" aimed to "defend the democratic principle by preserving the religious spirit, the dignity of the human being, and the love of liberty, with responsibility under God's inspiration"—as administered by the Generals with the technocrats at their side. The authors of the 1992 Republican Campaign platform would have been much impressed, along with 1980s-style "conservatives" rather generally.

The President announced in 1970 that repression would be "harsh and implacable," with no rights for "pseudo-Brazilians." Torture became "a grisly ritual, a calculated onslaught against body and soul," Skidmore writes, with such specialties as torture of children and gang rape of wives before the family. The "orgy of torture" provided "a stark warning" to anyone with the wrong thoughts. It was a "powerful instrument," that "made it even easier for Delfim and his technocrats to avoid public debate over fundamental economic and social priorities" while they "preached the virtues of the free market." The resumption of high economic growth, by these means, made Brazil "again attractive to foreign private investors," who took over substantial parts of the economy. By the late 1970s, "The industries dominated by local capital in Brazil [were] the same industries where small businesses flourish in the United States"; multinationals and their local associates dominated the more profitable growth areas, though with the changes in the global economy, about 60 percent of foreign capital was then non-US (Peter Evans).

Macroeconomic statistics continued to be satisfying, Skidmore continues, with rapid growth of GNP and foreign investment. A "dramatic" improvement in terms of trade in the early '70s also provided a shot in the arm to the Generals and technocrats. They held firm to the doctrine that "the real answer to poverty and unequal income distribution was rapid economic growth, thereby increasing the total economic pie," eliciting nods of approval in the West. A closer look shows other characteristic features of neoliberal doctrine. Growth rates in 1965-1982 under the National Security State averaged no higher than under the parliamentary governments from 1947-1964, economist David Felix observes, despite the advantages of authoritarian control the fascist neoliberals enjoyed; and the domestic savings rate hardly rose during the "miracle years" under the "right-wing consumerism" instituted by the Generals and technocrats. The domestic market was dominated by luxury goods for the rich. None of this will be unfamiliar to others subjected to the same doctrines, including North Americans during the "Reagan revolution."

Brazil became "the most rapidly growing of major overseas markets of American manufacturers," Evans observes, with high rates of return for investment, second only to Germany during the late '60s and early '70s. Meanwhile, the country became even more of a foreign-owned subsidiary. As for the population, a World Bank study in 1975—at the peak of the miracle years—reported that 68 percent had less than the minimum caloric requirement for normal physical activity and that 58 percent of children suffered from malnutrition. Ministry of Health expenditures were lower than in 1965, with the expected concomitant effects.[11]

After a visit to Brazil in 1972, Harvard political scientist Samuel Huntington urged some relaxation of the fascist terror, but with moderation: "relaxation of controls" might "have an explosive effect in which the process gets out of control," he warned. He suggested the model of Turkey or Mexican one-party rule, playing down the importance of liberal rights in comparison with the more significant values of "institutionalization" and stability.

A few years later, the bubble burst. Brazil was swept up in the global economic crisis of the '80s, particularly ruinous in Africa and Latin America. Terms of trade now rapidly declined, eliminating this crutch for those who held the purse strings and the whip. Inflation and debt raced out of control, income levels dropped substantially, many firms faced bankruptcy, and idle capacity reached 50 percent, "giving a new meaning to 'stagflation'," Skidmore observes. Delfim's neoliberal growth strategy was in "total collapse," he adds. After 4 years of severe economic decline, the economy began to recover, in large part thanks to the import-substituting industrialization decried by neoliberal economic doctrine. The Generals bowed out, leaving a civilian government to administer the economic and social wreckage.

5. "A Real American Success Story"

Writing in 1989, Gerald Haines describes the results of more than four decades of US dominance and tutelage as "a real American success story." "America's Brazilian policies were enormously successful," bringing about "impressive economic growth based solidly on capitalism." As for political success, as early as September 1945, when the "testing area" had barely been opened for experiment, Ambassador Berle wrote that "every Brazilian now has available to himself all of the resources available to any American during a political campaign: he can make a speech, hire a hall, circulate a petition, run a newspaper, post handbills, organize a parade, solicit support, get radio time, form committees, organize a political party, and otherwise make any peaceable bid for the suffrage and support of his countrymen"—just like "any American." We're all equal, one happy family in harmony, which is why government is so responsive to the needs of the people. And so "democratic"—in the doctrinally approved sense of the term, referring to unquestioned business rule.

This triumph of capitalist democracy stands in dramatic contrast to the failures of Communism, though admittedly the comparison is unfair—to the Communists, who had nothing remotely like the favorable conditions of this "testing area" for capitalism, with its huge resources, no foreign enemies, free access to international capital and aid, and benevolent US guidance for half a century. And the success is real. From the early years, US investments and profits boomed as "Washington intensified Brazil's financial dependence on the United States, influenced its government's decisions affecting the allocation of resources, and nudged Brazil into the U.S.-dominated trading system," Haines writes.

Within Brazil, the "modern scientific methods of development based solidly on capitalism" also brought great benefits, though to understand them, a bit more precision is necessary. There are two very different Brazils, Peter Evans wrote as the miracle peaked in the 1970s: "the fundamental conflict in Brazil is between the 1, or perhaps 5, percent of the population that comprises the elite and the 80 percent that has been left out of the 'Brazilian model' of development." The first Brazil, modern and westernized, has benefited greatly from the success story of capitalism. The second is sunk in the deepest misery. For three-quarters of the population of this "mighty realm of limitless potentialities," the conditions of Eastern Europe are dreams beyond reach, another triumph of the Free World.

The "real American success story" was spelled out in a 1986 study commissioned by the new civilian government. It presented "a by-now familiar picture of Brazil," Skidmore observes: "although boasting the eighth largest economy in the Western world, Brazil fell into the same category as the less developed African or Asian countries when it came to social welfare indices"; this was the result of "two decades of a free hand for the technocrats" and the approved neoliberal doctrines, which "increased the cake" while leaving "one of the most unequal income distributions in the world" and "appalling deficiencies" in health and welfare generally. A UN *Report on Human Development* (measuring education, health, etc.) ranked Brazil in 80th place, near Albania, Paraguay, and Thailand. Shortly after, in October 1990, the UN Food and Agriculture Organization (FAO) announced that more than 40 percent of the population (almost 53 million people) are hungry. The Brazilian Health Ministry estimates that hundreds of thousands of children die of hunger every year. Brazil's educational system ranks above only Guinea-Bissau and Bangladesh, according to 1990 UNESCO data.[12]

The "success story" is summarized in a May 1992 Americas Watch report: "Rich in natural resources and with a large industrial base, the country has the largest debt in the developing world and an economy that is entering its second decade of acute crisis. Tragically, Brazil is not able to provide an adequate standard of living for its 148 million people, two-thirds of whom were malnourished in 1985, their misery caused and compounded by lack of access to the land" in a country with "one of the highest degrees of concentration of land ownership in the world," and one of the most lopsided distributions of income as well.

Starvation and disease are rampant, along with slave labor by contract workers who are brutally treated or simply murdered if they seek to escape before working off their debts. In one of the nine cases of rural slavery unearthed by the Catholic Church Land Ministry Commission in the first few months of 1992, 4000 slave workers were found extracting charcoal in an agribusiness project established and subsidized by the military government as a "reforestation project" (of which nothing operates but the charcoal pits). In haciendas, slave laborers work 16 hours a day without pay and are frequently beaten and tortured, sometimes murdered, with almost complete impunity. Almost half the farmland is owned by 1 percent of farmers; government emphasis on export crops, following the precepts of the foreign masters, favors farmers with capital to invest, marginalizing the huge majority even further. In the north and northeast, rich landowners call in gunmen or the military police to burn houses and crops, shoot livestock, murder unionists, priests, nuns or lawyers trying to defend peasant rights, and drive the villagers into shantytowns or to the Amazon, where they are then blamed for deforestation as they clear land in a desperate attempt to survive. Brazilian medical researchers describe the population of the region as a new subspecies: "Pygmies," with 40 percent the brain capacity of humans—the result of severe malnutrition in a region with much fertile land, owned by large plantations that produce cash crops for export.[13]

Brazil is a world center of such triumphs as child slavery, with some 7 million children working as slaves and prostitutes, exploited, overworked, deprived of health and education, "or just deprived of their childhood," an International Labor Organization study estimates. The luckier children can look forward to work for drug traffickers in exchange for glue to sniff to "make the hunger go away." The figure worldwide is estimated at hundreds of millions, "one of the grimmer ironies of the age," George Moffett comments. Had the grim result been found in Eastern Europe it would have been a proof of the bestiality of the Communist enemy; since it is the normal situation in Western domains, it is only irony, the result of "endemic third-world poverty...exacerbated as financially strapped governments have cut expenditures for education," all with no cause.

Brazil also wins the prize for torture and murder of street children by the security forces—"a process of extermination of young people" according to the head of the Justice Department in Rio de Janeiro (Hélio Saboya), targeting the 7-8 million street children who "beg, steal, or sniff glue" and "for a few glorious moments forget who or where they are" (London *Guardian* correspondent Jan Rocha). In Rio, a congressional commission identified 15 death squads, most of them made up of police officers and financed by merchants. Bodies of children murdered by death squads are found outside metropolitan areas with their hands tied, showing signs of torture, riddled with bullet holes. Street girls are forced to work as prostitutes. The Legal Medical Institute recorded 427 children murdered in Rio alone in the first ten months of 1991, most by death squads. A Brazilian parliamentary study released in December 1991 reported that 7000 children had been killed in the past four years.[14]

Truly a tribute to our magnificence and the "modern scientific methods of development based solidly on capitalism" in a territory as much "worth exploitation" as any in the world.

We should not underestimate the scale of the achievement. It took real talent to create a nightmare in a country as favored and richly-endowed as Brazil. In the light of such triumphs, it is understandable that the ruling class of the new imperial age should be dedicated with such passion to helping others share the wonders, and that the ideological managers should celebrate the accomplishment with such enthusiasm and self-praise.

6. Fundamentalism Triumphant

One might object that despite its unusual advantages, Brazil is still not the optimal testing area to demonstrate the virtues of the neoliberal doctrines that "American-style capitalism" urges upon countries it deems "worth exploitation." Perhaps it would be better to try Venezuela, even more favorable terrain with its extraordinary resources, including the richest petroleum reserves outside the Middle East. We might, then, have a look at that success story.

In a major scholarly study of US-Venezuelan relations, Stephen Rabe writes that after World War II, the US "actively supported the vicious and venal regime of Juan Vicente Gómez," who opened the country wide to foreign exploitation. The State Department shelved the "Open Door" policy in the usual way, recognizing the possibility of "U.S. economic hegemony in Venezuela," hence pressuring its government to bar British concessions (while continuing to demand—and secure—US oil rights in the Middle East, where the British and French were in the lead). By 1928, Venezuela had become the world's leading oil exporter, with US companies in charge. During World War II, the US agreed to a Venezuelan demand for 50-50 profit-sharing. The effect, as predicted, was a vast expansion of oil production and "substantial profits for the [US] oil industry," which took control over the country's economy and "major economic decisions" in all areas. During the 1949-1958 dictatorship of the murderous thug Pérez Jiménez, "U.S. relations with Venezuela were harmonious and economically beneficial to U.S. businessmen"; torture, terror, and general repression passed without notice on the usual Cold War pretexts. In 1954, the dictator was awarded the Legion of Merit by President Eisenhower. The citation noted that "his wholesome policy in economic and financial matters has facilitated the expansion of foreign investment, his Administration thus contributing to the greater well-being of the country and the rapid development of its immense natural resources"—and, incidentally, huge profits for the US corporations that ran the country, including by then steel companies and others. About half of Standard Oil of New Jersey's profits came from its Venezuelan subsidiary, to cite just one example.

From World War II, in Venezuela the US followed the standard policy of taking total control of the military "to expand U.S. political and military influence in the Western Hemisphere and perhaps help keep the U.S. arms industry vigorous" (Rabe). As later explained by Kennedy's Ambassador Allan Stewart, "U.S.-oriented and anti-Communist armed forces are vital instruments to maintain our security interests." He illustrated the point with the case of Cuba, where the "armed forces disintegrated" while elsewhere they "remained intact and able to defend themselves and others from Communists," as demonstrated by the wave of National Security States that swept over the hemisphere. The Kennedy Administration increased its assistance to the Venezuelan security forces for "internal security and counterinsurgency operations against the political left," Rabe comments, also assigning personnel to advise in combat operations, as in Vietnam. Stewart urged the government to "dramatize" its arrests of radicals, which would make a good impression in Washington as well as among Venezuelans (those who matter, that is).

In 1970, Venezuela lost its position as world's leading oil exporter to Saudi Arabia and Iran. As in the Middle East, Venezuela nationalized its oil (and iron ore) in a manner quite satisfactory to Washington and US investors, who "found a newly rich Venezuela hospitable," Rabe writes, "one of the most unique markets in the world," in the words of a Commerce Department official.[15]

The return to office of social democrat Carlos Andrés Pérez in 1988 aroused some concerns, but they dissipated as he launched an IMF-approved structural readjustment program, resolutely maintained despite thousands of protests, many violent, including one in February 1989 in which 300 people were killed by security forces in the capital city of Caracas.

Though rarely reported in the US, protests continued along with strike waves severe enough to lead to fear that the country was headed towards "anarchy." Among other cases, three students were killed by police who attacked peaceful demonstrations in late November 1991; and two weeks later, police used tear gas to break up a peaceful march of 15,000 people in Caracas protesting Pérez's economic policies. In January 1992, the main trade union confederation predicted serious difficulties and conflicts as a result of the neoliberal programs, which had caused "massive impoverishment" including a 60 percent drop in workers' buying power in 3 years, while enriching financial groups and transnational corporations.[16]

By then, another "economic miracle" was in place: "a treasury brimming with foreign reserves, inflation at its lowest rate in five years, and an economy growing at the fastest rate in the Americas, 9.2 percent in 1991," Times correspondent James Brooke reported, noting also some familiar flaws, among them a fall in the real minimum wage in Caracas to 44 percent of the 1987 level, a decline in nutritional levels, and a "scandalous concentration of wealth," according to a right-wing Congressman he quotes. Other flaws were to come to light (in the US) a few weeks later after a coup attempt, among them, the government's admission that only 57 percent of Venezuelans could afford more than one meal a day in this country of enormous wealth. Other flaws in the miracle had been revealed in the report of an August 1991 Presidential Commission for the Rights of Children, not previously noticed, which found that "critical poverty, defined as the inability to meet at least one half of basic nutritional requirements," had tripled from 11 percent of the population in 1984 to 33 percent in 1991; and that real per capita income fell 55 percent from 1988 to 1991, falling at double the rate of 1980-1988.[17]

On February 4, 1992, an attempted military coup was crushed. "There was little jubilation," AP reported. "The coup attempt caps a crescendo of anger and frustration over the economic reforms that have written such a macroeconomic success story but have failed to benefit the lives of most Venezuelans and have embittered many" (*Financial Times*). It "was met by silent cheers from a large part of the population," Brooke reported, particularly in poor and working-class areas. Like the Brazilian technocrats, Pérez had done everything right, "cutting subsidies, privatizing state companies and opening a closed economy to competition." But something had unaccountably gone wrong. True, the growth rate was impressive, "but most economic analysts agree that the high price of oil in 1991 fueled Venezuela's growth more than Pérez's austerity moves," Stan Yarbro reported, and none can fail to see that "the new wealth has failed to trickle down to Venezuela's middle and lower classes, whose standard of living has fallen dramatically." Infant deaths "have soared in the past two years as a result of worsening malnutrition and other health problems in the shantytowns," a priest who had worked in poor neighborhoods for 16 years said. There is ample "new wealth," much of it "poured into financial speculation schemes rather than new investments in industry. In 1991 money made in real estate and financial services almost equaled the profits from manufactures."[18]

In short, a typical economic miracle, achieved under unusually favorable conditions for the evaluation of the neoliberal doctrines preached with such fervor by the priesthood of what Jeremy Seabrook calls the new "International Monetary Fundamentalism."[19]

7. Some Competitors for the Prize

It is a bit unfair to award Brazil the prize for enslavement, murder, and abuse of children; after all, it is the "colossus of the South," so opportunities abound and numbers are larger. In fact, the story is much the same throughout the continent. Take Guatemala, another country richly endowed with resources that offered fine prospects for a success story for capitalism after the US regained control in 1954—and another case that should inspire us with pride in our accomplishments, so impressive in comparison with the wreckage left by the despicable enemy.

Guatemala now boasts a higher level of child malnutrition than Haiti, according to UNICEF. The Health Ministry reports that 40 percent of students suffer from chronic malnutrition, while 2.5 million children in this country of 9 million suffer abuse that leads them to abandon school and become involved in crime. A quarter of a million have been orphaned by political violence. The condition of children is not very surprising when 87 percent of the population live below the poverty line (up from 79 percent in 1980), 72 percent cannot afford a minimum diet (52 percent in 1980), 6 million have no access to health service, 3.6 million lack drinking water, and concentration of land ownership continues to rise (2 percent now control 70 percent of the land). Purchasing power in 1989 was 22 percent of its 1972 level, dropping still further as the neoliberal measures of the 1980s were intensified.

We need not linger on the record of mass slaughter, genocide in the highlands, disappearance, torture, mutilation, and other standard accompaniments of Free World victories; admittedly, a display of imperial benevolence that has been somewhat excessive in the case of Guatemala. The contours, at least, should be recalled. The terror began as soon as the US-run military coup succeeded in overthrowing the reformist capitalist democracy. Some 8000 peasants were murdered in two months in a terror campaign that targeted particularly United Fruit Company union organizers and Indian village leaders. The US Embassy participated with considerable fervor, providing lists of "Communists" to be eliminated or imprisoned and tortured while Washington dedicated itself to making Guatemala "a showcase for democracy." At a comparable stage, the Khmer Rouge were condemned for genocide. Terror mounted again in the 1960s, with active US participation. The process resumed in the late 1970s, soon reaching new levels of barbarism. Over 440 villages were totally destroyed and well over 100,000 civilians were killed or "disappeared," up to 150,000 according to the Church and others, all with the enthusiastic support of the Reagan Administration. Huge areas of the highlands were destroyed in a frenzy of irreversible environmental devastation. The goal was to prevent a recurrence of popular organization or any further thought of freedom or social reform. The toll since the US regained control is estimated at about 200,000 unarmed civilians killed or "disappeared," and in the highlands, episodes that qualify as genocide, if the word has meaning. In an amazing triumph of the human spirit, popular forces and leaders continue their struggle against US-inspired neo-Nazism.[20]

The terror continues, still arousing little notice in the US or the West generally. The report of the Archbishop's Office of Human Rights for the first half of 1992 reported at least 399 assassinations, many of them "extra-judicial actions" of the state security forces and their allies. "Every day dozens of attacks upon constitutional rights are reported." The terror has its place in the neoliberal economic program. "Twenty union leaders fled into exile in 1991 because of death threats against themselves and their families," according to the State Department's annual human rights review. When workers began to form a legally recognized union in the US-owned Phillips-Van Heusen company in 1991, the result was death threats, raised production quotas and the shooting of an organizer to deter any threat to the working conditions that enable foreign-owned clothing assembly plants to make their contribution to the "economic miracle": under $2 wages for 16 hours of work, stifling warehouses with few fans and locked exits, and physical and sexual abuse, according to a complaint by US unions to the US Trade Representative Office.[21]

As for the "showcase of democracy," an election was scheduled for 1963, but it was prevented by a military coup backed by the Kennedy Administration to block the participation of Juan José Arévalo, the founder of Guatemalan democracy, who had been elected in 1945 after the over-throw of the US-backed Ubico dictatorship. A 1966 election extended military control over the country, setting off another wave of terror. The 1985 election was proclaimed by the US Embassy to be the "final step in the reestablishment of democracy in Guatemala." The November 1990 elections ended in a draw between two right-wing neoliberal candidates, who managed to stir up 30 percent of the electorate (counting valid votes). In the runoff election won by Jorge Serrano, abstention was even higher.

These achievements aside, the prevailing social conditions are the result of another successful experiment: the development model intro-duced by US advisers after the 1954 coup terminated the ten-year episode of capitalist democracy. As terror improved the investment climate, export-oriented economic programs led to rapid growth in production of agricul-tural commodities and beef for export, destruction of forests and traditional agriculture, sharp increase in hunger and general misery, the world cham-pionship for DDT in mothers' milk (185 times World Health Organization limits), and gratifying balance sheets for US agribusiness and local affiliates. The new maquiladoras are having a similar impact. Current economic plans, under the guidance of US advisers, are intensifying this range of effects.

No less predictably, in his January 1992 report to Congress, President Serrano declared the results of the properly neoliberal economic program (including the 100 percent increase for the military in the 1992 budget) to be an "economic miracle," while Western commentators applauded and looked forward to still further triumphs of capitalist democracy.

We may recall, in passing, that the main victims are indigenous people, who constitute over half the population. Their travail began long ago. "At no time before the [Spanish] conquest," Susanne Jonas writes, "did the Indians suffer the systematic material deprivation that has characterized Guatemala since 1524," and "although Bartolomé de Las Casas's figure of 4-5 million Indian deaths in Guatemala between 1524 and 1540 may be exaggerated, its thrust is accurate. An estimated two-thirds to six-sevenths of the Indian population in Central America and Mexico died between 1519 and 1650."[22]

Child slavery has long been documented in the traditional service areas. India alone is reported to have some 14 million child laborers, aged six and up, many working under conditions of virtual slavery for up to 16 hours a day. As always, this is a reflection of general social conditions. A detailed study in a leading Indian journal of "one of South India's most fertile and productive regions" found "a story of narrowing options, desolation and despair—and, increasingly, of death" from starvation and suicide, with at least 73 starvation deaths among weavers in two months of 1991. The deteriorating conditions result from the "frenzied export drive" and accompanying "strategy of taxing the poor and pampering the rich," policies to be accelerated under the IMF-designed structural adjustment policies for which India is now widely praised.[23]

The situation in Thailand has long been notorious, condemned by international and Thai human rights groups while Thailand is hailed in the West as another "success story for capitalism." The Bangkok press alone offers harrowing testimony. Cambodia specialist Michael Vickery provides a recent sample, including the case of teenagers "freed...from a factory where they were allegedly detained for slave labour and tortured," tied up and beaten when they became too tired to work after 18-hour shifts; eighteen girls aged 12-14 rescued from a textile mill where they worked over 15 hours a day "for almost no pay"; teenagers fleeing from poverty in the Northeast dragooned into factories or forced into brothels for European and Japanese tourists. A leading Thai political scientist comments:

> In Thailand, we occasionally hear stories about young children sold into bondage by their parents. These young indentured servants work under harsh conditions...and for many, the bondage will be renewed when the parents make out another loan from the employer. [Young girls] would be forced to work in a factory normally not registered with the Minister

of Industry... as young as nine—would be literally imprisoned by the boss for up to 12 hours a day...those who complained or attempted to escape would be harshly punished.

This is apart from the normal misery and brutal exploitation of the millions of poor.

"Year after year, such incidents are revealed in the Thai press," Vickery observes, "and although the authorities express shock each time, no substantial reform ever results. This is because such atrocities, and we must call them by their true name, are systemic in the Thai type of capitalism"—more generally, in the "economic miracles" that are the "success stories of capitalism." It is all more "irony," given the locus of the plague. Another "irony" is illustrated by Vickery's acid comment on the treatment of Cambodia and Vietnam, tortured and strangled by US-run economic warfare, in comparison to Thailand, a major aid recipient: "While Vietnamese farmers are getting greater control over land and its produce, Thai farmers are losing theirs and their children are forced into types of exploitation which have not been discovered in Vietnam since 1975, even by the most hostile observers."[24]

Surveying the Latin American region in a Peruvian Church journal, Uruguayan journalist Samuel Blixen reports that in Guatemala City, the majority of the 5000 street children work as prostitutes. In September 1990, three bodies of children were found with their ears cut off and eyes gouged out, a warning about what would happen to witnesses of abuse of children by the security forces, formal or informal. In Peru, children are sold to the highest bidder to pan for gold; according to a young campesina who escaped, they work 18 hours a day in water up to their knees and are paid with a daily ration sufficient to keep them alive. In Guayaquil, Ecuador, some 100,000 children from 4 to 14 work 10- to 12-hour shifts for low wages, many of them victims of sexual abuse. "In Panama the Minors Protective Tribunal buildings were bombed during the 1989 US invasion, rendering work nearly impossible. Following the invasion the number of criminal gangs robbing stores in search of food increased," with about 45 percent of robberies attributed to children using stolen military weapons. UNICEF reports that 69 million children in Latin America survive by menial labor, robbing, running drugs, and prostitution. A study released by the health ministers of the Central American countries in November 1991 estimated that 120,000 children under five die annually in Central America from malnutrition (one million are born annually), and that two-thirds of the survivors suffer from malnutrition.

"Until recently," Blixen writes, "the image of the abandoned Latin American child was of a ragged child sleeping in a doorway. Today the image is of a body, lacerated and dumped in a city slum—those who survive that far."[25]

A leading Mexican journal reports a study by Victor Carlos García Moreno of the Institute for Law Research at the Autonomous National University of Mexico (UNAM), presented at a conference on "International Traffic in Children" in Mexico City. He found that about 20,000 children are sent illegally to the United States each year "for supplying illegal traffic in vital organs, for sexual exploitation, or for experimental tests." Mexico's leading daily, *Excelsior*, reports that "Another element of abuses against minors [in Guatemala] is the existence of various illegal 'crib houses' responsible for the 'fattening' of newborns who are sent out of the country for their organs to be sold in the United States and Europe." A Professor of Theology at the University of São Paulo (Brazil), Father Barruel, informed the UN that "75 percent of the corpses [of murdered children] reveal internal mutilation and the majority have their eyes removed." The President of the Episcopal Council of Latin America, Archbishop Lopez Rodriguez of Santo Domingo, stated in July 1991 that the Church "is investigating all the charges concerning sale of children for illegal adoption or organ transplant."

There have been numerous allegations about kidnapping of children for organ transplant in Latin America; whether true or not, the fact that they are taken seriously, from the press to academic researchers and government agencies, is indicative of the conditions of existence for children.[26]

And other superfluous creatures as well. The *British Medical Journal* reported an Argentine judicial investigation that led to arrest of the director of a state-run mental hospital, doctors, businessmen and others, after "evidence of the trafficking of human organs" was unearthed, among other crimes. AFP reported that "Argentines were aghast at the near-hallucinatory revelations of the horrors involving disappearances, trafficking in corneas, blood, babies, contraband and corruption" for more than a decade at the hospital, and the discovery in Uruguay of a "gang of organ smugglers headed by Argentinians." "There is traffic in children and organs," the Argentine Minister of Health reported.

A novel idea was implemented in Colombia, where security guards of a medical school murdered poor people and sold the bodies to the school for student research; reports indicate that before they were killed, organs that could be sold on the black market were removed. These practices, however, scarcely make a dent in one of the worst human rights records in the continent, compiled by security forces that have long benefited from

US training and supply and have now become one of the hemisphere's top recipients of US military funding. As elsewhere, the main targets for muti- lation, torture, and murder are priests, union activists, political leaders and others who try to defend the poor, form cooperatives, or otherwise qualify as "subversives" by interfering with the neoliberal economic model imple- mented under instructions from the US and the World Bank.[27]

These development programs have other features, among them, an epidemic of pesticide poisoning that has reached the few corners of our little region over here that, for a time, escaped the deadly impact of the neoliberal doctrines. In Costa Rica, "legal pesticides—many of them im- ported from the United States—are making people sick, injuring them, even killing them," Christopher Scanlan reports in the *Miami Herald* from Pitahaya, where a 15-year old farm worker had just died of poisoning by a highly toxic American Cyanamid product. The village cemetery of Pitahaya, he continues, "is a stark symbol of a global death toll from pesticides estimated at 220,000 a year by the World Health Organization," along with 25 million incidents a year of illness, including chronic neurological dam- age; the Guaymí Indians who die from pesticide poisoning cleaning drain- age ditches at US-owned plantations in Costa Rica and Panama are unlikely to make it to a village cemetery. More than 99 percent of deaths from acute pesticide poisoning occur in Third World countries, which use 20 percent of agricultural chemicals.

With "markets closed at home" by regulations to protect the popula- tion and the environment, "chemical companies shifted sales of these banned chemicals to the Third World where government regulations are weak." The corporations have also devised new "nonpersistent" pesticides that "are generally much more acutely toxic" to farm workers and their families, including some "first developed as nerve gas by the Germans before World War II." Physicians in Costa Rica are calling for removal of killer chemicals from the Third World market, but "the Bush administration sides with the industry," Scanlan reports. Its position is that the solution does not lie in interference with the market—to translate to English: profits for the rich. Rather, in "educating people about the risk," William Jordan of the Environmental Protection Agency explains. Progress has its problems, he concedes, but "you cannot simply ignore progress." An American Cyanamid executive says "I sleep at night very comfortably." So do leaders and ideologists generally, except when their rest is disturbed by the faults of official enemies and their retrograde doctrines.[28]

The United States has never been very happy with Costa Rica, despite its almost total subordination to the wishes of US corporations and Wash- ington. Costa Rican social democracy and successes in state-guided development, unique in Central America, were a constant irritant. Concerns were relieved in the 1980s, as the huge debt and other problems gave the US government leverage to move Costa Rica closer to the "Central American mode" lauded by the press, but the Ticos still don't know their place. One problem arose in November 1991, when Costa Rica renewed its request to the US to extradite US rancher John Hull, who was charged with murder in the La Penca bombing in which six people were killed, as well as drug running and other crimes. This renewed call for extradition was particularly irritating because of the timing—just as the US was orchestrating a vociferous PR campaign against Libya for its insistence on keeping to international law and arranging for trial of two Libyans accused of air terrorism either in its own courts or by a neutral country or agency, instead of handing them over to the US. The unfortunate coincidence did not disrupt the Washington-media campaign against Libya, thanks to the scrupulous suppression of the Costa Rican request.

Yet another Costa Rican crime was its expropriation of property of US citizens, for which it was duly punished by the freezing of promised economic assistance. The most serious case was the confiscation of the property of a US businessman by President Oscar Arias, who incorporated it into a national park. Costa Rica offered compensation, but not enough, Washington determined. The land was expropriated when it was found that it had been used by the CIA for an illegal air strip for resupplying US terrorist forces in Nicaragua. Arias's expropriation without adequate compensation is a crime that naturally calls for retribution by Washington—and silence by the media, particularly as they are railing against Libyan terrorism.[29]

The effrontery of the powerful often leaves one virtually speechless.

Another *Miami Herald* reporter surveys the "barren future" that "looms for Central America" as forests there and in Mexico vanish at a rate "faster than any other region on Earth except West Africa," perhaps to "disappear within our lifetime." The accelerating destruction is caused by poor farmers, lumbermen, and people seeking firewood, but "experts throughout the region blame rapid deforestation on unfair land distribution" throughout the region, including even Costa Rica, which "boasts one of the highest rates of deforestation in the world." Another major factor is the US-initiated counterinsurgency doctrine, with its emphasis on blasting people out of their homes and lands with massive firepower if they cannot be controlled. The Central American Committee on Water Resources warned that the ecological disaster is also severely diminishing water supply. "The main lagoons and rivers which supply water to the people are about to be destroyed by continuous deforestation in the region," one high official said after a July 1992 regional meeting, also "setting back the generation of electricity and possible economic growth in the region."

"The concentration of the best land into vast coffee, cotton and sugar estates owned by a small elite meant hundreds of thousands of peasants were forced to eke a living off steep, marginal land," Tom Gibb reports from El Salvador, where firewood may disappear in a decade and 90 percent of rivers are contaminated. The destruction might still be averted, but that would "require a change in the political atmosphere that has dominated El Salvador for decades: peasant farmers are afraid to organize and work in groups for fear of being labeled 'subversive'."[30]

To rephrase in more realistic terms, farmers are aware that efforts to organize will call forth another US-sponsored wave of torture and massacre to bar any interference with our high ideals of economic liberalism for the Third World.

A study of the Costa Rican economy by the Washington World Resources Institute and the Tropical Science Center in Costa Rica concludes that each year, 5 percent of the Gross Domestic Product "has vanished without a trace" and that depreciation of natural resources has robbed the country of almost 30 percent of its potential net growth over the past 20 years. A quarter of the estimated growth rate from 1970 through 1989 disappears when these factors are considered.[31]

These effects will only increase as neoliberal models are more firmly implanted. In Costa Rica, they were firmly in place by 1985, earlier in much of the region—and in fact, they are only a variant of traditional US programs. After five years of IMF Fundamentalism in Costa Rica, the predicted growth had not occurred though the trade deficit grew substantially, fed primarily by imports from the US; the minimum wage had lost 25 percent of its buying power, with 37 percent of salaried workers paid below the legal minimum. Average family incomes declined by 10 percent through the 1980s, except for the top 5 percent, and buying power of workers continues its decline. The Ministry of Labor reported that under President Calderón's neoliberal rule, poverty had increased 18 percent in 1991 alone, leaving 35 percent of Costa Rican families unable to satisfy their most basic needs, a home census of the Ministry of Economy revealed. 1991 marks a sharp increase in the poverty rate, "a consequence of the kind of economic adjustment applied in recent years," a researcher added. "Representatives of the World Bank and USAID have showered the Calderón administration with praise for its economic program," CAR reports.[32]

Costa Rica is the Central American exception, a special case. When we turn to the "Central American mode," the situation is vastly worse. In Honduras, IMF measures "have provoked mass unemployment [to two-thirds of the population] and skyrocketing inflation," with sharply rising prices for fuel, food, and medicine *(CAR)*. President Callejas concedes that these policies have had "a negative effect on the vast majority of the population"; but, *CAR* observes, he "is willing to pay this price, however, to satisfy international lenders and continue promoting a free market economy." Callejas and his associates, needless to add, are not those who "pay the price." In El Salvador, 90 percent of the population live in poverty and only 40 percent have steady employment. The 1990 structural adjustment program put 25,000 more out of work and substantially reduced exports, and despite increase in minimum salaries, "the price of the basic family basket far outstrips workers' income." Almost 80 percent of private bank loans go to large businesses; of agricultural loans, 60 percent went to coffee growers, 3 percent to small-scale basic grain producers. Reserves have risen, the Central Bank reports, but not because of the austerity measures; rather, as a result of the $700 million sent by Salvadorans abroad, many of them refugees fleeing the state terror of the past decade, which, in this way, did produce an "economic success story." Mass terror has declined, but terror continues at a low level. On July 31, 1992, a top leftist union leader, Ivan Ramírez, was murdered by unidentified gunmen in the style of the death squads. We turn to Nicaragua directly.[33]

The effects of IMF Fundamentalism, now administered with renewed fervor, "have been catastrophic" in Central America, the Jesuit journal *Envío* reports. Inflation has increased. Fiscal deficits have not declined as anticipated, but GDP growth has stagnated since 1985 and declined since 1988. Real wages have substantially fallen almost everywhere in Latin America, and the distribution of income is becoming even more skewed than before. "The word 'development' has disappeared from Latin America's economic vocabulary"—though "profit" is on everyone's lips, for the foreigner and the domestic islands of privilege. The same can only be expected elsewhere. Discussing what lies ahead for India under IMF-designed restructuring, two economics professors at the Bombay Institute of Development Research review the consequences of such programs worldwide, drawing the "unambiguous" conclusion from "economic theory and the recent economic history of developing countries": the effects are "tremendous hardship for the poor and working people" and "great hardship on the economies of developing nations"; no less unambiguous are the benefits for the privileged sectors and their foreign associates, who call the tune.[34]

8. "Our Nature and Traditions"

There are many other "success stories" in the Caribbean and Central America, the Philippines, Africa, in fact wherever Western power and capitalist ideology have reached. The few partial exceptions, mostly in the Japanese orbit, have escaped by radically violating the prescribed rules of the game, under special circumstances that are not likely to recur.[35] These basic truths and their meaning, which would be taught in elementary schools in free societies, must be kept far removed from consciousness as we advance towards Year 501 of the Old World Order.

And so they are. Merely to take the case closest to hand, the US-run charnel house in Central America in the 1980s, we find that cultivated opinion takes pride in what we have wrought. Typical is a report by *Washington Post* Central America correspondent Lee Hockstader on a meeting in Guatemala of the new breed of conservative Presidents, freely elected at last without a trace of foreign influence. This "new wave of democracy" has "shifted politicians' priorities" from the days when they "traditionally represented the established order." The proof is that they have now dedicated themselves to serving the poor with an imaginative new approach: "Central Americans to use Trickle-down Strategy in War on Poverty," the headline reads. "Committed to free-market economics," the Presidents have abandoned vapid rhetoric about land reform and social welfare programs, adopting at last a serious idea: "a trickle-down approach to aid the poor." "The idea is to help the poor without threatening the basic power structure," a regional economist observes. This brilliant and innovative conception overturns the "preferential option for the poor" of the Latin American Bishops. Now that we have driven this naive idea from the heads of our little brown brothers by Pol Pot-style terror, we can return to our traditional vocation of serving the poor, somehow not drowning in our own hypocrisy—the one truly memorable achievement.

Barbara Crossette reports in the *New York Times* that Central America illustrates "what Bush Administration officials regard as one of their most successful foreign policy initiatives: to bring peace, disarmament and economic development to this tormented region"; she wastes no words on how and why it was tormented, and by whom. "The strategy was immeasurably assisted by the collapse of the Soviet Union," she continues, repeating the convenient fairy tale that the US assault was undertaken in defense against the Evil Empire. El Salvador is "the most violent theater of East-West conflict in the hemisphere," Tim Golden proclaims on the front page; perhaps some Soviet counterpart wrote in 1956 that Hungary is "the most violent theater of East-West conflict in Eastern Europe"—however shameful, a claim that would have been far more plausible, in the irrelevant real world.

For the larger picture, we naturally turn to *New York Times* chief diplomatic correspondent Thomas Friedman, who takes as his text Congressman Les Aspin's proclamation that "The emerging world is likely to lack the clarity of the cold war... The old world was good guys and bad guys. The new world is gray guys." Developing this theme, Friedman observes that "Normally, Washington gets rather exercised about the toppling of freely elected presidents." But now life is harder. Some of those elected may not be clean upstanding folk as in the past, and we may have to make sharper discriminations. It won't be as easy as when Washington got "exercised about the toppling of" Goulart, Arbenz, Allende, Bosch ....

Even before, we did not always support only good guys, Friedman recognizes, recalling such unpleasant folk as the Shah and Marcos. But that deviation from high principle is easily handled: "During the cold war the United States did not really have the luxury or burden of choosing its friends," but "simply had to identify who was with it in the grand struggle with the 'Evil Empire' led by Moscow." Our real values were demonstrated by the "fact" that "Washington did press for democracy, free markets and other ideals"—a declaration of some audacity, but safe enough in the reigning intellectual culture.

The "Soviet threat" forced on us "a degree of cynicism in foreign affairs, which was contrary to our nature and traditions," a senior Administration policymaker adds with the *Times* imprimatur. Neither tarries on some questions that come to mind. To mention a few: How are "our nature and traditions" illustrated by our practice before the Soviet Union threatened our existence in 1917? Or by the regular pattern of concocting "Soviet threats" on the most ludicrous pretexts to justify atrocities undertaken to preserve "stability" in our special sense of the term? Nor do they trouble to explain exactly what the Soviet threat had to do with our support for genocidal monsters from Indonesia to Guatemala, or how it explains the close correlation between torture and US aid.

The same official warns that we should not revert to our traditional stand "of granting idealism a near exclusive hold on our foreign policy." The world is still too harsh a place for us to "revert to form," slipping back unthinkingly to our role of world benefactor while ignoring "the national interest," bemused by "Wilsonian" idealism. The latter concept has an interesting status; it does not refer to what Wilson did—for example, his murderous interventions in Haiti and the Dominican Republic—or even what he said, when push came to shove. The same holds, more generally, of the concept "our values." Thus, Friedman quotes Harvard political philosopher Michael Sandel, who expresses his concern that we will persist in past practices instead of rising to the current challenge. "For years we have just pressed a shorthand version of our values—free elections and free markets—without realizing that the fullest expression of our values required more" than the limited mission of righteousness that has guided us heretofore. As in the case of Wilsonianism, the concept "our values" is entirely independent of what we do or even profess, except before the cameras.

With the global enemy out of the way, "the emerging yardstick is one of democratic values," Friedman concludes, doubtless thinking of George Bush's attitude towards Suharto, the Gulf emirates and Saddam Hussein (before his unfortunate error of August 2, 1990), and other attractive figures whose appeal has outlasted the Cold War—and had little to do with it in the first place.

"No satire of Funston could reach perfection, because Funston occupies that summit himself," Mark Twain wrote, referring to one of the heroes of the Philippine slaughter: he is "satire incarnated."[36]

The device of eliminating history by a wave at the Cold War, no matter how foolish the pretense, is one that is to be highly recommended to the aspiring servant of power, given what history actually tells us. This is only the most recent application of the technique of "change of course," regularly invoked when some ugliness finally breaks through the elegant and smoothly functioning mechanisms of suppression: Yes, there was an unfortunate lapse, but now we can march on behind the banner of our high ideals.

9. Some Tools of the Trade

The doctrine of "change of course" is only one of the devices that must be mastered by those who hope to attain respectability and prestige; several others have been mentioned, and we turn to other handy procedures below. The preceding discussion has touched upon a more subtle array of notions that are essential for the aspiring intellectual: "economic miracle," "American success story," "free market triumph," etc. These are elusive, and require a bit of care.

The term "economic miracle" refers to a complex of nice macroeconomic statistics, great profits for foreign investors, and a life of luxury for local elites; and, in the small print, increasing misery for the general population, quite typically. It is no wonder that these miracles are so admired by commentators in the press and elsewhere. As long as the façade remains in place, such societies are "American success stories" and "triumphs of capitalism and the free market." But when it collapses, the very same examples turn into a demonstration of the dread pitfalls of statism, socialism, Marxism-Leninism, and other sins.

The Brazilian case illustrates the doctrinal pattern. Gerald Haines was not alone in celebrating the triumph of capitalism and American know-how in Brazil, though his timing—1989—was a bit off. The brilliant achievements of the Generals and their right-thinking technocratic advisers made Brazil "the Latin American darling of the international business community,"*Business Latin America* reported in 1972. Arthur Burns, Chairman of the Federal Reserve, was full of praise for Delfim's "miraculous" work. As the "Chicago boys" were invited in by another collection of fascist killers after the overthrow of Allende in Chile a year later, Chicago school economist Arnold Harberger held up Brazil "as the exemplar of a glowing future under economic liberalism," David Felix recalls. A few years later, in a 1980 interview, he was to applaud Pinochet's successes under the same model: "Santiago has never looked better. Consumer goods from all over the world are readily available at cheap prices"; there are even jobs for people with the right qualifications, like police torturers. True, real wages had collapsed, but the real value of imports was up 38 percent by 1980, thanks to the increase of 276 percent in luxury goods while capital imports fell sharply. Foreign debt skyrocketed (to be paid off later by the poor), and unions and peasant movements had been crushed in a wave of terror. But the rich were doing just fine; everything was on course in Chile, as in Brazil, thanks to proper application of economic theory.

By the early '80s, the Brazilian economy was spinning towards disaster, and the tune changed. Brazil was dropped from the list of "neoliberal successes," Felix observed in 1986, though some had not heard the message. In a 1989 discussion of the Brazilian military regime, Harvard Government professor Frances Hagopian, like Haines, still admired "the impressive extent to which the military succeeded in its economic objectives," while expressing doubts as to whether this "extraordinary economic success" really required the repression and torture.[37]

While the "economic miracle" was churning merrily along, Brazil's achievements were heralded as a demonstration of the marvels of free-market capitalism, the happy result of American guidance and kind assistance. After the collapse, Brazil demonstrates the *failure* to follow US advice and the sound principles of economic liberalism. Brazil's plight is attributed to its state socialist deviation from economic orthodoxy. We thus derive yet another proof of the superiority of capitalism and the free market. To account for Brazil's sorry state, we may now invoke the very measures that brought about the "free market triumph" while it was still possible to be dazzled by the "economic miracle": the indefinite wage controls instituted by the much-praised neoliberal economist Delfim, the state corporations established to overcome the severe recession caused by monetarist strategies and to prevent a complete takeover of the economy by foreign corporations, and the import-substitution strategy that kept the economy afloat in the mid-1980s.

It all goes to show, once again, how supple an instrument ideology can be, in well-trained hands.

A great sigh of relief accompanied the victory in 1989 of the attractive representative of the Brazilian elite, Fernando Collor de Mello, in an election in which the two candidates could actually be distinguished without a microscope, the other being the labor leader Luís Inácio da Silva ("Lula"). With "the playing field levelled" by Collor's huge financial resources and clear warnings by those who own the country that they would sink it down the tube if the elections came out the wrong way, Collor was able to eke out a victory. There was great enthusiasm in the doctrinal institutions as he set forth on the approved neoliberal path, with expectations for yet another "success story for American-style capitalism." Briefly, however. The economy fell from 3.3 percent growth in 1989 to -4.6 percent in 1990. Per capita income fell by 6 percent from 1990 to 1992 as production continued to decline, health spending was cut by 33 percent, education spending sank further, and the tax burden on wage earners rose 60 percent. By mid-1992, James Brooke reports, "Mr. Collor's failed economic policies" were "feeding national discontent." And to top it off, Collor was facing impeachment after exposure of a corruption scandal that also set new records.[38]

As in the case of Brazil, "success stories of capitalism and democracy" achieve this status irrespective of the means employed. The import substitution strategy that saved Brazil from utter ruin was also an essential component of the "economic miracles" of the Pacific Rim. These miracles came into being under harsh authoritarian regimes that intervened massively in economic planning and kept tight control (by terror if necessary, as at Kwangju), not only of labor, as is the norm, but of capital as well (see chapter 4.2). The achievements of the NICs, constituting an "economic miracle," thereby illustrate the virtues of democracy and the free market. Thus the *New York Times* cites South Korea, Taiwan, Singapore, and Hong Kong to teach the lesson that "as an economic mechanism, democracy demonstrably works." And democratic socialist Dennis Wrong writes admiringly of the "striking capitalist successes" of the same grand democracies "under capitalist economies free from control by rickety authoritarian governments"—correct, in that the authoritarian state capitalist governments were efficient, powerful, and interventionist, not "rickety" (in contrast, he explains, Cuba, Nicaragua, and other officially designated enemies demonstrate the failure of Marxist-Leninist dogma, no other factor in their travail being detectable to the properly blinkered eye). *Washington Quarterly* editor Brad Roberts writes that "Nondemocratic governments have on the whole shown themselves incapable of providing the framework necessary for economic adaptation...," thinking perhaps of the NICs, or in earlier years, Hitler Germany—though in this case, we have to ask just what he means by "democratic," given his faith in "the US commitment to democracy abroad" and to the "protection of human rights," particularly in the 1980s.[39]

It is recognized that "economic miracles" have some attendant flaws. Discussing "Menem's Miracle" in Argentina, British correspondent John Simpson notes that "The miracle is not perfect." There are "unpleasant signs of corruption," "large sections of the middle class have sunk without trace" while "the new entrepeneurs and the old rich" happily shop in the "expensive shops," and there is substantial poverty. Unconstrained by the conventional reserve, James Petras and Pablo Pozzi fill in a few of the details. Since the onset of "Menem's Miracle" in 1989, "Neo-liberal private pillage has set up a system where individual wealth depends on public decay and economic regression," with some 40 percent of the economically active population unemployed or underemployed, proliferating shantytowns, factories closed and not replaced by new enterprises, exploitation of the state as "an instrument for personal enrichment and private pillage," reduction of expenditures for health, education and welfare to all time lows, negative growth rates, decreasing yearly rate of investment, and declining real wages. By now, over 60 percent of the 12 million inhabitants of Buenos Aires are not connected to the sewer system, one reason for the return of diseases that had been eradicated decades ago. The "speculative economy, reinforced by a neo-liberal economic policy, which impoverishes most of the population while destroying Argentina's internal market and productive capacity, and scarce resources has generated a Hobbesian world, a savage struggle to survive while the elite continue to reap windfall profits." The "privileged minority whose wealth, level of consumption and standard of living have flourished" are enthusiastic about the neoliberal policies. "Menem's miracle" also includes "privatization," the new shibboleth, but with a twist: thus the government sold the state telephone monopoly to Spanish and Italian state corporations, and the national airline to the Spanish government airline Iberia, so that "management is merely transferred from Argentine to Spanish and Italian bureaucrats," David Felix observes.[40]

In short, an "economic miracle," in the technical sense.

The proper deployment of these ideas is also illustrated in the case of Mexico, where another gratifying "economic miracle" is in process, though "'Economic Miracle' Has Yet to Reach Mexico's Poorest," a front-page headline reads, followed by the familiar story. Elsewhere we learn that wages are at their lowest level in history, having dropped 60 percent under the neoliberal policies of the 1980s (National Autonomous University (UNAM) Institute of Economic Research and other economists); that half of all newborns in Mexico City have lead levels in their blood high enough to impair neurological and motor-physical development; and that nutritional levels have sharply declined. GDP has risen since 1987, UNAM economists observe, "but this larger production of wealth advanced in one direction, contrary to the gradual impoverishing of millions of Mexicans," concentrating "in the hands of businessmen." The 1990 census reports that 60 percent of households were unable to cover basic needs. Despite the growth of maquila production (foreign-owned, export-oriented), "the industrial sector employs fewer people now than it did a decade ago," economist David Barkin writes, and labor's participation in personal income declined from 36 percent in the mid-'70s to 23 percent in 1992 while rewards for the rich and to foreign investors are "fabulous," developments that have "aroused the admiration of the international press."

Attempting to entice foreign investors, the Mexican Secretary of Commerce stressed the sharp decline of the price of labor in Mexico, from $1.38 per hour in 1982 to $0.45 in 1990, an appealing prospect for GM, Ford, Zenith, and other foreign corporations, along with the useful absence of effective environmental restrictions. The wage level is ensured by brutal government repression of labor, with the participation of corrupt union leaders linked closely to the one-party state. The 1980s have been a particularly dim era in that respect. Typical is the experience of Ford workers at one major plant. In 1987, Dan LaBotz observes in a study of labor rights in Mexico, "the company fired the entire work force, eliminated the union contract, and then rehired the workers at a far inferior salary. When the workers attempted to win the right to democratic union elections, and to fight for their legally mandated benefits, they were subjected to beatings, kidnappings, and murder blatantly conducted through collusion between the Ford Motor Company" and officials of the union run by the always-ruling party. These are little-discussed but critical features of the North American Free Trade Agreement (NAFTA), crafted so as to guarantee optimal conditions for profit, whatever the human cost may be.

Foreign debt is increasing, along with the trade deficit, electoral fraud, government repression to bar labor organizing or critical public commentary (murder of several journalists a year makes the message clearer still), and torture that is "endemic" according to Amnesty International. As NAFTA is currently designed "most Mexicans will become irrelevant," Barkin predicts in a review of the crisis that has resulted from "more than 35 years of *successful* capitalist development" oriented to the needs of domestic wealth and foreign capital. But foreign investors are happy, as is the business-professional sector that benefits. Mexico is therefore put forth by Secretary of State James Baker as "a model" for reform in Eastern Europe and the Third World, an authentic "economic miracle."[41]

Lead headlines herald the good news: "A Breath of Fresh Economic Air Brings Change to Latin America," though we also learn that "Latin Debt Load Keeps Climbing Despite Accords" (Nathaniel Nash, *NYT*). Another reads: "South Americans Find Economic Reform Has Initial Social Costs, People Say the New Wealth Is Slow to Trickle Down" (Thomas Kamm, *WSJ*). Just hang in there; all will be well. As usual, we do not learn that the famed "trickle down" policies have, in the past, produced a tiny trickle indeed, though read closely, the current reports indicate why the same can be expected this time around. The indicators look fine from Washington and Europe, Kamm reports, but they conceal rapid concentration of wealth, increased poverty including "critical poverty," declining real wages, and the other usual concomitants of "miracles." Former Brazilian President José Sarney writes that "in all countries" of Latin America, the foreign banks and other usual beneficiaries reap their rewards, "and what's left is unemployment, slave wages, and terrible social indicators." "The rich continue to get richer, the gap between them and the middle and lower classes widen," and none of the policies that are so promising "have been able to wipe out poverty" (Nash), a curious and unexpected failure to achieve their goal, we are to understand.[42]

The most phenomenal success story of all is Chile, with its "prospering free-market economy generated by Gen. August Pinochet" (Nash). That is an established truth, repeated everywhere. True, Pinochet was tough, but the "economic miracle" carried out by his Chicago Boys from 1974 to 1989 is there for all to see. To see, if they do not look too closely.

Pinochet's "miracle" turned into the "Chilean catastrophe" in under a decade, David Felix writes; virtually the entire banking system was taken over by the government in an attempt to salvage the economy, leading some to describe the transition from Allende to Pinochet as "a transition from utopian to scientific socialism, since the means of production are ending up in the hands of the state" (Felix), or "the Chicago Road to socialism." The militantly anti-socialist London *Economist Intelligence Unit* wrote that "the believer in free markets, President Pinochet, had a more comprehensive grip on the 'controlling heights of the economy' than

President Allende had dared dream of." The government-controlled portion of the economy in 1983 was comparable to the Allende years after the state took over failing enterprises, which it sold off at bargain rates to the private sector when they were resuscitated, along with efficient and profitable public enterprises that were generating 25 percent of the government's revenues, Joseph Collins and John Lear note. Multinational corporations did very nicely in the process, gaining control over large parts of the Chilean economy. Citing Chilean economists, James Petras and Steve Vieux report that "an estimated $600 million in subsidies were provided to purchasers in the 1986-1987 wave of privatizations," including "efficiently run, surplus-producing operations"; the operation is expected to reduce government surplus by $100 to $165 million during 1990-1995.

Until 1980, Chile's GDP per capita did not approach the 1972 (Allende) level, and investment was still below the late 1960s while unemployment was far higher. Per capita health care was more than halved from 1973 to 1985, setting off explosive growth in poverty-related diseases such as typhoid and viral hepatitis. Since 1973, consumption dropped 30 percent for the poorest 20 percent in Santiago and increased 15 percent for the top 20 percent. Private hospitals proudly display their high-tech equipment for the rich, while public ones offer mothers an appointment months away and medicines they cannot afford. College education, free for everyone under Allende, is now for the more privileged; and they will not be exposed to the "subversives" who have been purged, but offered "sociology, political science, and economics courses...more like religious instruction in the revealed truth of free markets and the red peril" (Tina Rosenberg), as in Brazil under the generals, or other places that come to mind. Macroeconomic statistics in the Pinochet years are generally below those for the preceding two decades; the average GNP growth from 1974-1979 was just over half that of 1961-1971, while per capita GNP fell 6.4 percent and per capita consumption 23 percent from 1972-1987. The capital city of Santiago is now "among the most polluted cities in the world," Nathaniel Nash observes, thanks to the free market Friedmanite model with its slogan "Produce, produce, produce," come what may—what we denounce as the "Stalinist model" when there are points to be scored thereby. What "came" was "the daunting cost of cleaning up, ...and the daunting cost of not cleaning up" in a country with "some of the world's dirtiest factories," no regulations, severe pollution of water supplies, and general environmental ruin with much-feared consequences for the health of the population.

And thanks to the miracle, along with a little US help in "making the economy scream" under the Allende government, the proportion of the population that fell below the poverty line (minimum income required for basic food and housing) increased from 20 percent to 44.4 percent from 1970 to 1987.

"Not much of a miracle," Edward Herman comments.[43]

In the bad old days, according to the doctrinal truths of 1992, our Latin American wards didn't listen to our sage counsel. Now, however, with the worldwide victory of economic liberalism and free trade, they understand, at last, the wisdom of our words. The chorus of self-adulation is untroubled by the usual problems, such as the fact that we never followed that model ourselves, nor did any other country that has developed except when it conferred advantage; and that contrary to the doctrine, Latin America quite commonly did follow our advice, as the review of Brazil illustrates. It is hardly the only case. The Kennedy-Johnson Alliance for Progress is another. One of its most highly touted success stories was Somoza's Nicaragua. The catastrophic "miracle" provided a popular base for the Sandinista revolution in 1979. The most respected Nicaraguan economist during the US war against Nicaragua was Francisco Mayorga, who became economic Czar under the US-backed UNO government (soon to be dispatched to oblivion when the recovery policies he initiated to much US acclaim proved an utter failure). During his day in the sun, the media and others who hailed Mayorga were careful to ignore his major scholarly work. This interesting 1986 study examined the failure of the "monetarist paradigm" that had been advocated and enthusiastically backed by the US, which left the economy "on the verge of collapse" by 1978, perhaps unresurrectable, Mayorga argued, no matter what economic policies had been pursued, even without the immense costs of US terror and economic warfare.[44]

Blithely ignoring all relevant facts (and crucially, the unmentionable US contribution), Latin America specialists in the press now inform us that "To the commercial pioneers of the post-Sandinista era, Nicaragua is ripe for a comeback after a decade of revolutionary mismanagement and two years of fiscal rehabilitation under President Violeta Chamorro" (Pamela Constable). True, businessmen still see problems, Constable notes: "the continuing threat of violence from labor unions" and armed factions in the countryside, and "the unresolved status of property" confiscated by the Sandinistas. But the "commercial pioneers" are optimistic. Particularly cheerful are private bankers and their clients. The Sandinistas nationalized banks "and began channeling state loans to farmers, rural cooperatives and small industry high-risk sectors," Tim Johnson writes in the *Miami Herald*. But, thankfully, such misbehavior is now over, and "the public is beginning to demand a lot more services from their banks," a private banker comments.

"The public" does not include the campesinos whose march against hunger was reported in the Mexican press a few days later, or the huge number of unemployed, or the children sniffing glue, or the semi-human figures celebrating the victory of capitalism and democracy while scavenging in the Managua garbage dump.

Shortly after, the government's National Development Bank (BND) announced a new credit policy under pressure from international lending institutions, *CAR* reported: "Under the Sandinista government, the BND provided subsidies and low-interest credit to cooperatives and small farmers with very few prerequisites, but those days are over." Now there will be "only guaranteed loans to clients with substantial collateral, leaving most peasant farmers out in the cold." Another feature of the new credit policy is that it "is expected to make it impossible for workers to pay off debts or make monthly bank payments on the companies they intend to buy." That will overcome a serious defect in the privatization process that the US demands as a condition for calling off its economic warfare: under the evil influence of the Sandinistas, the process allowed the wrong class of people—workers in the enterprise—to gain a share in ownership. That is quite improper, and inconsistent with the concept of "economic miracle."

To be sure, traditional US idealism will see to it that free market policies are not carried to excessive lengths: "the BND is considering financing large producers...at up to 70 percent of production costs," *CAR* notes.

The guiding US hand can also be seen in the measures to overcome "the unresolved status of property" that troubles the "commercial pioneers" and their cheerleaders in the US press. *Envío* reports that "The retrenching of the state banks towards medium- and large-scale production became evident in 1991, when the BND closed 16 branch offices in small towns throughout the country's central regions. Traditional financing mechanisms such as usury credit, futures sales, and sharecropping—whose costs to the peasantry are well-known—are coming into use again." Campesinos will be forced to leave their land, and it will return to its rightful owners.

To help the natural evolution along, the Army and National Police have been "utilizing all forms of violence and humiliation" to evacuate rural farmers from their lands, *CAR* reports; these lands had been distributed by constitutional decrees introduced by the Sandinistas, under which "farmlands and other properties abandoned or liquidated...were parceled out to landless campesinos in the form of small family subsistence plots or cooperative farms." In June 1992, 21 farms were violently "cleaned out" by the security forces, to be returned to their former owners; in 11 cases, to members of the Somoza family, according to the Nicaraguan Center for Human Rights (CENIDH). On June 30, *CAR* continues, 300 police and army troops "violently evicted 40 campesino families" with attack dogs, beating men, women, and children and threatening to kill campesinos who did not leave, burning homes and crops, and arresting activists of the Rural Workers Association. The security forces have imposed "a state of terror and blackmail" to prevent campesinos from organizing, CENIDH charged.

The police are now almost half ex-contras, it is estimated. The US failure to regain total control of the security forces has caused much outrage in Washington and the press. One major reason for the US war against Nicaragua was to restore that traditional control, so that the security forces can once again impose the "regional standards" of El Salvador, Guatemala, and Honduras, as in the Somoza days.[45]

Since the US-backed UNO government won the February 1990 election, rural poverty has "drastically increased" because of the acceleration of neoliberal policies, which has "wreaked havoc on Nicaragua's small and medium-sized farmers," *CAR* reports. In much of the countryside, people are "becoming more desperate each day, with more than 70 percent of the children in these areas suffering malnutrition and between 65 percent to 89 percent of the population unemployed." In the Atlantic Coast region, "not only are farmers suffering, but fishermen are losing 80 percent of their livelihood to foreign companies which the UNO government has authorized to fish in the Atlantic Coast waters." Serious diseases that were eradicated under the Sandinistas are now common in the region, where 90 percent of residents are unable to satisfy basic needs. A representative of the National Union of Farmers and Cattle Ranchers (UNAG) says that the stringent credit requirements for peasant farmers "are killing us": "Large nontraditional farms get all the funding they need, but a subsistence farmer growing beans or corn to feed his family is allowed to go bankrupt and starve." Thirty-two-thousand families are surviving on "roots and empty tortillas with salt," UNAG reports. Opening of the economy, reeling under the impact of the US embargo and the terrorist war, has "forced Nicaragua's homegrown industries to compete with giant multinational companies," John Otis observes. As the country is flooded with foreign products, small industries have declined from 3800 when Chamorro took office to 2500 two years later; Nicaragua even imports its own national beer from Wisconsin, under a Nicaraguan label. Importers, middlemen, luxury goods shops, and the local wealthy are doing fine, along with the foreigners for whom the policies are designed. The rest can wait for "trickle down," including the 50 percent or more unemployed.[46]

Per capita income has fallen to the level of 1945; real wages amount to 13 percent of their 1980 value, still falling. Infant mortality and low birth weight are increasing, reversing earlier progress. The reduction of the health care budget by 40 percent in March 1991 has seriously affected the already insufficient supply of medicines. Hospitals for the general public barely function, though the rich can have what they need as the country returns to the "Central American mode." "The right to health care no longer exists in post-war Nicaragua," apart from those rich enough to pay, the Evangelical Church (CEPAD) reports. A survey of prostitutes found that 80 percent had taken up the trade in the last year, many of them teenagers.

In May 1992, the US Congress suspended over $100 million of already approved aid, objecting to alleged government assistance to Sandinista organizations and failure to return property to former owners. "Extraofficially, it was learned that the government will give priority to United States citizens, to prominent Nicaraguan business people and to leaders of the former contras," the Mexican press reported, notably the North American Rosario Mining Co., which claims the gold mining installations in the northeast. The central issue is "whether the more than 100,000 peasant families who received land or title to land which they were already working under the Sandinista Administration will be able to keep their lands," as had been promised in the UNO program, Lisa Haugaard of the Central American Historical Institute observes.

Another issue is the independence of the security forces. In accord with longstanding policy, Washington insists that they be under US control—that Sandinista officials be dismissed, to use the code words preferred by government-media propaganda. Other industrial countries, not having the traditional interest in running "our little region over here," dismiss these demands as absurd, considering the Sandinista FSLN to be a "solidly structured [party] with a significant political weight," the only large popular-based party in the country (Detlev Nolte, head of Germany's Institute of Ibero-American Studies). They object to the US policy of "again polarizing the situation," another German Latin American specialist adds. When the congressional hold on aid was dropped, the Bush Administration held it back anyway, in line with its deep commitment to bar even a minimal show of independence.[47]

As we gaze on what we have accomplished and envision the glorious future that awaits, we can take pride in "having served as an inspiration for the triumph of democracy in our time," as the *New Republic* exulted after the elections had been won by "the right side" in Nicaragua, a "level playing field" having been established by Washington's stern warning that any other outcome would be followed by continued economic strangulation and terror. We can, in short, join the editors in their praise for Washington's terror and violence, giving "Reagan & Co. good marks" for the gratifying mounds of mutilated corpses and hordes of starving children in Central America, recognizing, as they advised, that we must send military aid to "Latin-style fascists... regardless of how many are murdered" because "there are higher American priorities than Salvadoran human rights."[48]

Recall that in accord with official convention, the economic catastrophe of the past years in Latin America is the result of statism, populism, Marxism, and other evils, now to be cured by the newly discovered virtues of monetarism and the free market. This picture is "a complete fabrication," James Petras and Steve Vieux point out. The highly-touted new discoveries are just those that have led to catastrophe in the past—with no little aid from US-sponsored terror and economic warfare. Furthermore, neoliberal dogma has ruled for years in these US-run "testing areas." Social expenditures dropped sharply from 1980, leading to public health disaster and educational collapse, except for the rich; growth stagnated or declined. There was one area of progress: privatization, providing great advantages to wealthy sectors at home and abroad, and diminishing public revenues still further when "efficiently run, surplus-producing operations" were sold off, as in Chile. "The brutal austerity programs of the 1980s were obviously the work of doctrinaire neoliberals," they point out, and the "dismal results" are directly traceable to their ideological fervor. The huge debt accumulated through the partnership of domestic military-economic elites and foreign banks awash with petrodollars is to be paid by the poor. "Wage earners sacrificed the most in making available the surplus needed to make payments on the external debt," the UN World Economic Survey 1990 observed.

"More than any geographic area in the world," correspondent Marc Cooper writes, "Latin America over the past decade took seriously the promise of the Reagan revolution"—not quite by choice. The decade was marked by privatization, deregulation, "free trade," destruction of unions and popular organizations, opening of resources (including national parks and reserves) to foreign investors, and all the rest of the package. The effects have been disastrous, predictably.[49]

The celebration in the doctrinal institutions is also entirely predictable. Blame for past catastrophes has to be shifted to the shoulders of others. Any role that the US masters have played is, by definition, marginal at most, to be attributed to Cold War imperatives. And as the old doctrines produce new "economic miracles," there is every reason for the ideologues of privilege to applaud, as they always have, and as they will continue to do as long as power offers them that task.

CHAPTER 8

THE TRAGEDY OF HAITI

1. "The First Free Nation of Free Men"

"Haiti was more than the New World's second oldest republic," anthropologist Ira Lowenthal observed, "more than even the first black republic of the modern world. Haiti was the first *free* nation of *free* men to arise within, and in resistance to, the emerging constellation of Western European empire." The interaction of the New World's two oldest republics for 200 years again illustrates the persistence of basic themes of policy, their institutional roots and cultural concomitants.

The Republic of Haiti was established on January 1, 1804, after a slave revolt expelled the French colonial rulers and their allies. The revolutionary chiefs discarded the French "Saint-Domingue" in favor of the name used by the people who had greeted Columbus in 1492, as he arrived to establish his first settlement in Europe's New World. The descendants of the original inhabitants could not celebrate the liberation. They had been reduced to a few hundred within 50 years from a pre-Colombian population estimated variously from hundreds of thousands to 8 million, with none remaining at all, according to contemporary French scholars, when France took the western third of Hispaniola, now Haiti, from Spain in 1697. The leader of the revolt, Toussaint L'Ouverture, could not celebrate the victory either. He had been captured by deceit and sent to a French prison to die a "slow death from cold and misery," in the words of a 19th century French historian. Medical anthropologist Paul Farmer observes that Haitian schoolchildren to this day know by heart his final words as he was led to prison: "In overthrowing me, you have cut down in Saint-Domingue only the tree of liberty. It will spring up again by the roots for they are numerous and deep."[1]

The tree of liberty broke through the soil again in 1985, as the population revolted against the murderous Duvalier dictatorship. After many bitter struggles, the popular revolution led to the overwhelming victory of Haiti's first freely elected president, the populist priest Jean-Bertrand Aristide. Seven months after his February 1991 inauguration he was driven from office by the military and commercial elite who had ruled for 200 years, and would not tolerate loss of their traditional rights of terror and exploitation.

"As soon as the last Duvalier had fled Haiti," Puerto Rican ethnohistorian Jalil Sued-Badillo recounts, "an angry crowd toppled the statue of Christopher Columbus in Port-au-Prince and threw it in the sea," protesting "the ravages of colonialism" under "a long line of despots" from Columbus to Duvalier, and on to today's rulers, who have reinstated Duvalier savagery. There were similar scenes in the neighboring Dominican Republic, subjected to a US-imposed terror regime after another Marine invasion in 1965 and a victim of IMF Fundamentalism from the early 1980s. In February 1992, President Balaguer "unleashed his security forces to beat peaceful demonstrators who were protesting the exorbitant expenditures shelled out for the 500-year celebration while the average Dominican starves," the Council on Hemispheric Affairs reported. Its centerpiece is a multi-million-dollar 100-foot-high half-mile-long recumbent cross with powerful search-lights that "rises above a slum of rat-infested shacks where malnourished, illiterate children slosh through the fetid water that washes through the streets during tropical rainstorms," the news services reported. Slums were cleared to accommodate its sprawling terraced gardens, and a stone wall conceals "the desperate poverty that its beams will soon illuminate." The huge expenses "coincide with one of the worst economic crises since the '30s," the former president of the Central Bank pointed out. After ten years of structural adjustment, health care and education have radically declined, electricity cutoffs up to 24 hours are used to ration power, unemployment exceeds 25 percent, and poverty is rampant. "The big fish eat the little ones," one old women says in the nearby slum.[2]

Columbus described the people he found as "lovable, tractable, peaceable, gentle, decorous," and their land as rich and bountiful. Hispaniola was "perhaps the most densely populated place in the world," Las Casas wrote, "a beehive of people," who "of all the infinite universe of humanity, ...are the most guileless, the most devoid of wickedness and duplicity." Driven by "insatiable greed and ambition," the Spanish fell upon them "like ravening wild beasts, ... killing, terrorizing, afflicting, torturing, and destroying the native peoples" with "the strangest and most varied new methods of cruelty, never seen or heard of before, and to such a degree" that the population is barely 200 persons, he wrote in 1552, "from my own knowledge of the acts I witnessed." "It was a general rule among Spaniards to be cruel," he wrote: "not just cruel, but extraordinarily cruel so that harsh and bitter treatment would prevent Indians from daring to think of themselves as human beings." "As they saw themselves each day perishing by the cruel and inhuman treatment of the Spaniards, crushed to the earth by the horses, cut in pieces by swords, eaten and torn by dogs, many buried alive and suffering all kinds of exquisite tortures, ...[they] decided to abandon themselves to their unhappy fate with no further struggles, placing themselves in the hands of their enemies that they might do with them as they liked."

As the propaganda mills ground away, the picture was revised to provide retrospective justification for what had been done. By 1776, the story was that Columbus found "nothing but a country quite covered with wood, uncultivated, and inhabited only by some tribes of naked and miserable savages" (Adam Smith). As noted earlier, it was not until the 1960s that the truth began to break through, eliciting scorn and protest from outraged loyalists.[3]

The Spanish effort to plunder the island's riches by enslaving its gentle people were unsuccessful; they died too quickly, if not killed by the "wild beasts" or in mass suicide. African slaves were sent from the early 1500s, later in a flood as the plantation economy was established. "Saint Domingue was the wealthiest European colonial possession in the Americas," Hans Schmidt writes, producing three-quarters of the world's sugar by 1789, also leading the world in production of coffee, cotton, indigo, and rum. The slave masters provided France with enormous wealth from the labor of their 450,000 slaves, much as in the British West Indian colonies. The white population, including poor overseers and artisans, numbered 40,000. Some 30,000 mulattoes and free Negroes enjoyed economic privileges but not social and political equality, the origins of the class difference that led to harsh repression after independence, with renewed violence today.

Cubans may have seemed "of dubious whiteness," but the rebels who overthrew colonial rule did not approach that status. The slave revolt, which had reached serious proportions by the end of 1791, appalled Europe, as well as the European outpost that had just declared its own independence. Britain invaded in 1793; victory would offer "a monopoly of sugar, indigo, cotton and coffee" from an island which "for ages, would give such aid and force to industry as would be most happily felt in every part of the empire," a British military officer wrote to Prime Minister Pitt. The United States, which had lively commerce with the French colony, sent its French rulers $750,000 in military aid as well as some troops to help quell the revolt. France dispatched a huge army, including Polish, Dutch, German, and Swiss troops. Its commander finally wrote Napoleon that it would be necessary to wipe out virtually the entire black population to impose French rule. His campaign failed, and Haiti became the only case in history "of an enslaved people breaking its own chains and using military might to beat back a powerful colonial power" (Farmer).

The rebellion had broad consequences. It established British dominance of the Caribbean, and impelled its former colonies a long step further on their westward course as Napoleon, abandoning his hopes for an empire in the New World, sold the Louisiana territory to the United States. The rebel victory came at tremendous cost. Much of the agricultural wealth of the country was destroyed, along with perhaps a third of the population. The victory horrified Haiti's slave-holding neighbors, who backed France's claims for huge reparations, finally accepted in 1825 by Haiti's ruling elite, who recognized them to be a precondition for entry into the global market. The result was "decades of French domination of Haitian finance" with "a catastrophic effect on the new nation's delicate economy," Farmer observes. France then recognized Haiti, as did Britain in 1833. Simon Bolívar, whose struggles against Spanish rule were aided by the Haitian Republic on condition that he free slaves, refused to establish diplomatic relations with Haiti on becoming President of Greater Colombia, claiming that Haiti was "fomenting racial conflict"—a refusal "typical of Haiti's welcome in a monolithically racist world," Farmer comments. Haitian elites continued to be haunted by fear of conquest and a renewal of slavery, a factor in their costly and destructive invasions of the Dominican Republic in the 1850s.

The US was the last major power to insist that Haiti be ostracized, recognizing it only in 1862. With the American Civil War underway, Haiti's liberation of slaves no longer posed a barrier to recognition; on the contrary, President Lincoln and others saw Haiti as a place that might absorb blacks induced to leave the United States (Liberia was recognized in the same year, in part for the same reason). Haitian ports were used for Union operations against the rebels. Haiti's strategic role in control of the Caribbean became increasingly important in US planning in later years, as Haiti became a plaything among the competing imperial powers. Meanwhile its ruling elite monopolized trade, while the peasant producers in the interior remained isolated from the outside world.

2. "Unselfish Intervention"

Between 1849 and 1913, US Navy ships entered Haitian waters 24 times to "protect American lives and property." Haiti's independence was scarcely given even "token recognition," Schmidt observes in his standard history, and there was little consideration for the rights of its people. They are "an inferior people," unable "to maintain the degree of civilization left them by the French or to develop any capacity of self government entitling them to international respect and confidence," Assistant Secretary of State

William Phillips wrote, recommending the policy of invasion and US military government that President Woodrow Wilson soon adopted. Few words need be wasted on the civilization left to 90 percent of the population by the French, who, as an ex-slave related, "hung up men with heads downward, drowned them in sacks, crucified them on planks, buried them alive, crushed them in mortars..., forced them to eat shit, ... cast them alive to be devoured by worms, or onto anthills, or lashed them to stakes in the swamp to be devoured by mosquitos, ...threw them into boiling cauldrons of cane syrup"—when not "flaying them with the lash" to extract the wealth that helped give France its entry ticket to the rich men's club.

Phillips captured prevailing attitudes with accuracy, though some, like Secretary of State William Jennings Bryan, found the Haitian elite rather amusing: "Dear me, think of it, Niggers speaking French," he remarked. The effective ruler of Haiti, Marine Colonel L.W.T. Waller, who arrived fresh from appalling atrocities in the conquest of the Philippines, was not amused: "they are real nigger and no mistake...real nigs beneath the surface," he said, rejecting any negotiations or other "bowing and scraping to these coons," particularly the educated Haitians for whom this blood-thirsty lout had a special hatred. Assistant Secretary of the Navy Franklin Delano Roosevelt, while never approaching the racist fanaticism and thuggery of his distant relative Theodore Roosevelt, shared the feelings of his colleagues. On a visit to occupied Haiti in 1917, he recorded in his diary a comment by his travelling companion, who later became the Occupation's leading civilian official. Fascinated by the Haitian Minister of Agriculture, he "couldn't help saying to myself," he told FDR, "that man would have brought $1,500 at auction in New Orleans in 1860 for stud purposes." "Roosevelt appears to have relished the story," Schmidt notes, "and retold it to American Minister Norman Armour when he visited Haiti as President in 1934." The element of racism in policy formation should not be discounted, to the present day.

Such thoughts were not unusual at the time of Wilson's intervention, not only in the United States. We may recall that shortly after, Winston Churchill authorized the use of chemical weapons "against recalcitrant Arabs as experiment," denouncing the "squeamishness" of those who objected to "using poisoned gas against uncivilised tribes," mainly Kurds, a policy that he strongly favored, expecting that it "would spread a lively terror." For England itself, he had somewhat different plans. As Home Secretary in 1910 he had secretly proposed sterilization of 100,000 "mental degenerates" and the dispatch of tens of thousands of others to state-run labor camps so as to save the "British race" from inevitable decline if its "inferior" members are allowed to breed—ideas that were within the bounds of enlightened opinion of the day, but have been kept secret in Home Office files because of their sensitivity, particularly after they were taken up by Hitler.[4]

Given the cultural climate of the day, the character of Wilson's 1915 invasion comes as no great surprise. It was even more savage and destructive than his invasion of the Dominican Republic in the same years. Wilson's troops murdered, destroyed, reinstituted virtual slavery, and demolished the constitutional system. After ruling for 20 years, the US left "the inferior people" in the hands of the National Guard it had established and the traditional rulers. In the 1950s, the Duvalier dictatorship took over, running the show in Guatemalan style, always with firm US support.

The brutality and racism of the invaders, and the dispossession of peasants as US corporations took over the spoils, elicited resistance. The Marine response was savage, including the first recorded instance of coordinated air-ground combat: bombing of rebels (Cacos) who were surrounded by Marines in the bush. An in-house Marine inquiry, undertaken after atrocities were publicly revealed, found that 3250 rebels were killed, at least 400 executed, while the Marines and their locally recruited gendarmerie suffered 98 casualties (killed and wounded). Leaked Marine orders call for an end to "indiscriminate killing of natives" that "has gone on for some time." Haitian historian Roger Gaillard estimates total deaths at 15,000, counting victims "of repression and *consequences* of the war," which "resembled a massacre." Major Smedley Butler recalled that his troops "hunted the Cacos like pigs." His exploits impressed FDR, who ordered that he be awarded the Congressional Medal of Honor for an engagement in which 200 Cacos were killed and no prisoners taken, while one Marine was struck by a rock and lost two teeth.

The leader of the revolt, Charlemagne Péralte, was killed by Marines who sneaked into his camp at night in disguise. In an attempt at psywar that prefigured some of Colonel Edward Lansdale's later exploits in the Philippines, the Marines circulated photos of his body in the hope of demoralizing the guerrillas. The tactic backfired, however; the photo resembled Christ on the cross, and became a nationalist symbol. Péralte took his place in the nationalist Pantheon alongside of Toussaint.

The invaders "legalized" the Occupation with a unilateral declaration they called a "treaty," which the client regime was forced to accept; it was then cited as imposing on the US a solemn commitment to maintain the Occupation. While supervising the takeover of Haiti and the Dominican Republic, Wilson built his reputation as a lofty idealist defending self-determination and the rights of small nations with impressive oratory. There is no contradiction. Wilsonian doctrine was restricted to people of the right sort: those "at a low stage of civilization" need not apply, though the civilized colonial powers should give them "friendly protection, guidance, and assistance," he explained. Wilson's Fourteen Points did not call for self-determination and national independence, but rather held that in questions of sovereignty, "the interests of the populations concerned must have equal weight with the equitable claims of the government whose title is to be determined," the colonial ruler. The interests of the populations "would be ascertained by the advanced nations, who best comprehended the needs and welfare of the less advanced peoples," William Stivers comments, analyzing the actual import of Wilson's language and thinking. To mention one case with long-term consequences, a supplicant who sought Wilson's support for Vietnamese representation in the French Parliament was chased away from his doors with the appeal undelivered, later surfacing under the name Ho Chi Minh.[5]

Another achievement of Wilson's occupation was a new Constitution, imposed on the hapless country after its National Assembly was dissolved by the Marines for refusing to ratify it. The US-designed Constitution overturned laws preventing foreigners from owning land, thus enabling US corporations to take what they wanted. FDR later took credit for having written the Constitution, falsely it appears, though he did hope to be one of its beneficiaries, intending to use Haiti "for his own personal enrichment," Schmidt notes. Ten years later, in 1927, the State Department conceded that the US had used "rather highhanded methods to get the Constitution adopted by the people of Haiti" (with 99.9 percent approval in a Marine-run plebiscite, under 5 percent of the population participating). But these methods were unavoidable: "It was obvious that if our occupation was to be beneficial to Haiti and further her progress it was necessary that foreign capital should come to Haiti..., [and] Americans could hardly be expected to put their money into plantations and big agricultural enterprises in Haiti if they could not themselves own the land on which their money was to be spent." It was out of a sincere desire to help the poor Haitians that the US forced them to allow US investors to take the country over, the State Department explained, the usual form that benevolence assumes.

Elections were not permitted because it was recognized that anti-American candidates would win, hindering the US programs to help the suffering people. These programs were described as "An Experiment in Pragmatism" by one not untypical intellectual commentator, who observed that "The pragmatists insist that intelligent guidance from without may sometimes accelerate the process of national growth and save much waste." We have already seen some illustrations of that "intelligent guidance" in the case of beneficiaries from Bengal to Brazil and Guatemala. We turn to the Haitian experience in the next chapter.[6]

The Occupation "consistently suppressed local democratic institutions and denied elementary political liberties," Schmidt writes. "Instead of building from existing democratic institutions which, on paper, were quite impressive and had long incorporated the liberal democratic philosophy and governmental machinery associated with the French Revolution, the United States blatantly overrode them and illegally forced through its own authoritarian, antidemocratic system." "The establishment of foreign-dominated plantation agriculture necessitated destruction of the existing minifundia land-tenure system with its myriad peasant freeholders," who were forced into peonage. The US supported "a minority of collaborators" from the local elite who admired European fascism but lacked the mass appeal of their fascist models. "In effect," Schmidt observes, "the Occupation embodied all the progressive attitudes of contemporary Italian fascism, but was crippled by failures in human relationships" (lack of popular support). The only local leadership it could mobilize was the traditional mulatto elite, its racist contempt for the great mass of the population now heightened by the even harsher attitudes of "ethnic and racial contempt" of the foreigner with the gun and the dollar, who brought "concepts of racial discrimination" not seen since before independence, and the "racist colonial realities" that went along with them.

The Occupation thus reinforced the internal class/race oppression that goes back to the days of French colonialism. One consequence was the rise of the ideology of *Noirisme,* in response to the racism of the occupiers and their elite collaborators. "Papa Doc" Duvalier would later exploit this backlash when, 20 years after the Marines left, he took the reins with the pretense of handing power to the black majority—in reality, to himself, his personal killers (the Tontons Macoutes), and the traditional elite, who continued to prosper under his murderous kleptocracy.

"The Occupation worsened the economic crisis by augmenting the peasantry's forced contribution to the maintenance of the State," Haitian historian Michel-Rolph Trouillot writes. "It worsened the crisis of power by centralizing the Haitian army and disarming [citizens in] the provinces," "putting in place the structures of military, fiscal, and commercial centralization" that were to yield a "bloody finale" under the Duvalier dynasty.

Through the bloodiest years of the occupation, the media were silent or supportive. The *New York Times* index has no entries for Haiti for 1917-1918. In a press survey, John Blassingame found "widespread editorial support" for the repeated interventions in Haiti and the Dominican Republic from 1904 to 1919, until major atrocity stories surfaced in 1920, setting off congressional inquiry. Haitians and Dominicans were described as "coons," "mongrels," "unwholesome," "a horde of naked niggers," the Haitians even more "retrograde" than the Dominicans. They needed "energetic Anglo-Saxon influence." "We are simply going in there...to help our black brother put his disorderly house in order," one journal wrote. Furthermore, The US had a right to intervene to protect "our peace and safety" (*New York Times*).

Times editors lauded the "unselfish and helpful" attitude that the US had always shown, now once again as it responded "in a fatherly way" as Haiti "sought help here." Our "unselfish intervention has been moved almost exclusively by a desire to give the benefits of peace to people tormented by repeated revolutions," with no thought of "preferential advantages, commercial or otherwise," for ourselves. "The people of the island should realize that [the US government] is their best friend." The US sought only to ensure that "the people were cured of the habit of insurrection and taught how to work and live"; they "would have to be reformed, guided and educated," and this "duty was undertaken by the United States." There is a further benefit for our "black brother": "To wean these peoples away from their shot-gun habit of government is to safeguard them against our own exasperation," which might lead to further intervention. "The good-will and unselfish purposes of our own government" are demonstrated by the consequences, the editors wrote in 1922, when they were all too apparent and the Marine atrocities had already aroused a storm of protest.

Some contemporary scholars adopt the same stance. As Haiti reentered the sphere of public awareness with the fall of Duvalier, Harvard historian David Landes presented some background, explaining that the Marines had "provided the stability needed to make the political system work and to facilitate trade with the outside," though "even a benevolent occupation creates resistance...among the beneficiaries" and protest by "more enlightened members of the dominant society," a constant problem faced by benefactors. Another noted scholar, Professor Hewson Ryan of the Fletcher School of Law and Diplomacy, was even more effusive in his praise for what we had accomplished in "two centuries of well-intentioned involvement." Indeed, he observed, Haiti has been uniquely privileged: "Few nations have been the object over such a sustained period of so much well-intentioned guidance and support." He described the achievements with no little awe, particularly our kind insistence on eliminating such "unprogressive" features of the constitutional system as the provisions against takeover of lands by foreigners.[7]

With the barriers to foreign ownership of the country now overcome—admittedly, by somewhat "high handed methods"—US investors quickly moved in to take large tracts of land for new plantations. Extremely cheap labor was another inducement. A New York business daily described Haiti in 1926 as "a marvelous opportunity for American investment": "The run-of-the-mill Haitian is handy, easily directed, and gives a hard day's labor for 20 cents, while in Panama the same day's work cost $3." These advantages gained prominence as the remnants of Haiti's agricultural wealth were steadily destroyed. From the 1960s, assembly operations for US corporations grew rapidly in the Caribbean region, in Haiti, from 13 companies in 1966 to 154 in 1981. These enterprises furnished about 40 percent of Haitian exports (100 percent having been primary commodities in 1960), though limited employment or other benefits for Haitians, apart from new opportunities for enrichment for the traditional elite.

In the 1980s, IMF Fundamentalism began to take its customary toll as the economy deteriorated under the impact of the structural adjustment programs, which caused agricultural production to decline along with investment, trade and consumption. Poverty became still more terrible. By the time "Baby Doc" Duvalier was driven out in 1986, 60 percent of the population had an annual per capita income of $60 or less according to the World Bank, child malnutrition had soared, the rate of infant mortality was shockingly high, and the country had become an ecological and human disaster, perhaps beyond hope of recovery. Through the 1970s, thousands of boat people fled the ravaged island, virtually all forced to return by US officials with little notice here, the usual treatment of refugees whose suffering lacks propaganda value. In 1981, the Reagan Administration initiated a new interdiction policy. Of the more than 24,000 Haitians intercepted by the US Coast Guard in the next ten years, 11 were granted asylum as victims of political persecution, in comparison with 75,000 out of 75,000 Cubans. During Aristide's brief tenure, the flow of refugees dropped dramatically as terror abated and there were hopes for a better future. The US response was to approve far more asylum claims. Twenty-eight had been allowed during the ten years of Duvalier and post-Duvalier terror; 20 during Aristide's seven and a half months in office. After Aristide's overthrow, a new surge of boat people reached several thousand a month, most of them forcibly returned in callous disregard of the grim circumstances that awaited them. For the few permitted to apply for asylum under a new policy, treatment was hardly better. One of the first was an Aristide supporter whose application was rejected on the grounds that he suffered only "petty harassment" when soldiers raked his home with gunfire and destroyed his shop.

A USAID-World Bank development strategy was initiated in 1981-1982, based on assembly plant and agro-industrial exports. The effect was to shift

30 percent of cultivated land from food for local consumption to export crops. AID forecast "a historic change toward deeper market interdependence with the United States" in this rising "Taiwan of the Caribbean." A 1985 World Bank report, "Haiti: Policy Proposals for Growth," developed the usual ideas further, calling for an export-oriented development strategy, with domestic consumption "markedly restrained in order to shift the required share of output increases into exports." Emphasis should be placed on "the expansion of private enterprises," the Bank recommended. Costs for education should be "minimized," and such "social objectives" as persist should be privatized. "Private projects with high economic returns should be strongly supported" in preference to "public expenditures in the social sectors," and "less emphasis should be placed on social objectives which increase consumption"—"temporarily," until the famed trickle-down effects are detected, some time after the Messiah arrives. The recommendations, it is understood, are a precondition to aid, and a bright future is sure to follow.

Of the array of predictions, one came to pass: the intended migration of the rural population to urban areas, and for many, to leaky boats attempting the dangerous 800-mile passage to Florida, to face forcible return if they make it (many don't). Haiti remains Haiti, not Taiwan.

Reviewing US aid and development strategy for Haiti, Amy Wilentz writes that it "achieves two strategic U.S. goals—one, a restructured and dependent agriculture that exports to U.S. markets and is open to American exploitation, and the other, a displaced rural population that not only can be employed in offshore U.S. industries in the towns, but is more susceptible to army control."[8]

4. "Politics, not Principle"

In June 1985, the Haitian legislature unanimously adopted a new law requiring that every political party must recognize President-for-Life Jean-Claude Duvalier as the supreme arbiter of the nation, outlawing the Christian Democrats, and granting the government the right to suspend the rights of any party without reasons. The law was ratified by a majority of 99.98 percent. Washington was impressed. It was "an encouraging step forward," the US Ambassador informed his guests at a July 4 celebration. The Reagan Administration certified to Congress that "democratic development" was progressing, so that military and economic aid could continue to flow—mainly into the pockets of Baby Doc and his entourage. The Administration also informed Congress that the human rights situation was improving, as it always is when some regime requires military aid to suppress the population in a good cause. The Democrat-controlled House Foreign Affairs Committee had given its approval in advance, calling on the Administration "to maintain friendly relations with Duvalier's non-Communist government."

These gratifying developments were short-lived, however. By December, popular protests were straining the resources of state terror. What happened next was described by the *Wall Street Journal* two months later with engaging frankness:

> An administration official said that the White House concluded late last year, following huge demonstrations that hadn't been seen on such a scale before, that the regime was unraveling...U.S. analysts learned that Haiti's ruling inner circle had lost faith in the 34-year-old president for life. As a result, U.S. officials, including Secretary of State George Shultz, began openly calling for a "democratic process" in Haiti.

The cynicism was underscored by the fact that the very same scenario was then being enacted in the Philippines, where the army and elite made it clear they would no longer support another gangster for whom Reagan and Bush had expressed their admiration, even "love," not long before, so that the White House "began openly calling for a 'democratic process'" there as well. Both events have, accordingly, entered the canon as a demonstration of how, particularly in the 1980s, we have "served as inspiration for the triumph of democracy in our time" (*New Republic*).[9]

Duvalier was duly removed, flown out in a US Air Force jet and sent to comfortable exile in France. Armed Forces chief General Henri Namphy took power. This long-time US favorite and close Duvalier associate was "Haiti's best chance for democracy," Assistant Secretary of State Elliott Abrams announced, revealing once again the dedication to democracy for which he was famous. Not all were pleased. A rural priest in a small church, Father Jean-Bertrand Aristide, said that "we're glad Duvalier is gone" but "what we now have is Duvalierism without Duvalier." Few listened, but events were to prove him right in short order.

Elections were scheduled for November 1987, but Namphy and his associates, the army and the old elite, were determined that nothing would go wrong. The Tontons Macoutes were reorganized, terror continued. A particularly gruesome massacre took place in July 1987, involving the army and the Macoutes. The same groups sponsored escalating violence, leading up to an election day massacre that provided Namphy with a pretext to cancel the elections. Throughout, US military aid continued on grounds that it helped the army keep order—which was disrupted by army-Macoute violence and atrocities. Military aid was finally suspended after the election day terror, with over 95 percent of the 1987 funds already disbursed.

A fraudulent military-run election followed, then a coup restoring Namphy to power and a rash of Duvalierism-without-Duvalier atrocities by the army and Macoutes, including repeated attacks on union offices and peasant groups. Asked about these events by US human-rights organizations, Ambassador Brunson McKinley said, "I don't see any evidence of a policy against human rights." True, there is violence, but it is just "part of the culture." Whose, one might wonder.[10]

A month later, a gang of killers attacked Aristide's church as he was saying mass, leaving at least 13 dead and 77 wounded. Aristide fled underground. In yet another coup, Duvalierist General Prosper Avril arrested Namphy and expelled him. The Haitian head of Aristide's Salesian order authorized him to return to his church, but not for long. To the dismay of the conservative Church hierarchy, Aristide continued to call for freedom and an end to terror. He was duly ordered by his superiors in Rome to leave the country. Popular protests blocked his departure, and he went into hiding. At the last minute, Aristide decided to take part in the December 1990 elections. In a stunning upset, he won 67 percent of the vote, defeating the US candidate, former World Bank official Marc Bazin, who came in second with 14 percent. The courageous liberation theologist, committed to "the preferential option for the poor" of the Latin American bishops, took office in February as the first democratically elected President in Haiti's history—briefly; he was overthrown by a military coup on September 30.

"Under Aristide, for the first time in the republic's tortured history, Haiti seemed to be on the verge of tearing free from the fabric of despotism and tyranny which had smothered all previous attempts at democratic expression and self-determination," the Washington Council on Hemispheric Affairs observed in a post-coup review. His victory "represented more than a decade of civic engagement and education on his part," spearheaded by local activists of the Church, small grassroots-based communities, and other popular organizations that formed the basis of the Lavalas ("flood") movement that swept him into power, "a textbook example of participatory, 'bottom-up' and democratic political development." With this popular base, his government was committed to "the empowerment of the poor," a "populist model" with international implications that frightened Washington, whose model of "democracy" does not entertain popular movements committed to "social and economic justice, popular political participation and openness in all governmental affairs" rather than "the international market or some other current shibboleth." Furthermore, Aristide's balancing of the budget and "trimming of a bloated bureaucracy" led to a "stunning success" that made White House planners "extremely uncomfortable": he secured over half a billion dollars in aid from the international lending community, very little of it from the US, indicating "that Haiti was slipping out of Washington's financial orbit" and "demonstrating a degree of sovereignty in its political affairs." A rotten apple was in the making.[11]

Washington was definitely not pleased. With its ally Duvalier gone, the US had in mind the usual form of democracy committed to the preferential option for the rich, particularly US investors. To facilitate this outcome, the bipartisan National Endowment for Democracy (NED) directed its "democracy building" grants to the Haitian International Institute for Research and Development (IHRED) and two conservative unions. IHRED was associated with Bazin and other political figures with little popular base beyond the NED, which portrayed them as the democratic movement. The State Department approached AIFLD, the AFL-CIO affiliate with a notorious record of anti-labor activities in the Third World, to join its efforts in Haiti "because of the presence of radical labor unions and the high risk that other unions may become radicalized." AIFLD joined in, expanding the support it had given from 1984 to a union group run in part by Duvalier's security police. In preparation for the elections, NED extended its support to several other organizations, among them a human rights organization headed by Jean-Jacques Honorat, former Minister of Tourism under Duvalier and later an opponent of his regime. By way of the right wing Puebla Institute, NED also provided pre-election funding to Radio Soleil, which had been anti-Duvalier but shifted well to the right under the influence of the conservative Catholic hierarchy.

Following Aristide's victory, US funding for political activities sharply increased, mainly through USAID. According to Kenneth Roth, deputy director of Human Rights Watch, the aid was intended to strengthen conservative groups that could "act as an institutional check on Aristide," in an effort to "move the country in a rightward direction." After Aristide was overthrown and the elite returned to power, Honorat became de facto Prime Minister under the military regime. The popular organizations that supported Aristide were violently suppressed, while those backed by NED and AID were spared.[12]

One of the closest observers of events in Haiti, Amy Wilentz, writes that Aristide's brief term was "the first time in the post-Duvalier era that the United States government has been so deeply concerned with human rights and the rule of law in Haiti" (not that there was more than rhetoric under the Duvaliers). The State Department is reported to have "circulated a thick notebook filled with alleged human rights violations" under Aristide—

"something it had not done under the previous rulers, Duvalierists and military men," who were deemed proper recipients for aid, including military aid, "based on unsubstantiated human-rights improvements":

> During the four regimes that preceded Aristide, international human-rights advocates and democratic observers had begged the State Department to consider helping the democratic opposition in Haiti. But no steps were taken by the United States to strengthen anything but the executive and the military until Aristide won the presidency. Then, all of a sudden, the United States began to think about how it could help those Haitians eager to limit the powers of the executive or to replace the government constitutionally.

USAID's huge "Democracy Enhancement" project was "specifically designed to fund those sectors of the Haitian political spectrum where opposition to the Aristide government could be encouraged."[13]

All absolutely normal, simply further evidence that "democracy" and "human rights" are regarded purely as power instruments, of no intrinsic value, even dangerous and objectionable; precisely as any rational person with some knowledge of history and institutions would expect.

Before deciding to run for office, Aristide had observed that "Of course, the U.S. has its own agenda here," adding that it was natural for the rich to make investments and want to maximize return. "This is normal, capitalist behavior, and I don't care if the U.S. wants to do it at home... But it is monstrous to come down here and impose your will on another people," whom you do not understand and for whom you care nothing. "I cannot accept that Haiti should be whatever the United States wants it to be." It's obvious why he had to go.[14]

There are few surprises here, well into the post-Cold War era with its heralded New World Order.

Immediately after taking power on September 30, 1991, the army "embarked on a systematic and continuing campaign to stamp out the vibrant civil society that has taken root in Haiti since the fall of the Duvalier dictatorship," Americas Watch reported in December. At least 1000 people were killed in the first two weeks of the coup and hundreds more by December, "generally reliable Haitian human rights groups" estimated, though they knew little about what is happening in the countryside, traditionally the locus of the worst atrocities. Terror increased in the months that followed, particularly after the reconstituted Macoutes were unleashed in late December. Tens, perhaps hundreds of thousands are in hiding. Many regard the terror as "worse than Papa Doc." "The goal of the repression is twofold: first, to destroy the political and social gains made since the downfall of the Duvalier dynasty; and second, to ensure that no matter what Haiti's political future may hold, all structures for duplicating those gains will have been laid waste." Accordingly, unions and popular organizations were specifically targeted for violent repression, and the "lively and combative radio stations—the main form of communication with Haiti's dispersed and largely illiterate population"—were suppressed. The rascal multitude must remain dispersed and scattered, without unions or other popular organizations through which they might act to formulate and express their interests, and without independent means of communication and information.

If it sounds familiar, that's because it is. In the Haitis of the world, the means can be quite direct.

De facto Prime Minister Jean-Jacques Honorat justified the coup. "There is no relationship between elections and democracy," he said. Haiti is being defamed by foreign "racists" in the press and French Embassy. It is right to return Duvalier thugs to power as rural section chiefs because "No society can exist without police." Along with landholders, they "are taking revenge against those who were persecuting them," notably priests, Christian base communities, and the nonviolent Papaye Peasant Movement, who are guilty of "terrorism." "The military was systematically persecuted" by these elements, who believed "they could do anything" under Aristide's rule, he informed the visiting human rights delegation, blaming Aristide for the coup. When a press conference of the Federation of Haitian Students at the national university was attacked by armed soldiers, clubbing and arresting participants, Honorat's wife "offered fifty of the students their freedom if they taped a statement saying they had been treated well in detention," Kenneth Roth reports.

"As Haitians began in early November to flee this violence and persecution in large numbers," the Americas Watch report continues, "the Bush Administration changed from an outspoken proponent of human rights and democracy in Haiti to a shameful apologist." The State Department "issued a fraudulent opinion asserting that political persecution of Aristide's supporters had ceased," providing "rhetorical cover to the army's ongoing campaign of repression" and laying the basis for the forcible return of fleeing refugees to the terror of the coup regime. "Evidently fearful that continuing honest and outspoken criticism of military abuses in Haiti would jeopardize the legal defense of its interdiction efforts, which had come under challenge in U.S. courts, the Administration stopped public criticism altogether. Since late October, Haiti has been immune from censure by the State Department on human rights grounds."[15]

The Bush Administration quickly "distanced itself from" deposed President Aristide "in light of concerns over his human rights record," the press reported with no detectable embarrassment; the White House "refus[ed] to say that his return to power was a necessary precondition for Washington to feel that democracy has been restored in Haiti" (Thomas Friedman). The same day, the head of the OAS delegation stated that "We have come down with an extremely clear mandate that Aristide must be restored."

It was the notes sounded by Washington, however, that reverberated in the press. Aristide was regarded as "an insular and menacing leader who saw his own raw popularity as a substitute for the give and take of politics," *Times* correspondent Howard French wrote. He governed "with the aid of fear," leaning "heavily on Lavalas, an unstructured movement of affluent idealists and long-exiled leftists" whose model was China's Cultural Revolution—the *Times* version of the "textbook example of participatory, 'bottom-up' and democratic political development" depicted by the Council on Hemispheric Affairs. Aristide's power hunger led to "troubles with civil society," another concept of *Times*-speak, excluding the large majority of the population, which continued to support him with passion and courage. Furthermore, "Haitian political leaders and diplomats say, the growing climate of vigilantism as well as increasingly strident statements by Father Aristide blaming the wealthier classes for the poverty of the masses encouraged" the coup; such statements are outrageous and absurd, we are to understand. "Although he retains much of the popular support that enabled him to win 67 percent of the popular vote in the country's December 1990 elections, Father Aristide was overthrown in part because of concerns among politically active people over his commitment to the Constitution, and growing fears of political and class-based violence, which many believe the President endorsed."

As this well-informed correspondent knew, the "political and class-based violence" was a near monopoly of the military and the elite, whose "commitment to the Constitution" was invisible and who turned at once to terror to demolish the "politically active people" and their organizations—which were much too "structured" and effective for the tastes of those who qualify as "civil society" by Administration-*Times* standards. What they call "civil society" intends to retain their traditional power and privilege, and the army, which, French assures us, "made it clear that it had no desire to hold on to power," will doubtless be happy to permit "civil society" to rule as in the past, on condition that the army can "hang on to effective control of the country and resume its highly lucrative activities such as the transshipment of narcotics from South America to North America" (*Financial Times*).[16]

Ruminating on the dilemmas of the post-Cold War era, the editor of *Foreign Affairs*, William Hyland, observed that "In Haiti it has not been so easy to differentiate among the democrats and the dictators"; the distinction between Aristide, on the one hand, and Duvalier and his latter-day clones, on the other, is too subtle even for the discriminating eye. It should not be thought that Hyland is lacking in human concerns. Our worthy commitment to "pragmatism," he warned, should be tempered by the recognition that the US "owes a moral debt to the people of Israel"; accordingly, we must not allow policy to succumb to the "virulent antisemitism" that lies "beneath the veneer of support for Israel," and is "beginning to break through in the debate over Israeli settlements." In Haiti, in contrast, it is hard to detect anyone who might merit our support.

Commentators who found it possible to distinguish Aristide from Papa Doc and the ruling generals hoped that he would find some way to convince the White House of his good faith. A visit to Washington, Pamela Constable wrote, might "bolster his image as a reasonable leader committed to democracy and thus win him a strong public endorsement by the Bush administration"—which, surely, was holding back only because of its reservations on this score.[17]

The OAS at once imposed an embargo, which the US joined, suspending trade on October 29. It was denounced by the ruling elite, and cheered by those who suffer most from its effects. In the slums, "news of the O.A.S. embargo was the only thing many people could find to cheer about as hundreds of people squeezed into overloaded buses to the countryside to flee the expected nightly violence by soldiers," Howard French reported on October 9. Trade should be cut off, "anxious-looking residents" told reporters: "It doesn't matter how much misery we get. We'll die if necessary." Months later, the mood remained the same. "Keep the Embargo" was the popular refrain among the poor: "Titid [Aristide] gave us dignity and hope... We are ready to suffer if it means Titid will come back."

The embargo was loosely observed and ineffectual. Europe disregarded it, and members of "civil society" continued to fly to Miami and New York to satisfy their wants, or to trade with the Dominican Republic, a practice that provided alms for the Dominican military as well. Washington, which knows how to twist arms when some serious power or profit interest is at stake, could find no way, in this case, to call upon its allies to save Haitian democracy and stop the terror. One recalls the delicate sensibilities that prevented Bush from lending any support to Kuwaiti democrats after the Gulf war, so profound as to bar mention of the word "democracy" even in private communications to the Emir, because, officials explained, "You can't pick out one country to lean on over another." Oil tankers, mainly from Europe, arrived faster "than they can unload," a senior State Department official said in April 1992.[18]

The Administration had not carried out such obvious measures as "freezing any U.S. assets of military officers who participated in the coup, and of their wealthy Haitian backers," or even "temporarily lifting U.S. visas to these people, who travel frequently to the U.S.," *Wall Street Journal* Washington correspondent Robert Greenberger reported in January 1992. But there is a reason: Aristide's defects. Liberal Democrat Robert Torricelli, Chairman of the House Foreign Affairs subcommittee on Western Hemisphere affairs, took time from his democracy-inspired efforts to tighten the embargo on Cuba to explain that "The democratic process doesn't always produce perfect results"; given "Mr. Aristide's record," it isn't easy to gain support for stronger action against Haiti. Cuban terrorists pose no such problems. Though "overwhelmingly elected in Haiti's first free election" and "immensely popular with the poor," Greenberger continues, "his fiery rhetoric sometimes incited class violence," something that always deeply disturbs the *Journal* whenever their keen eyes discern traces of it in Haiti, Guatemala, Brazil, Indonesia, and elsewhere.

Torricelli called for an end to the Haitian embargo and supported the forcible repatriation of Haitian refugees from Guantanamo, illustrating still more clearly the passion for democracy and human rights that inspires his Cuban initiatives.[19]

Many pondered the difficult choices faced by the Bush Administration. *Time* suggested that Bush might "ease the toll on Haitians by loosening the embargo on plants that assemble goods for U.S. companies, restoring as many as 40,000 jobs"—and, incidentally restoring profits to US investors, though the motive could only be to "ease the toll on Haitians" who are calling on the US to "keep the embargo," as the same article reports.

We might take note of another standard item of PC usage. The word "jobs" has taken on an entirely new meaning: "profits." Thus when George Bush takes off to Japan with a bevy of auto executives in tow, he waves the banner "jobs, jobs, jobs," meaning "profits, profits, profits," as a look at his social and economic policies demonstrates without equivocation. The press and air waves resound with impassioned proposals to increase "jobs," put forth by those who do what is in their power to send them to low-wage, high-repression regions, and to destroy what remains of meaningful work and workers' rights, all in the interest of some unmentionable seven-letter word.

Bush had wasted no time in following *Time's* advice. On February 4, the US lifted the embargo for the assembly plants that use cheap Haitian labor for goods for export to the US, most of them US-owned. A few months later, it was reported in the small print that while "the Administration is tightening rules on ships trading with Haiti" in accord with a May 17 OAS resolution, "it is apparently continuing to relax controls on goods going to Port-au-Prince from the United States," allowing export of seeds, fertilizers, and pesticides from the US to Haiti. All for "jobs, jobs, jobs."

The Administration had been "under heavy pressure from American businesses with interests in Haiti," the *Washington Post* reported. The editors felt that the February 4 decision was wise: the embargo was a "fundamental political miscalculation" that "has caused great suffering, but not among the gunmen. Since it hasn't served its purpose, it is good that it is being relaxed"—not tightened so as to serve the professed purpose, as those undergoing the great suffering plead. But for the US to repatriate refugees by force, the editors continue, is not in keeping with "its deep commitment to human rights"—which they see manifested wherever they turn.[20]

Washington's unilateral relaxation of the OAS embargo was condemned by the Secretary General of the OAS, who had urged the State Department against this action. The forcible return of refugees was condemned by the UN High Commission on Refugees (UNCHR), which rarely confronts the US, knowing what that entails. In November 1991, UNCHR had called on the US to admit all refugees "for determination of their refugee status." UNCHR pointed out that the UN Conventions on refugees proscribe their return "in any manner whatsoever" to territories where their lives or freedom would be endangered, with "no exception." In May 1992, UNCHR again declared the forced return to be in violation of international agreements; the adjacent column in the *New York Times* quotes a conservative businessman with close ties to the US, who reports "a tremendous increase" in death squad-style killings: "People are being terrorized, and a bunch of people are being killed," a "spate of violence" that coincided with Washington's decision to "directly repatriate" Haitians trying to reach the US.[21]

The relaxation of the embargo "was greeted enthusiastically by assembly plant owners," Lee Hockstader reported, but not by "many of the workers most directly affected by the sanctions," who have "applauded them as the best way to promote the return of Aristide." "All indications are that Aristide's massive popular support among the poor majority...remains intact... It is difficult to find anyone on the street, either in the capital or in the provinces, who does not support the priest-turned-politician." His associates bitterly condemned the US move. A priest who is a close adviser to Aristide denounced Washington as having "totally" betrayed him "from the beginning." US policy, he said, is "the most cynical thing you can ever find on earth... I don't think the U.S. wants Aristide back," because he "is not under their control. He is not their puppet."[22]

The assessment is plausible enough. That the US should have sought to establish "Duvalierism without Duvalier" could surprise only the willfully blind. For similar reasons, the Carter Administration sought desperately to institute "Somocismo without Somoza" after its efforts to salvage the tyrant collapsed, and its successor turned to more violent means to achieve the same end, with the general approval of enlightened opinion, tactical disagreement aside.[23]

Superfluously perhaps, the priest's assessment is reinforced by a leaked secret document allegedly authored by a staff member of the US Embassy in Port-au-Prince at the behest of Prime Minister Honorat and other Haitian officials. Its authenticity was questioned by the Council on Hemispheric Affairs (COHA), and denied by the State Department, but "later research has now validated [it] as being completely reliable," COHA concluded. The document lays out a plan to allow a symbolic "restoration" of Aristide as a PR ploy, with his complete removal later on, when attention has declined.

By the time the document surfaced in January 1992, most of its applicable recommendations had been implemented, COHA noted. Others were to follow shortly. The embargo was rendered still more toothless on February 4. Three weeks later, Aristide accepted what COHA described as "a near-total defeat for Haitian democracy," "a tragic sell-out by a desperate man" who was forced to agree to a "government of national unity" in which he would have only a symbolic role. Aristide "was effectively left with no option but to mutilate his own stature by signing away his powers in exchange for the still uncertain prospect of his restoration to what will now be a figurehead presidency," COHA stated. The "national unity" government brought together two partners: a group headed by René Théodore, who represented 1.5 percent of the electorate, the Haitian military and elite, and the US government; and another led by Aristide, with 67 percent of the electorate but no other assets. Given the balance, the outcome is not obscure; and it is not surprising that Assistant Secretary of State Bernard Aronson declared his satisfaction with the agreement.

COHA raised an obvious question. Suppose that "after a hypothetical coup [in Nicaragua] in which [President Violeta Chamorro] was forced to flee for her life, she had been made to accept a major Sandinista figure as her prime minister who would exercise effective control of the country in order to be allowed back. Would Aronson be pleased with such a formula if the FSLN had overthrown and exiled her, violently had beaten and killed at least 2,000 of those who backed her, and had induced her to give up real powers in order to be restored?" Or to make the analogy more exact, if in addition the FSLN were a party with no popular base and a record of terror in the style of US clients? No one troubled to respond.

The military in Haiti celebrated the agreement, along with "civil society." One Haitian Senator commented happily that "it would be surrealistic to believe or to print that [Aristide] can return by June 30, or any other specific date for that matter." "The military thugs down there understand...that they have got a nod and a wink from the U.S. government," Congressman John Conyers said.

All that was left was to replace Théodore by the original US favorite Marc Bazin. That result was achieved in June 1992, when Bazin was inaugurated as Prime Minister. "The Vatican and the Haitian bishops' conference...walked into the National Palace and blessed Haiti's new army-backed government," the *National Catholic Reporter (NCR)* commented, though the Vatican was alone in extending formal recognition. The Vatican had waited until Aristide was exiled to fill the position of papal nuncio. The formal recognition "shows they're really out to get Aristide and to align themselves with Haiti's traditional powers—the army and the bourgeoisie," a Western diplomat told *NCR*. Liberation and human rights were a grand cause in Eastern Europe; in the Caribbean and Central America, they must be crushed, in the service of traditional privilege, and "the preferential option for the poor" is definitely not welcome. Bazin delivered his inauguration address in French to a "stifling official gathering of men in dark suits and perfumed women in white dresses," Howard French reported; Aristide had given his in Creole, the language of the population, receiving the presidential sash from a peasant woman.[24]

Democracy marches on.

An adviser of the Bazin government, echoing Aristide, said that "all it would take is one phone call" from Washington to send the army leadership packing. "Virtually all observers agree" that little more would be necessary, Howard French writes. But "Washington's deep-seated ambivalence about a leftward-tilting nationalist whose style diplomats say has sometimes been disquietingly erratic" precludes any meaningful pressure. "Despite much blood on the army's hands, United States diplomats consider it a vital counterweight to Father Aristide, whose class-struggle rhetoric...threatened or antagonized traditional power centers at home and abroad." The "counterweight" will therefore hold power with the "erratic" nationalist in exile, and class-struggle rhetoric and terror will continue with the tacit support of traditional power centers.[25]

The *New York Times* sought to place the proper spin on the February 4 decision to advance the anti-Aristide scenario and benefit US businesses. Under the headline "U.S. Plans to Sharpen Focus of Its Sanctions Against Haiti," Barbara Crossette reported from Washington that "The Bush Administration said today that it would modify its embargo against Haiti's military Government to punish anti-democratic forces and ease the plight of workers who lost jobs because of the ban on trade." The State Department would be "fine tuning" its economic sanctions, the "latest move" in Administration efforts to find "more effective ways to hasten the collapse of what the Administration calls an illegal Government in Haiti." The naive may find the logic a bit obscure: how the move punishes the anti-democratic forces who applauded it, while easing the plight of workers who strenuously opposed it, is left a mystery. Until we translate from PC to English, that is. Then all is clear.[26]

A more straightforward account appeared a few days later in a report from Port-au-Prince under the heading: "Democracy Push in Haiti Blunted: Leaders of Coup Gleeful After U.S. Loosens Its Embargo and Returns Refugees." Howard French writes that "the mood in army and political circles began to turn from anxiety to confidence that the United States, *feeling no particular domestic pressure now from Haiti's problems,* would leave them in peace." The same day, the anniversary of Aristide's inauguration, New York traffic was tied up by a large protest march against the US actions, as in Miami. That is not what is meant by "domestic pressure," however; mostly black, the protestors merited little notice—though the actions were reported in the Alaska press, where one could also read the statement by Haiti's consul general in New York, who said "There is a tacit collaboration between the Haitian military and the State Department. The Americans will have the last word. And the Americans don't want Aristide's return." *Time* quoted a "disillusioned Republican congressional staffer" who said, "The White House is banking on the fact that people won't care. Politics, not principle, is the overriding consideration."[27]

That much seems beyond dispute. For those who choose to hear, the italicized words tell the story that is solidly based on two centuries of history. Without popular support here, Toussaint's tree of liberty will remain deeply buried, at best a dream—not in Haiti alone.

CHAPTER 9

THE BURDEN OF RESPONSIBILITY

1. Irrational Disdain

As the US proceeded to "assume, out of self-interest, responsibility for the welfare of the world capitalist system" after World War II, it also extended the "experiments in pragmatism" that it had been conducting in its narrower domains to "accelerate the process of national growth and save much waste" (Gerald Haines, Ulysses Weatherby). One striking feature of the "scientific methods of development" designed for our wards is what Hans Schmidt calls the "irrational disdain for the agricultural experience of local peasants." This was the source of "a series of disastrous failures" as US experts attempted to apply "the latest developments in scientific agriculture" to their Haitian testing area—as always, sincerely believing that they were doing good while (by the sheerest accident) benefiting US corporations. A 1929 study found that "Haitian peasants were growing cotton more successfully than American plantations which employed the latest scientific methods," Schmidt observes. The chief US agricultural expert reported to the State Department that US ventures "had failed because promoters had been unwilling to study the techniques employed by local people who had, through generations of practical experience, developed locally viable methods," which enabled the natives to raise cotton more successfully than the plantations that were "scientifically cultivated."[1]

The story continued after the government was handed over to Haitian overseers. In 1941, the Haitian-American Company for Agricultural Development (SHADA) was set up as an aid project under the guidance of US agronomists, who dismissed the advice and protests of Haitian experts with the usual contempt. With millions of dollars of US government credits, SHADA undertook to raise sisal and rubber, needed at the time for war purposes. The project acquired 5 percent of Haiti's finest agricultural lands, expelling 40,000 peasant families, who, if lucky, might be rehired as day laborers. After four years of production, the project harvested a laughable five tons of rubber. It was then abandoned, in part because the market was gone. Some peasants returned to their former lands, but were unable to resume cultivation because the land had been ruined by the SHADA project. Many could not even find their own fields after trees, hills and bushes had been bulldozed away.

··"Haitian objections to U.S. aid projects sound paranoid,ʼ Amy Wilentz remarks after reviewing this not untypical instance.[2] Sometimes, however, there really is a man with an ax chasing the fellow with the irksome complaint.

In 1978, US experts became concerned that swine fever in the Dominican Republic might threaten the US pig industry. The US initiated a $23 million extermination and restocking program aimed at replacing all of the 1.3 million pigs in Haiti, which were among the peasants' most important possessions, even considered a "bank account" in case of need. Though some Haitian pigs had been found to be infected, few had died, possibly because of their remarkable disease-resistance, some veterinary experts felt. Peasants were skeptical, speculating that the affair had been staged so that "Americans could make money selling their pigs." The program was initiated in 1982, well after traces of disease had disappeared. Two years later, there were no pigs in Haiti.

Peasants regarded this as "the very last thing left in the possible punishments that have afflicted us." A Haitian economist described the enterprise as "the worst calamity to ever befall the peasant," even apart from the $600 million value of the destroyed livestock: "The real loss to the peasant is incalculable... [The peasant economy] is reeling from the impact of being without pigs. A whole way of life has been destroyed in this survival economy." School registration dropped 40-50 percent and sales of merchandise plummeted, as the marginal economy collapsed. A USAID-OAS program then sent pigs from Iowa—for many peasants, confirming their suspicions. These were, however, to be made available only to peasants who could show that they had the capital necessary to feed the new arrivals and to house them according to specifications. Unlike the native Haitian pigs, the Iowa replacements often succumbed to disease, and could survive only on expensive feed, at a cost that ran up to $250 a year, a huge sum for impoverished peasants. One predictable result was new fortunes for the Duvalier clique and their successors who gained control of the feed market. A Church-based Haitian development program that had sought to deal with the problems abandoned the effort as "a waste of time." "These pigs will never become acclimated to Haiti... Next they'll ask us to install a generator and air conditioning."[3]

Other experiments have often turned out the same way. In his study of another long-time "testing area," Liberia, anthropologist Gordon

Thomasson found the same "irrational disdain" for native intellectual achievement, and the same severe costs—for the locals. Over the centuries, the Kpelle had developed hundreds of varieties of rice that were matched precisely to microenvironments in particular ecosystems; dozens of different seeds might be planted in a small field, with very high yields. US agronomists advised capital-intensive "green revolution" techniques using petrochemical inputs which, apart from being far too costly for a poor country, bring lower yields and loss of the traditional knowledge and the wide variety of seeds that have been bred, selected, diversified, and maintained over centuries. Thomasson estimates that agricultural productivity will be cut by as much as 50 percent if the rich genetic pool of rice varieties, "the product of centuries of self-conscious breeding and selection," is lost and replaced by foreign inputs: "many areas of rural Liberia will for all intents and purposes cease to exist, and so will many of Liberia's indigenous cultures."

The disdain of the experts was heightened by the fact that this is "women's knowledge," transmitted by older women to young girls who spent much time acquiring the skills and lore. The same attitudes extend more broadly. Max Allen, curator of one of the world's leading textile museums, observes that "In most Northern-hemisphere traditional societies, the most impressive man-made artifacts are not made by men at all, but by women," namely textile products, which "are certainly *artistic*," though not regarded as "art" by Western tradition. They are assigned to the category of crafts, not art. The fact that the artistic traditions extending over thousands of years are "women's work," may contribute to these dubious interpretations, Allen suggests.[4]

The "suspicious" will not fail to observe that, however ruinous to Liberia, the "scientific methods of development" offer many benefits to the western corporate sector, perhaps well beyond the usual beneficiaries, agribusiness and petrochemicals. As the variety of crops is reduced, and disease and blight become an increasing threat, genetic engineering may have to come to the rescue with artificially designed crops, offering the rising biotech industries alluring prospects for growth and profit.

Following standard doctrine, US experts advised Liberia to convert farmland to plantation cash crops (which, incidentally, also happens to benefit US corporations). The resulting shortfalls led USAID to push the development of paddy rice in swamps, ignoring a World Health Organization effort to keep people out of these regions because of extreme health hazards.

The Kpelle had also developed sophisticated metallurgical technology, enabling them to produce highly efficient tools. In this case, Thomasson writes, their achievements were "killed by colonialism and monopoly capitalism, not because the product it produced was in any way inferior or overpriced in the marketplace," but by means of subsidies to coastal merchants and other market distortions designed by the economic experts and imposed by the US-controlled governments, "eventually destroying the economy, currency, and indigenous industry." Again, there were beneficiaries: multinational mining concessions, foreign producers who supplied the importers, and banks outside Liberia to which they ship their profits.[5]

Chalk up another victory for "free market" values.

Some might consider it unfair to take Liberia and Haiti as illustrations. As Wilson's Secretary of State Robert Lansing explained:

> The experience of Liberia and Haiti show that the African race are devoid of any capacity for political organization and lack genius for government. Unquestionably there is an inherent tendency to revert to savagery and to cast aside the shackles of civilization which are irksome to their physical nature. Of course, there are many exceptions to this racial weakness, but it is true of the mass, as we know from experience in this country. It is that which makes the negro problem practically unsolvable.[6]

Perhaps it is this racial weakness that accounts for the results of the experiments in Liberia and Haiti—which are duplicated throughout the subject domains.

These regular features of the 500-year conquest will have growing significance in the years ahead as the ecological consequences of unsustainable capital-intensive agriculture reach a scale that cannot be neglected even by the rich. At that point, they will enter the agenda, like the ozone layer, which became "important" when it seemed likely to endanger rich white folk. Meanwhile, the experiments will continue in the testing areas.

2. Laboratory Animals

The concept "testing area" merits particular notice. Similarly, "American strategists have described the civil war in El Salvador as the 'ideal testing ground' for implementing low-intensity conflict doctrine" (a.k.a. international terrorism), a DOD-sponsored RAND Corporation report on the experiment concludes. In earlier days, Vietnam was described as "a going laboratory where we see subversive insurgency…being applied in all its forms" (Maxwell Taylor), providing opportunities for "experiments with population and resource control methods" and "nation building." The

Marine occupation of Haiti was described in similar terms, as we have seen. The technical posturing appears to sustain the self-image, at least.[7]

One finds no intimation that the experimental subjects might have the right to sign consent forms, or even to know what is happening to them. On the contrary, they scarcely have the rights of laboratory animals. *We* will determine what is best for them, as we always have; another hallmark of the 500 years.

The wise among us just *know*, for example, that maximizing consumption is a core human value: "If we weren't influencing the world" in this direction, "it would be someone else because what we are seeing everywhere is an expression of the basic human desire to consume," Boston University professor of management Lawrence Wortzel explains. US entrepreneurs are fortunate indeed to be so in tune with human nature. True, slow learners sometimes have to be helped to understand their true nature. The advertising industry devotes billions of dollars to stimulating this self-awareness, and in the early days of the industrial revolution, it was no small problem to bring independent farmers to realize that they wished to be tools of production so as to be able to gratify their "basic human desire to consume." The very "visible hand" of government has also helped. As radio was becoming a major medium, the Federal Radio Commission "equated capitalist broadcasting with 'general public service' broadcasting" since it would provide whatever "the market desired," Robert McChesney writes, while attempts by labor, other popular sectors, or educational programming were deemed "propaganda." It was therefore necessary "to favor the capitalist broadcasters" with access to channels and other assistance.[8]

Apart from the regular bombardment of the senses through advertising and media portrayal of life-as-it-should-be-lived, corporate-government initiatives are undertaken on an enormous scale to shape consumer tastes. One dramatic example is the "Los Angelizing" of the US economy, a huge state-corporate campaign to direct consumer preferences to "suburban sprawl and individualized transport—as opposed to clustered suburbanization compatible with a mix of rail, bus, and motor car transport," Richard Du Boff observes in his economic history of the United States, a policy that involved "massive destruction of central city capital stock" and "relocating rather than augmenting the supply of housing, commercial structures, and public infrastructure." The role of the federal government was to provide funds for "complete motorization and the crippling of surface mass transit"; this was the major thrust of the Federal Highway Acts of 1944, 1956, and 1968, implementing a strategy designed by GM chairman Alfred Sloan. Huge sums were spent on interstate highways without interference, as Congress surrendered control to the Bureau of Public Roads;

about 1 percent of the sum was devoted to rail transit. The Federal Highway Administration estimated total expenditures at $80 billion by 1981, with another $40 billion planned for the next decade. State and local governments managed the process on the scene.

The private sector operated in parallel: "Between 1936 and 1950, National City Lines, a holding company sponsored and funded by GM, Firestone, and Standard Oil of California, bought out more than 100 electric surface-traction systems in 45 cities (including New York, Philadelphia, St. Louis, Salt Lake City, Tulsa, and Los Angeles) to be dismantled and replaced with GM buses... In 1949 GM and its partners were convicted in U.S. district court in Chicago of criminal conspiracy in this matter and fined $5,000." By the mid-1960s, one out of six business enterprises was directly dependent on the motor vehicle industry. The federal spending helped keep the economy afloat. Eisenhower's fears of "another Depression setting in after the Korean War" were allayed, a US Transportation Department official reported. A congressional architect of the highway program, John Blatnik of Minnesota, observed that "It put a nice solid floor across the whole economy in times of recession." These government programs supplemented the huge subsidy to high technology industry through the military system, which provided the primary stimulus and support needed to sustain the moribund system of private enterprise that had collapsed in the 1930s.[9]

The general impact on culture and society was immense, apart from the economy itself. Democratic decision-making played little role in this massive project of redesigning the contemporary world, and only in marginal respects was it a reflection of consumer choice. Consumers made choices no doubt, as voters do, within a narrowly determined framework of options designed by those who own the society and manage it with their own interests in mind. The real world bears little resemblance to the dreamy fantasies now fashionable about History converging to an ideal of liberal democracy that is the ultimate realization of Freedom.

The primitive people to whose needs we minister also commonly lack self-awareness, and need a little help to discover what they really want. The efforts of the Jesuits who sought to raise their Amerindian charges from "their natural condition of rudeness and barbarism...were first, and very wisely, directed to the creation of wants—the springs of human activity," in which these creatures were so sorely lacking, Hegel learnedly explained. A century later, the US proconsul in Haiti, Financial Adviser Arthur Millspaugh, observed that "the peasants, living lives which to us seem indolent and shiftless, are enviably carefree and contented; but, if they are to be citizens of an independent self-governing nation, they must acquire, or at least a larger number of them must acquire, a new set of wants"—

which the advertising industry will be happy to stimulate, and US exporters will generously fulfill.[10]

Abolition of slavery raised in a sharp form the problem of creating wants, a problem that was addressed over a much longer period as peasants were driven to wage labor in the early stages of industrialization. Given the suddenness of the transition in the case of abolition, the problem had to be faced squarely, and with self-awareness. Thomas Holt has an interesting study of the case of Jamaica, where after a slave revolt, the British rulers abolished slavery in 1834. The problem was to ensure that the plantation system would be maintained without essential change. Officials understood that freedmen must be prevented from relapsing "into barbarous indolence." "Should things be left to their natural course," Colonial Secretary Lord Glenelg observed, "labour would not be attracted to the cultivation of exportable produce," meaning sugar. He therefore urged a variety of government measures to prevent freed slaves from acquiring the ample fertile lands then available, liberal doctrine notwithstanding. Another colonial official recognized that more is needed: the creation of "artificial wants," which "become in time real wants." As abolition was being prepared, a British Parliamentarian observed (1833) that "To make them labour, and give them a taste for luxuries and comforts, they must be gradually taught to desire those objects which could be attained by human labour. There was a regular progress from the possession of necessaries to the desire of luxuries; and what once were luxuries, gradually came…to be necessaries. This was the sort of progress the negroes had to go through, and this was the sort of education to which they ought to be subject in their period of probation" after emancipation. Otherwise, "they would hardly have any inducement to labour," a high-ranking colonial official, Governor Charles Metcalfe, later observed (1840). By such means, another official noted, it would be possible to attain the desired end: "to change a slavish multitude into an orderly and happy peasantry," performing essentially the same tasks as under slavery, while the "slave driving oligarchy" becomes "a natural upper class."[11]

The same problem was faced by the United Fruit Company (UFCO) in its Central American plantations. Under conditions of free labor, workers had to be prevented somehow from retreating to a self-sustaining economy, no simple matter. People chose to work "only when forced to and that was not often, for the land would give them what little they needed," an UFCO historian wrote in 1929. To overcome the problem, UFCO sought to instill consumer values, recognizing that "The desire for goods…is something that has to be cultivated." The company was able to "arouse desires by advertising and salesmanship," the same historian wrote approvingly; this had "its effect in awakening desires, ...the same effect as in the United States," where, as industry knew well, "desires" had to be artificially stimulated and shaped. The newly-awakened desires—for silk stockings instead of cotton, expensive Stetson hats and "a flashy silk shirt while their feet were bare," and so on—could then be satisfied at UFCO stores. The device was "repeatedly abused" by the company, its official historian concedes, as goods were sold "at outrageous prices to the workers—all too frequently on credit," driving them on "a straight road to peonage."[12]

The problems had been addressed on a different scale in opening China to the West. Again, it was not easy. A British mission was admitted to Beijing in 1793, offering samples of virtually everything Britain could produce. It was "the most elaborate and expensive diplomatic initiative ever undertaken by a British government," John Keay writes in his history of the East India Company, which held its monopoly on trade with China until well into the 19th century. The Emperor graciously accepted the offerings as "Tribute from the Kingdom of England," commending the "respectful spirit of submission" of the British emissary. There would be no trade however: "Our celestial empire possesses all things in prolific abundance," the Emperor informed him, though "I do not forget the lonely remoteness of your island, cut off from the world by intervening wastes of sea." European merchants made inroads in the south, but were blocked elsewhere by imperial power.

One commodity for which Britain did find a market was Bengali opium. By the early 19th century, the East India Company's revenues from opium sales to China were second only to land revenue, "showing profits high enough both to stifle any moral scruples felt by the British and to negate the prohibitions frequently invoked by the Chinese," Keay writes. A few years later China sought to halt the flow, now truly offending British moral scruples. Pleading the virtues of free trade, Britain forced China to open its doors to lethal narcotics, exploiting the great superiority in violence that so revived the spirits of British jingoists during the 1991 Gulf War. "It took the construction and despatch of an ironclad steamship, the *Nemesis,* to reduce the Central Kingdom to reason," military historian Geoffrey Parker comments sardonically: the guns of the *Nemesis* "managed to destroy, in just one day in February 1841, nine war-junks, five forts, two military stations and a shore battery in the Pearl River," and China was soon able to enjoy the benefits of liberal internationalism. The US sought to match the privileges that Britain gained, also pleading high principle. China's refusal to accept opium from Britain's Indian colony was denounced by John Quincy Adams as a violation of the Christian principle of "love thy neighbor" and "an enormous outrage upon the rights of human

nature, and upon the first principles of the rights of nations," while mission-
aries lauded the "great design of Providence to make the wickedness of
men subserve his purposes of mercy toward China, in breaking through
her wall of exclusion, and bringing the empire into more immediate contact
with western and christian nations."

In such ways, Britain succeeded in creating new wants in China, much
as the US does today as it compels Asian countries, on pain of severe trade
sanctions, to admit US-grown lethal narcotics that kill perhaps 50 to 100
times as many people a year as all hard drugs combined in the United States,
and to advertise to open new markets, particularly women and children.[13]

3. Indian Removal and the Vile Maxim

The problem of driving an awareness of their true wants into the
heads of "rude barbarians" also beset the US government in the course of
its program of Indian removal and annexation. The most striking instance,
perhaps, arose in the 1880s, as Washington prepared to rescind the solemn
treaties recognizing ownership of Eastern Oklahoma by the Five Civilized
Tribes. The Indian Territory had been granted to these nations in perpetuity
after they had been brutally expelled from their traditional homes under an
1835 "treaty" that several Indian leaders were forced to accept, recognizing
that "they are strong and we are weak"; "We were all opposed to selling
our country east," the signers wrote to Congress, condemning the US
government for "making us outcasts and outlaws in our own land, plunging
us at the same time into an abyss of moral degradation which was hurling
our people to swift destruction." For the English settlers, peace treaties had
a special meaning, explained by the Council of State in Virginia in the 17th
century: when the Indians "grow secure uppon the treatie, we shall have
the better Advantage both to surprise them, & cutt downe theire Corne."
The concept survives to the present.

The 1835 treaty replaced earlier ones, going back to 1785, when the
newly liberated colonies forced a treaty on the Cherokees (who had, not
surprisingly, supported the British in the revolutionary war), taking lands
held by the Cherokees under earlier treaties while stating that Congress
"want none of your lands, nor anything else which belongs to you." This
was a "humane and generous act of the United States," the US representative
declared. In 1790, George Washington assured the Cherokees that "In
future you cannot be defrauded of your lands": the new government "will
protect you in all your just rights...The United States will be true and faithful
to their engagements." President Jefferson added that "I sincerely wish you

may succeed in your laudable endeavors to save the remnant of your nation by adopting industrious occupations, and a government of regular law. In this you may always rely on the counsel and assistance of the United States." In the years that followed, settlers encroached on Indian territory and new treaties were dictated, imposing further cessions of land. In what remained, a successful agricultural society was established, with textile manufacture from 1800, schools, printing presses, and a well-functioning government that was much admired by outsiders. A report submitted to the War Department in 1825 gave a "glowing description of the Cherokee country and nation at the time," Helen Jackson writes in her exceptional (in many ways) 19th century history of Indian removal, quoting extensive passages of praise for the advanced civilization that the Cherokees had developed and the "republican principles" on which it was based. Meanwhile, the leading thinkers of Europe lectured on the strange lack of "psychic power" that caused the Indians to "vanish" and "expire as soon as Spirit approached" with the European presence.

However impressive, progress was being made by the wrong people, who once again stood in the way of the advance of "progress" in the Politically Correct sense of the term. Andrew Jackson's Indian Removal Act of 1830 was followed by the imposed treaty of 1835, in which the signers relinquished all claims of the Civilized Nations to their lands east of the Mississippi. Jackson was deeply moved by his generosity in "having done my duty to my red children"; "if any failure of my good intention arises, it will be attributable to their want of duty to themselves, not to me." He was not only granting "these children of the forest" an opportunity "to better their condition in an unknown land" as "our forefathers" did, but even paying "the expense of his removal," an act of "friendly feeling" that "thousands of our own people would gladly embrace" if only it were extended to them.

Three years later, 17,000 Cherokees were driven at bayonet point to Oklahoma by the US Army "over a route so marked with new-dug graves that it was ever afterwards known as the Trail of Tears" (Thurman Wilkins); perhaps half survived "the generous and enlightened policy" of the US government, as the operation was described by the Secretary of War, with the routine self-acclaim for unspeakable atrocities.

Reviewing the remarkable achievements of the Cherokee nation before and after, and the treatment accorded them, Helen Jackson writes that "In the whole history of our Government's dealing with the Indian tribes, there is no record so black as the record of perfidy to this nation. There will come a time in the remote future when, to the student of American history, it will seem well-nigh incredible"—a judgment with which it is hard to quarrel, though the future is still remote.[14]

In 1870, the Department of the Interior recognized that "the Cherokees, and the other civilized Indian nations [of the Oklahoma territory] no less, hold lands in perpetuity by titles defined by the supreme law of the land," a "permanent home" granted "under the most solemn guarantee of the United States," to "remain theirs forever—a home that shall never in all future time be embarrassed by having extended around it the lines or placed over it the jurisdiction of a Territory or State," or be disturbed in any other way. Six years later, the Department declared that affairs in the Indian Territory are "complicated and embarrassing, and the question is directly raised whether an extensive section of the country is to be allowed to remain for an indefinite period practically an uncultivated waste, or whether the Government shall determine to reduce the size of the reservation." The Department had previously described the "uncultivated waste" as a miracle of progress, with successful production by people living in considerable comfort, a level of education "equal to that furnished by an ordinary college in the States," flourishing industry and commerce, an effective constitutional government, a high level of literacy, and a state of "civilization and enlightenment" comparable to anything known: "What required five hundred years for the Britons to accomplish in this direction they have accomplished in one hundred years," the Department declared in wonder.[15]

Jackson ends her account in 1880 with a question: "Will the United States Government determine 'to reduce the size of the reservation'?" It was soon to be answered, in just the way she anticipated. Again, the advanced civilization of the Indians stood in the way of civilization, properly conceived.

What followed is described by Angie Debo in her classic study *And Still the Waters Run*. In the independent Indian Territory, land was held collectively and life was contented and prosperous. The Federal Indian Office opposed communal land tenure by ideological dogma, as well as for its practical effect: preventing takeover by white intruders. In 1883, a group of self-styled philanthropists and humanitarians began to meet to consider problems of the Indians. Their third meeting was addressed by Senator Henry Dawes of Massachusetts, considered a "distinguished Indian theorist," who had just concluded a visit of inspection to the Indian Territory. Like earlier observers, he described what he found in glowing terms: "There was not a pauper in that nation, and the nation did not owe a dollar. It built its own capitol, in which we had this examination, and it built its schools and its hospitals." No family lacked a home.

Dawes then recommended that the society be dissolved, because of a fatal flaw, of which the benighted natives were unaware:

Yet the defect of the system was apparent. They have got as far as they can go, because they own their land in common. It is Henry George's system, and under that there is no enterprise to make your home any better than that of your neighbors. There is no selfishness, which is the bottom of civilization. Till this people will consent to give up their lands, and divide them among their citizens so that each can own the land he cultivates, they will not make much more progress.

In brief, though superficially civilized and advanced, the people remained culturally deprived, unable to recognize their "basic human drive to consume" and to best their neighbors, ignorant of the "vile maxim of the masters."

Dawes's proposal to bring enlightenment to the savages was approved by the Eastern humanitarians, and soon implemented. He introduced legislation that barred communal landholding and headed the Commission that oversaw the dispossession of the Indians that inevitably ensued. Their lands and property were looted, and they were scattered to remote urban areas where they suffered appalling poverty and destitution.

Such is the way with experiments; they don't always succeed. In fact, the regular experiments conducted in our various "testing areas" typically do succeed quite well, as this one did, for those who design and execute them, Adam Smith's architects of policy—honorable men, always guided by the most benevolent intentions, which, fortuitously, happen to coincide with their own interests. If the experiments do not succeed for the indigenous people of North America—or Brazilians, or Haitians, or Guatemalans, or Africans, or Bengalis, or welfare mothers, or others who stand in the way of the rich men who rule—we may seek the reasons in their genes, "defects," and inadequacies. Or we may muse on the ironies of history.

One can readily understand the appeal to postwar intellectuals of the work of Reinhold Niebuhr, "the theologian of the establishment," the guru of the Kennedy intellectuals, George Kennan, and many others. How comforting it must be to ponder the "paradox of grace" that was his key idea: the inescapable "taint of sin on all historical achievements," the need to make "conscious choices of evil for the sake of good"—soothing doctrines for those preparing to "face the responsibilities of power," or in plain English, to set forth on a life of crime.[16]

4. "The American Psyche"

The state-corporate nexus has always devoted substantial efforts and resources to ensure that the rascal multitude recognize their wants and needs, never an easy task, from the days when independent farmers had to be turned into wage earners and consumers. Many of them remained mired in darkest ignorance and superstitious belief, sometimes even heeding the words of such scoundrels as Uriah Stephens, a founder and the first grandmaster workman of the Knights of Labor, who outlined labor's task in 1871 as "The complete emancipation of the wealth producers from the thralldom and loss of wage slavery," a conception that can be traced to the leading principles of classical liberalism. Many took the conditions of "free labor" to be "a system of slavery as absolute if not as degrading as that which lately prevailed in the South," as a *New York Times* reporter described the new era in which "manufacturing capitalists" are the masters.[17]

Even today, after a century of intense and dedicated efforts by cultural managers, the general population often fail to perceive their inner wants. The debate over health care provides some useful illustrations. A case in point is a major article in the *Boston Globe* by Thomas Palmer, well to the liberal side of the spectrum. Palmer opens by reporting that almost 70 percent of Americans prefer a Canadian-style health-care system—a surprising figure, given that this retrograde socialism is regularly denounced as un-American. But the general public is just wrong, for two reasons, Palmer explains.

The first reason is technical: it was clarified by President Bush, who "emphasized the importance of avoiding the problems of bureaucratized, universal-care systems like Canada's." Mr. Bush, *New York Times* correspondent Robert Pear reports, "accuses the Democratic nominee of favoring a state-run system that would have Soviet-like elements," a "back door national health insurance" in the words of Presidential adviser Gail Wilensky. This is "a charge that Mr. Clinton and other Democrats deny," Pears adds with proper journalistic objectivity, keeping the balance between the charges of crypto-Communism and the angry denials. It is a matter of logic that Commie-style systems of the kind that exist throughout the industrial world apart from the United States (and South Africa) are inefficient. Accordingly, the fact that the highly bureaucratized private sector system in the US is vastly more inefficient is simply irrelevant. It is, for example, of no relevance that Blue Cross of Massachusetts employs 6680 people, more than are employed in all of Canada's health programs, which insure 10 times as many people; or that the share of the health dollar for administrative costs is over twice as high in the US as in Canada. Logic

cannot be confuted by mere fact, by Hegel's "negative, worthless existence."

More interesting is the second reason, which is "spiritual," Palmer
continues. There is a "difference in outlook" north and south of the border,
"theoretical differences that students of the two nations see in the psyches
of the average American and Canadian." The studies of these penetrating
scholars show that the Canadian system would cause "the kind of rationing
of health care that Americans would never accept... The US system rations
by price; if you can afford it, it's there. Canadians ration their health care
by providing the same care for everyone and simply making those seeking
elective or less urgent procedures wait."

Plainly, that would not accord with "American-style impatience," one
"student of the two nations" explains. Imagine, he says, that "no matter how
poor you are, you will sit in a hospital bed and receive care as the richest
in your community. No matter what contacts you have and no matter how
rich you are, you can get no better than that." Americans would never accept
that, we learn from this expert (incidentally, the president of a health-care
consulting firm). Further insights into the American psyche are given by the
deputy director of a trade group of commercial health insurers.[18]

The 70 percent of Americans who don't understand their own psyches
are not sampled. That is not unreasonable, after all. They are not students
of the American psyche, and it has long been common understanding that
they need instruction in self-awareness.

Part IV
Memories

CHAPTER 10

MURDERING HISTORY

A few months before the end of Year 500, the *Times Book Review* appeared with a front-page headline reading: "You Can't Murder History." The review-article dedicated to this lesson keeps to a single case: "History in the old Soviet Union was like cancer in the human body, an invisible presence whose existence is bravely denied but against which every conceivable weapon is mobilized." It takes up one striking example of "this disease within the Soviet body politic," the depiction of the murder of the Tsar and his family, recalling "those all-powerful Soviet officials whose job it was to suppress the public's memory of this grisly episode," but who, in the end, "could not hold back the tide."[1]

These reflections did not touch upon a few other examples of murdering history that might come to mind, particularly at this historical moment. Convention has it that multiples of 10 provide the occasion to reflect on the meaning of history and the questions it poses; and perhaps also on the murder of history by its guardians, who, in every society, are acutely sensitive to the faults of official enemies. The convention is useful. By adopting it and examining some of the anniversaries that fall within the 500th year, we can learn something about ourselves, in particular, about the doctrinal foundations of Western culture, a topic of much importance, given the resources of violence, coercion, and denial at its core.

2. The Date which will Live in Infamy

As Year 500 opened in October 1991, other memories displaced the coming quincentennial. December 7 would be the 50th anniversary of the Japanese bombing of Pearl Harbor, the "date which will live in infamy." Accordingly, Japanese attitudes and practices were subjected to close scrutiny, and found wanting. Some profound defect left the aberrant Japanese unwilling to offer regrets for their nefarious deed.

In an interview in the *Washington Post,* Foreign Minister Michio Watanabe expressed "deep remorse over the unbearable suffering and sorrow Japan inflicted on the American people and the peoples of Asia and the Pacific during the Pacific War, a war that Japan started by the surprise attack on Pearl Harbor." He said that the National Parliament would pass a resolution on the 50th anniversary of the crime, expressing Japan's remorse. But this turned out to be just more Japanese treachery. Penetrating the disguise, *New York Times* Tokyo Bureau Chief Steven Weisman revealed that Watanabe had used the word *hansei*, "which is usually translated as 'self-reflection' rather than 'remorse'." The statement of the Foreign Minister does not count as authentic apology. Furthermore, Japan's Parliament is unlikely to pass the resolution, he added, in the light of President Bush's firm rejection of any apology for the Hiroshima and Nagasaki bombings.

No one considers an apology for the 1000-plane raid five days after Nagasaki on what remained of major Japanese cities, a triumph of military management skills designed to be "as big a finale as possible," the official Air Force history relates; even Stormin' Norman would have been impressed. Thousands of civilians were killed, while amidst the bombs, leaflets fluttered down proclaiming: "Your Government has surrendered. The war is over." General Spaatz wanted to use the third atom bomb on Tokyo for this grand finale, but concluded that further devastation of the "battered city" would not make the intended point. Tokyo had been removed from the first list of targets for the same reason: it was "practically rubble," analysts determined, so that the power of the bomb would not be adequately revealed. The final 1000-plane raid was therefore dispersed to seven targets, the Air Force history adds.[2]

Some went beyond George Bush's dismissal of any thought of apology for the use of nuclear weapons to kill 200,000 civilians. Democratic Senator Ernest Hollings told South Carolina workers they "should draw a mushroom cloud and put underneath it: 'Made in America by lazy and illiterate Americans and tested in Japan'," drawing applause from the crowd. Hollings defended his remark as a "joke," a reaction to Japan's "America bashing." The humorless Japanese did not find the joke amusing. The event was briefly reported, provoking no inquiries into the American psyche.[3]

Japan's obsessions with the bomb, which provoke much scorn here, were also revealed after the Texas air shows where the atomic bombing was reenacted annually for many years (perhaps still is) before an admiring audience of tens of thousands, with a B-29 flown by retired Air Force General Paul Tibbets, who lifted the curtain on the atomic age at Hiroshima. Japan condemned the display as "in bad taste and offensive to the Japanese people," to no avail. Perhaps the hypersensitive Japanese would have expressed similar reservations about the showing of a film entitled "Hiroshima" in the early 1950s in Boston's "combat zone," a red-light district where pornographic films were featured: it was a Japanese documentary with live footage of scenes too horrendous to describe, eliciting gales of laughter and enthusiastic applause.

In more sedate intellectual circles, few have considered the observation by Justice Röling of the Netherlands after the Tokyo Tribunal where Japanese war criminals were tried and convicted: "From the Second World War above all two things are remembered: the German gas chambers and the American atomic bombings." Or the impressive dissent by the one independent Asian Justice, Radhabinod Pal of India, who wrote: "When the conduct of the nations is taken into account the law will perhaps be found to be *that only a lost cause is a crime*... if any indiscriminate destruction of civilian life and property is still illegitimate in warfare, then, in the Pacific war, this decision to use the atom bomb is the only near approach to the directives...of the Nazi leaders... Nothing like this could be traced to the present accused" at Tokyo, seven of whom were hanged along with over 900 other Japanese executed for war crimes; among them General Yamashita, executed for atrocities committed by troops over whom he had no control at the war's end. Even the reactions of high-ranking US military officials have been little noted, for example, Admiral William Leahy, chief of staff under the Roosevelt and Truman Administrations, who regarded nuclear weapons as "new and terrible instruments of uncivilized warfare," "a modern type of barbarism not worthy of Christian man," a reversion to the "ethical standard common to the barbarians of the Dark Ages"; its use "would take us back in cruelty toward noncombatants to the days of Genghis Khan."[4]

Recognizing where power lies, Prime Minister Watanabe adopted US conventions in expressing Japan's regrets: he traced Japan's crimes to December 7, 1941, thus implicitly discounting hideous atrocities that killed 10 to 13 million Chinese, by conservative estimate, from 1937 through 1945, not to speak of earlier crimes.[5]

Passing silently over Watanabe's dating of the guilt, Weisman raises only one question: the evasiveness of the gesture at apology. The anniversary commemoration was based upon the same principle: killing, torturing, and otherwise abusing tens of millions of people may not be wholly meritorious, but a "sneak attack" on a naval base in a US colony is a crime of a completely different order. True, to heighten the recognition of Japan's iniquity, its atrocities and aggression in Asia are regularly tacked on to the indictment, but as an afterthought: the Pearl Harbor attack is the real crime, the initial act of aggression.

That decision has many merits. It enables us to ruminate on the strange defects of the Japanese character without having to confront some facts that are better removed from history. For example, the fact that pre-Pearl Harbor, much of the American business community and many US officials rejected "the generally accepted theory that Japan has been a big bully and China the downtrodden victim" (Ambassador Joseph Grew, an influential figure in Far East policy). The US objection to Japan's New Order in Asia, Grew explained in a speech in Tokyo in 1939, was that it imposed "a system of closed economy, ... depriving Americans of their long-established rights in China." He had nothing to say about China's right to national independence, the rape of Nanking, the invasion of Manchuria, and other such marginal issues. Secretary of State Cordell Hull adopted much the same priorities in the negotiations with Japanese Admiral Nomura before the Pearl Harbor attack, stressing US rights to equal access to the territories conquered by Japan in China. On November 7, Japan finally agreed to the US demand, offering to accept "the principle of nondiscrimination in commercial relations" in the Pacific, including China. But the wily Japanese added a qualifying clause: they would accept the principle only if it "were adopted throughout the world."

Hull was greatly shocked at this insolence. The principle was to apply in the Japanese sphere alone, he admonished the impudent *arrivistes*. The US and other Western powers could not be expected to respond in kind in their dominions, including India, Indonesia, the Philippines, Cuba, and other vast regions from which the Japanese had been effectively barred by extremely high tariffs when they unfairly began to win the competitive game in the 1920s.

Dismissing Japan's frivolous appeal to the British and American precedent, Hull deplored the "simplicity of mind that made it difficult for...[Japanese generals]...to see why the United States, on the one hand, should assert leadership in the Western Hemisphere with the Monroe Doctrine and, on the other, want to interfere with Japan's assuming leadership in Asia." He urged the Japanese government to "educate the generals" about this elementary distinction, reminding his backward pupils that the Monroe Doctrine, "as we interpret and apply it uniformly since 1823 only contemplates steps for our physical safety." Respected scholars chimed in with their endorsement, expressing their outrage over the inability of the little yellow men to perceive the difference between a great power like the US and a small-time operator like Japan, and to recognize that "The United States does not need to use military force to induce the Caribbean republics to permit American capital to find profitable investment. The doors are voluntarily open"—as even the most cursory look at history will show.[6]

3. Missing Pieces

Also unmentioned in the historical musings is an air of familiarity about Japan's actions in Manchuria, as they established the "independent" state of Manchukuo in 1932 under the former Manchu emperor. The procedure was "a familiar one," Walter Lippmann wrote at the time, not unlike US precedents "in Nicaragua, Haiti, and elsewhere." Manchuria had claims to independent status, surely stronger claims than, say, South Vietnam 25 years later, a fact recognized by the US client regime, which always defined itself as the Government of all of Vietnam, even in an unamendable article of its US-imposed Constitution. Scholars noted that had it not been for Western intervention in support of Chinese rule over the outer regions, motivated by the desire to increase "the sphere of future Western investment and exploitation," the Tibetans, Mongols, and Manchurians might well have moved towards independence (Owen Lattimore, 1934). Japan undertook to "defend" the "independent state" against "bandits" who attacked it from China. The goal of Japan's Kwantung army was to "liberate the masses" from exploitation by military and feudal cliques and to protect them from Communist terrorists. Adopting the policies favored by Kennedy doves in later years, its military leadership undertook counterinsurgency campaigns, complete with "collective hamlets," earnest measures to win hearts and minds, and other ideas that have a certain resonance. Among a series of unpleasant—hence unmentionable—facts is the similarity of these operations to the no less brutal and atrocious ones conducted by the United States a few years later near China's southern border, operations that peaked in murderous violence shortly after the Japanese documents on Manchuria were released by the RAND Corporation in 1967, to be shelved with appropriate silence by the cultural managers.[7]

The similarity is not entirely accidental. Apart from the fact that the same thoughts naturally come to the minds of similar actors facing similar circumstances, US counterinsurgency doctrine was consciously modelled on the practices and achievements of World War II fascism, though it was the Nazis who were the preferred model. Reviewing US Army manuals of the 1950s, Michael McClintock notes the "disturbing similarity between the Nazi's view of the world and the American stance in the Cold War." The manuals recognize Hitler's tasks to have been much the same as those undertaken by the US worldwide as it took over the struggle against the anti-fascist resistance and other criminals (labelled "Communists" or "terrorists"). They adopt the Nazi frame of reference as a matter of course: the partisans were "terrorists," while the Nazis were "protecting" the population from their violence and coercion. Killing of anyone "furnishing aid or comfort, directly or indirectly, to such partisans, or any person withholding information on partisans," was "legally well within the provisions of the Geneva Convention," the manuals explain. The Germans and their collaborators were the "liberators" of the Russian people. Former *Wehrmacht* officers helped to prepare the army manuals, which culled important lessons from the practices of their models: for example, the utility of "evacuation of all natives from partisan-infested areas and the destruction of all farms, villages, and buildings in the areas following the evacuations"—the policies advocated by Kennedy's dovish advisors, and standard US practice in Central America. The same logic was adopted by the civilian leadership from the late 1940s, as Nazi war criminals were resurrected and reassigned to their former tasks (Reinhard Gehlen, Klaus Barbie, and others), or spirited to safety in Latin America and elsewhere to pursue their work, if they could no longer be protected at home.[8]

The notions were refined in the Kennedy years, under the impetus of the President's well-known fascination with unconventional warfare. US military manuals and "antiterrorism experts" of the period advocate "the tactic of intimidating, kidnapping, or assassinating carefully selected members of the opposition in a manner that will reap the maximum psychological benefit," the objective being "to frighten everyone from collaborating with the guerrilla movement." Respected American historians and moralists were later to provide the intellectual and moral underpinnings, notably Guenter Lewy, who explains in his much-admired history of the Vietnam war that the US was guilty of no crimes against "innocent civilians," indeed could not be. Those who joined our righteous cause were free from harm's way (except by inadvertence, at worst a crime of involuntary manslaughter). Those who failed to cooperate with the "legitimate government" imposed by US violence are not innocent, by definition; they lose any such claim if they refuse to flee to the "safety" provided by their liberators: infants in a village in the Mekong Delta or inner Cambodia, for example. They therefore deserve their fate.[9]

Some lack innocence because they happened to be in the wrong place; for example, the population of the city of Vinh, "the Vietnamese Dresden," Philip Shenon casually observes in a *Times Magazine* cover story on the belated victory of capitalism in Vietnam: it was "leveled by American B-52 bombers" because it was "cursed by location" and hence "was a natural target" for the bombers, much like Rotterdam and Coventry. This city of 60,000 was "flattened" in 1965, Canadian officials reported, while vast surrounding areas were turned into a moonscape.[10] One could learn the facts outside the mainstream, where they were generally ignored, or even flatly denied; for example, by Lewy, who assures us, on the authority of US government pronouncements, that the bombing was aimed at military targets and damage to civilians was minimal.

Plainly, it is better to keep the history under wraps. The Politically Correct approach, adopted without notable deviation on the anniversary, is to date Japan's criminal course to the "sneak attack" on Pearl Harbor; to bring in Japan's earlier atrocities only as a device to sharpen the distinction between their evil nature and our purity; to put aside the uneasy relation between the doctrine that the war began on December 7, 1941 and the fact that we denounce Japan for atrocities committed through the 1930s, which were, furthermore, deemed acceptable in influential circles; and more generally, to eliminate from the mind discordant notes from past and present history.

It is interesting to see the reaction when the rules of decorum are occasionally violated by comparisons between Japan's policies and actions and ours in Vietnam. For the most part, the comparisons are so unthinkable as to be unnoticed, or are dismissed as absurdity. Or they may be denounced as apologetics for Japan's crimes, an interpretation that is quite natural. Given that our perfection is axiomatic, it follows that any comparison drawn confers upon others a share of our nobility, and thus counts as apologetics for their crimes. By the same irrefutable logic, it follows that applause for our crimes is not apologetics, but merely a proper tribute to our magnificence; and silence about them is only a shade less meritorious than enthusiastic approval. Those who fail to comprehend these truths can be condemned for their "irrational hatred of America." Or, if not so completely beyond the pale, they can be offered a course of instruction, like the Japanese generals.

The ban on such subversive thoughts was revealed on the Pearl Harbor anniversary in a striking way, to which we return (section 8). Another example is provided by a commentary on the anniversary by the noted Japan scholar John Dower, solicited by the *Washington Post*. Dower commented that there is "more than a little irony in observing Americans ramble on about other people's military violence and historical amnesia," considering how Vietnam and Korea have entered officially-sanctioned memory. The invited column was rejected.[11]

Another pertinent question was omitted from the deliberations on the aggression launched by Japan on December 7, 1941: How did we happen to have a military base at Pearl Harbor, or to hold our Hawaiian colony altogether? The answer is that we stole Hawaii from its inhabitants, by force and guile, just half a century before the infamous date, in part so as to gain the Pearl Harbor naval base. The centenary of that achievement falls shortly after the opening of Year 501, and might have merited a word as we lamented Japan's failure to face up to its perfidy. Lifting the veil, we find an instructive story.

As long as the British deterrent remained in force, the US government vigorously defended Hawaiian independence. In 1842, President Tyler declared that the US desired "no peculiar advantages, no exclusive control over the Hawaiian Government, but is content with its independent existence and anxiously wishes for its security and prosperity." Accordingly, Washington would oppose any attempt by any nation "to take possession of the islands, colonize them, and subvert the native Government." With this declaration, Tyler extended the Monroe Doctrine to Hawaii. Its independence was also recognized by the major European countries and others, and confirmed by numerous treaties and declarations.

As the century progressed, the balance of power shifted in favor of the United States, offering new opportunities, as in Latin America. US colonists established a thriving sugar industry, and the value of the island as a stepping stone towards broader Pacific horizons became increasingly apparent. Admiral DuPont had observed that "It is impossible to estimate too highly the value and importance of the Hawaiian Islands, whether in a commercial or a military sense." Plainly, our sphere of legitimate self-defense must be extended to include this prize. But there was an impediment: the independence of the island kingdom, and the "demographic problem" posed by the 90 percent majority of native Hawaiians (already reduced to one-sixth the pre-contact era). The colonists therefore undertook to guide and assist these people, so "low in mental culture," and to provide them with the gift of good government—by their betters.

Planters' Monthly observed in 1886 that the Hawaiian "does not yet realize" the "bounds and limits fixed" and the "moral and personal obligations attending" the gift we have offered them: "The white man has organized for the native a Government, placed the ballot in his hands, and set him up as a lawmaker and a ruler; but the placing of these powers in his hands before he knows how to use them, is like placing sharp knives, pointed instruments and dangerous tools in the hands of infants." Similar concerns about the "rascal multitude" and their innate stupidity and worthlessness have been voiced by the "men of best quality" throughout the modern period, forming a major strand in democratic theory.[12]

The first Marine landing to support the colonists took place in 1873, just 30 years after Tyler's ringing endorsement of Hawaii's independence. After failing to take power in the 1886 elections, the plantation oligarchy prepared for a coup d'état, which took place a year later with the help of their military arm, the Hawaiian Rifles. The "Bayonet Constitution" forced upon the king granted US citizens the right to vote, while excluding a large part of the native population through property qualifications and barring Asian immigrants as aliens. Another consequence of the coup was the delivery of the Pearl River estuary to the United States as a naval base.

Exhibiting the "uniform" interpretation of the Monroe Doctrine that so impressed Secretary of State Hull, his predecessor James Blaine observed in 1889 that "there are only three places that are of value enough to be taken. One is Hawaii. The others are Cuba and Puerto Rico." All were shortly to fall into the proper hands.

Regular military interventions ensured good behavior by the locals. In 1891, the USS *Pensacola* was dispatched "in order to guard American interests," which now included ownership of four-fifths of the arable land. In January 1893, Queen Liliuokalani made a last ditch effort to preserve Hawaiian sovereignty, granting the right to vote in Hawaiian elections only to Hawaiians, rich or poor, without discrimination. At the order of US Minister John Stevens, US troops landed and imposed martial law—to support "the best citizens and nine-tenths of the property owners of the country," in the words of the commanding officer. Stevens informed the Secretary of State that "The Hawaiian pear is now fully ripe and this is the golden hour for the United States to pluck it." Long before, John Quincy Adams had used the same imagery with regard to the second of "the places of value," Cuba, a "ripe fruit" that would fall into our hands once the British deterrent is removed (see chapter 6).

The US planters and their native collaborators produced a declaration proclaiming the conviction of the "overwhelming majority of the conservative and responsible members of the community"—who numbered a few hundred men—"that independent, constitutional, representative and responsible government, able to protect itself from revolutionary uprisings and royal aggression, is no longer possible in Hawaii under the existing system of government." Under protest, the Queen surrendered to the "superior force of the United States of America" and its troops, abdicating in the hope of saving her followers from the death penalty; she herself was fined $5000 and sentenced to five years at hard labor for her crimes against good order (commuted in 1896). The Republic of Hawaii was established with American planter Sanford Dole proclaiming himself President on July 4, 1894. Each sip of Dole pineapple juice offers an occasion to celebrate another triumph of Western civilization.

Congress passed a joint resolution for annexation in 1898, as the US went to war with Spain and Commander George Dewey's naval squadron sank a decrepit Spanish fleet in Manila, setting the stage for the slaughter of hundreds of thousands of Filipinos as another ripe fruit was plucked from the tree. President McKinley signed the annexation resolution on July 7, 1898, creating "The First Outpost of a Greater America," a journal of the "conservative and responsible members of the community" triumphantly proclaimed. Their iron-fisted rule eliminated any residual interference by the "ignorant majority," as the planters called them, still about 90 percent of the population, soon to become dispersed, impoverished, and oppressed, their culture suppressed, their lands stolen.[13]

In this manner, Pearl Harbor became a major military base in the US colony of Hawaii, to be subjected a half-century later to a scandalous "sneak attack" by Japanese monsters setting forth on their criminal path.

On January 2, 1992, the Institute for the Advancement of Hawaiian Affairs published a document entitled "The Cause of Hawaiian Sovereignty," reviewing the history, in preparation for "the 100th anniversary of the overthrow of Hawaii" in January 1993.[14] Short of a dramatic change in the reigning culture, that anniversary is destined to remain deeply buried in the memory hole, joining many others that commemorate the fate of the victims of the 500 year conquest.

4. Some Lessons in Political Correctness

Let us return to the public commemoration of the 50th anniversary of the infamous date, carefully sanitized and insulated from improper thoughts. Americans are much annoyed by the unwillingness of the Japanese to face their guilt for the Pearl Harbor crime, Urban Lehner reports in a lengthy *Wall Street Journal* article on Japanese "revisionism." He quotes the Pearl Harbor memorial park historian on "the complete absence of a sense in Japan of their own history." To illustrate "Japan's ambivalence toward remembering history," Lehner describes a visit to the home of a "courtly" Japanese military historian, who "can't understand why the U.S. won't forget it. 'If the U.S. and Japan are partners, why talk about Pearl Harbor forever? That's what Japanese people are thinking,' he says. 'Why do you keep reminding us?'"[15]

So the article ends, no comment being necessary on the unique sins of the Japanese exhibited with such clarity.

The *New York Times Magazine* devoted a cover story to this peculiarly Japanese malady by Tokyo Bureau Chief Weisman, entitled "Pearl Harbor in the Mind of Japan." There is "little sound of remorse," the subtitle reads, and "no commemorative ceremonies of the bombing in Japan." The US will approach the event "from a completely different perspective," Weisman writes, reflexively taking that perspective to be right and proper, no questions asked. His study of this topic exemplifies the general style and provides useful instruction in the techniques of Political Correctness, encapsulating many of the standard gambits.[16]

Americans were not always so clear as they are today about the simple verities, Weisman observes. In the late '60s, "guilt-ridden over the Vietnam conflict...American historians were more willing to question American motives in Asia. Today, their tone is much less apologetic"—the last word, an interesting choice. With the Persian Gulf war and the collapse of communism, "Times have changed," and "Roosevelt's drawing a line in the sand is no longer seen as improper."

Weisman's claims about the late '60s contain a particle of truth: younger historians associated with the antiwar movement did indeed begin to raise previously forbidden questions. They were compelled to form their own professional association (the Committee of Concerned Asian Scholars), with very few senior faculty involved, to discuss subversive thoughts about possible flaws in "American motives." Though they were the cream of the graduate student crop at the time, not many survived the authoritarian structure of the ideological disciplines; some were eliminated from the academic world in straight political firings, some marginalized in other familiar ways. The young scholars did receive some support in the mainstream, notably from John King Fairbank, the dean of Asian scholarship and a figure at the dissident extreme, often accused of crossing the line to Communist apologetics. He outlined his own position on the Vietnam war in his presidential address to the American Historical Association in December 1968, well after the corporate sector had called for terminating the enterprise. The war was an "error," Fairbank explained, based on misunderstanding and naiveté, yet another example of "our excess of righteousness and disinterested benevolence."[17]

One will find very little questioning of American motives in respectable circles then, or since.

Conventional falsehoods commonly retain their appeal because they are functional, serving the interests of established authority. Weisman's tales about the late '60s are a case in point: they buttress the view that the academy, the media, and intellectual life generally have been taken over by a left-wing onslaught, leaving only a few last brave defenders of simple truths and intellectual values, who therefore must be given every bit of support that can be mustered for their lonely cause, a project well-suited to current doctrinal needs (see chapter 2.4).

Like all right-thinking people, Weisman takes it as axiomatic that the US stance in the Persian Gulf and the Cold War is subject to no imaginable qualification, surely no questioning of "American motives." Also following convention, he evades entirely the issue of shared responsibility for the Pacific war. The issue is not "Roosevelt's drawing a line in the sand," but rather the decision of the traditional imperial powers (Britain, France, Holland, US) to close the doors of their domains to Japan after it had followed the rules of "free trade" with too much success; and the US position, maintained to the end, that the US-Japan conflict might be resolved if Japan would permit the US to share in exploiting all of Asia, while not demanding comparable rights in US-dominated regions. Weisman indeed recognizes that such issues have been raised, making sure to frame them in a proper way. He does not refer to the discussion of the actions of the imperial powers in Western scholarship as events unfolded, or since. Rather, these are the "startling" words of Prime Minister Hideki Tojo, hanged in 1948 as a Class A war criminal, who "defiantly defended the attack on Pearl Harbor as forced by 'inhuman' economic sanctions imposed by Washington," which "would have meant the destruction of the nation," had Japan not reacted. Could there be a particle of truth lurking behind the thought? The question need not be answered, since it cannot rise to consciousness.

Weisman writes that "of course, most American historians would have little trouble rendering a judgment on Japan's singular responsibility, if not guilt," noting Japan's "annex[ation] of Manchuria in 1931," and its "bloody sweep through China" in 1937 and later into Indochina, driving out the French colonial regime. No words here on the US attitude towards all of this at the time, except for an oblique hint: "Beginning with the decision to move naval vessels in 1940, the United States responded to Japanese military aggression with warnings and protests"—nine years after the invasion of Manchuria, three years after the murderous escalation in China. Why the delay? Weisman also puts aside other questions: Why were Western claims to their colonial domains stronger than those of Japan, and why did indigenous nationalists often welcome the Japanese conquest, driving out the traditional oppressors? Nor is he troubled by a simple fact of logic: If these were Japan's crimes, then why do we commemorate a much later event as the "date which will live in infamy"? Why is it "the tragedy of 50 years ago" that evokes Weisman's inquiry into Japan's flawed psyche?

Weisman does concede a measure of US responsibility: not for what happened, but for Japan's failure to face up to its crimes. The US wanted "to create a democracy" after the war, but "After China fell to the Communists in 1949 and the Korean War broke out a year later, Washington changed its mind, deciding to foster a stable conservative Government in

Japan to challenge Communism in Asia," even sometimes allowing war criminals to regain authority.

This revision of history also has its functional utility: under the laws of Political Correctness, it is permissible to recognize our occasional lapses from perfection if they can be interpreted as an all-too-understandable overreaction to the evil deeds of selected malefactors. In fact, as Weisman surely knows, Washington's "reverse course" was in 1947, hence well before the "fall of China" (to translate: the overthrow of a corrupt US-backed tyranny by an indigenous movement); and 3 years before the officially-recognized Korean war, at a time when the pre-official phase was charging full-speed ahead, as the US-imposed regime, aided by fascist collaborators restored by the US occupying army, was busy slaughtering some 100,000 anti-fascists and other adherents of the popular movements that the US clients could never hope to face in political competition.

Washington's "reverse course" called a halt to democratic experiments that threatened established power. The US moved decisively to break Japanese unions and reconstruct the traditional industrial-financial conglomerates, supporting fascist collaborators, excluding anti-fascist elements, and restoring traditional conservative business rule. As explained in a 1947 paper prepared under the direction of the primary author of the reverse course, George Kennan, the US had "a moral right to intervene" to preserve "stability" against "stooge groups" of the Communists: "Recognizing that the former industrial and commercial leaders of Japan are the ablest leaders in the country, that they are the most stable element, that they have the strongest natural ties with the US, it should be US policy to remove obstacles to their finding their natural level in Japanese leadership." The purge of war criminals was ended, and the essential structure of the fascist regime restored. The reverse course in Japan was one element in a worldwide US campaign at the same time with the same goals, all prior to 1949.[18]

The reconstruction of what US technical experts angrily condemned as "totalitarian state capitalism," with popular and democratic forces suppressed, was underway well before the reverse course of 1947. The Occupation also determined at once that the basic issues of war guilt would be shelved. General MacArthur "would neither allow the emperor to be indicted, nor take the stand as a witness, nor even be interviewed by International Prosecution investigators" at the War Crimes trials, Herbert Bix writes, despite ample evidence of his direct responsibility for Japanese war crimes—available to MacArthur, but kept secret. This whitewashing of the monarchy had "momentous" consequences for reestablishing the traditional conservative order and defeating a far more democratic alternative, Bix concludes.[19]

Weisman observes correctly that Japan's "goal was to assure access to natural resources, markets and freedom of the seas." These goals it has now attained, he adds, by "its own hard work" and "the generosity (and self-interest) of the United States." The implication is that Japan could have achieved the same goals 50 years ago, had it not been in the grip of fascist ideology and primitive delusion. Overlooked are some obvious questions. If Japan could have achieved these ends by accepting Western norms, then why did the British, the Americans, and the other imperial states not simply abandon the high tariff walls they had erected around their colonies to bar Japan? Or, assuming that such idealism would be too much to ask, why did Hull not at least accept the Japanese offer for mutuality of exploitation? Such thoughts go beyond legitimate bounds, reaching into the forbidden territory of "American motives."

In the real world, Japan's aggression gave an impetus to the nationalist movements that displaced colonial rule in favor of the more subtle mechanisms of domination of the postwar period. Furthermore, the war left the US in a position to design the new world order. Under these new conditions, Japan could be offered its "Empire toward the South" (as Kennan put it) under US control, though within limits: the US intended to maintain its "power over what Japan imports in the way of oil and such other things" so that "we would have veto power on what she does need in the military and industrial field," as Kennan advised in 1949.[20] This stance was maintained until unexpected factors intervened, notably the Vietnam war with its costs to the US and benefits to Japan and other industrial rivals.

Yet another fault of the Japanese, Weisman observes, is the "bellicose terms" in which they frame Japanese-American relations, thus revealing their penchant for militarism. The Japanese speak of "their 'second strike': if Washington cuts off Japanese imports, Tokyo can strangle the American economy by cutting off investments or purchases of Treasury bonds." Even if we adopt Weisman's unexamined judgment on the impropriety of such retaliation, it would hardly seem to rank high in comparison to standard US practices: for example, the devastating and illegal economic warfare regularly waged against such enemies as Cuba, Chile, Nicaragua, and Vietnam; or the efforts of Jacksonian Democrats to "place all other nations at our feet," primarily the British enemy, by gaining a monopoly over the most important commodity in world trade.

Japan's worst sin, however, is its tendency towards "self-pity," its refusal to offer reparations to its victims, its "clumsy attempts to sanitize the past" and in general, its failure to "come forward with a definitive statement of wartime responsibility." Here Weisman is on firm ground—or would be, if he, or his editors, or their colleagues in the doctrinal system were even to consider the principles they espouse for others. They do not, not for a moment, as the record shows with utter clarity.

5. "Self-Pity" and other Character Flaws

The 50th anniversary was commemorated with cover stories in the major newsweeklies, articles in the press, and TV documentaries. Several were applauded by *Wall Street Journal* critic Dorothy Rabinowitz for their "unrelentingly tough historic view of the Pearl Harbor attack," with no ambiguities about the distinction between pure righteousness and absolute evil (December 2). She reserves her condemnations for the "journalists of the fashionable Left and the terminal Right" who "invariably" portray the Japanese "as victims" of the dastardly Americans. Examples of these lunacies are omitted; the actual historical issues receive not a phrase.

The opposite side of the page carries an article by Robert Greenberger headlined "U.S.-Vietnam Ties Remain Held Back By the MIA Issue," describing a Vietnamese plan "to solve the main issue blocking a resumption of relations: accounting for Americans missing since the Vietnam War." This news report is so conventional as to merit no particular notice, apart from the interesting layout. It is a staple of the media, and the culture generally, that we were the injured party in Vietnam. We were innocent victims of what John F. Kennedy called "the assault from the inside" (November 12, 1963), the "internal aggression" by South Vietnamese peasants against their legitimate government and the saviors who imposed it upon them and defended their country from them.[21] Later we were treacherously assaulted by the North Vietnamese. Not content with attacking us, they also imprisoned Americans who had mysteriously fallen into their hands. Unrelenting, the Vietnamese aggressors proceeded to abuse us shamefully after the war's end, refusing to cooperate fully on the fate of US pilots and MIAs, even failing to devote themselves with proper dedication to locating the remains of pilots they had viciously blasted from the skies.

Our suffering at the hands of these barbarians is the sole moral issue that remains after a quarter-century of violence, in which we vigorously backed the French effort to reconquer their former colonies; instantly demolished the 1954 diplomatic settlement; installed a regime of corrupt and murderous thugs and torturers in the southern sector where we had imposed our rule; attacked that sector directly when the terror and repression of our clients elicited a reaction that they could not withstand; expanded our aggression to all of Indochina with saturation bombing of densely-populated areas, chemical warfare attacks to destroy crops and vegetation, bombing of dikes, and huge mass murder operations and terror programs when refugee-generation, population removal, and bulldozing of villages failed; ultimately leaving three countries destroyed, perhaps beyond the hope of recovery, the devastated land strewn with millions of corpses and unexploded ordnance, with countless destitute and maimed, deformed fetuses in the hospitals of the South that do not touch the heartstrings of "pro-life" enthusiasts, and other horrors too awful to recount in a region "threatened with extinction...as a cultural and historic entity...as the countryside literally dies under the blows of the largest military machine ever unleashed on an area of this size," in the words of the hawkish historian Bernard Fall, one of the leading experts on Vietnam, in 1967—that is, *before* the major US atrocities were set in motion.[22]

From all of this, one single element remains: the terrible abuse we have suffered at the hands of our tormenters.

Reactions to our adversity are not entirely uniform. At the dovish extreme, we find Senator John Kerry, who warns that we should never again fight a war "without committing enough resources to win"; no other flaw is mentioned. And there is President Carter, the noted moral teacher and human rights apostle, who assured us that we owe Vietnam no debt and have no responsibility to render it any assistance because "the destruction was mutual," an observation so uncontroversial as to pass with no reaction. Others less inclined to turn the other cheek forthrightly assign the blame to the Vietnamese Communists alone, denouncing the anti-American extremists who labor to detect lingering ambiguities.[23]

In the *New York Times,* we read stories headlined "Vietnam, Trying to be Nicer, Still has a Long Way to Go," with Asia correspondent Barbara Crossette reporting that though the Vietnamese are making some progress "on the missing Americans," they are still far from approaching our lofty moral standards. And a hundred others with the same tone and content. Properly statesmanlike, President Bush announces that "It was a bitter conflict, but Hanoi knows today that we seek only answers without the threat of retribution for the past." Their crimes against us can never be forgotten, but "we can begin writing the last chapter of the Vietnam war" if they dedicate themselves with sufficient zeal to the MIAs. We might even "begin helping the Vietnamese find and identify their own combatants missing in action," Crossette reports. The adjacent front-page story reports Japan's failure, once again, to "unambiguously" accept the blame "for its wartime aggression."[24]

As the 1992 presidential campaign heated up, Vietnam's savage maltreatment of suffering America flared up into a major issue: had Washington done enough to end these abuses, or had it conspired to efface them.

A front-page *New York Times* story by Patrick Tyler captured the mood. Tyler reported that the White House had rejected Ross Perot's 1987 proposal that easing the pressures against Hanoi might be "a way to win the repatriation of any American servicemen still held in Southeast Asia." "At the time," Tyler observes, "Washington was taking a harder diplomatic line with Hanoi to achieve the same end." "History has shown that concessions prior to performance is death," said Richard Childress, NSC official supervising POW/MIA policy. "They'll take and take and take," he added. "We've learned that over 25 years." "United States negotiators were holding onto their leverage until Hanoi made progress on a step-by-step 'roadmap' to improved relations, through cooperation on P.O.W./M.I.A. investigations," Tyler adds, without even the most timid query about Washington's declared intentions or a hint, however faint, that someone might fail to appreciate their righteousness.[25]

As the country solemnly contemplated "the Mind of Japan," deploring the disgraceful "self-pity" of the Japanese, their failure to offer reparations to their victims, or even to "come forward with a definitive statement of wartime responsibility," the US government and press escalated their bitter denunciations of the criminals in Hanoi who not only refuse to confess their guilt but persist in their shameful mistreatment of innocent America. In a lengthy report on this rising indignation over Vietnam's morbid insistence on punishing us 17 years after the war's official end, Crossette wrote that expectations for diplomatic relations between the US and Vietnam "may be set back by a resurgence of interest in one piece of unfinished business that will not go away: the fate of missing Americans." Properly incensed by Vietnam's iniquity, George Bush, opened Year 500 in October 1991 by intervening once again to block European and Japanese efforts to end the embargo that the US imposed in 1975, while Defense Secretary Dick Cheney reported to Congress that "despite improved cooperation," the Vietnamese will have to do more before we grant them entry into the civilized world. "Substantial progress" on the MIA issue is required as a condition for normalizing ties, Secretary of State James Baker said, a process that could take several years. Meanwhile, officials in one of the world's poorest countries continue to show irritation, as they did "last week when the United States blocked a French proposal calling for the International Monetary Fund to lend money to Vietnam," the *Times* reported.[26]

For a time, the embargo was imposed to punish Vietnam for yet another crime: its assault against Pol Pot in response to murderous Khmer Rouge attacks on Vietnamese border areas. The US had striven to normalize relations despite Vietnam's cruel treatment of us, Barbara Crossette reports under the heading "Indochina's Missing: An Issue That Refused to Die." But, she continues, "President Carter's efforts to open links to Hanoi were thwarted by Vietnam's invasion of Cambodia in 1978." Naturally, the saintly moralist could not overlook unprovoked aggression; had George Bush been in charge, he doubtless would have sent Stormin' Norman to crush the aggressor (at least, if there had been a guarantee that no one would shoot back).[27]

Carter's deep feelings about the war crime of aggression had been demonstrated for all to see by his reaction to Indonesia's invasion of East Timor—in this case, not terminating a murderous assault on the population but initiating a comparable one. As Indonesian violence approached genocidal levels in 1978 and its military supplies were running low, the Carter Administration sharply stepped up the flow of arms to its Indonesian ally, also sending jets via the Israeli connection to evade congressional restrictions; 90 percent of Indonesian arms were US-supplied, on the strict condition that they be used only for defensive purposes. From his moral pinnacle, Carter surveyed the Vietnamese crime of aggression and reluctantly terminated his efforts to bring Vietnam into the community of civilized nations, so we are instructed. The principled US opposition to the use of force in international affairs was revealed again through the 1980s; for example, by Washington's decisive support for Israel's invasion of Lebanon and the accompanying slaughter, the government-media reaction to the World Court judgment in 1986 ordering the US to desist from its "unlawful use of force" against Nicaragua, Bush's invasion of Panama to celebrate the fall of the Berlin wall and the end of the Cold War, and much else.[28]

According to the USG-*Times* version, Washington "refused to normalize relations as long as a Vietnamese-backed Government in Cambodia resisted a negotiated settlement to its civil war" (Steven Greenhouse); that is, the conflict with the Khmer Rouge, supplied by China and Thailand (and, indirectly, the US and its allies), and attacking Cambodian rural areas from their Thai sanctuaries.[29]

The reality is a bit different. The Carter Administration "[chose] not to accept the Vietnamese offer to reestablish relations," Raymond Garthoff observes, impelled primarily by its early 1978 "tilt towards China" and, accordingly, toward China's Khmer Rouge ally, well before Vietnam invaded Cambodia. Pol Pot proceeded to carry out the worst atrocities of his reign, concealed by the CIA in its later demographic study, presumably because of the US connection. Unlike many European countries, the US did not abstain at the UN on the "legitimate" government of Cambodia after the Khmer Rouge were expelled by the Vietnamese, but "joined China in supporting the Khmer Rouge" (Garthoff). The US backed China's invasion to "punish Vietnam," and turned to supporting the Thai-based coalition in which the Khmer Rouge was the major military element. The US "encouraged the Chinese to support Pol Pot," as Carter's National Security Adviser, Zbigniew Brzezinski, later commented. Deng Xiaoping, a particular favorite of the Reagan-Bush Administrations, elaborated: "It is wise to force the Vietnamese to stay in Kampuchea because they will suffer more and will not be able to extend their hand to Thailand, Malaysia, and Singapore," which they no doubt would have proceeded to conquer had they not been stopped in time. After helping to reconstruct Pol Pot's shattered forces, the US-China-Thailand coalition (and the West generally) lent its diplomatic support to Pol Pot; imposed an embargo on Cambodia and blocked aid from other sources, including humanitarian aid; and undermined any moves toward a negotiated settlement that did not offer the Khmer Rouge an influential role. The US even threatened Thailand with loss of trade privileges if it refused to support the Khmer Rouge, the *Far Eastern Economic Review* reported in 1989.

It was under the pressure of the five permanent members of the UN Security Council that "the Cambodians were forced...to accept the return of the Khmer Rouge," Sihanouk pointed out in his first speech after his triumphant return to Cambodia in November 1991. A year earlier, he had informed US journalist T.D. Allman that "To save Cambodia...all you had to do [in 1979] was to let Pol Pot die. Pol Pot was dying and you brought him back to life."[30]

A more accurate rendering of *Times*-speak, then, is that Vietnam's efforts to restore relations were thwarted by the Carter Administration's turn towards China and the Khmer Rouge, that the US exploited the pretext of the invasion to punish the people of Vietnam and Cambodia as severely as possible, and that Washington refused to allow any diplomatic settlement that did not guarantee the Khmer Rouge a leading role.

By expelling this tacit US ally from Cambodia, bringing to an end atrocities that peaked after Carter's "tilt toward China" (hence toward Pol Pot), and then keeping him at bay, Vietnam "may have earned the thanks of most Cambodians," *Globe* editor H.D.S. Greenway writes. But these actions "earned it the opprobrium of most of the rest of the world"—notably, those parts of the world that follow US whims. But Vietnam's withdrawal from Cambodia eliminated this pretext for the embargo, leaving only Vietnam's mistreatment of us on the MIA issue. This continuing crime, US moralists in press and government explain, requires that we keep the embargo in force, thus depriving Vietnam of loans and investments from the international financial institutions that the US controls and the Europeans and Japanese, wary of stepping on the toes of their powerful and relentless ally.[31]

The Pearl Harbor anniversary itself was marked by a *Washington Post* editorial noting that although Vietnam had made progress, "some MIA advocates" allege that it "is holding back remains." "It will take considerable openness on Hanoi's part and diligent investigation on Washington's to clear up this question," the editors sternly conclude. If the Vietnamese are willing to cooperate fully, we may allow them to join the world community, though we will never forgive them for the harm and pain they have inflicted upon us for over 40 years, any more than we can forget the Japanese infamy of just a few years earlier.[32]

Turning again to the real world, it is largely US business interests that are complaining over the fanatical commitment to "bleed Vietnam"; they fear that they may be cut out of opportunities for profit by competitors abroad, that they may not get their "fair share of trade in Vietnam," as one executive puts it. These considerations do provide some reason to rethink our stand. We might relent, the press reports, if Vietnam agrees to two years of excavations, takes steps to open our way to Laos and Cambodia, promises to turn over any remains that may ever be found, and grants us "immediate access to the Vietnamese countryside" and to military archives; as the aggrieved party, we meanwhile confine Vietnamese diplomats at the UN to the immediate vicinity, and as for military archives, ...[33]

"There are Vietnamese like Deputy Foreign Minister Le Mai, who 'says he understands the need of the American government to convince the American people on the MIAs'," Greenway writes. "The Vietnamese also understand that the issue of missing Americans is the single greatest barrier to lifting the American-imposed trade embargo, establishing diplomatic relations with the US, and rejoining the world community." But, Greenway adds, "there are also Vietnamese who speak with great bitterness against what they see as America making a political issue of its own loss with a country that has 200,000 to 300,000 of its soldiers missing and unaccounted for." One Vietnamese war veteran suggests that Americans "come back and tell us where Vietnamese are buried." "What a task," Greenway writes from ample direct experience as a war correspondent, "recalling long-suppressed memories of bulldozers shoveling Vietnamese corpses into pits and helicopter sling loads, with arms and legs protruding from the mesh, being carted off to some unmarked grave."[34]

Greenway deserves credit for this rare departure from the ranks, though we might take note of a few other problems that some might attribute to an agent who remains unnamed.

None of this, hardly a secret, stands in the way of allowing the US to "rejoin the world community," or calls for *hansei* —whether "remorse" or even "self-reflection"—not to speak of reparations for ghastly crimes.

Other voices are too faint to penetrate our orgy of self-pity over the abuse we suffer; for example, the surgeon who carried out a delicate operation in February 1990 to remove a US-made shell from the arm of one of the many victims killed or maimed by unexploded ordnance after the fighting ended. The miserable Commies were berated with much scorn when they released maps of mines in Afghanistan so that civilians could be protected from the deadly legacy of their aggression. There were no such denunciations of the United States, for a simple reason: Washington refused to provide mine maps to civilian mine-deactivation teams in Indochina. As a Pentagon spokesman explained, "people should not live in those areas. They know the problem." What is more, as a matter of elementary logic, no condemnation could be in order for seeding the countryside with mines or anti-personnel bomblets in "our excess of righteousness and disinterested benevolence."[35]

Readers of the foreign press can hear the voice of 11-year-old Tran Viet Cuong in the city of Vinh—which had the misfortune of being "cursed by location," as the *Times* thoughtfully explained (p. 242). His parents desperately want him to obtain an education, and since the town cannot afford schoolbooks, Tran must go without breakfast so that his parents can buy them (if he's lucky, his teacher will buy chalk out of a salary eked from two or three jobs). The local government also "cannot afford to repair many of the roads, hospitals and sewage drains destroyed 20 years ago by U.S. bombers," John Stackhouse reports from the shattered city. In 1991, the children's hospital was forced to close 50 of 250 beds and to ask patients to provide medicines. Doctors perform surgical operations on a table donated by Poland, largely without equipment. At the Vinh Medical Center, where the hospital's pharmacy remains "a pile of rubble," a doctor states the obvious: "the problems here are a consequence of the American war, and the embargo has made it worse."

The embargo, Stackhouse notes, has "isolated Vietnam internationally, cutting it off from trade and aid flows," blocking aid from development organizations where the US has "an effective veto," including the Manila-based Asian Development Bank, which is prepared to lend $300 million, including funds for an irrigation project that could increase farm yields by one-third. Though Vietnam undertook the structural adjustment programs required by the official lenders well before Eastern Europe, it cannot receive any of the low-cost World Bank funds designed to ease the severe impact, thanks to the stern US veto. The result is that child deaths are two to three times higher than in Bangladesh, and the education system, "which once produced an overwhelmingly literate population," has collapsed. Commercial banks and other donors and investors will not move until the US permits it, and foreign markets are largely closed, so there is no prospect for private sector jobs. Even a UNICEF appeal failed, because "No one wants to offend the U.S.," the director of UNICEF's Ho Chi Minh city office observes.[36]

Readers of the foreign press may also hear the voices of mountain tribesmen in October 1991, as they "asked authorities for permission to shoot down a U.S. helicopter when they heard it was on the way to investigate evidence of U.S. soldiers missing in action." "It is not difficult to uncover the source of the pent-up aggression" here, Canadian correspondent Philip Smucker reports: "It is only a matter of locating which village has had a child recently maimed or killed by a 'bomblet,' a tiny bomb left hidden in the soil for the past 18 years" in a region where "carpet bombing and dioxin spraying by U.S. aircraft...devastated the forests, leaving much of the countryside looking like a mountainous moonscape perforated with craters the size of Cadillacs," the soil "drenched with more than 200 litres [of chemical poisons] a square hectare," so that "the number of deformed children is much higher here than in the North where there was no spraying." In this isolated region alone, "more than 5,000 people have been injured and killed" from unexploded bombs since 1975. "I hate the man who dropped this bomb," a peasant says "standing in front of a crater 10 times his size that is literally at his doorstep," one of the relics of the B-52 carpet bombings that killed his wife in 1969. Another tells of his 8-year-old son, who had just been blown to pieces a few weeks earlier when he picked up a round metal object in the mud, another child's death that "will go unrecorded in the annals of the Vietnam War."[37]

Surely there is nothing here to trouble our unsullied conscience as we scrutinize the deformed minds of the perfidious Japanese and the psychic disorders that so puzzle and intrigue us. Those who have memorized the guiding doctrine of the 500-year conquest will have no difficulty perceiving the moral chasm that lies between us and the Japanese: Morality comes from the barrel of a gun—and we have the guns.

As if to highlight the point, the *New York Times* Science Section ran an article headlined "Study of Dioxin's Effect in Vietnam Is Hampered by Diplomatic Freeze." The "diplomatic freeze" is depicted with the symmetry that objective journalism demands ("Vietnamese and American officials move at a glacial pace in negotiations to improve ties," etc.), but the article is unusual in noting some unfortunate consequences of this curious mutual disorder. The problem is that the "17-year freeze in relations between Vietnam and the United States is hindering vital research into long-term effects of Agent Orange and other sources of dioxin on both military and civilian populations." This is most unfortunate, since much might be learned "about the potential dangers of industrial dioxin in the West by studying the people in areas sprayed during the Vietnam War with large doses of American defoliants containing dioxin."

"Vietnam is an ideal location for more research into potential links between dioxin and cancer, reproductive dysfunction, hormone problems, immune deficiencies, disorders of the central nervous system, liver damage, diabetes and altered lipid metabolism," the article continues, and may help solve the "critical" problem of determining "the level at which it might become dangerous to humans." That the creatures under inquiry might have some needs to be addressed, perhaps by the hidden agent, is a thought too exotic to be addressed, even hinted.

There are two reasons why "Vietnam could provide excellent opportunities for study." "First, a large number of Vietnamese of all ages and both sexes have been exposed to dioxin," including "many women and children," while in the West, industrial accidents or "neighborhood contamination" as in Seveso, Italy, and Love Canal "have involved small groups in confined areas," mostly men. Second, Vietnam "furnishes an extensive control group," since northerners "were not sprayed." Another useful feature is that "Many Vietnamese had substantial exposures to dioxin." "Eighty percent of the Vietnamese lived in rural areas and were frequently barefoot or in sandals," an American researcher comments. "Cooperation in Vietnam couldn't be better," but "we're letting a unique opportunity fade" to "study the health consequences for all of us" because of the continuing freeze; "Time is running out for studies of people exposed to spraying."[38]

Perhaps this interesting research project might include a look at the children dying of cancer and birth defects or the women with rare malignant tumors in hospitals in the South (not the North, spared this particular atrocity), the sealed containers with hideously deformed babies, and other "terrifying" scenes reported occasionally in the foreign press or far from the public eye here. That inquiry too might yield benefits for the United States.[39]

This critique of the mutual disorder departs from convention in at least suggesting that something may be awry. Like all too much else, it may raise in some minds the question whether the intellectual culture is real, or a script by Jonathan Swift. The critique recalls the occasional complaints about the heavy censorship in Japan under the American occupation, imposed in secret (references to it were censored) while the US designed a Constitution for Japan stating that "No censorship shall be maintained, nor shall the secrecy of any means of communication be violated," and General MacArthur "was emphatically telling the Japanese people and

Japanese journalists that freedom of the press and freedom of speech were very close to his heart and were freedoms for which the Allies had fought the war" (Monica Braw). The censorship had been instituted at once and was maintained for four years, by which time the purge of dissidents made it less important. One motive, from the first days, was to prevent any discussion of the atom bomb or its effects. These were kept as secret as possible within Japan because of concerns that the truth might "disturb public tranquility" and imply that "the bombing was a crime against humanity," one censor declared as he barred an eyewitness account of the Nagasaki atrocity. Even Japanese scientific papers were barred. That did elicit some objections, but not because the censorship hindered treatment of survivors, an issue largely ignored; rather, because a unique opportunity to learn more about radiation damage was being lost.[40]

As America contemplated Japan's crimes on the fiftieth anniversary, a new book appeared on the one American atrocity that has indeed been recognized: the My Lai massacre in March 1968. American reviewers were shocked to learn that "the infamous Lt. Calley," who commanded the killers, "served less than three years of confinement in his bachelor officer quarters before he was paroled" and now enjoys life as a Georgia businessman, driving his Mercedes sedan from his pleasant home to the shopping mall where his jewelry store is located. Concluding his reflections on the massacre, the *Washington Post* reviewer observes: "Any book on this subject ultimately shirks its responsibility unless it clearly tracks the fault down to the complex light and dark of the individual human soul."

In the London *Financial Times*, Justin Wintle had a different reaction:

> Like nearly every other book about Vietnam published in the West, *Four Hours in My Lai* focuses on America, and the damage done to the American self-esteem. The other half of the equation is marginalised. Although [the authors] dutifully record the eye-witness accounts of a handful of survivors of My Lai, the engulfing sorrow that still pervades Quang Ngai as a result of eight years' occupation by US and South Korean forces is here unsung. Instead the reader is swamped by any amount of often trivial biographical detail pertaining to the lives of nearly every American mentioned in the text.

That pattern had been set early on. Few winced when the *New York Times* published a think piece from My Lai on the fifth anniversary of the massacre, in March 1973, noting that the village and region remained "silent and unsafe," though the Americans were still "trying to make it safe" by relentless bombardment and shelling. The reporter quoted villagers who accused the Americans of killing many people, adding philosophically:

"They are in no position to appreciate what the name My Lai means to Americans."[41]

The *Washington Post* review observes the laws of Political Correctness by enjoining us to plumb the depths of "the individual human soul" with its dark complexities, to seek the answer to My Lai in some universal fault of the human species, not in US policies and institutions. The laws prescribe that the US only reacts to the crimes of others, and has no policies beyond a general benevolence; in Quang Ngai province, no policies beyond "trying to make it safe" for the suffering Vietnamese who we are "protecting." True, there was destruction in Indochina, but, quite commonly, with no agent. There were "substantial tracts of land made fallow by the war," the *Times* leading Asia hand, Fox Butterfield, reports, coining a phrase that would have made Orwell gasp. His colleague Craig Whitney summarized "the legacy of the war": "the punishment inflicted on [the Vietnamese] and their land when the Communists were allowed to operate in it" and the villagers "driven from the ancestral homes by the fighting." It was all some natural disaster, inexplicable, except by musing on the darkness of the individual human soul, perhaps.[42]

The British reviewer recommended a step beyond: a look at "the objectives of Washington's policy makers," not merely the soul of Lt. Calley and the half-crazed GIs in the field who carried out the brutal massacre, knowing only that every Vietnamese in the ruins of a Quang Ngai village— man, woman, or child—was a potential threat to their lives. As a first step in determining these objectives, we might inspect Operation Wheeler Wallawa, in which the official body count listed 10,000 enemy, including the victims of My Lai. In his detailed study of this and other mass murder operations of the period, *Newsweek* Bureau Chief Kevin Buckley writes that My Lai was "a particularly gruesome application of a wider policy which had the same effect in many places at many times," for example, in one area of four villages where the population was reduced from 16,000 to 1,600, or another where the US military command's location plots reveal that B-52 bombings were targeted precisely on villages, and where helicopters chased and killed people working in the fields. "Of course, the blame for that could not have been dumped on a stumblebum lieutenant," Buckley commented: "Calley was an aberration, but 'Wheeler Wallawa' was not." Or many other operations like it, a fact that brings certain thoughts to mind.[43]

North American relief workers in Quang Ngai knew of the My Lai massacre at once, but, like the local population, took no particular notice because it was not considered out of the ordinary. Retired army officer Edward King wrote that "My Lai represented to the average professional soldier nothing more than being caught up in a cover-up of something which he knew had been going on for a long time on a smaller scale." By accident, the military panel investigating the My Lai massacre found another much like it a few miles away, at My Khe, but dismissed charges against the commanding officer on the grounds that it was a perfectly normal operation in which a village was destroyed with about 100 people killed and the remnants forcibly relocated—much like the remnants of My Lai, sent to a waterless camp on Batangan Peninsula over which floated a banner reading: "We thank you for liberating us from communist terror." There, they were subjected to Operation Bold Mariner, which "tried to make that region safe" with probably even greater slaughter and ecological devastation.[44]

Could there be another candidate for war crimes trials, beyond General Yamashita and 1000 others executed for their crimes in the Pacific War?

6. On Sensitivity to History

Recall that one of the character flaws we discover in exploring "the Mind of Japan" is their "clumsy attempts to sanitize the past" and "the complete absence of a sense in Japan of their own history," much like the Soviet officials who mobilized "every conceivable weapon...to suppress the public's memory" of the "grisly episodes" that form "the larger cancer" of history, finally in vain, because "You Can't Murder History."

Or can you? The fate of the Indochina wars in US ideology illustrates our right to pontificate on this issue. A still more recent example is the Central America episode of the past decade: some future historian will gaze in wonder at our self-adulation over the monstrous atrocities we perpetrated there, surpassing even the earlier achievements that have helped to keep our "backyard" in deepest misery.

The very idea of an American intellectual judging others on how they come to terms with their history is so astounding as to leave one virtually speechless. Who among us, from the earliest days, has failed to come to terms with the truth about slavery or the extermination of the native population? Can there be a resident of civilized New England, for example, who has not committed to memory the gruesome details of the first major act of genocide, the slaughter of the Pequot Indians in 1637, the remnants sold into slavery? Who has not learned the proud words of the 1643 Puritan account of these inspiring acts, describing the official dissolution of the Pequot nation by the colonial authorities, who outlawed even the designation *Pequot* "so that the name of the Pequots (as of Amalech) is blotted out from under heaven, there being not one that is, or (at least) dare call himself a Pequot"? Surely every American child who pledges allegiance to our nation "under God" is instructed as to how the Puritans borrowed the rhetoric and imagery of the Old Testament, consciously modelling themselves on His Chosen People as they followed God's command, "'smiting' the Canaanites and driving them from the Promised Land" (Neil Salisbury). Who has not shown *hansei* while studying the chroniclers who extolled our revered forebears as they did the Lord's work in accord with the admonitions of their religious leaders, fulfilling their "divine mission" with a pre-dawn surprise attack on the main Pequot village while most of the men were away, slaughtering women, children, and old men in true Biblical style? In their own words, the Puritans turned the huts into a "fiery Oven" in which the victims of "the most terrible death that may be" were left "frying in the fire and the streams of blood quenching the same," while the servants of the Lord "gave the praise thereof to God, who had wrought so wonderfully for them." Can there be anyone who has not asked whether our history might offer some later resonances of this exultation over the extermination of those who had "exalted themselves in their great Pride," arrogantly refusing to grant us what they have?[45]

Or if southern Connecticut is too remote for intellectual and moral guides in our greatest city, then surely they could not have failed to immerse themselves in the records of the actions that cleared the New York region of the native scourge only a few years later. For example, the account by David de Vries of his experiences in Lower Manhattan in February 1643, while Dutch soldiers massacred peaceful Algonquin Indians right across the Hudson, finally exterminating or expelling almost all Native Americans from the New York Metropolitan area. The killers in this case preferred another favored model of the Founding Fathers,

> considering they had done a deed of Roman valor in murdering so many in their sleep; where infants were torn from their mother's breasts, and hacked to pieces in the presence of the parents, and the pieces thrown into the fire and in the water, and other sucklings, being bound to small [cradle] boards, were cut, stuck, and pierced, and miserably massacred in a manner to move a heart of stone. Some were thrown into the river, and when the fathers and mothers endeavored to save them, the soldiers would not let them come on land but made both parents and children drown.

Not unlike the Rio Sumpul massacre on the Salvador-Honduras border in 1980, the first major atrocity of the US-run war in El Salvador, which some day perhaps the *New York Times* may even discover; and countless other operations of the elite battalions fresh from their US training, armed with US arms, and guided by the doctrines we have taught them for many years.[46]

No one can accuse us of concealing the actions that cleared the New York area; the facts are, after all, readily available to everyone in *Native American Place Names in New York City*, prominently published by the Museum of the City of New York.

The spectacle of our "sensitivity to history" is too obscene to merit review, though neglect would not be quite the right word. Anyone who can recall the images and lessons of their childhood will know why; at least those whose childhood years came before the impact of the popular movements of the 1960s was finally felt, arousing a chorus of revulsion over the PC takeover of our previously saintly culture. My own memories were reawakened a few weeks after the exposure of the My Lai massacre in 1969, while thumbing through a fourth-grade text on colonial New England assigned in a Boston suburb noted for the quality of its schools. The children indeed read a fairly accurate account of the slaughter of the Pequots— which was applauded, much in the manner of the Puritan record of 1643.[47]

And so the story continues right through the 500th year. In the *Times Book Review*, historian Caleb Carr reviews a book on the 1862 Sioux Uprising in Minnesota. The "Minnesota encounter," he explains, was "a total war between rival nations for control of a territory both groups were willing to die for." But there was a crucial asymmetry. For one nation, "settlement was generally their last hope"; they were "staking not only their fortunes but also their very lives on the hope of building new lives in untried country." For the natives, at least at first, "the terms of the conflict" were "less mortal"; they could, after all, trudge off further West. Carr describes the "encounter" as "less than inspiring," and praises the author for recognizing that both nations were guilty of crimes. Those of the Sioux are outlined in gory detail ("atrocious behavior," "sadism and blood lust," "a particular penchant for torturing infants and children," etc.); the tune changes markedly when Carr turns to the settlers seeking to build new lives (broken treaties, hanging of 38 Sioux, expulsion even of some who were not "guilty" of resistance, etc.). But the radical difference is only fair, given the asymmetry of need in the "encounter."

To conjure up a nightmare, suppose the Nazis had won the European war. Perhaps some later German ideologue might have conceded that the "encounter" between Germans and Slavs on the Eastern front was "less than inspiring," though for balance, we must recall that it was "a total war between rival nations for control of a territory both groups were willing to die for"; and for the Slavs "the terms of the conflict" were "less mortal" than for the Germans needing *Lebensraum,* "staking not only their fortunes but also their very lives on the hope of building new lives in untried country." The Slavs, after all, could trudge off to Siberia.[48]

It is noteworthy that Carr's review opens with the predictable frothing at the mouth about the evils of PC, that is, the efforts of a misguided few to face some of the truths of history. That is a common posture; in the *Times, de rigueur* on this topic (among others). In a typical case, another *Times* reviewer, with bitterness dripping from every line, writes that a novel on Columbus "adheres closely to the new multi-cultural perspective," focusing on what the author "sees as the devastating effects that Columbus's arrival in the New World had on the native populations," including "the supposed deaths of thousands of people." Who but a fashionable "multi-culturalist" could believe that the effects of the conquest were "devastating" or could "suppose" that "thousands" of Native Americans died? A second *Times* reviewer of the same book, former *Newsweek* senior book critic Paul Prescott, chimes in with a hysterical denunciation of the "ideologically correct" author for daring to write that the Spanish harmed the natives of Hispaniola while suppressing "the kind of history is not politically correct": that the natives "told [Columbus] that their immediate problem was that they were being eaten by the Caribs." How they "told" Columbus this tale of woe, and why no record exists, Prescott does not explain; on the "immediate problem" as seen by the contemporary observer Las Casas, who denied the cannibalism charge concocted by Columbus, see pp. 198-9.[49]

It is not unreasonable to suppose that the extremely crude but quite effective propaganda campaign about the takeover of our culture by PC left fascists was in part motivated by the forthcoming quincentennial, with the danger that it might elicit some "self-reflection," perhaps even "remorse."

7. "Thief! Thief!"

The renewal of the punishment of Vietnam for its crimes, the voices of the unheard victims, the search into the depths of the "individual human soul" (but nothing more) in the case of our admitted departure from purity, and our contemplation of "the Mind of Japan"—all of these fall on the 50th anniversary of Pearl Harbor, along with the resurgence of self-pity over our tragic fate.

Those who might believe that the POW-MIA issue reflects the profound humanitarian impulses of our leaders will quickly be disabused of this naive idea by a look at a few comparisons. Walter Wouk, a Vietnam veteran who chairs the New York State Senate Vietnam Veterans Advisory Council, writes:

> At the end of World War II the U.S. had 78,751 MIAs, 27 percent of the war's U.S. battle deaths. The Korean War resulted in 8,177 MIAs which represented 15.2 percent of the Americans killed-in-action. Of the 2.6 million Americans who served in Vietnam, 2,505—less than 5.5 percent of the U.S. battle deaths—are listed as missing in action. But even that figure is misleading. Of that number 1,113 were killed in action, but their bodies were not recovered. Another 631 were presumed dead because of the circumstances of their loss—i.e., airmen known to have crashed into the sea—and 33 died in captivity. The remaining 728 are missing. It should be noted that 590 of the missing Americans (81 percent) were airmen; and there were strong indications that more than 442 of these individuals (75 percent) went down with their aircraft.

Are the Vietnam MIAs in a special category because of the refusal of the savage Communists to allow a thorough search? In the major study of the MIA campaign, Bruce Franklin points out that remains of MIAs from World War II are discovered almost every year in the European countryside, where no one has hampered any search for 45 years. Remains from General Custer's 1876 battle were still being located in the 1980s, as were skeletons of Confederate soldiers and US soldiers killed in Canada during the War of 1812.[50]

The truth of the matter is not hard to perceive. The state-media complex has been resorting to a trick familiar to every petty crook and tenth-rate lawyer: when you are caught with your hand in someone's pocket, cry "Thief! Thief!" Don't try to defend yourself, thus conceding that there is an issue to confront: rather, shift the onus to your accusers, who must then defend themselves against your charge. The technique can be highly effective when control over the doctrinal system is assured. The device is familiar to propagandists, virtually a reflex, adopted unthinkingly. The PC propaganda operation is a transparent example (chapter 2.4).

The device also comes naturally to the corporate rulers, who commonly present themselves as pathetic and embattled, desperately trying to survive the onslaught of the liberal media, powerful unions, and hostile government forces that keep them from earning an honest dollar. Their media propagandists play the same game. During the Pittston mine workers strike in 1989-1990, the company president ran daily press conferences, though it was hardly necessary, since the media were eager to do his work for him. In the first (and only) TV gesture toward coverage, Robert Kulwich of CBS commented that Pittston Coal Group president "Mike Odom is willing to say that the union has done a very slick public relations job, and that he has some catching up to do." That takes care of the fact that the national media—to the limited extent that they covered this historic labor struggle at all—adopted the company point of view reflexively, deflecting union efforts to present the issues as the workers saw them with their practiced efficiency.[51]

The same device is standard in debate over the media. It is child's play to demonstrate their subordination to state power with regard to Indochina, Central America, and the Middle East. Accordingly, the sole issue we are permitted to discuss is whether the media went too far in their adversarial zeal, perhaps even undermining the foundations of democracy (the questions pondered in the solemn deliberations of the Trilateral Commission and Freedom House). An academic study of the media on Central America and the Middle East, led by a man with proper liberal credentials, considers only the question of the anti-establishment fervor of the media: Was it too extreme, or did they manage to keep it within tolerable bounds? As in this case, the "Thief! Thief!" technique is particularly effective when the analyst can be placed at the outer limits of dissidence. Thus long-time NPR Middle East correspondent Jim Lederman inquires into the fervent support of the US media for the cause of the Palestinians, their manipulation by Yasser Arafat, and their consuming hatred of Israel—all so obvious to any reader. Exhibiting his left-liberal credentials, he concludes that there is no proof of a conscious anti-Semitic conspiracy, despite appearances.[52]

In such ways, mountains of evidence can be made to disappear with a mere flick of the wrist. The technique requires lock-step loyalty on the part of the cultural managers. But the unwashed masses are sometimes more difficult to handle.

In the case of Vietnam, by the late 1960s substantial sectors of the public were joining those whom Kennedy-Johnson National Security adviser McGeorge Bundy called "the wild men in the wings," questioning the "first team" that was running the war, and even the justice of the US cause.[53] With all the help provided by the mass media, things were reaching the point where the murderous barbarism of the US war could no longer be concealed or defended. The predictable response was to cry "Thief! Thief!" Of course, there was nothing new in this. But the Indochina wars were reaching the stage where something was needed beyond the norm.

By the late '60s, schoolchildren were given assignments in the *Weekly Reader*, which goes to elementary schools throughout the country, to write letters to Ho Chi Minh pleading with him to release the Americans he had captured—the implication being that the evil Communists had snatched them as they strolled peacefully on Main Street, Iowa, spiriting them off to

Hanoi for the purpose of torturing them. The PR campaign went into full gear in 1969, for two major reasons. First, US atrocities were reaching a scale that surpassed any hope of denial. Defense against the charges being impossible, the debate must be transferred to the evil nature of the enemy: *his* crimes against *us*. Second, corporate America had determined that the war must end. It would therefore no longer be possible to evade diplomacy and negotiations. But the Eisenhower-Kennedy-Johnson doctrine still held firm: diplomacy is not an option because the US and its clients were too weak politically to hope to prevail in the arena of peaceful competition. Accordingly, Nixon and Kissinger radically accelerated and expanded the violence, and sought in every way to deflect unwanted negotiations. The device used was to raise demands on prisoner return that no belligerent had ever so much as considered in the past, in the hope that Hanoi would keep to traditional Western standards and reject them, so that the Commie rats could be denounced for their infamy and the negotiations could be delayed.

After the war's end, a new motive arose. The destruction of Indochina was not considered a sufficient victory: it was necessary to continue to strangle and crush the Vietnamese enemy by other means—refusal of diplomatic relations, economic warfare, and the other devices available to the toughest guy on the block. The cause was taken up by President Carter, accelerated as he made his "tilt toward China" in early 1978. It has been pursued since by his successors, with the support of the political class generally. Its current manifestations, we have just reviewed.

This resort to the "Thief! Thief!" technique was a brilliant success throughout, thanks to the compliance of the institutions of indoctrination. Franklin reviews the matter in some detail, showing how the press leaped into the fray on command while film-makers and TV pursued the ingenious strategy of selecting the best-publicized atrocities of the US and its client and rearranging personnel to transform them into crimes of the enemy. The supreme cynicism of the enterprise is highlighted by the maneuvers that had to be undertaken to shift from professed outrage over Pol Pot atrocities—itself an utter fraud in elite circles, as demonstrated conclusively by their reaction to US atrocities in Cambodia a few years earlier and to those of the US-backed Indonesian client in Timor in the very same years[54]—to a complex stand in which Pol Pot is condemned as the very symbol of Communist horror, while the Vietnamese invasion that saved Cambodia from his atrocities is shaped into a still more monstrous Communist atrocity, and the quiet US support for Pol Pot is somehow finessed. Even that task was effortlessly accomplished. And the ideological institutions shifted gears smoothly when the Cambodia pretext was lost and only the POW/MIA issue remained to justify the torture of the people of Indochina.

Michael Vickery makes the important point that every time Vietnam has had a chance, however slight, to escape from the conditions left from the cruel and destructive era of French colonialism, the US has stepped in to block that opportunity. When the Geneva settlement of 1954 laid the basis for unification with countrywide elections, the US barred that option, recognizing that the wrong side would surely win. Though the DRV (North Vietnam) was cut off from the traditional food surplus areas in the south, by 1958 it had achieved food self-sufficiency while industry was developing—a prospect of success that caused much dismay among US planners, who urged secretly that the US do what it could to retard the economic progress of the Communist Asian states, with its dangerous demonstration effect. They were particularly concerned over the progress in the DRV in comparison to the failures of the US-imposed regime in the south: US intelligence in 1959 expected development in the South to "lag behind that in the North," where economic growth was proceeding and was "concentrated on building for the future." The Kennedy escalation and its aftermath took care of that threat.

After the war, Vietnam was admitted to the IMF, and in a confidential report of 1977, a World Bank team "praised the Vietnamese government's efforts to mobilize its resources and tap its vast potential." The US made short shrift of that danger as well, blocking any assistance and imposing an economic stranglehold. In 1988-1990, Vickery observes further, "in spite of an extremely unfavorable international position, Vietnam had come through with a surprising economic success," leading the IMF to present a "glowing report," the *Far Eastern Economic Review* reported. The response was George Bush's renewal of the embargo; and in the ideological institutions, a revival of lagging fervor over the abuse we endure at the hands of the criminal aggressors.[55]

There is method in the madness. Apart from the principled opposition to Third World development out of US control, it is important for subject peoples to understand that they dare not raise their heads in the presence of the master. If they do, not only will they be devastated by overwhelming violence, but they will continue to suffer, as long as we deem it in our interests. Current treatment of Nicaragua illustrates the pattern, as of Iraq, where Bush's friend and ally stepped out of line, so we must see to it that tens of thousands of his Iraqi victims die of starvation and disease after the war's end. The West sternly destroys the weapons of mass destruction it provided to this monster when it was profitable and advantageous to do so, while unleashing "the destructive power of another weapon of mass destruction—the effective withdrawal of food and other necessities from the Iraqi people," two specialists on world hunger observe.[56] The lower orders must understand their place in a world of order and "stability."

In its editorial on Vietnam marking the Pearl Harbor anniversary, the editors of the *Washington Post* note the

> abiding irony that the United States lost the war in a military sense but ended up imposing a victor's terms for normalization. It could do so because it remained a country representing dominant global values, powerfully influencing the regional balance and the international economy. This is how all the concessions came to be made by Vietnam.

The statement has merit, though a little amplification is in order. The "dominant global values" extolled by the *Post* editors are the values of those who wield the sword and thereby set the rules.[57]

It would be difficult to find an example in the 500-year conquest as sordid, dishonest, and cowardly as the carefully contrived display of self-pity on the part of the murderous aggressors who destroyed three countries, leaving mountains of corpses and countless others maimed and orphaned, in order to block a political settlement that they knew their clients were too weak to sustain—a fact that is clear from the internal record, has been developed in detail by military historians, and is recognized even by the most fanatic government "scholars."[58] The "abiding irony" is that this shameful performance proceeds, untroubled, alongside our musings about the defects of the Japanese psyche.

8. A Date which does not Live in Infamy

The irony—to use a word that hardly meets the need—is heightened by another anniversary that did not reach threshold. The 50th anniversary of the "date which will live in infamy" coincided with the 30th anniversary of John F. Kennedy's escalation of the Vietnam conflict from large-scale international terrorism to outright aggression. On October 11, 1961, Kennedy ordered dispatch of a US Air Force Farmgate squadron to South Vietnam, 12 planes especially equipped for counterinsurgency warfare (combat modified T-28 fighter bomber trainers, SC-47s, and B-26 bombers), soon authorized "to fly coordinated missions with Vietnamese personnel in support of Vietnamese ground forces." On December 16, Defense Secretary McNamara authorized their participation in combat operations. These were the first steps in engaging US forces directly in bombing and other combat operations in South Vietnam from 1962, along with sabotage missions in the North. These 1961-1962 actions laid the groundwork for the huge expansion of the war in later years.[59]

As we have seen, the anniversary did not pass entirely unmarked: Bush chose the occasion—almost 30 years to the day after Kennedy's first major step in this fateful direction—to block the admission of Vietnam to the world community, and the propaganda apparatus orchestrated a revival of its POW/MIA hypocrisies. To the best of my knowledge, the conjunction of anniversaries reached the media three times: Michael Albert (*Z magazine*), and Alexander Cockburn (*Nation, Los Angeles Times*).[60]

In a world of truth and honesty, that failure could be attributed to the distinction between the two cases, so large as to make the comparison irrelevant and unfair. It hardly makes sense to draw a comparison between Japan's attack on a naval facility in a US colony, after some relevant earlier interactions, and the first major act of aggression against a defenseless civilian society 10,000 miles away. History offers no controlled experiments, but those who seek an analogy might, perhaps, compare Japan's sneak attack to the US bombing of Libya in 1986, carefully timed for the 7pm EST national evening news; the Reagan PR folks borrowed a leaf from Lyndon Johnson, who had ordered the bombing of North Vietnam in retaliation for the alleged Tonkin Gulf incident in August 1964 for 7pm EST, though the military could not oblige in that case. But this comparison too, one might argue, is still unfair to the Japanese. The US attack on Libya was aimed at civilian targets, on fraudulent pretexts; the Tonkin Gulf "retaliation" too was readily detected to be a fraud, outside the compliant mainstream.[61]

Such thoughts are doubtless too outlandish to pursue. Let us therefore put them aside, though some might find something in them to consider as we turn to Year 501.

The coincidences of 1991-1992 are striking: great indignation on the 50th anniversary of Pearl Harbor, the backgrounds carefully sanitized; sober contemplation of the Mind of Japan and the social and cultural flaws revealed therein; silence on the 30th anniversary of John F. Kennedy's direct attack against the civilian society of South Vietnam. The combination is a rare tribute to the moral cowardice and intellectual corruption that are the natural concomitants of unchallenged privilege.

One last coincidence might be noted, of no small interest in itself. The forgotten 30th anniversary of JFK's aggression happened to be the occasion for an outpouring of adulation for the fallen leader who, it was claimed with some passion, intended to withdraw from Vietnam, a fact suppressed by the media; and had been assassinated for that reason, it was prominently charged. The awed admiration for Kennedy the lonely hero, struck down as (and perhaps because) he sought to prevent a US war in Vietnam, adds an interesting touch to the questions of *hansei* that might find some small place in the 500th year. This 1991-1992 drama proceeded at several levels, from cinema to scholarship, engaging some of the best-known Kennedy intellectuals as well as substantial segments of the popular movements that in large part grew from opposition to the Vietnam war. Much as they differ on parts of the picture and other issues, there is a shared belief across this spectrum that history changed course dramatically when Kennedy was assassinated in November 1963, an event that casts a dark shadow over all that followed. Specific timing apart, the renewal of Camelot enthusiasms is an interesting and enlightening manifestation of the cultural and political climate of the early 1990s.

There is no doubt about the import of what followed Kennedy's 1961 aggression. The nature of his plans and the reaction to them is therefore of great interest. The perception of current reality, the shaping of memories, and ideas about a better future could be significantly affected by the truth of the matter: At one end of the spectrum of views, the murder of the President, however tragic the killing of an individual may be, was an event of indeterminate political consequence, though one may speculate one way or another without firm basis[62]; at the other, it was a momentous historical event, with extraordinary long-term significance and ominous portent.

There are many sources of evidence that bear on the question: in particular, the record of internal deliberations is available far beyond the norm. While history never permits anything like definitive conclusions, in this case the richness of the record, and its consistency, permit some unusually confident judgments, in my opinion. The issue has aroused sufficient interest to merit a separate discussion, presented elsewhere, which I will only summarize here. The basic story that emerges from the historical and documentary record seems to me, in brief, as follows.[63]

Policy towards Vietnam fell within the general framework of doctrine that had been established for the post-World War II global order, and faced little challenge until the general framework was modified in the early 1970s. The US quickly threw in its lot with France, fully aware from the start that it was opposing the forces of Indochinese nationalism and that its own clients could not withstand political competition. Accordingly, resort to peaceful means was never an option; rather, a dire threat to be avoided. It was also understood, throughout, that domestic support for the US wars and subversion was thin. It was therefore necessary to wind the operation up as quickly as possible, leaving Indochina under the control of client regimes, to the extent feasible.

Basic policies held firm in planning circles (and among elites generally) from 1950 into the early 1970s, though by the end questions of feasibility and cost were seriously raised. The Geneva agreements of 1954 were at once subverted. The US imposed a fragile client regime in what came to be called "South Vietnam." Lacking popular support, the regime resorted to large-scale terror to control the population, finally eliciting resistance, which it could not control. As Kennedy took office, collapse of the US position seemed imminent. Kennedy therefore escalated the war to direct US aggression in 1961-1962. The military command was exuberant over the success of the enhanced violence, and thought that the war could soon be wound up, leading to US withdrawal after victory. Kennedy went along with these predictions though with reservations, never willing to commit himself to the withdrawal proposals. By mid-1963, coercive measures appeared to be successful in the countryside, but internal repression had evoked large-scale urban protest. Furthermore, the client regime was calling for a reduction of the US role or even US withdrawal, and was making overtures for a peaceful settlement with the North. The Kennedy Administration therefore resolved to overthrow its client in favor of a military regime that would be fully committed to military victory. This result was achieved with the military coup of November 1, 1963.

As the US command had predicted, the coup simply led to further disintegration, and as the bureaucratic structure of the former regime dissolved, to a belated recognition that reports of military progress were built on sand. Tactics were then modified in the light of two new factors: (1) the hope that at last a stable basis had been established for expanded military action, and (2) recognition that the military situation in the countryside was a shambles. The first factor made escalation possible, the second made it necessary, even more so as the former hopes were seen to be a mirage. The plans to withdraw, always predicated on victory, had to be abandoned as the precondition collapsed. By early 1965, only large-scale US aggression could prevent a political settlement. The unchallenged policy assumptions allowed few options: the attack against South Vietnam was sharply escalated in early 1965, and the war was extended to the North.

The January 1968 Tet offensive revealed that the war could not be quickly won. By that time, internal protest and deterioration of the US economy vis-à-vis its industrial rivals convinced domestic elites that the US should move towards disengagement.

These decisions set in motion the withdrawal of US ground forces, combined with another sharp escalation of the military assault against South Vietnam and by now all of Indochina in the hope that the basic policies could still somehow be salvaged. Negotiations continued to be deferred as long as possible, and when the US was finally compelled to sign a "peace treaty" in January 1973, Washington announced at once, in the clearest and most explicit terms, that it would subvert the treaty in every crucial respect. That it proceeded to do, in particular, by increasing the violence in the South in violation of the treaty, to much domestic acclaim as the tactic appeared to be successful. The dissident press could tell the story, but the mainstream was entirely closed to such heretical truths, and still is, a ban maintained with impressive rigor.[64] These actions of the US and its client again elicited a reaction, and the client regime again collapsed. This time the US could not enter to rescue it. By 1975, the war ended.

The US had achieved only a partial victory. On the negative side, the client regimes had fallen. On the positive side, the entire region was in ruins, and there was no fear that the "virus" of successful independent development might "infect" others. Improving the picture further, the region was now insulated from any residual danger by murderous military regimes that the US helped install and strongly supported. Another consequence, predictable years earlier, was that the indigenous forces in South Vietnam and Laos, unable to resist the US onslaught, had been decimated, leaving North Vietnam as the dominant force in Indochina.[65] As to what would have happened had these forces survived and the countries allowed to develop in their own ways, one can only speculate. The press and journals of opinion are happy to serve up the desired formulas, but these, as usual, reflect doctrinal requirements, nothing more.

Basic policy remained constant in essentials: disentanglement from an unpopular and costly venture as soon as possible, but after the virus was destroyed and victory assured (by the 1970s, with increasing doubt that US client regimes could be sustained). Tactics were modified with changing circumstances and perceptions. Changes of Administration, including the Kennedy assassination, had no large-scale effect on policy, and not even any great effect on tactics, when account is taken of the objective situation and how it was perceived.

The scale of these colonial wars and their destructiveness was extraordinary, and the long-term import for international and domestic society correspondingly great. But in their essentials, the Indochina wars fall well within the history of the 500-year conquest, and more specifically, within the framework of the period of US hegemony.

CHAPTER 11

THE THIRD WORLD AT HOME

---

1. "The Paradox of '92"

The basic theme of the 500-year conquest is misread if it sets Europe—broadly construed—against the subject domains. As Adam Smith stressed, the interests of the architects of policy are not those of the general population; the internal class war is an inextricable element of the global conquest. One of the memories that reverberates through the 500 years is that "European societies were also colonized and plundered," though the "better-organized" communities with "institutions for economic regulation and political self-government" and traditions of resistance were able to retain basic rights and even extend them through continuing struggle.[1]

The end of the affluent alliance and the onset of the "new imperial age" have intensified the internal class war. A corollary to the globalization of the economy is the entrenchment of Third World features at home: the steady drift towards a two-tiered society in which large sectors are superfluous for wealth-enhancement for the privileged. Even more than before, the rabble must be ideologically and physically controlled, deprived of organization and interchange, the prerequisite for constructive thinking and social action. "The paper has taken us one at a time and convinced us 'how good the times' are," Wobbly writer T-Bone Slim commented: "We have no opportunity to consult our neighbor to find out if the press speaketh the truth."[2] A large majority of the population regard the economic system as "inherently unfair," look back at the Vietnam war as not a "mistake" but "fundamentally wrong and immoral," favored diplomacy not war as the US prepared to bomb Iraq, and so on. But these are private thoughts; they do not raise the dread threat of democracy and freedom as long as there is no systematic way "to consult our neighbor." Whatever the individual thoughts may be, collectively we march in the parade. No presidential candidate, for example, could possibly say "I opposed the Vietnam war on principled grounds and honor those who refused to obey the order to fight a war that was 'fundamentally wrong and immoral'."

In any system of governance, a major problem is to secure obedience. We therefore expect to find ideological institutions and cultural managers to direct and staff them. The only exception would be a society with an equitable distribution of resources and popular engagement in decision-making; that is, a democratic society with libertarian social forms. But meaningful democracy is a remote ideal, regarded as a danger to be averted, not a value to be achieved: the "ignorant and meddlesome outsiders" must be reduced to their spectator status, as Walter Lippmann phrased the theme that has long been common coin. The current mission is to ensure that any thought of controlling their destiny must be driven from the minds of the rascal multitude. Each person is to be an isolated receptacle of propaganda, helpless in the face of two external and hostile forces: the government and the private sector, with its sacred right to determine the basic character of social life. The second of these forces, furthermore, is to be veiled: its rights and power must be not only beyond challenge, but invisible, part of the natural order of things. We have travelled a fair distance on this path.

The rhetoric of the 1992 election campaign illustrates the process. The Republicans call for faith in the entrepreneur, accusing the "other party" of being the tool of social engineers who have brought the disaster of Communism and the welfare state (virtually indistinguishable). The Democrats counter that they only intend to improve the efficiency of the private sector, leaving its dictatorial rights over most of life and the political sphere unchallenged. Candidates say "vote for me," and I will do so-and-so for you. Few believe them, but more important, a different process is unthinkable: that in their unions, political clubs, and other popular organizations people should formulate their own plans and projects and put forth candidates to represent them. Even more unthinkable is that the general public should have a voice in decisions about investment, production, the character of work, and other basic aspects of life. The minimal conditions for functioning democracy have been removed far beyond thought, a remarkable victory of the doctrinal system.

Toward the more totalitarian end of the spectrum, self-styled "conservatives" seek to distract the rascal multitude with jingoist and religious fanaticism, family values, and other standard tools of the trade. The spectacle has elicited some bemused commentary abroad. Observing the 1992 Republican convention, from the pre-Enlightenment God and Country Rally on opening day to the party platform crafted by evangelical extremists, and the fact that the Democratic candidate "mentioned God six times in his acceptance speech" and "quoted from scriptures," the *Economist* wondered at a society "not ready yet for openly secular leaders," alone in the industrial world. Others watched with amazement as a debate between the

Vice-President and a TV character occupied center stage. These are signs of the success in defanging democratic forms, to eliminate any threat to private power.[3]

Contemporary right-wing discourse can hardly fail to bring to mind earlier denunciations of "liberalism," with its call "for women's equality" and denial of the ancient truth that a woman's "world is her husband, her family, her children, and her home" (Adolf Hitler). Or the warning, from the same voice, that it is "a sin against the will of the Almighty that hundreds upon thousands of his most gifted creatures should be made to sink in the proletarian swamp while Kaffirs and Hottentots are trained for the liberal professions"—however the current version may be masked in code words. The resort to "cultural" themes and religious-jingoist fervor revives the classic fascist technique of mobilizing the people who are under assault. The encouragement of religious "enthusiasm," in particular, has a long history within what E.P. Thompson called "the psychic processes of counter-revolution" used to tame the masses, breeding "the chiliasm of despair," the desperate hope for some other world than this one, which can offer little.[4]

Studies of public opinion bring out other strands. A June 1992 Gallup poll found that 75 percent of the population do not expect life to improve for the next generation of Americans—not too surprising, given that real wages have been dropping for 20 years, with an accelerated decline under Reaganite "conservatism," which also managed to extend the cloud over the college-educated. Public attitudes are illuminated further by the current popularity of ex-presidents: Carter is well in the lead (74 percent) followed by the virtually unknown Ford (68 percent), with Reagan at 58 percent, barely above Nixon (54 percent). Dislike of Reagan is particularly high among working people and "Reagan Democrats," who gave him "the highest unfavorable rating [63 percent] of a wide range of public officials," one study found. Reagan's popularity was always largely a media concoction; the "great communicator" was quickly dismissed when the farce would no longer play.[5]

The Harris polling organization has been measuring alienation from institutions for 25 years. Its latest survey, for 1991, found the numbers at an all-time high of 66 percent. Eighty-three percent of the population feel that "the rich are getting richer and the poor are getting poorer," saying that "the economic system is inherently unfair," Harris president Humphrey Taylor comments. The concerns of the overwhelming majority, however, cannot be addressed within the political system; even the words can barely be spoken or heard. The journalist who reports these facts sees only people who are angry at "their well-paid politicians" and want "more power to the

people," not "more power to the government." We are not allowed to think
that government might be of and by the people, or that they might seek to
change an economic system that 83 percent regard as "inherently unfair."[6]

Another poll revealed that "faith in God is the most important part of
Americans' lives." Forty percent "said they valued their relationship with
God above all else"; 29 percent chose "good health" and 21 percent a
"happy marriage." Satisfying work was chosen by 5 percent, respect of
people in the community by 2 percent. That this world might offer basic
features of a human existence is hardly to be contemplated. These are the
kinds of results one might find in a shattered peasant society. Chiliastic
visions are reported to be particularly prevalent among blacks; again, not
surprising, when we learn from the *New England Journal of Medicine* that
"black men in Harlem were less likely to reach the age of 65 than men in
Bangladesh."[7]

Also driven from the mind is any sense of solidarity and community.
Educational reform is designed for those whose parents can pay, or at least
are motivated to "get ahead." The idea that there might be some general
concern for children—not to speak of others—must be suppressed. We
must make "the true costs of bearing a child out of wedlock clear" by letting
"them be felt when they are incurred—namely at the child's birth"; the
teenage high-school dropout must realize that her child will get no help
from us (Michael Kaus). In the rising "culture of cruelty," Ruth Conniff
writes, "the middle-class taxpayer, the politician, and the wealthy upper
class are all victims" of the undeserving poor, who must be disciplined and
punished for their depravity, down to future generations.

When the Caterpillar corporation recruited scabs to break a strike by
the United Auto Workers, the union was "stunned" to find that unemployed
workers crossed the picket line with no remorse, while Caterpillar workers
found little "moral support" in their community. The union, which had
"lifted the standard of living for entire communities in which its members
lived," had "failed to realize how public sympathy had deserted organized
labor," a study by three *Chicago Tribune* reporters concludes—another
victory in an unremitting business campaign of many decades that the
union leadership refused to see. It was only in 1978 that UAW President
Doug Fraser criticized the "leaders of the business community" for having
"chosen to wage a one-sided class war in this country—a war against
working people, the unemployed, the poor, the minorities, the very young
and the very old, and even many in the middle class of our society," and
having "broken and discarded the fragile, unwritten compact previously
existing during a period of growth and progress." That was far too late, and

the tactics of the abject servant of the rich who soon took office destroyed a good bit of what was left.[8]

The *Tribune* study sees the defeat of the union as "the end of an era, the end of what may be the proudest creation of the American labor movement in the 20th century: a large blue-collar middle class." That era, based on a corporation-union compact in a state-subsidized private economy, had come to an end 20 years earlier, and the "one-sided class war" had been underway long before. Another component of the compact was "the exchange of political power for money" by the union leaders (David Milton), a bargain that lasted as long as the rulers found it to their advantage. Trust in the good faith and benevolence of the masters will yield no other outcome.

A crucial component of the state-corporate campaign is the ideological offensive to overcome "the crisis of democracy" caused by the efforts of the rabble to enter the political arena, reserved for their betters. Undermining of solidarity with working people is one facet of that offensive. In his study of media coverage of labor, Walter Puette provides ample evidence that in the movies, TV, and the press the portrayal of unions has generally "been both unrepresentative and virulently negative." Unions are depicted as corrupt, outside the mainstream, "special interests" that are either irrelevant or actually harmful to the interests of workers and the general public, "un-American in their values, strategies, and membership." The theme "runs deep and long through the history of media treatment," and "has helped push the values and goals of the American labor movement off the liberal agenda." This is, of course, the historic project, intensified when need arises.[9]

Caterpillar decided in the '80s that its labor contract with the UAW was "a thing of the past," the *Tribune* study observes: the company would "permanently change it with the threat of replacement workers." That tactic, standard in the 19th century, was reinstituted by Ronald Reagan to destroy the air traffic controllers union (PATCO) in 1981, one of the many devices adopted to undermine labor and bring the Third World model home. In 1990, Caterpillar shifted some production to a small steel processor that had broken a Teamsters Local by hiring scabs, "a swift and stunning blow to the workers, a harbinger" of what was to come. Two years later, the hammer struck. For the first time in 60 years, a major US manufacturer felt free to use the ultimate anti-labor weapon. Congress followed shortly after by effectively denying railroad workers the right to strike after an employer lockout that stopped the trains.

Congress's General Accounting Office found that companies felt much more free to threaten to call in "permanent replacement workers" after Reagan used the device in 1981. From 1985 to 1989, employers resorted to the threat in one-third of all strikes, and fulfilled it in 17 percent of strikes in 1990. A 1992 study showed that "four of five employers are willing to wield the replacement-worker weapon," the *Wall Street Journal* reported after the Caterpillar strike, and one-third said they would use it at once.

Labor reporter John Hoerr points out that the decline in workers' income from the early 1970s has been paralleled by decline in strikes, now at the lowest ebb since World War II. Militant labor organizing during the Great Depression brought about labor's first—and last—political victories, notably the National Labor Relations Act (Wagner Act) of 1935, which granted labor rights that had long been established in other industrial societies. Though the right to organize was quickly weakened by Supreme Court rulings, it was not until the 1980s that corporate America felt strong enough to return to the good old days, moving the US off the international spectrum once again. The International Labor Organization (ILO), taking up an AFL-CIO complaint in 1991, noted that the right to strike is lost when workers run the risk of losing their jobs to permanent replacements and recommended that the US reassess its policies in the light of international standards—strong words, from an organization traditionally beholden to its powerful sponsors. Among industrial countries the US is alone, apart from South Africa, in tolerating the ancient union-busting devices.[10]

"Paradox of '92: Weak Economy, Strong Profits." The headline of a lead article in the *Times* business section captures the consequences of the "one-sided class war" waged with renewed intensity since the end of the affluent alliance. "America is not doing very well, but its corporations are doing just fine," the article opens, with corporate profits "hitting new highs as profit margins expand." A paradox, inexplicable and insoluble. One that will only deepen as the architects of policy proceed without interference from "meddlesome outsiders."[11]

What the "paradox" entails for the general population is demonstrated by numerous studies of income distribution, real wages, poverty, hunger, infant mortality, and other social indices. A study released by the Economic Policy Institute on Labor Day, 1992, fleshed out the details of what people know from their experience: after a decade of Reaganism, "most Americans are working longer hours for lower wages and considerably less security," and "the vast majority" are "in many ways worse off" than in the late 1970s. From 1987, real wages have declined even for the college educated. "Poverty rates were high by historic standards," and "those in poverty in 1989 were significantly poorer than the poor in 1979." The poverty rate rose further in 1991, the Census Bureau reported. A congressional report released a few days later estimates that hunger has grown by 50 percent since the mid-1980s to some 30 million people. Other studies show that one of eight children under 12 suffers from hunger, a problem that reappeared in 1982 after having been overcome by government programs from the 1960s. Two researchers report that in New York, the proportion of children raised in poverty more than doubled to 40 percent, while nationwide, "the number of hungry American children grew by 26 percent" as aid for the poor shrank during "the booming 1980s"—"one of the great golden moments that humanity has ever experienced," a spokesman for the culture of cruelty proclaimed (Tom Wolfe).[12]

The impact is brought out forcefully in more narrowly-focused studies; for example, at the Boston City Hospital, where researchers found that "the number of malnourished, low-weight children jumped dramatically following the coldest winter months," when parents had to face the agonizing choice between heat or food. At the hospital's clinic for malnourished children, more were treated in the first nine months of 1992 than in all of 1991; the wait for care reached two months, compelling the staff to "resort to triage." Some suffer from Third World levels of malnutrition and require hospitalization, victims of "the social and financial calamities that have befallen families" and the "massive retrenchment in social service programs."[13] By the side of a road, men hold signs that read "Will Work for Food," a sight that recalls the darkest days of the Great Depression.

But with a significant difference. Hope seems to have been lost to a far greater extent today, though the current recession is far less severe. For the first time in the modern history of industrial society, there is a widespread feeling that things will not be getting better, that there is no way out.

2. "Fight to the Death"

The victory for working people and for democracy in 1935 sent a chill through the business community. The National Association of Manufacturers warned in 1938 of the "hazard facing industrialists" in "the newly realized political power of the masses"; "Unless their thinking is directed we are definitely headed for adversity." A counteroffensive was quickly launched, including the traditional recourse to murderous state violence. Recognizing that more would be needed, corporate America turned to "scientific methods of strike-breaking," "human relations," huge PR campaigns to mobilize communities against "outsiders" preaching "communism and anarchy" and seeking to destroy our communities, and so on. These devices, building upon corporate projects of earlier years, were put on hold during the war, but revived immediately after, as legislation and propaganda chipped away at labor's gains, with no little help from the union leadership, leading finally to the situation now prevailing.[14]

The shock of the labor victories of the New Deal period was particularly intense because of the prevailing assumption in the business community that labor organizing and popular democracy had been buried forever. The first warning was sounded in 1932, when the Norris-LaGuardia Act exempted unions from antitrust prosecution, granting labor rights that it had received in England sixty years earlier. The Wagner Act was entirely unacceptable, and has by now been effectively reversed by the business-state-media complex.

In the late 19th century, American workers made progress despite the extremely hostile climate. In the steel industry, the heart of the developing economy, union organization reached roughly the level of Britain in the 1880s. That was soon to change. A state-business offensive destroyed the unions with considerable violence, in other industries as well. In the business euphoria of the 1920s, it was assumed that the beast had been slain.

American labor history is unusually violent, considerably more so than in other industrial societies. Noting that there is no serious study, Patricia Sexton reports an estimate of 700 strikers killed and thousands injured from 1877 to 1968, a figure that may "grossly understate the total casualties"; in comparison, one British striker was killed since 1911.[15]

A major blow against working people was struck in 1892, when Andrew Carnegie destroyed the 60,000 member Amalgamated Association of Iron and Steel Workers (AAISW) by hiring scabs—yet another anniversary that might have been commemorated in 1992, when the UAW was laid low by the very same methods, revived after a sixty-year lapse. The leading social historian Herbert Gutman describes 1892 as "the really critical year" that "shaped and reshaped the consciousness of working-class leaders and radicals, of trade unionists." The use of state power for corporate goals at that time "was staggering," and led to "a growing awareness among workers that the state had become more and more inaccessible to them and especially to their political and economic needs and demands." It was to remain so until the Great Depression.

The 1892 confrontation at Homestead, commonly called "the Homestead strike," was actually a lockout by Carnegie and his manager on the scene, the thuggish Henry Clay Frick; Carnegie chose to vacation in Scotland, dedicating libraries he had donated. On July 1 the newly-formed Carnegie Steel Corporation announced that "No trade union will ever be recognized at the Homestead Steel Works hereafter." The locked-out workers could reapply individually, nothing more. It was to be "a Finish Fight against Organized Labor," the Pittsburgh press proclaimed, a fight "to the death between the Carnegie Steel Company, limited, with its $25,000,000 capital, and the workmen of Homestead," the *New York Times* reported.

Carnegie and Frick overcame the workers of Homestead by force, first sending Pinkerton guards, then the Pennsylvania National Guard when the Pinkertons were defeated and expelled by the local population. "The lockout crushed the largest trade union in America, the AAISW, and it wrecked the lives of its most devoted members," Paul Krause writes in his comprehensive history. Unionism was not revived in Homestead for 45 years. The impact was far broader.

Destruction of unions was only one aspect of the general project of disciplining labor. Workers were to be deskilled, turned into pliable tools under the control of "scientific management." Management was particularly incensed that "the men ran the mill and the foreman had little authority" in Homestead, one official later said. As discussed earlier, it has been plausibly argued that the current malaise of US industry can be traced in part to the success of the project of making working people "as stupid and ignorant as it is possible for a human creature to be," in defiance of Adam Smith's warning that government must "take pains to prevent" this fate for the "labouring poor" as the "invisible hand" does its grim work (see pp. 18, 103). On the contrary, business called upon state power to accelerate the process. Elimination of the mechanisms "to consult our neighbor" is a companion process in the taming of the herd.

Homestead was a particularly tempting target because workers there were "thoroughly organized," and in control of local political life as well. Homestead held firm through the 1880s while a few miles away, in Pittsburgh, labor suffered severe defeats. Its multi-ethnic work force demanded their "rights as freeborn American citizens" in what Krause describes as "a workers' version of a modern American Republic," in which workers would have freedom and dignity. Homestead was "the nation's preeminent labor town," Krause writes, and Carnegie's next target in his ongoing campaign to destroy the right to organize.[16]

Carnegie's victory at Homestead enabled him to slash wages, impose twelve-hour workdays, eliminate jobs, and gain monumental profits. This "magnificent record was to a great extent made possible by the company's victory at Homestead," a historian of the company wrote in 1903. Carnegie's "free enterprise" achievements relied on more than the use of state violence to break the union. As in the case of other industries from textiles to electronics, state protection and public subsidy were critical to Carnegie's success. "Under the beauties of the protective tariff system the manufacturing interests of the country are experiencing unparalleled prosperity," the *Pittsburgh Post* reported on the eve of the lockout, while Carnegie and others like him were preparing "an enormous reduction in the wages of their men." Carnegie was also a master swindler, defrauding the city of Pittsburgh in collusion with city bosses. Famed as a pacifist as well as philanthropist, Carnegie looked forward to "millions for us in armor" in construction of battleships—purely for defense, he explained, hence in accord with his pacifist principles. In 1890 Carnegie had won a large naval contract for his new Homestead plant. "It was with the help of...powerful politicians and crafty financiers who operated in the grand arenas of national and international government—as well as in the backrooms of Pittsburgh's businesses and city hall—that Carnegie was able to construct his immense industrial fiefdom," Krause writes: the world's first billion-dollar corporation, US Steel. Meanwhile, the new imperial navy was "defending" the US off the coasts of Brazil and Chile and across the Pacific.[17]

The press gave overwhelming support to the Company, as usual. The British press presented a different picture. The *London Times* ridiculed "this Scotch-Yankee plutocrat meandering through Scotland in a four-in-hand opening public libraries, while the wretched workmen who supply him with ways and means for his self-glorification are starving in Pittsburgh." The far-right British press ridiculed Carnegie's preachings on "the rights and duties of wealth," describing his self-congratulatory book *Triumphant Democracy* as "a wholesome piece of satire" in the light of his brutal methods of strike-breaking, which should be neither "permitted nor required in a civilized community," the *London Times* added.

In the US, strikers were depicted as "brigands," "blackmailers whom all the world loathes" (*Harper's Weekly*), a "Mob Bent on Ruin" (*Chicago Tribune*), "anarchists and socialist[s]...preparing to blow up...the Federal building and take possession" of the money in the treasury vaults (*Washington Post*). Eugene Debs was a "lawbreaker at large, an enemy of the human race," who should be jailed (he soon was), "and the disorder his bad teachings has engendered must be squelched" (*New York Times*). When Governor John Altgeld of Illinois wired President Cleveland that press accounts of abuses by strikers were often "pure fabrications" or "wild exaggerations," the *Nation* condemned him as "boorish, impudent, and ignorant"; the President should put him in his place forthwith for his "bad manners" and "the bad odor of his own principles." The strikers are "untaught men" of "the lowest class," the *Nation* continued: they must learn that society is "impregnable" and cannot allow them to "suspend, even for a day, the traffic and industry of a great nation, merely as a means of extorting ten or twenty cents a day more wages from their employers."

The press was not alone in taking up the cudgels for the suffering businessman. The highly respected Reverend Henry Ward Beecher denounced "the importation of the communistic and like European notions as abominations. Their notions and theories that the Government should be paternal and take care of the welfare of its subjects [sic] and provide them with labor, is un-American... God has intended the great to be great, and the little to be little." How much has changed over a century.[18]

After its victory at Homestead, the company moved to destroy any vestige of workers' independence. Strike leaders were blacklisted, many jailed for lengthy periods. A European visitor to Homestead in 1900 described Carnegie's "Triumphant Democracy" as "Feudalism Restored." He found the atmosphere "heavy with disappointment and hopelessness," the men "afraid to talk." Ten years later, John Fitch, who took part in a study of Homestead by urban sociologists, wrote that employees of the company refuse to talk to strangers, even in their homes. "They are suspicious of one another, of their neighbors, and of their friends." They "do not dare openly express their convictions," or "assemble and talk over affairs pertaining to their welfare as mill men." Many were discharged "for daring to attend a public meeting." A national union journal described Homestead as "the most despotic principality of them all" in 1919, when the 89-year-old Mother Jones was dragged "to their filthy jail for daring to speak in behalf of the enslaved steel workers," though some were later "allowed to speak for the first time in 28 years" in Homestead, Mother Jones recalled. So matters continued until the movements of the 1930s broke the barriers. The relation between popular organization and democracy is vividly illustrated in this record.[19]

We cannot really say that the current corporate offensive has driven working class organization and culture back to the level of a century ago. At that time working people and the poor were nowhere near as isolated, nor subject to the ideological monopoly of the business media. "At the turn of the century," Jon Bekken writes, "the U.S. labor movement published hundreds of newspapers," ranging from local and regional to national weeklies and monthlies. These were "an integral part of working class communities, not only reporting the news of the day or week, but offering a venue where readers could debate political, economic and cultural issues." Some were "as large, and in many ways as professional, as many of the capitalist newspapers they co-existed with." "Like the labor movement itself, this press spanned the range from a fairly narrow focus on workplace conditions to advocacy of social revolution." The socialist press alone had a circulation of over 2 million before World War I; its leading journal, the weekly *Appeal To Reason*, reached over 760,000 subscribers.

Workers also "built a rich array of ethnic, community, workplace and political organizations," all part of "vibrant working class cultures" that extended to every domain and retained their vitality until World War II despite harsh government repression, particularly under the Wilson Administration. Repression aside, the labor press ultimately succumbed to the natural effects of the concentration of wealth: advertisers kept to capitalist competitors that could produce below cost, and other market factors took their toll, as happened to the mass working class press in England as late as the 1960s. Similar factors, along with federal government policy, undermined efforts in the 1930s to prevent radio from becoming, in effect, a corporate monopoly.[20]

Left intellectuals took an active part in the lively working class culture. Some sought to compensate for the class character of the cultural institutions through programs of workers' education, or by writing best-selling books on mathematics, science, and other topics for the general public. Remarkably, their left counterparts today often seek to deprive working people of these tools of emancipation, informing us that the "project of the Enlightenment" is dead, that we must abandon the "illusions" of science and rationality—a message that will gladden the hearts of the powerful, delighted to monopolize these instruments for their own use. One recalls the days when the evangelical church taught not-dissimilar lessons to the unruly masses, as their heirs do today in peasant societies of Central America.

It is particularly striking that these self-destructive tendencies should appear at a time when the overwhelming majority of the population wants to change the "inherently unfair" economic system, and belief in the basic moral principles of traditional socialism is surprisingly high (see p. 76). What is more, with Soviet tyranny finally overthrown, one long-standing impediment to the realization of these ideals is now removed. However meritorious personal motives may be, these phenomena in left intellectual circles, in my opinion, reflect yet another ideological victory for the culture of the privileged, and contribute to it. The same tendencies make a notable contribution to the endless project of murdering history as well. During periods of popular activism, it is often possible to salvage elements of truth from the miasma of "information" disseminated by the servants of power, and many people not only "consult their neighbors" but learn a good deal about the world; Indochina and Central America are two striking recent examples. When activism declines, the commissar class, which never falters in its task, regains command. While left intellectuals discourse polysyllabically to one another, truths that were once understood are buried, history is reshaped into an instrument of power, and the ground is laid for the enterprises to come.

3. "To Consult Our Neighbor"

"The men and women who fought for hearth and home in 1892 provided a lesson as important for our age as it was for their own," labor historian David Montgomery writes in summarizing a collection of reports on Homestead. "People work in order to provide their own material needs, but that everyday effort also builds a community with purposes more important than anyone's personal enrichment. The last 100 years have shown how heavily the health of political democracy in a modern industrial society depends on the success of working people in overcoming personal and group differences to create their own effective voice in the shaping of their own futures. The fight for hearth and home is still with us."[21]

The community of labor in Homestead was destroyed by state violence "mobilized to protect the claims of business enterprises to undisturbed use of their property in their pursuit of personal gain," Montgomery writes. The impact on workers' lives was enormous. By 1919, after organizing efforts were broken once again—in this case, with the help of Wilson's Red Scare—"the average compulsory work week in American steel mills was twenty hours longer than in British ones, and American hours were longer than they had been in 1914 or even 1910," Patricia Sexton observes. Communal values disintegrated. When Homestead was a union town, large steps were taken towards overcoming traditional barriers between skilled and unskilled workers, and the rampant anti-immigrant racism. Immigrant workers, bitterly despised at the time, were in the forefront of the struggle, and were saluted as "brave Hungarians, sons of toil, ...seeking which is right." "Such praise from 'American' workers was seldom heard" in later years, Montgomery points out.[22]

Democracy and civil liberties collapsed with the union. "If you want to talk in Homestead, you talk to yourself," residents said; outsiders were struck by the atmosphere of suspicion and fear, as we have seen. In 1892, the working class population was in charge of local politics. In 1919, town officials denied union organizers the right to hold meetings and barred "foreign speakers"; and when forced by court order to tolerate meetings, placed state police on the platform "to warn speakers against inflammatory remarks or criticism of local or national authorities" (Montgomery). The experience of Mother Jones outraged others, but few could speak about it in Homestead.

Forty years after the crushing of the union and freedom, "the establishment of rights at work through union recognition and the reawakening of democracy in political life appeared hand in hand" in Homestead, Montgomery continues. Working people organized, democracy revived; as always, the opportunity to consult our neighbors in an ongoing and systematic fashion is decisive in establishing democracy, a lesson understood by priests in El Salvador as well as labor organizers in Homestead, and understood no less by those who use what means they can to keep the rabble scattered and bewildered. The struggle continues along an uneven path. During the past several decades, the institutions of power and their priesthood have gained some impressive victories, and sustained some serious defeats.

The tendencies towards the new imperial age heralded by the international financial press are obvious and understandable, along with the extension of the North-South divide to the habitations of the rich. There are also countertendencies. Throughout the North, notably in the United States, much has changed in the past 30 years, at least in the cultural and moral spheres, if not at the institutional level. Had the quincentennial of the Old World Order fallen in 1962, it would have been celebrated once again as the liberation of the hemisphere. In 1992, that was impossible, just as few can blandly talk of our task of "felling trees and Indians." The European invasion is now officially an "encounter," though large sectors of the population reject that euphemism as only somewhat less offensive.

The domestic constraints on state violence that are fully recognized by the US political leadership are another case in point. Many were depressed by the inability of the peace movement to prevent the Gulf war, failing to recall that perhaps for the first time ever, large-scale protests actually preceded the bombing, a radical change from the US assault against South Vietnam 30 years earlier, in that case without even the shreds of a pretext. The ferment of the '60s reached much wider circles in the years that followed, eliciting new sensitivity to racist and sexist oppression, concern for the environment, respect for other cultures and for human rights. One of the most striking examples is the Third World solidarity movements of the 1980s, with their unprecedented engagement in the lives and fate of the victims. This process of democratization and concern for social justice could have large significance.

Such developments are perceived to be dangerous and subversive by the powerful, and bitterly denounced. That too is understandable: they do threaten the vile maxim of the masters, and all that follows from it. They also offer the only real hope for the great mass of people in the world, even for the survival of the human species in an era of environmental and other global problems that cannot be faced by primitive social and cultural structures that are driven by short term material gain, and that regard human beings as mere instruments, not ends.

Glossary

Periodicals/News Organizations

AP	Associated Press
BG	Boston Globe
BMJ	British Medical Journal
BW	Business Week
CAHI	Central America Historical Institute
CAN	Central America Newspak
CAR	Central America Report
CIIR	Catholic Institute of International Relations
COHA	Council on Hemispheric Affairs
CSM	Christian Science Monitor
CT	Chicago Tribune
FEER	Far Eastern Economic Review
FT	Financial Times
G&M	Toronto Globe and Mail
IHT	International Herald Tribune
IPS	Inter Press Service
LANU	Latin America News Update
LAT	Los Angeles Times
MH	Miami Herald
NCR	National Catholic Reporter
NR	The New Republic
NYRB	The New York Review of Books
NYT	The New York Times
SFC	San Francisco Chronicle
SFE	San Francisco Examiner
WOLA	Washington Office on Latin America
WP	The Washington Post
WP-MG	Washington Post-Manchester Guardian Weekly
WSJ	The Wall Street Journal

Books

APNM	American Power and the New Mandarins
AWWA	At War with Asia
COT	Culture of Terrorism
DD	Deterring Democracy
FRS	For Reasons of State
FTR	The Fateful Triangle
MC	Manufacturing Consent
NI	Necessary Illusions
P&E	Pirates and Emperors
PEHR	Political Economy and Human Rights
PI	On Power and Ideology
PPV	Pentagon Papers
RC	Rethinking Camelot
TNCW	Towards a New Cold War
TTT	Turning the Tide

Notes

Notes to Chapter 1

1. Höfer, *Fünfhundert-jährige Reich*. See Stannard, *American Holocaust*.
2. Stavrianos, *Global Rift*, 276.
3. Smith, *Wealth of Nations*, Bk. IV, Ch. VII, Pt. III (ii, 141); Bk. IV, Ch. I (i, 470). Hegel, *Philosophy*, 108-9, 81-2, 93-6; "the German world" presumably takes in Northwest Europe. On the fate of the mere savages lacking in Spirit, and the evasion of it, see Jennings, *Invasion;* Lenore Stiffarm with Phil Lane in Jaimes, *State;* Stannard, *American Holocaust*.
4. Jan Carew, Davidson, *Race & Class,* Jan.-March 1992.
5. Pearson, in Tracy, Merchant Empires, citing Niels Steensgaard. Brewer, *Sinews*, xv, 64.
6. Keynes, *A Treatise on Money,* cited by Hewlett, *Cruel Dilemmas*. Pearson, Brady, in Tracy, *Merchant Empires* (Andrews and Angus Calder (on Celts) cited by Brady); Brewer, *Sinews*, 11, 169 (Anglo-Dutch wars). Hill, *Nation*. Smith, *Wealth,* Bk. IV, Ch. II (i, 484f.); Bk. IV, Ch. VII, Pt. III (ii, 110ff.). On the transfer to North America of skills developed in the Celtic fringe, see Jennings, *Invasion, Empire*. For a graphic account of the British-Dutch-Portuguese wars, see Keay, *Honorable Company*.
7. *Ibid.,* 281; Parker, K.N. Chaudhuri (quoting Ibn Jubayr), in Tracy, *Merchant Empires*. Smith, *Wealth,* Bk. V, Ch. III (ii, 486). See ch. 1.2.
8. Tracy, Pearson, in Tracy, *Merchant Empires*.
9. Brewer, *Sinews,* xiiif., 186, 89f. 100, 127, 167.
10. Pearson, *op. cit.* Smith, *Wealth,* Ch. VII, Pt. III (ii, 110ff.); Bk. IV, Ch. II (i, 483).
11. *Ibid.,* Bk. I, Ch. X, Pt. II (i, 150). Stigler, preface. Morris, *American Revolution,* 34. On the Pacific War, see ch. 10, below.
12. Keay, *Honorable Company,* 170, 220-1, 321; Parker, *op. cit.* Thompson and Garrett, *Rise and Fulfillment of British Rule in India,* 1935, cited by Nehru, *Discovery,* 297.
13. Hartman and Boyce, *Quiet Violence,* ch. 1. Bolts, *Considerations on Indian Affairs,* 1772, cited by Hartman and Boyce and by the editor of Smith, *Wealth,* ii, 156n. *Ibid.,* Bk. I, Ch. VIII (i, 82); Bk. IV, Ch. V (ii, 33); Bk. IV, Ch. VII, Pt. III (ii, 153); Bk. IV, Ch. VII, Pt. II (ii, 94-5). Trevelyan, Bentinck, cited by Clairmonte, *Economic Liberalism,* 86n., 98. Nehru, *Discovery,* 285, 299, 304.
14. De Schweinitz, *Rise and Fall,* 120-1, citing economic historian Paul Mantoux (on the Acts) and Clapham's "cautious" economic history of Britain.

Clairmonte, *Economic Liberalism,* 73, 87 (Wilson). Jeremy Seabrook, *Race & Class,* July-Sept. 1992. Hewlett, *Cruel Dilemmas,* 7.

15. Nehru, *Discovery,* 296-9, 284. See Clairmonte, *Economic Liberalism,* ch. 2, for much confirming evidence.

16. Arruda, Pearson, in Tracy, *Merchant Empires.*

17. Smith, *Wealth,* Bk. IV, Ch. VII, Pt. III (ii, 131-3, 147); Bk. IV, Ch. VIII (ii, 180-1).

18. Brady, in Tracy, *Merchant Empires.* Brenner, in Aston and Philpin, *Brenner Debate,* 62; see particularly ch. 10. *DD,* ch. 12.

19. Smith, *Wealth,* Bk. I, Ch. I (i, 7); Bk. V, Ch. I, Pt. III, Art. II (ii, 302-3). In the detailed index, the entry for "division of labor" does not list Smith's condemnation of its consequences. Humboldt, see *FRS.*

20. Smith, *Wealth,* Bk. III, Ch. IV (i, 437).

21. Herman Merivale, cited by Clairmonte, *Economic Liberalism,* 92. Cromer, Curzon, cited by de Schweinitz, *Rise and Fall,* 16. Dutch Governor-General J. P. Coen cited by Tracy, in Tracy, *Merchant Empires,* 10-11. Seal, Jenning, *Invasion,* 228.

22. David Gergen, *Foreign Affairs, America and the World,* 1991-92.

23. Nehru, *Discovery,* 293, 326, 301.

24. *Britannica,* 9th edition, 1910; Cobban's 1963 *History* (vol. 1, 74), cited by Edward Herman, *Z magazine,* April 1992.

25. Miller, *Founding Finaglers;* Keay, *Honorable Company,* 185. Virginia, Jennings, *Invasion, Empire* (447 on germ warfare, ordered by "their highest authority in America, Commander in Chief Amherst" at Fort Pitt; also Stannard, *American Holocaust,* 335n).

26. Saxton, *Rise and Fall,* 41. Mannix and Cowley, *Black Cargoes,* 274. Alfred Rubin, "Who Isn't Cooperating on Libyan Terrorists?," *CSM,* Feb. 5, 1992.

27. Bailey, *Diplomatic History,* 163.

28. Drinnon, *Facing West,* 65, 43; *White Savage,* 157, 169-71; also his "The Metaphysics of Empire-Building," ms, Bucknell, 1972. Jennings, *Invasion,* 60, 149ff.

29. *TTT,* 87 (Theodore Roosevelt), 126 (Churchill; for further details, *DD,* 182f., Omissi, *Air Power,* 160). Stannard, *American Holocaust,* 134 (Theodore Roosevelt). Kiernan, *European Empires,* 200 (Lloyd George). On Bush as the inheritor of Theodore Roosevelt, see John Aloysius Farrell, *BG Magazine,* March 31, 1991, and much other fascist-racist rhetoric of the moment. For a sample from the liberal press, see my articles in *Z magazine,* May 1991, and Peters, *Collateral Damage.* Indochina, *APNM,* chap. 3, n. 42.

30. Perkins, *Monroe Doctrine,* I, 131, 167, 176f. See *TTT,* 69.

31. Morris, *American Revolution,* 57, 47. *DD,* ch. 1.3. See also Jan Carew, *Monthly Review,* July-August 1992.

32. On the civil conflict and the flight of refugees, see *PEHR,* II, 2.2; Morris, *Forging,* 12ff. *Caroline* test, commonly adduced in discussion of the UN Charter, cited by law professor Detlev Vagts, "Reconsidering the Invasion of Panama," *Reconstruction,* I.2 1990.

33. Lawrence Kaplan, *Diplomatic History,* Summer 1992.

34. Appleby, *Capitalism,* 1f.

35. Hietala, *Manifest Design;* Horsman, *Race.* Fredonia, Drinnon, *White Savage,* 192, 201-21; emphasis in original. Emerson, cited by Clarence Karier, "The Educational Legacy of War," ms., U. of Illinois, July 1992.

36. Hietala, *Manifest Design,* 193, 170, 259, 266.

37. Howard, *Harper's,* March 1985; Morris, *American Revolution,* 4, 124; Bernstein, *NYT,* Feb. 2, 1992.

38. *Military Sales: the United States Continuing Munition Supply Relationship with Guatemala,* US General Accounting office, Jan. 1986, report to Committee on Foreign Affairs, House of Representatives, 4. "Inter-Agency Task Force, Africa Recovery Program/Economic Commission," *South African Destabilization: the Economic Cost of Frontline Resistance to Apartheid,* NY, UN, 1989, 13, cited by Merle Bowen, *Fletcher Forum,* Winter 1991.

39. *CAR,* Nov. 22, 1991; *Economist,* July 20, 1991; Freed, *LAT,* May 7, 1990. Shelley Emling, *WP,* Jan. 6, 1992. Gramajo refused to respond to the Court charges and was found guilty by default of massive human rights violations; the plaintiffs were awarded over $10 million in damages—symbolic, doubtless.

40. See *PI,* Lect. I; *DD,* ch. 1. Generally, see Kolko, *Confronting.* Schoultz, *Human Rights,* 7.

41. Jackson, *Century.* Zwick, *Mark Twain's Weapons;* 190, 162. Hassett and Lacey, *Towards a Society; DD,* ch. 12. *Economist,* Dec. 21, 1991. Las Casas, cited by Todorov, *Conquest,* 245.

Notes to Chapter 2

1. For details and sources, see *TTT, PI, DD.* Kennan and other documents, *TTT,* ch. 2.2, *PI,* Lect. I.

2. Green, *Containment,* VII.2. See ch. 7.1, below.

3. Cumings, *Origins,* 172-3. On the contempt for Japan's prospects, see *DD,* 337-8. *Ibid.,* ch. 6 and "Afterword," on the Middle East; and *TNCW,* ch. 8. British and Dulles, Stivers, *Supremacy,* 28, 34; *America's Confrontation,* 20f.

4. *DD,* 49-51, 27; and generally.

5. *Ibid.,* 259; *TTT,* 270; *COT,* 219-221; *NI,* 71-2. Kissinger, *TTT,* 67-8.

6. *DD,* 395. Russell, *Practice and Theory,* 68.

7. Gleijeses, *Shattered Hope,* 365. *Foreign Relations of the United States,* 1952-1954, Vol. IV, 1131ff.; no other evidence was cited. The Attorney-General invoked "self-defense and self-preservation" to justify the blockade imposed in violation of international law. Memorandum of NSC discussion, May 27, 1954.

8. *APNM,* 33ff.; *TNCW,* 67-9, 89-90.

9. Friedman, *NYT,* July 7, 1991. Iraqi democrats, *DD,* ch. 6.4, "Afterword," sec. 4, and earlier articles in *Z magazine.*

10. Friedman, *NYT,* June 24; Haberman, *NYT,* June 28, 1992; see Nabeel Abraham, *Lies of Our Times,* Sept. 1992. On US-vs.-peace process, and background, see *DD,* "Afterword"; for an ongoing record, *TNCW, FTR, NI.* On official PC, see Herman, *Decoding Democracy.*

11. Eisenhower quoted by Richard Immerman, *Diplomatic History* (Summer 1990). John Foster Dulles, Telephone Call to Allen Dulles, June 19, 1958, "Minutes of telephone conversations of John Foster Dulles and Christian Herter," Eisenhower Library, Abilene KA.

12. Leffler, *Preponderance,* 258, 90-1. *TNCW,* chs. 8, 11; *DD,* chs. 1, 6, 8, 11. Frank Costigliola, in Paterson, *Kennedy's Quest.* On Japan, see Schaller, *American Occupation.* See references of n. 16.

13. Leffler, *Preponderance,* 71. Jeffrey-Jones, *CIA,* 51. Pisani, *CIA,* 106-7. See ch. 1.2, above. Nicaraguan election, *MC, NI, DD. DD,* ch. 11, on US and Italy, in the context of the broader struggle to deter the threat of democracy in the industrial societies after World War II.

14. Pisani, *CIA,* 114f., 91f. Chace, *NYT Magazine,* May 22, 1977. On racist attitudes towards the "wops" in both the internal and public record, see *DD,* chs. 1.4, 11.5.

15. Stimson; Kolko, *Politics,* 471. Wood, *Dismantling,* 193, 197 (citing Woodward, personal letter; Dreier, *The Organization of the American States* (1962)). Pastor, *Condemned,* 32, his emphasis.

16. Leffler, *Preponderance,* 165. For earlier discussion of these matters, see among others *AWWA,* introduction; essays by Gabriel Kolko, Richard Du Boff, and John Dower in *PP* V; *FRS,* 31ff. Important recent studies include Borden, *Pacific Alliance;* Schaller, *American Occupation;* Rotter, *Path to Vietnam.* Leffler's very useful study, summarizing much recent work and adding significant new information, places this thinking within the general matrix of Truman era planning. Recent scholarship largely confirms and extends the pioneering work of Gabriel and Joyce Kolko 20-25 years ago. For a partial update, see Kolko, *Confronting.* See also *DD,* chs. 1, 11, and sources cited.

17. South Commission, *Challenge,* 216ff., 71f., 287.

18. Kissinger, *American Foreign Policy;* Leffler, *Preponderance,* 17, 449, 463.

19. *Ibid.,* 282f.

20. *Ibid.,* 284, 156. Acheson, Kennan, cited by Gaddis, *Strategies,* 76.

21. Leffler, *Preponderance,* 117, 119. *DD,* ch. 11. On "aggression," see *FRS,* 114f.

22. Costigliola, in Paterson, *Kennedy's Quest,* quoting Theodore Sorenson; also George Ball. Wachtel, *Money Mandarins,* 64f. On Kennedy and Vietnam, see *RC.* On the impact of "international military Keynesianism" after the failure of the aid programs, see particularly Borden, *Pacific Alliance; DD,* ch. 1, for other sources and comment.

23. Garthoff, *Détente,* 487f.

24. Excerpts, *NYT,* March 8; Patrick Tyler, *NYT,* March 8, 11; Barton Gellman, *WP Weekly,* March 16-22, 1992.

25. Patrick Tyler, *NYT,* May 24, 1992. Frederick Kempe, "U.S., Bonn Clash Over Pact with France," *WSJ,* May 27, 1992.

26. See *DD,* introduction. Christopher Bellamy, *International Affairs,* July 1992.

27. Strange, *International Economic Relations of the Western World* (1976), cited in Wachtel, *Money Mandarins,* 79; 137, on profitability.

28. *Ibid.* Du Boff, *Accumulation,* 153f.; Calleo, *Imperious Economy,* 63, 116, 75.

29. See particularly Rand, *Making Democracy Safe;* and on the effects, my 1977 article reprinted in *TNCW,* ch. 11; also ch. 2. *DD,* ch. 6.1. See also Yergin, *Prize.*

30. See *DD,* 98, on capital flow.

31. *NI,* 84f., App. IV.4. *DD,* ch. 6, "Afterword," sec. 5; my essay in Peters, *Collateral.* UNESCO, Preston et al., *Hope & Folly.*

32. *TTT,* ch. 5, and sources cited; *NI,* ch. 1. *LAT, Extra!* (FAIR), July/August 1992, the six months before the April 1992 Rodney King verdict. Maynes, editor, *Foreign Policy,* Summer 1990.

33. G. Rees, Alain Besançon, *Encounter,* Dec. 1976, June 1980.

34. See below, ch. 7; *DD,* ch. 7. Nancy Wright, *Multinational Monitor,* April 1990, cited in Gar Alperovitz and Kai Bird, *Diplomatic History,* Spring 1992. See also James Petras, *Monthly Review,* May 1992.

35. Fitzgerald, *Between.* Foreign staff, "US and Japan shy from investing in UK," *FT,* Sept. 25, 1992.

36. Marc Fisher, "Why Are German Workers Striking? To Preserve Their Soft Life," *WP* service, *IHT,* May 4; Andrew Fisher, *FT,* May 20; Christopher Parkes, *FT;* Kevin Done, *FT,* Sept. 24 (GM); *FT,* June 4, 1992. Elaine Bernard, "The Defeat at Caterpillar," ms. Harvard Trade Union Program, May 1992.

37. Sexton, *War on Labor,* 83f. See ch. 11, below.

38. Barnaby Feder, *NYT,* May 25, 1992.

39. Jim Stanford, "Going South: Cheap Labour as an Unfair Subsidy in North American Free Trade," Canadian Centre for Policy Alternatives, Dec. 1991; Andrew Reding, *World Policy Journal,* Summer 1992. Edward Goldsmith, Mark Ritchie, *The Ecologist,* Nov./Dec. 1990; Watkins, *Fixing,* 103-4. Brief amicus curiae of Government of Canada, US Court of Appeals, "Corrosion Proof Fittings, et al., vs. EPA and William K. Riley," May 22, 1990. See ch. 3, n. 43.

40. "Drug war" and media, *DD,* ch. 4; ch. 7, on comparative study. Jonathan Kaufman, *BG,* May 26, 1992.

41. Bob Hohler, *BG,* May 26, 1992.

42. "Interview," *Multinational Monitor,* May 1992.

43. Reding, *op. cit.*

44. Rose Gutfeld, *WSJ,* May 27, 1992.

45. Arthur MacEwan, *Socialist Review,* July-Dec. 1991; Du Boff, *Accumulation;* World Bank, *Global Economic Prospects and the Developing Countries 1992,* cited by Doug Henwood, *Left Business Observer,* No. 54, Aug. 4, 1992; Watkins, *Fixing,* 5, 24.

46. World Bank, in *Trócaire Development Review* (Catholic Agency for World Development, Dublin, 1990); Chakravarti Raghavan and Martin Khor, *Third World Economics* (Penang), March 16-31, 1991; *Economist,* April 25, 1992; Watkins, *Fixing,* 75, 49, 64; Frances Williams, *FT,* June 11, 1992; Kent Jones, *Fletcher Forum,* Winter 1992. On Reaganite protectionism, see *DD,* ch. 3; and for extensive detail, Bhagwati and Patrick, *Aggressive Unilateralism;* Bovard, *Fair Trade Fraud.*

47. George Graham, *FT,* Sept. 25; Nancy Dunne, *FT,* Sept. 24, 1992.

48. Wachtel, *Money Mandarins*, 146; Greider, *Secrets*, 521f. *FT*, May 16/17, 1992.
49. *Economist*, May 16; Jonathan Hicks, *NYT*, March 31, 1992.
50. Preliminary Report, LAC, Sept. 16, 1992.
51. *DD*, ch. 12; Wilbur Edel, "Diplomatic History—State Department Style," *Political Science Quarterly*, 106.4 1991/2.

Notes to Chapter 3

1. Brenner, in Aston and Philpin, *Brenner Debate*, 277ff., 40ff. Stavrianos, *Global Rift*, chs. 3, 16; Feffer, *Shock Waves*, 22; Shanin, *Russia* (quoting historian D. Mirsky). Zeman, *Communist Europe*, 15-16 (citing T. Masaryk), 57-8. Gerschenkron, *Economic Backwardness*.
2. Leffler, *Preponderance*, 359. Gaddis, *Long Peace*, 10.
3. Gerschenkron, *Economic Backwardness*, 146, 150. Du Boff, *Accumulation*, 176, citing Kuznets.
4. See *FRS*, 51-2, for details on Indochina. Wood, 177, on Guatemala; US and Fascism-Nazism, Mexico, *DD*, chs. 1.3-4, 11. Sklar, *Washington's War*, and a substantial further literature on Nicaragua.
5. *DD*, ch. 11. FDR, Zeman, *Communist Europe*, 172n.; Kimball, *Juggler*, 34. Truman, Garthoff, *Détente*, 6, citing *NYT*, June 24, 1941.
6. Leffler, *Preponderance*, 78; Indochina, see *RC*.
7. *NI*, 185f., on the Red Scare; 272f. on Libya, and *P&E*, ch. 3.
8. Leffler, *Preponderance*, 58-9, 15.
9. Leffler gives a detailed and largely sympathetic account of the actual fears and their basis. On the UN, see references of n. 10, ch. 2.
10. *DD*, 103.
11. Leffler, *Preponderance*, 284-5.
12. *DD*, ch. 1. Khrushchev's moves were revealed by Raymond Garthoff, *International Security*, Spring 1990, as an "interesting precedent" to Gorbachev's; see p. 365, below. Kennedy, *Strategy of Peace*, 5; cited by Leacock, *Requiem*, 7.
13. *Defense Monitor*, Jan. 1980. Zeman, *Communist Europe*, 267-8.
14. See Charles S. Maier, *Why Did Communism Collapse in 1989?*, Program on Central and Eastern Europe, Working Paper Series #7, Jan. 1991.
15. World Bank statement published in *Trócaire Development Review*, *op. cit.* (ch. 2, n. 46).
16. Quotes from *TNCW*, 3, 204. On NSC 68, see *DD*, ch. 1.1. Meyer, cited by Pisani, *CIA*, from his *Peace or Anarchy*.
17. Holzman, *Challenge*, May/June 1992. Garthoff, *Détente*, 793-800. In an addendum of June 11, 1992, Holzman notes that a Review Committee of 5 distinguished economists set up by the House Permanent Select Committee on Intelligence found the same technical problems and was unable to get satisfactory explanations in face-to-face meetings with the responsible CIA analysts, who were described as lacking in "candor."
18. Leiken, *Foreign Policy*, Spring 1981; cited by Schoultz, *National Security*, a useful review of the delusional systems of planners, whether real or contrived,

one can only speculate. See *DD*, ch. 3.6, for further discussion. Thompson, *Diplomatic History*, Winter 1992.

19. Carnegie, cited in Krause, *Homestead*, 235. 1987 poll cited by Lobel, *Less than Perfect*, 3. See *APNM*, ch. 1; "Intellectuals and the State," reprinted in *TNCW*.

20. Feffer, *Shock Waves*, 22, 112, 129. Brumberg, *NYRB*, Jan. 30; *FT*, Feb. 3; Robinson, *FT*, April 28, 1992. Haynes, *European Business and Economic Development*, Sept. 1992. Economic indicators; *FT*, Sept. 28, 1992. Engelberg, *NYT*, Feb. 9; *WSJ*, Feb. 4; Glaser, *NYT*, April 19; Bohlen, *NYT*, Aug. 30, 1992. Continental Illinois, see p. 63. Children, see *DD*, ch. 7; ch. 9.5, below. Polanyi, *Great Transformation*. Miller, *Founding Finaglers*. On the Costa Rican exception and US attitudes towards it from the 1940s, see *NI*, 111f., App. V.1; *DD*, 221f., 273ff.

21. Gowan, *World Policy Journal*, Winter 1991-92.

22. See Deere, *In the Shadows*, 213; McAfee, *Storm Signals*.

23. See *DD*, chs. 1.6, 3.3. Kaslow, *CSM*, Aug. 12, 1992.

24. Burke, *Current History*, Feb. 1991; Morales, *Third World Quarterly*, vol. 13.2, 1992. See also Peter Andreas et al., "Dead-End Drug Wars," *Foreign Policy*, Winter 1991-92.

25. McAfee, *Storm Signals*, ch. 7. Bourne, *Orlando Sentinel*, April 12, 1992. Suskind, *WSJ*, Oct. 29, 1991. *DD*, 162. On the suppressed history, see *NI*, 177f.

26. *CAR*, Sept. 27, 1991; June 5, 1992. *Latinamerica press* (Lima), June 4, 1992. AFP, Chicago Sun-Times, Dec. 22, 1991. Sheppard, *CT*, June 18, May 22, Sept. 1, 1992. *Proceso* (Mexico), Dec. 2, 1992 *(LANU)*. Kenneth Sharpe, *CT*, Dec. 19, 1991. Andreas, *op. cit.* Joachim Bamrud, *CSM*, Jan. 24, 1991.

27. *CAR*, Sept.20, Nov. 29, May 3, 1991. *Links* (National Central America Health Rights Network), Summer 1992.

28. Felipe Jaime, IPS, *Subtext* (Seattle), Sept. 3-16; Nusser, *NYT* news service, Sept. 26; Johnson, *MH*, Dec. 3, 1991.

29. *CAR*, Oct. 11, 1991. Gómez, *NYT*, Jan. 28, 1992. See Americas Watch, *'Drug War'*; WOLA, *Clear and Present Dangers*.

30. Simes, *NYT*, Dec. 27, 1988. For further detail, see *DD*, 97f.

31. See *Daedalus*, Winter 1990; *NYT*, Jan. 4, Aug. 31, 1990. *DD*, 61, for more.

32. Lionel Barber and Alan Friedman, *FT* (London), May 3, 1991. Serious mainstream coverage of the topic in the US began with the *Los Angeles Times*, Feb. 23, 25, 26, 1992. On information available before the invasion of Kuwait, often ignored in the mainstream, see *DD*, 152, 194f.

33. *DD*, chs. 4-5.

34. *DD*, ch. 6 and "Afterword." For fuller detail, my article in Peters, *Collateral Damage*. "Iron fist," p. 38, above.

35. *DD*, 141f., ch. 10. See *COT*, *NI*, *DD*, for an ongoing record of subversion of the peace process and media complicity. See Robinson, *Faustian Bargain*, on US subversion of the election itself.

36. Van Niekerk, *G&M*, Jan. 25, 29, 1992. Britain, *Guardian* (London), March 30; *Guardian Weekly*, April 5, 1992. See George Wright, *Z magazine*, May/June, 1992, for background.

37. Lewis, *NYT*, Aug. 24, 1992.

38. *Latin America Strategy Development Workshop,* Sept. 26 & 27, 1990, minutes, 3.

39. *DD,* 29-30, for further detail.

40. Maureen Dowd, *NYT,* Feb. 23, 1991; see *DD,* "Afterword."

41. Khor, *Uruguay Round,* 10. See also Raghavan, *Recolonization.*

42. Wachtel, *Money Mandarins,* 266; Peter Phillips, *Challenge,* Jan.-Feb. 1992.

43. Virginia Galt, *G&M,* Dec. 15, 1990. John Maclean, *CT,* May 27, 1991; *WSJ,* Nov. 28, 1990.

44. *Monthly Review,* March 1992.

Notes to Chapter 4

1. Rabe, *Road,* 129.

2. Asia Watch, *Human Rights;* Shorrock, *Third World Quarterly,* Oct. 1986. *Harvard Human Rights Journal* 4, Spring 1991; see my article in Peters, *Collateral Damage.*

3. Fitzgerald, *Between,* citing Ryutaro Komiya, et al., *Industry Policy of Japan* (Tokyo, 1984; Academic press, 1988). Johnson, *National Interest,* Fall 1989.

4. Amsden, "Diffusion of Development: the Late-Industrializing Model and Greater East Asia," AEA Papers and Proceedings, 81.2, May 1991. See particularly her *Asia's Next Giant.* Smith, *Industrial Policy;* citing Hollis Chenery, Sherman Robinson, and Moises Syrquin, *Industrialization and Growth: A Comparative Study* (Oxford, 1986). Brazil, see ch. 7. Comparisons, see *DD,* ch. 7.7.

5. Francis, *CSM,* May 14, 1992. Amsden, *op.cit.* Huelshoff, Sperling, in Merkl, *Federal.* Ronald van de Krol, *FT,* Sept. 28; *Economist,* May 23, 1992. Dertouzos et al., *Made in America.* Felix, "On Financial Blowups and Authoritarian Regimes in Latin America," in Jonathan Hartlyn and Samuel A. Morley, eds., *Latin American Political Economy* (Westview, 1986). Also Lazonick, *Business Organization,* 43. *Ibid.,* on the role of banks in German industrial development. Gerschenkron, *Economic Backwardness,* Landes, *Unbound,* for extensive discussion.

6. Bils, cited by Du Boff, *Accumulation,* 56. Bartel, editor, *Challenge,* July/August 1992. See Du Boff on the general topic. Brady, *Business,* on 1920s and '30s. A classical study of the abandonment of the free market is Polanyi, *Great Transformation.* For further references, see *DD,* ch. 1, n. 19.

7. Lazonick, *Business Organization.*

8. Taylor, *Dollars & Sense,* Nov. 1991.

9. Steven Elliott-Gower, Assistant Director, Center for East-West Trade Policy, U. of Georgia, *NYT News Service,* Dec., 23, 1991. Jeffrey Smith, *WP* weekly, May 18-24; Korb, *CSM,* Jan. 30; Schweid, *BG,* Feb. 15, 1992. Hartung, *World Policy Journal,* Spring 1992. The ambitious plans were not realized, the Congressional Research Service reported in July 1992, with sales declining in 1991 though the US still accounted for 57 percent of all arms sales to the Third World; Robert Pear, *NYT,* July 21, 1992.

10. On Food for Peace, see *NI*, 363, and sources cited, particularly Borden, *Pacific Alliance*. Hogan, *Marshall Plan*, 42-3, 45. Commerce Department analysis, Wachtel, *Money Mandarins*, 44f. *BW*, April 7, 1975.
11. Nasar, *NYT*, Feb. 7; "Furor on Memo at World Bank," *NYT*, Feb. 7; Reuters and Peter Gosselin, *BG*, Feb. 7, 1992. *Economist*, Feb. 8, Feb. 15 (Summers's letter), 1992.
12. MacEwan, *Dollars & Sense*, Nov. 1991. Hegel, *Philosophy*, 36.
13. "Criminalizing the Seriously Mentally Ill"; Anita Diamant, *BG*, Sept. 10, 1992. Falco, and other articles, *Daedalus*, "Political Pharmacology," Summer 1992. James McGregor, *WSJ*, Sept. 29, 1992; this front-page story on Burmese opium in China manages to avoid entirely the major CIA role in creating the curse; see McCoy, *Politics*. Victoria Benning, *BG*, June 27, 1992.
14. Paul Hemp, *BG*, Aug. 30, 1992.
15. Louis Ferleger and Jay Mandle, *Challenge*, July/Aug. 1991. US tax rate is 95 percent of Japan's and 71 percent of Western Europe's, according to figures cited by economist Herbert Stein, criticizing the "myth" that US taxes are high by international or historical standards; *WP Weekly*, Sept. 7, 1992.
16. Sonia Nazario, *WSJ*, Oct. 5, 1992. Wachtel, *op. cit.*, "Afterword"; John Zysman, "US power, trade and technology," *International Affairs* (London), Jan. 1991. Benjamin Friedman, *NYRB*, Aug. 13; *CSM*, Aug. 14; *Science*, Aug. 21; Pollin, *Guardian* (NY), August 1992.
17. Uchitelle, *NYT*, A1, Aug. 12, 1992.
18. Michael Waldholz and Hilary Stout, "Rights to Life," *WSJ*, April 7; Leslie Roberts, *Science*, May 29, 1992. *The Blue Sheet*, April 8, 15, 1992.
19. Gina Kolata, *NYT*, July 28, 1992.
20. *Economist*, Aug. 22, 1992. Richard Knox, *BG*, Sept. 11, 1992, study by Families USA Foundation; drug manufacturers conceded its accuracy. Fazlur Rahman, *NYT*, April 26; William Stevens, *NYT*, May 24, 1992.
21. Watkins, *Fixing*, 94-5.
22. "Intellectual Property Rights," *Anthropology Today* (UK), Aug. 1990.
23. Jeremy Seabrook, *Race & Class*, July 1992. Watkins, *Fixing*, 96.
24. David Hirst, *Guardian* (London), March 23, 1992.

Notes to Chapter 5

1. Thomas Friedman, *NYT*, Jan. 12, 1992; see p. 183. Taylor, *Swords*, 159. Pfaff and Hoopes, virtually identical commentary with no cross-reference, so it is unclear who should receive the credit; see *AWWA*, 297-300, *FRS*, 94-5. Wohlstetter, *WSJ*, Aug. 25, 1992. Hegel, *Philosophy*, 96.
2. Schoultz, *Comparative Politics*, Jan. 1981. Herman, in *PEHR*, I, ch. 2.1.1; *Real Terror Network*, 126ff. *PEHR, MC*, for comparative analysis. And a huge literature on case studies.
3. See *TNCW*, 73f., for further discussion. Also *NI, DD*, among others.
4. Leffler, *Preponderance*, 260, 165. See ch. 10.4, and for the background, ch. 2.1-2. On Japan-SEA, see *RC*, ch. 2.1. Below, unless otherwise indicated, see Peter Dale Scott, "Exporting Military-Economic Development," in Caldwell,

Ten Years, and "The United States and the Overthrow of Sukarno," *Pacific Affairs,* Summer 1985; *PEHR,* vol. I, ch. 4.1; Kolko, *Confronting.*

5. *FIR,* 457ff.; *COT,* ch. 8. Marshall, et al., *Iran-Contra,* chs. 7, 8.
6. McGehee, *Nation,* April 11, 1981. Also *News from Asia Watch,* June 21, 1990.
7. *Ibid.* Rusk cited by Kolko.
8. Brands, "The Limits of Manipulation: How the United States Didn't Topple Sukarno," *J. of American History,* Dec. 1989.
9. Johnson cited by Kolko, *Confronting.* McNamara and congressional report cited in Wolpin, *Military Aid,* 8, 128. McNamara to Johnson, Brands, *op. cit.* Ch. 7.3.
10. *Public Papers of the Presidents,* 1966 (Washington, 1987), Book II, 563.
11. *NYT,* March 29, 1973. See ch. 10, n. 64.
12. Frankel, *NYT,* Oct. 11, 1965.
13. Quoted in *NYT,* Oct. 17, 1965.
14. Robert Martin, *U.S. News,* June 6, 1966. *Time,* July 15, 1966.
15. *NYT,* June 19, 1966.
16. Editorials, *NYT,* Dec. 22, 1965; Feb. 17, Aug. 25, Sept. 29, 1966.
17. *IHT,* Dec. 5, 1977, from *LAT.*
18. *PEHR,* I, ch. 3.4.4; *TNCW,* ch. 13; Peck, *Chomsky Reader,* 303-13. For an overview, Taylor, *Indonesia's Forgotten War.*
19. John Murray Brown, *CSM,* Feb. 6, 1987; Shenon, *NYT,* Sept. 3, 1992; *Economist,* Aug. 15, 1987.
20. Wain, *WSJ,* April 25, 1989; *Asia Week,* Feb. 24, 1989, cited in *TAPOL Bulletin,* April 1989. Richard Borsuk, *WSJ,* June 8, 1992.
21. Kadane, *SFE,* May 20, 1990. *WP,* May 21; AP, May 21; *Guardian* (London), May 22; BG, May 23, 1990. One exception to the general dismissal was the *New Yorker,* "Talk of the Town," July 2, 1990. Guatemala, ch. 7.7.
22. Wines, *NYT,* July 12; Martens, letter, *WP,* June 2, 1990.
23. Budiarjo, letters, *WP,* June 13; Rosenfeld, *WP,* July 13, July 20, 1990.
24. Moynihan, *NYRB,* June 28, 1990.
25. See *TNCW,* ch. 13. Lewis, *NYT,* April 16, 1992.
26. Shawcross, see *MC,* 284f.; for more detail, Peck, *op. cit.* Chaliand, *Nouvelles littéraires,* Nov. 10, 1981; Fallows, *Atlantic Monthly,* Feb., June 1982. Halliday, *Guardian Weekly,* Aug. 16, 1992.
27. *Daily Hansard* SENATE (Australia), 1 November, 1989, 2707. *Indonesia News Service,* Nov. 1, 1990. Green left mideast.gulf.346, electronic communication, Feb. 18, 1991. *Monthly Record,* Parliament (Australia), March 1991. Reuters, Canberra, Feb. 24; Communiqué, International Court of Justice, Feb. 22, 1991. *PEHR,* I, 163-6. Taylor, *Indonesia's Forgotten War,* 171.
28. *FEER,* 25 July, 1991. Carey, letter, *Guardian Weekly,* July 12, 1992.
29. ABC (Australia) radio, "Background briefing; East Timor," Feb. 17, 1991; Osborne, *Indonesia's Secret Wars;* Monbiot, *Poisoned Arrows;* Anti-Slavery Society, *West Papua.*
30. *Age* (Australia), Jan. 11, Feb. 18; IPS, Kupang, Jan. 20; *Australian,* July 6; Carey, *op. cit.; The Engineer,* March 26, 1992. See also *TAPOL Bulletin,* Aug. 1992.

Notes to Chapter 6

1. Jennings, "The Indians' Revolution"; Berlin, "The revolution in black life"; both in Young, *American Revolution*. Morris, *American Revolution*, 72. Higginbotham, *In the Matter of Color*. Hamilton, cited by Vine Deloria, in Lobel, *Less than Perfect*. See references of n. 32, ch. 1.

2. Gleijeses, "The Limits of Sympathy: the United States and the Independence of Spanish America," ms., Johns Hopkins, 1991.

3. Lawrence Kaplan, *Diplomatic History,* Summer 1992; see ch. 1.2.

4. See Bernal, *Black Athena*.

5. *North American Review,* April 12, 1821, cited by Gleijeses. Crossette, *NYT,* Jan. 18; Stephen Fidler, *FT,* Jan. 29, 1992.

6. Jefferson cited by van Alstyne, *Rising American Empire,* 81.

7. Gleijeses, "Limits of Sympathy." Drinnon, *White Savage,* 158. Also *PI,* 12f., 71f., and sources cited.

8. *Ibid.*

9. Green, *Containment,* 13-18. On the Good Neighbor Policy and its backgrounds, see LaFeber, *Inevitable Revolutions;* Krenn, *US Policy.* See also Salisbury, *Anti-Imperialism.*

10. Benjamin, *US and Origins,* 186ff. Paterson, in Paterson, *Kennedy's Quest;* Mexican diplomat quoted in Leacock, *Requiem,* 33.

11. *NI,* 177, 101. Shirley Christian, *NYT,* Sept. 4, 1992.

12. "Patriotic America," 1903; Zwick, *Mark Twain's Weapons,* 161.

13. *Envío,* Jesuit Central American University (UCA), Managua, Jan.-Feb. 1992; *NI,* 176f., 67-8; *PI.* 22f.

14. For a review of terrorist operations, see Blum, *CIA.* Nixon, Garthoff, *Détente,* 76n. See McClintock, *Instruments,* for recent discussion, including Gilpatric interview. Also Garthoff, *Reflections* and Smith, *Closest of Enemies,* for accounts from well-informed US government sources.

15. Paterson, *op. cit.;* Martin Tolchin, *NYT,* Jan. 15, 1992. Garthoff, *Reflections,* 17.

16. On scholarly discipline, see, among others, *NI,* App. V.2 (on Walter Laqueur), and several articles in George, *Western. NYT* editorial, Sept. 8, 1991. French, *NYT,* April 19; Constable, *BG,* July 15, Oct. 26; Krauss, *NYT Book Review,* Aug. 30, 1992. See ch. 3.5.

17. See *DD,* 280-1.

18. For a particularly shameful example, see *NI,* App. I.1. On the general pattern, see *PEHR, MC,* and a voluminous further literature. On media coverage of Cuba, see Platt, *Tropical Gulag.*

19. *Envío, op. cit.;* Stavrianos, *Global Rift,* 747; *Latinamerica press,* April 5, 1990; Morris Morley and Chris McGillion, *Sydney Morning Herald,* Jan. 7, 1992. Ellacuría, "Utopia and Prophecy in Latin America" (1989), in Hassett & Lacey, *Towards a Society.*

20. Smith, *Closest of Enemies;* Gillian Gunn, *Current History,* Feb. 1992. Thomas Friedman, *NYT,* Sept. 12, 1991. Michael Kranish, *BG,* April 19; *NYT,* April 19, 1992. Nicaraguan coffee, *NI,* 98.

21. Detlev Vagts, "Reconsidering the Invasion of Panama," *Reconstruction,* vol. 1.2, 1990. See *DD,* ch. 5.

22. *WP weekly*, Jan. 20-26, 1992; *Post*, see *DD*, 103, 141; *NI*, for more extensive review of *Times-Post* dogmas. Benjamin, *US and Origins*, 59; *PI*, 72.

Notes to Chapter 7

1. Evans, *Dependent Development*, 51ff. *WP*, May 6, 1929; *New York Herald Tribune*, Dec. 23, 1926; *CSM*, Dec. 22, 1928; *NY Post*, Dec. 21, 1928; *WSJ*, Sept. 10, 1924; cited by Smith, *Unequal Giants*, 186f., 135f., 82. Krenn, *US Policy*, 122. Green, *Containment*, 8f.

2. Smith, *Unequal Giants*, 3ff., 35f., 134.

3. Evans, *Dependent Development*, 70; Rabe, *Road to OPEC*, 110.

4. Haines, *Americanization;* Leffler, *Preponderance*, 258, 339. Ch. 2.2.

5. Cited by Kolko, *Politics*, 302f. Green, *Containment*, ch. 11. The situation is more complex; see ch. 2.2.

6. See *TTT*, ch. 2.3. Bismarck quoted by Nancy Mitchell, ms., SAIS, Johns Hopkins, 1991, forthcoming in *Prologue*. Stimson, p. 42, above.

7. Green, *Containment*, 74f., 315n.; ch. 2.1, above.

8. NSC 5432, August 1954; *Memorandum for the Special Assistant to the President for National Security Affairs* (McGeorge Bundy), "Study of U.S. Policy Toward Latin American Military Forces," Secretary of Defense, 11 June 1965. See *PI*, lecture I, for further details. Green, *Containment*, 180f., 259f., 103, 147f., 174f., 188. On Latin American military, see also Leffler, *Preponderance*, 59f. On the aftermath in Bolivia, see, *DD*, 395f.; and ch. 3.4, above.

9. See ch. 5, n. 5. Agee, *Inside*, 361-2.

10. Parker, *Brazil;* Leacock, *Requiem;* Skidmore, *Politics;* Hewlett, *Cruel Dilemmas*. See also Black, *US Penetration*.

11. Felix, "Financial Blowups" (ch. 4, n. 5); Evans, *op. cit.;* Herman, *Real Terror Network*, 97.

12. Skidmore; Evans, 4. Mario de Carvalho Garnero, chairman of Brasilinvest Informations and Telecommunications, *O Estado de São Paulo*, Aug. 8 (*LANU*, Sept. 1990); *Latin America Commentary*, October, 1990. CIIR, *Brazil*. On the broader context, see *DD*, ch. 7.

13. Americas Watch, *Struggle for Land;* Brazilian journalist José Pedro Martins, *Latinamerica press*, June 4, 1992; George Monbiot, *Index on Censorship* (London), May 1992; Isabel Vincent, *G&M*, Dec. 17, 1991. Generally, see Hecht and Cockburn, *Fate*.

14. Dimerstein, *Brazil;* Blixen, "'War' waged on Latin American street kids," *Latinamerica press*, November 7, 1991; Gabriel Canihuante, *Ibid.*, May 14, 1992; Moffett, *CSM*, July 21, 1992; Maité Pinero, *Le Monde diplomatique*, August 1992.

15. Rabe, *Road*. Krenn, *US Policy*, on earlier period.

16. *Excelsior* (Mexico City), Nov. 11, Nov. 21, Dec. 4, 1991; Jan. 30, 1992 (*LANU*).

17. Brooke, *NYT*, Jan. 21; AP, *NYT*, Feb. 5; Douglas Farah, *BG*, Feb. 10; Stan Yarbro, *CSM*, Feb. 12, 1992.

18. AP, *NYT*, Feb. 5; Joseph Mann, *FT*, Feb. 5; Brooke, *NYT*, Feb. 9; Yarbro, *CSM*, Feb. 11, 12, 1992.

19. Seabrook, *Race & Class* (London), 34.1, 1992.

20. *TTT, MC;* Jonas, *Battle.*

21. *Excelsior,* July 21, 1992; Shelley Emling, *WP,* Aug. 1, 1992.

22. Jonas, *Battle.* David Santos, *Excelsior,* June 20, 1992 (*CAN*); *CAR,* Jan. 17, 1992; Florence Gardner, "Guatemala's Deadly Harvest," *Multinational Monitor,* Jan./Feb. 1991; *Report from Guatemala,* Spring 1992. On US government perspectives on Guatemalan democracy, see *DD,* chs.3.6, 8.3, 12.5.

23. Edward Gargan, *NYT,* July 9, 1992. *Frontline* (India), Dec. 6, 1991.

24. Vickery, "Cambodia After the 'Peace'," ms. (Penang, Malaysia, Dec. 1991). See his *Cambodia* for comparative discussion of Cambodia and Thailand. For a small sample of the plague of child slavery, see *TNCW,* 202, 283.

25. Blixen, *op. cit.; Excelsior* (Mexico), Nov. 5, 1991 (*CAN*).

26. *Unomásuno,* Oct. 13, 1990; David Santos, *Excelsior,* June 20, 1992; Pinero, *op. cit.* "Honduras: A Growing Market in Children?," *CAR,* June 5, 1992. See also UN Economic and Social Council, Commission on Human Rights, E/CN.4/Sub.2/1992/34, 23 June 1992. *DD,* ch. 7.

27. "Argentina uncovers patients killed for organs," *BMJ,* summer 1992; AFP, March 8, 1992, cited in *LANU,* April-May 1992; Pinero, *op. cit..* For additional reports from Latin America, see *DD,* 220-1. Colombia, also Reuters, *BG,* March 3, 5, 1992; Ruth Conniff, *Progressive,* May 1992, On the US role, see *DD,* ch. 4.5.

28. Scanlan, *MH,* May 28, 1991; *CT,* 243.

29. US-Costa Rica, ch. 3, n. 20. My "Letter from Lexington," *Lies of our Times,* Jan. 1992.

30. Tim Johnson, *MH,* June 14, 1992; Inter Press Service (IPS), July 31, 1992; Gibb, *SFC,* June 17, 1992 (*CAN*).

31. *Science,* Dec. 20, 1991; *Economist,* Jan. 4, 1992.

32. *CAR,* June 14; Aug. 16, 1991; Aug. 21, 1992. IPS, San José, Feb. 23; *Excelsior,* July 31, 1992 (*CAN*).

33. *CAR,* Oct. 18, 1991; Reuters, *SFC,* Aug. 1, 1992 (*CAN*).

34. *Envío* (Managua), April 1991. Madhura Swaminathan and V.K. Ramachandran, *Frontline* (India), Dec. 6, 1991. See Herman, *Real Terror Network,* ch. 3, on the pre-1980 version.

35. Ch. 4.2. See *DD,* ch. 1, n. 19; ch. 7.7. Also Bello and Rosenfeld, *Dragons.*

36. Hockstader, *WP,* June 20, 1990; Crossette, *NYT,* Jan. 18; Tim Golden, *NYT,* Jan 17; Friedman, *NYT,* Jan. 12, 1992. Aid-torture, p. 120. Zwick, *Twain,* 111.

37. Skidmore, Evans, Felix, *op. cit.* Hagopian, review of Skidmore, *Politics, Fletcher Forum,* Summer 1989. Chile, Herman, *Real Terror Network,* 189f. (citing Harberger interview, Norman Gall, *Forbes,* March 31, 1980).

38. James Petras and Steve Vieux, "Myths and Realities: Latin America's Free Markets," *Monthly Review,* May 1992; update, ms, SUNY Binghamton. CIIR, *Brazil.* Brooke, *NYT,* Aug. 28, 1992.

39. James Markham, *NYT Week in Review,* Sept. 25, 1988; Wrong, *Dissent,* Spring 1989. Roberts, "Democracy and World Order," *Fletcher Forum,* Summer 1991.

40. Simpson, *Spectator,* March 21, 1992; Petras and Pozzi, *Against the Current,* March/April 1992; Felix, "Reflections on Privatizing and Rolling Back the Latin American State," ms., Washington University, July 1991.

41. David Clark Scott, *CSM,* July 30, 1992; Salvador Corro, *Proceso* (Mexico), Nov. 18, 1991 (*LANU,* Jan. 1992); UN Report on the Environment, AP, May 7, 1992; La Botz, *Mask,* 165, 158; Andrew Reding and Christopher Whalen, *Fragile Stability,* Mexico Project, World Policy Institute, 1991. Barkin, *Report on the Americas* (NACLA), May 1991; "Salinastroika," ms., Aug. 1992. Baker, *WP,* Sept. 10, 1991, cited by Reding and Whalen.

42. Nash, *NYT,* Nov. 13, 1991; Aug. 1, 1992. Kamm, *WSJ,* April 16, 1992.

43. Felix, "Financial Blowups"; "Reflections on Privatizing"; "Latin American Monetarism in Crisis," in *'Monetarism' and the Third World,* Institute of Development Studies, Sussex, 1981. Data compiled by Chilean economist Patricio Meller; UN ECLA Poverty Study (Santiago, 1990) (Felix, p.c.). Petras and Vieux, "Myths and Realities." *Economist Intelligence Unit* cited by Doug Henwood, *Left Business Observer,* no. 50, July 7, 1992. Collins and Lear, "Pinochet's Giveaway," *Multinational Monitor,* May 1991. Rosenberg, *Dissent,* Summer 1989. Herman, letter, *Washington Report on the Hemisphere,* June 3, 1992. Nash, *NYT,* July 6, 1992.

44. Mayorga, *Nicaraguan Economic Experience.* See *DD* for further discussion.

45. Constable, *BG,* March 4 (see p. 150); Golden, *MH,* March 5; wire services, *Excelsior,* March 12, 1992 (*CAN*). *CAR,* July 31, 1992.

46. *CAR,* Oct. 18, 1991; May 8, 1992; Otis, *SFC,* Aug. 1, 1992.

47. *Links* (National Central America Health Rights Network), Summer 1992; *CEPAD Report,* Jan.-Feb. 1992; *Excelsior,* June 11, 1992 *(CAN);* Haugaard, CAHI, Georgetown University; IPS, Aug. 9, 1992 *(CAN).*

48. For more on the matter, see *TTT,* ch. 3.9; *DD,* ch. 10.

49. Petras and Vieux, "Myths and Realities." Cooper, *New Statesman & Society* (London), Aug. 7, 1992. On US-IMF programs in the Caribbean, see Deere, *In the Shadows;* McAfee, *Storm Signals.* For an ongoing record on Central America, see *PEHR, TNCW, TT, COT, NI, DD,* and sources cited.

Notes to Chapter 8

1. Lowenthal, *Reviews in Anthropology,* 1976, cited in Farmer, *AIDS and Accusation,* the source for much of which follows along with Schmidt, *US Occupation.* The classic account of the revolution is C.L.R. James, *The Black Jacobins.* The high population estimates are from Sherburne Cook and Woodrow Borah, *Essays in Population History: Mexico and the Caribbean* (California, 1971) (see Farmer, Stannard, *American Holocaust*).

2. Sued-Badillo, *Monthly Review,* July/August 1992. COHA press release, Feb. 18; Anne-Marie O'Connor, Cox News Service, April 12, 1992. On the IMF programs, see McAfee, *Storm Signals; DD,* 7.3.

3. Farmer, *AIDS,* 153; Las Casas, passages in Chicago Religious Task Force, *Dangerous Memories,* Stannard, *American Holocaust,* Sale, *Conquest.* See also Koning, *Columbus.* Smith, *Wealth,* Bk. IV, Ch. VII, Pt. I (ii, 70).

4. Ch. 1, n. 29. Sterilization, Churchill biographer Clive Ponting, *Sunday Age* (Australia), June 21, 1992. Racism-policymakers, *DD,* 52-3.

5. *TTT,* 46. Stivers, *Supremacy,* 66-73.

6. Ulysses B. Weatherly, "Haiti: an Experiment in Pragmatism," 1926, cited by Schmidt.

7. Trouillot, cited by Farmer, *AIDS*. Blassingame, *Caribbean Studies,* July 1969. *Times* editorials, *DD,* 280. Landes, *NR,* March 10; Ryan, *CSM,* Feb. 14, 1986. For more on these and other scholarly analyses, see *PI,* 68-9, *TTT,* 153f.

8. Deere, *Shadows,* 144, 35, 174-5 (excerpt from Josh DeWind and David Kinley, *Aiding Migration* [Westview, 1988]). McAfee, 17; *PI,* 68; Wilentz, *Rainy Season,* 272ff. Refugees, *PEHR,* II 50, 56 (1970s); Wilentz, *NR,* March 9; Bill Frelick, NACLA *Report on the Americas,* July 1992; Pamela Constable, *BG,* Aug. 21, 1992.

9. *PI,* 69f.; *WSJ,* Feb. 10, 1986. *NR,* p. 194, above.

10. Wilentz, *Rainy Season,* 341, 55, 326, 358. Wilentz gives a vivid eyewitness account of the years 1986-89.

11. COHA, "Sun Setting on Hopes for Haitian Democracy," Jan. 6, 1992.

12. *The NED Backgrounder,* Inter-Hemispheric Education Resource Center (Albuquerque), April 1992.

13. Wilentz, *Reconstruction,* vol. 1.4 (1992).

14. Wilentz, *Rainy Season,* 275.

15. Americas Watch, National Coalition for Haitian Refugees, and Physicians for Human Rights, "Return to the Darkest Days," Dec. 30, 1991. Roth, "Haiti: the Shadows of Terror," *NYRB,* March 26, 1992.

16. Friedman, French, *NYT,* Oct. 8, 1991. French, *NYT,* Oct. 22, 1991; Jan. 12, 1992. Canute James, *FT,* March 10, 1992.

17. Hyland, "The Case for Pragmatism," *Foreign Affairs, America and the World,* 1991-92. Constable, *BG,* March 13, 1992.

18. Americas Watch, "Return." French, *NYT,* Oct. 10, 1991. *Time,* Feb. 10; *FT,* April 3, 1992. Bush-Kuwait, Andrew Rosenthal, *NYT,* April 3, 1991.

19. Greenberger, *WSJ,* Jan. 13, 1992. COHA press release, Feb. 5, 1992.

20. *Time,* Feb. 10; Barbara Crossette, *NYT,* May 28; Lee Hockstader, *WP weekly,* Feb. 17; editorial, *WP weekly,* Feb. 10, 1992.

21. Frelick, *op. cit.;* Lee Hockstader, *WP weekly,* Feb. 10; Barbara Crossette, French, *NYT,* May 28, 1992.

22. Hockstader, *WP weekly,* Feb. 10; *WP-MG,* Feb. 16, 1992.

23. *DD,* chs. 8, 10; *NI,* 61-6; Sklar, *War.*

24. COHA press release, Jan. 10, Feb. 25, 1992. Barbara Crossette, *NYT,* Feb. 26; French, *NYT,* Feb. 27, June 21; James Slavin, *NCR,* Aug. 14, 1992.

25. French, *NYT,* Sept. 27, 1992.

26. Barbara Crossette, *NYT,* Feb. 5, 1992.

27. French, *NYT,* Feb. 7, my emphasis; Pierre-Yves Glass, AP, *Anchorage Times,* Feb. 17; *Time,* Feb. 17, 1992.

Notes to Chapter 9

1. Schmidt, *US Occupation,* 16, 181.

2. Wilentz, *Rainy Season,* 271-2.

3. Farmer, *AIDS,* 37ff

4. Allen, *Birth Symbol*.
5. Thomasson, *Cultural Survival Quarterly*, Summer 1991.
6. Cited by Schmidt, *US Occupation*, 62-3.
7. Schwarz, *American Counterinsurgency Doctrine. FRS*, 246; *APNM*, ch. 1.
8. David Holstrom, *CSM*, April 30, 1992. McChesney, *Labor*.
9. Du Boff, *Accumulation*, 101-3.
10. Hegel, *Philosophy*, 82. Schmidt, *US Occupation*, 158.
11. Holt, *Problem*, 45, 71ff., 54f.
12. A. Chomsky, *Plantation Society*.
13. De Schweinitz, *Rise and Fall*, 165; Keay, *Honorable Company*, 435f., 454f. M.N. Pearson, Parker, in Tracy, *Merchant Empires. DD*, ch. 4; ch. 2.4, above.
14. Jackson, *Century*. Wilkins, *Cherokee Tragedy*, 3, 4, 287. Peace treaty, Stannard, *American Holocaust*, 106. Andrew Jackson, Rogin, *Fathers*, 215f. On estimates of the toll, see Lenore Stiffarm with Phil Lane, "The Demography of Native North America," in Jaimes, *State*.
15. Jackson, *Century*.
16. For details, see my "Divine License to Kill," discussing works by and on Niebuhr, published in large part in *Grand Street*, Winter 1987.
17. Krause, *Battle*, 82-3.
18. Palmer, *BG*, Feb. 9; Pear, *NYT*, Aug. 12, 1992. Data from Nancy Watzman, *Multinational Monitor*, May 1992.

Notes to Chapter 10

1. Frederick Starr, *NYT Book Review*, July 19, 1992.
2. *WP-BG*, Dec. 4; Weisman, *NYT*, Dec. 6, 1991. On the August 14 bombings, see *APNM*, ch. 2, including an excerpt from the Air Force history and from Japanese novelist Makoto Oda's eyewitness report from Osaka. On Tokyo as target, see Barton Bernstein, *International Security*, Spring 1991.
3. AP, *NYT*, March 4, 5, 1992. Longer stories in the *Boston Globe*, same days.
4. See *PEHR*, II 32f., 39. On the principles of justice employed, see also *FRS*, ch. 3, reprinted from a *Yale Law Review* symposium on Nuremberg and Vietnam. For excerpts from Pal's dissent, see *APNM*. See Minnear, *Victor's Justice*. Leahy, cited by Braw, *Atomic Bomb*, from his 1950 autobiography, *I Was There*.
5. Japan historian Herbert Bix, *BG*, April 19, 1992.
6. *APNM*, ch. 2, for further material and sources.
7. *Ibid.*, for excerpts.
8. See *TTT*, 194f.; Simpson, *Blowback;* Reese, *Gehlen*.
9. McClintock, *Instruments*, 59ff., 230ff. Lewy, *America in Vietnam*. For discussion of this parody of history, see the review by Chomsky and Edward Herman, reprinted in *TNCW*. For Lewy's thoughts on how to eliminate the plague of independent thought on the home front, see *NI*, 350f.
10. Bernard Fall, *Ramparts*, Dec. 1965, reprinted in *Last Reflections*. For a postwar eyewitness description, see John Pilger, *New Statesman*, Sept. 15, 1978. Shenon, *NYT magazine*, Jan. 5, 1992.

11. Dower, "Remembering (and Forgetting) War," ms, MIT.
12. Hietala, *Manifest Design*, 61; Kent, *Hawaii*, 41f. Daws, *Shoal of Time*, 241. Poka Laenui, "The Theft of the Hawaiian Nation," *Indigenous Thought*, Oct. 1991. See pp. 17-18, 38, above; *DD*, ch. 12.
13. Kent, Daws, Laenui, *op. cit.*
14. Institute for the Advancement of Hawaiian Affairs, 86-649 Puuhulu Rd., Wai'anae Hawaii 96792.
15. Lehner, *WSJ*, Dec. 6, 1991.
16. Weisman, *NYT magazine*, Nov. 3, 1991.
17. On Fairbank's views, see *TNCW*, 400-1.
18. *DD*, ch. 11, and sources cited. Kennan, cited in Cumings, *Origins*, II, 57; see volumes I, II on the mass murder campaign in US-occupied Korea prior to what is called "the Korean war."
19. Sherwood Fine, quoted by Moore, *Japanese Workers*, p. 18; Moore, on the general topic. Bix, "The Showa Emperor's 'Monologue' and the Problem of War Responsibility," *J. of Japanese Studies*, 18.2, 1992 (citing John Dower, *Japan Times*, Jan. 9, 1989).
20. Cumings, *Origins*, II, 57.
21. Adlai Stevenson, defending the US war at the UN. See *FRS*, p. 114f.
22. Fall, *Last Reflections*.
23. Elizabeth Neuffer, *BG*, Feb. 27; Pamela Constable, *BG*, Feb. 21, 1992. Carter, news conference, March 24, 1977; see *MC*, 240.
24. *Ibid.*, 240ff. and *NI*, 33ff., for samples from the press. *NYT*, Oct. 24, 1992.
25. Tyler, *NYT*, July 5, 1992.
26. Crossette, *NYT*, Jan. 6, 1992. Mary Kay Magistad, *BG*, Oct. 20; Eric Schmitt, *NYT*, Nov. 6; Steven Greenhouse, *NYT*, Oct. 24, 1991.
27. Barbara Crossette, *NYT*, Aug. 14, 1992.
28. See ch. 5, n. 18. On media coverage of Pol Pot and Timor atrocities, see *PEHR*. On the illuminating reaction to these exposures, see *MC*, 6.2.8; *NI*, app. I. sec 1.
29. Greenhouse, *NYT*, Oct. 24, 1991.
30. See *MC*, 6.2.7, and sources cited. Garthoff, *Détente*, 701, 751. Sihanouk cited by Ben Kiernan, *Broadside* (Sydney, Australia), June 3, 1992; Allman, *Vanity Fair*, April 1990, cited by Michael Vickery, "Cambodia After the 'Peace'" (ch. 7, n. 24). For a review and update, see Kiernan, "Cambodia's Missed Chance: Superpower obstruction of a viable path to peace," *Indochina Newsletter*, Nov.-Dec. 1991, citing *FEER*. See also Kiernan, *Bulletin of Concerned Asian Scholars*, Vol. 21, 2-4, 1989; Vol. 24, 2, 1992. For extensive background, see Vickery, *Cambodia*, and Chandler, *Cambodia*.
31. Greenway, *BG*, Dec. 13; Uli Schmetzer, *CT*, Sept. 2, 1991. Susumu Awanohara, *FEER*, April 30, 1992.
32. Editorial, *WP weekly*, Dec. 2-8, 1991.
33. Barbara Crossette, *NYT*, March 31, 1992.
34. Greenway, *BG*, Dec. 20, 1991.
35. AP, March 14, 1990; *NI*, 35.
36. John Stockhouse, *G&M*, June 12, 1992.
37. Smucker, *G&M*, Oct. 7, 1991.

38. Barbara Crossette, *NYT,* Aug. 18, 1992.

39. See *NI,* 38-9, citing Israeli journalist Amnon Kapeliouk and US researcher Dr. Grace Ziem.

40. Braw, *Atomic Bomb.*

41. Robert Olen Butler, *WP-MG,* April 5; Wintle, *FT,* May 16-17, 1992; reviews of Michael Bilton and Kevin Sim, *Four Hours in My Lai.* AP, "Five years later, My Lai is a no man's town, silent and unsafe," *NYT,* March 16, 1973.

42. Butterfield, *NYT,* May 1, 1977; Whitney, *NYT,* April 1, 1973.

43. Buckley's unpublished notes. See *PEHR,* I, sec. 5.1.3.

44. *Ibid.; FRS,* 222. King, *The Death of the Army* (1972), cited by Kinnard, *War Managers.*

45. John Underhill, John Mason, and William Bradford. See Laurence Hauptman, in Hauptman and Wherry, *Pequots;* Salisbury, *Manitou,* 218ff. See Jennings, *Invasion,* for discussion and general background.

46. Robert Venables, "The Cost of Columbus: Was There a Holocaust?," *View from the Shore, Northeast Indian Quarterly* (Cornell, Fall 1990). Rio Sumpul, see *TNCW.*

47. For details, see *AWWA,* 102-3.

48. Carr, *NYT Book Review,* March 22, 1992. Of some interest, perhaps, is Carr's response to the comments above, which had appeared (in essence) in *Lies of Our Times,* May 1992. In toto: "The notion that there have been, in American history, episodes in which *neither* side behaved like much more than bloodthirsty animals is apparently too morally complex for many to bear" (Letters, *NYT Book Review,* Aug. 23, 1992, inserted irrelevantly into a response to criticism on totally different matters). I leave it to the reader to construct the Nazi analogue.

49. Regular *Times* reviewer Michio Kakutani, *NYT,* Aug. 28; Prescott, *NYT Book Review,* Sept. 20, 1992; reviews of Jay Parini, *Bay of Arrows.* On the cannibalism mythology that so enthralls Western ideologists, see Sale, *Conquest.* Ethnohistorian Jalil Sued-Badillo writes that "Archeological studies have not to this day been able to confirm cannibal practices anywhere in America"; *Monthly Review,* July-Aug. 1992. For a second-hand report of ritual cannibalism in North America, see Axtell, *Invasion,* 263; for Indian reports, Jennings, *Empire,* 446-7.

50. Wouk, *CT,* June 2, 1992. Franklin, *MIA.*

51. Puette, *Through Jaundiced Eyes,* ch. 7.

52. For discussion of these examples, see *TNCW,* 68f., 89f. *MC,* secs. 5.1, 5.5.2, App. 3. *NI,* App. I, sec. 2. Lederman, *Battle Lines;* see my "Letter from Lexington," *Lies of Our Times,* Sept. 1992, for details.

53. Bundy, *Foreign Affairs,* Jan. 1967. See *MC,* 175.

54. On these enlightening and therefore intolerable comparisons, see *PEHR,* vols. I, II; *MC.*

55. Vickery, *Cambodia After the 'Peace'.* On the internal US documents, see *FRS,* 31f., 36f.

56. Drèze and Gazdar, *Hunger and Poverty.*

57. See note 32. On the belief that the US "lost the war," and its significance, see *MC,* 241ff.; and below.

58. E.g., Douglas Pike. For sources and discussion, see *MC*, 180f.; *PEHR*, vol. I, 338f. See *RC*, ch. 2.3.
59. *Foreign Relations of the United States*, Vietnam, 1961-1963, I, 343; III, 4n. Gibbons, *US Government*, 70-1, citing Air Force history.
60. Albert, *Z magazine*, Dec., 1991; Cockburn, *LAT*, Dec. 5; *Nation*, Dec. 23, 1991.
61. See ch. 2.1-2. Tonkin Gulf, *MC*, 5.5.1; and *RC*. On timing, see *Foreign Relations of the United States*, Vietnam, 1964-1968, 609.
62. One speculation is that in Vietnam, Kennedy might have leaned towards an enclave strategy of the type advocated by General Maxwell Taylor and others or a Nixonian modification with intensified bombing and murderous "accelerated pacification" but many fewer US ground combat forces; while at home, he might not have proceeded so vigorously with Johnson's "Great Society" programs.
63. See my article "Vain Hopes, False Dreams," *Z magazine*, October 1992, and for a much more extensive review and discussion, see *Rethinking Camelot*. Sources already cited, and others in the dissident literature, gave a generally accurate picture as events proceeded, requiring little modification in the light of what is now known. For a summary, see *MC*.
64. On the remarkable complicity of the intellectual community in suppressing the readily-available facts about US subversion of diplomacy, see *TNCW*, ch. 3; *MC*, ch. 5.5.3. The full story of this suppression—in some cases, deliberate—has yet to be told.
65. On this prospect, see *AWWA*, 286.

Notes to Chapter 11

1. Pp. 17, 65.
2. T-Bone Slim, *Juice*, 68.
3. *Economist*, Aug. 22, 1992.
4. Brady, *Spirit*, ch. VI; Schoenbaum, *Hitler's Social Revolution*, ch. VI. Thompson, *Making*, ch. 11.
5. Steven Greenhouse, *NYT*, "Income Data Show Years of Erosion for U.S. Workers," *NYT*, Sept. 7; Adam Pertman, *BG*, July 15; Garry Wills, *NYRB*, Sept. 24, 1992. On the extraordinary efforts of government and right-wing analysts to conceal and distort the economic facts, see Paul Krugman, "The Right, the Rich, and the Facts," *American Prospects*, Fall 1992.
6. John Dillin, *CSM*, July 14, 1992.
7. AP, *BG*, April 4, 1991. *NEJ. of Med.*, Jan. 1990, cited by Melvin Konner, *NYT*, Feb. 24, 1990.
8. See ch. 4.3. Conniff, *Progressive*, Sept. 1992, reviewing Kaus, *End of Equality*. Stephen Franklin, Peter Kendall and Colin McMahon, "Caterpillar strikers face the bitter truth," pt. 3 of series, *CT*, Sept. 6, 7, 9, 1992. Fraser cited in Moody, *Injury*, 147.
9. Milton, *Politics*, 155; Puette, *Through Jaundiced Eyes*.
10. Franklin, et al., *op. cit.*; RR lockout, Alexander Cockburn, *LAT*, July 13; Robert Rose, *WSJ*, April 20, 1992. Hoerr, *American Prospect*, Summer 1992.

11. Floyd Norris, *NYT*, Aug. 30, 1992.
12. Peter Gosselin, *BG*, Sept. 7; Frank Swoboda, *WP weekly*, Sept. 14-20, 1992. Shlomo Maital and Kim Morgan, *Challenge*, July 1992. Wolfe, *BG*, Feb. 18, 1990.
13. Diego Ribadeneira and Cheong Chow, *BG*, Sept. 8; Ribadeneira, *BG*, Sept. 25, 1992.
14. See Alex Carey, "Managing Public Opinion: The Corporate Offensive," ms., U. of New South Wales, 1986; Milton, Moody, *op. cit.*, Sexton, *War*. Also Ginger and Christiano, *Cold War*.
15. Sexton, *War*, 76, 55.
16. Demarest, *"River,"* 44, 55, 216. Krause, *Battle*, 287, 13, 294, 205ff. 152, 178, 253, 486 (quoting Gutman interview).
17. Demarest, *"River,"* 32; Krause, *Battle*, 361, 274ff. Hagan, *People's Navy*.
18. Demarest, *"River,"* 159; Sexton, *War*, 83, 106ff.
19. Demarest, *"River,"* 199, 210f.; Krause, ch. 22.
20. Bekken, in Solomon and McChesney, *New Perspectives*. McChesney, *Labor*. England, see *MC*, ch. 1.1-2.
21. Demarest, *"River,"* Afterword.
22. *Ibid.*; Sexton, *War*, 87.

Bibliography

Agee, Philip. *Inside the Company* (Stonehill, 1975)

Allen, Max. *The Birth Symbol in Traditional Women's Art* (Museum of Textiles, Toronto, 1981)

Americas Watch. *The 'Drug War' in Colombia* (October 1990)

—*The Struggle for Land in Brazil* (Human Rights Watch, 1992)

Amsden, Alice. *Asia's Next Giant: South Korea and Late Industrialization* (Oxford, 1989)

Anti-Slavery Society. *West Papua* (London, 1990)

Appleby, Joyce. *Capitalism and a New Social Order* (NYU, 1984)

Asia Watch. *Human Rights in Korea* (Jan. 1986)

Aston, T.H., and C.H.E. Philpin. *The Brenner Debate: Agrarian Class Structure and Economic Development in Pre-Industrial Europe* (Cambridge, 1985)

Axtell, James. *The Invasion Within* (Oxford, 1985)

Bailey, Thomas. *A Diplomatic History of the American People* (New York, 1969)

Ball, George. *The Past has another Pattern* (Norton, 1982)

Bello, Walden, and Stephanie Rosenfeld. *Dragons in Distress* (Institute for Food and Development Policy, 1990)

Benjamin, Jules. *The United States and the Origins of the Cuban Revolution* (Princeton, 1990)

Bernal, Martin. *Black Athena* (Rutgers, 1987)

Bhagwati, Jagdish, and Hugh Patrick, eds. *Aggressive Unilateralism* (Michigan, 1990)

Black, Jan Knippers. *United States Penetration of Brazil* (Pennsylvania, 1977)

Blum, William. *The CIA: a forgotten history* (Zed, 1986)

Borden, William. *The Pacific Alliance* (Wisconsin, 1984)

Bovard, James. *Fair Trade Fraud* (St. Martin's, 1991)

Brady, Robert. *The Spirit and Structure of German Fascism* (Viking, 1937)

—*Business as a System of Power* (Columbia, 1943)

Braw, Monica. *The Atomic Bomb Suppressed: American Censorship in Japan* (M.E. Sharpe, 1991)

Brewer, John. *Sinews of Power: War, Money and the English State, 1688-1783* (Knopf, 1989)

Caldwell, Malcolm, ed. *Ten Years Military Terror in Indonesia* (Spokesman, 1975)

Calleo, David. *The Imperious Economy* (Harvard, 1982)

Catholic Institute of International Relations (CIIR). *Brazil: Democracy and Development* (London, 1992)

Chandler, David. *The Tragedy of Cambodian History* (Yale, 1992)

Chicago Religious Task Force on Central America. *Dangerous Memories: Invasion and Resistance since 1492* (Chicago, 1991)

Chomsky, Aviva. *Plantation Society, Land and Labor in Costa Rica's Atlantic Coast, 1870-1940* (PhD dissertation, UC Berkeley, 1990)

Chomsky, Noam. *American Power and the New Mandarins* (Pantheon, 1969) [*APNM*]

—*At War with Asia* (Pantheon, 1970) [*AWWA*]

—*For Reasons of State* (Pantheon, 1973) [*FRS*]

—Towards a New Cold War (Pantheon, 1982) [*TNCW*]

—Fateful Triangle (South End, 1983) [*FT*]

—Turning the Tide (South End, 1985) [*TTT*]

—Pirates and Emperors (Claremont, Black Rose, 1986; Amana, 1988) [*P&E*]

—On Power and Ideology (South End, 1986) [*PI*]

—Culture of Terrorism (South End, 1988) [*CT*]

—Necessary Illusions (South End, 1989) [*NI*]

—Deterring Democracy (Verso, 1990; updated edition, Hill & Wang, 1991) [*DD*]

—*Rethinking Camelot,* (South End Press, 1993) [*RC*]

—, and Edward Herman. *Political Economy of Human Rights* (South End, 1979) [*PEHR*]

—, and Howard Zinn, eds. *Pentagon Papers,* vol. 5, Analytic Essays and Index (Beacon, 1972) [*PPV*]

Clairmonte, Frederick. *Economic Liberalism and Underdevelopment* (Asia Publishing House, 1960)

Cooper, Chester. *The Lost Crusade* (Dodd, Mead, 1970)

Cumings, Bruce. *The Origins of the Korean War,* vol. II (Princeton, 1990)

Daws, Gavan, *Shoal of Time* (Macmillan, 1968)

Debo, Angie. *And Still the Waters Run* (1940; Princeton, 1991, updated)

Deere, Carmen Diana, et al. *In the Shadows of the Sun* (Westview, 1990)

Demarest, David, ed. *"The River Ran Red": Homestead 1892* (Pittsburgh, 1992)

Dertouzos, Michael, Richard Lester, and Robert Solow. *Made in America* (MIT, 1989)

Dimerstein, Gilberto. *Brazil: War on Children* (Latin America Bureau, London, 1991)

Drèze, Jean, and Haris Gazdar. *Hunger and Poverty in Iraq, 1991* (Development Economics Research Programme, London School of Economics, No. 32, Sept. 1991)

Drinnon, Richard. *White Savage: the Case of John Dunn Hunter* (Schocken, 1972)

—*Facing West* (Minnesota, 1980)

Du Boff, Richard. *Accumulation and Power* (M.E. Sharpe, 1989)

Evans, Peter. *Dependent Development* (Princeton, 1979)

Fall, Bernard. *Last Reflections on a War* (Doubleday, 1967)

Farmer, Paul. *AIDS and Accusation: Haiti and the Geography of Blame* (California, 1992)

Feffer, John. *Shock Waves: Eastern Europe After the Revolution* (South End, 1992)

Fitzgerald, Tom. *Between Life and Economics* (1990 Boyer lectures of the Australian Broadcasting Company, ABC, 1990)

Franklin, Bruce. *M.I.A., or Mythmaking in America* (Lawrence Hill, 1992)

Gaddis, John Lewis. *Strategies of Containment* (Oxford, 1982)

—*The Long Peace* (Oxford, 1987)

Garthoff, Raymond. *Détente and Confrontation* (Brookings, 1985)

—*Reflections on the Cuban Missile Crisis* (Brookings, 1987)

George, Alexander, ed. *Western State Terrorism* (Polity, 1991)

Gerschenkron, Alexander. *Economic Backwardness in Historical Perspective* (Harvard, 1962)

Ginger, Ann Fagan, and David Christiano, eds. *The Cold War Against Labor* (Meiklejohn Civil Liberties Institute, 1987), two vols.

Gleijeses, Piero. *Shattered Hope* (Princeton, 1991)

Green, David. *The Containment of Latin America* (Quadrangle, 1971)

Greider, William. *Secrets of the Temple* (Simon & Schuster, 1987)

Hagan, Kenneth. *This People's Navy* (Free Press, 1991)

Haines, Gerald. *The Americanization of Brazil* (Scholarly Resources, 1989)

Hartmann, Betsy, and James Boyce. *A Quiet Violence: View from a Bangladesh Village* (Zed, 1983)

Hassett, John, & Hugh Lacey, eds. *Towards a Society that Serves its People: The Intellectual Contributions of El Salvador's Murdered Jesuits* (Georgetown, 1991)

Hauptman, Laurence, and James Wherry, eds. *The Pequots in Southern New England* (Oklahoma, 1990)

Hecht, Susanna, and Alexander Cockburn. *The Fate of the Forest* (Verso, 1989)

Hegel, Georg Wilhelm Friedrich. *The Philosophy of History* (Dover, 1956; Lectures of 1830-31)

Herman, Edward. *The Real Terror Network* (South End, 1982)

—*Beyond Hypocrisy: Decoding the News in an Age of Propaganda* (South End, 1992)

—, and Frank Brodhead. *Demonstration Elections* (South End, 1984)

—, and Noam Chomsky. *Manufacturing Consent* (Pantheon, 1988) [*MC*]

Hewlett, Sylvia Ann, The Cruel Dilemmas of Development (Basic Books, 1980)

Hietala, Thomas. *Manifest Design* (Cornell, 1985)

Higginbotham, Leon. *In the Matter of Color* (Oxford, 1978)

Hill, Christopher. *A Nation of Change & Novelty* (Routledge & Kegan Paul, 1990)

Höfer, Bruni, Heinz Dieterich, and Klaus Meyer, eds., *Das Fünfhundert-jährige Reich* (Médico International, 1990)

Hogan, Michael. *The Marshall Plan* (Cambridge, 1987)

Holt, Thomas. *The Problem of Freedom* (Johns Hopkins, 1992)

Horsman, Reginald. *Race and Manifest Destiny* (Harvard, 1981)

Jackson, Helen. *A Century of Dishonor* (1880; reprinted in limited edition by Ross & Haines, Minneapolis, 1964)

Jaimes, Annette, ed. *The State of Native America* (South End, 1992)

—, and Andrew Lownie, eds. *North American Spies* (Edinburgh, 1992)

Jennings, Francis. *The Invasion of America* (North Carolina, 1975)
—*Empire of Fortune* (Norton, 1988)
Jonas, Susanne. *The Battle for Guatemala* (Westview, 1991)
Keay, John. *The Honorable Company: A History of the English East India Company* (HarperCollins, 1991)
Kent, Noel. *Hawaii* (Monthly Review, 1983)
Khor Kok Peng, Martin. *The Uruguay Round and Third World Sovereignty* (Third World Network, Penang, 1990)
Kiernan, V. G. *European Empires from Conquest to Collapse* (Fontana, 1982)
Kimball, Warren. *The Juggler* (Princeton, 1991)
Kinnard, Douglas. *The War Managers* (University Press of New England, 1977)
Kissinger, Henry. *American Foreign Policy* (Norton, 1974; expanded edition)
Kolko, Gabriel. *The Politics of War* (Random House, 1968)
—*Confronting the Third World* (Pantheon, 1988)
Koning, Hans. *Columbus: His Enterprise* (Monthly Review, 1976)
Krause, Paul. *The Battle for Homestead, 1880-1892* (Pittsburgh, 1992)
Krenn, Michael. *U.S. Policy toward Economic Nationalism in Latin America, 1917-1929* (Scholarly Resources, 1990)
La Botz, Dan. *Mask of Democracy: Labor Suppression in Mexico Today* (South End, 1992)
LaFeber, Walter. *Inevitable Revolutions* (Norton, 1983)
Landes, David. *The Unbound Prometheus* (Cambridge, 1969)
Lazonick, William. *Business Organization and the Myth of the Market Economy* (Cambridge, 1991)
Leacock, Ruth. *Requiem for Revolution* (Kent State, 1990)
Lederman, Jim. *Battle Lines* (Holt, 1992)
Leffler, Melvyn. *A Preponderance of Power* (Stanford, 1992)
Lewy, Guenter. *America in Vietnam* (Oxford, 1978)
Lobel, Jules, ed. *A Less than Perfect Union* (Monthly Review, 1988)
Maguire, Andrew, and Janet W. Brown, eds. *Bordering on Trouble* (Adler & Adler, 1986)
Mannix, Daniel, and Malcolm Cowley. *Black Cargoes* (Viking, 1962)
Marshall, John, Peter Dale Scott, and Jane Hunter. *The Iran-Contra Connection* (South End, 1987)
Mayorga, Francisco. *The Nicaraguan Economic Experience, 1950-1984: Development and exhaustion of an agroindustrial model* (PhD dissertation, Yale, 1986)
McAfee, Kathy. *Storm Signals* (South End, 1991)
McClintock, Michael. *Instruments of Statecraft* (Pantheon, 1992)
McCoy, Alfred. *The Politics of Heroin* (Lawrence Hill, 1991; revision of 1972 edition)
Merkl, Peter, ed. *The Federal Republic of German at Forty* (NYU press, 1989)
Miller, Nathan. *The Founding Finaglers* (McKay, 1976)
Milton, David. *The Politics of U.S. Labor* (Monthly Review, 1982)
Minnear, Richard. *Victor's Justice* (Princeton, 1971)
Monbiot, George. *Poisoned Arrows* (Abacus, London, 1989)
Moody, Kim. *An Injury to All* (Verso, 1988)

Moore, Joe. *Japanese Workers and the Struggle for Power, 1945-1947* (Wisconsin, 1983)

Morris, Richard. *The American Revolution Reconsidered* (Harper & Row, 1967)

—*The Forging of the Union* (Harper & Row, 1987)

Nehru, Jawaharlal. *The Discovery of India* (Asia Publishing House, 1961)

Omissi, David. *Air Power and Colonial Control* (Manchester, 1990)

Osborne, Robin. *Indonesia's Secret Wars* (Allen & Unwin, 1985)

Parker, Phyllis. *Brazil and the Quiet Intervention, 1964* (Texas, 1979)

Pastor, Robert. *Condemned to Repetition* (Princeton, 1987)

Paterson, Thomas, ed. *Kennedy's Quest for Victory* (Oxford, 1989)

Peck, James, ed. *The Chomsky Reader* (Pantheon, 1987)

Perkins, Dexter. *The Monroe Doctrine* (1927; reprinted by Peter Smith, 1965)

Peters, Cynthia, ed. *Collateral Damage* (South End, 1992)

Pisani, Sallie. *The CIA and the Marshall Plan* (Kansas, 1991)

Platt, Tony, ed. *Tropical Gulag* (Global Options, 1987)

Polanyi, Karl. *The Great Transformation* (Beacon, 1957)

Preston, William, Edward Herman, and Herbert Schiller. *Hope and Folly* (Minnesota, 1989)

Puette, William. *Through Jaundiced Eyes: How the Media View Organized Labor* (Cornell, 1992)

Rabe, Stephen. *The Road to OPEC* (Texas, 1982)

Raghavan, Chakravarthi. *Recolonization: GATT, the Uruguay Round & the Third World* (Third World Network, Penang, 1990)

Rand, Christopher. *Making Democracy Safe for Oil* (Little, Brown, 1975).

Reese, Mary Ellen. *General Reinhard Gehlen: the CIA Connection* (George Mason, 1990)

Robinson, William. *A Faustian Bargain* (Westview, 1992)

Rogin, Michael Paul. *Fathers and Children* (Random House, 1975)

Rotter, Andrew. *The Path to Vietnam* (Cornell, 1987)

Russell, Bertrand. *The Practice and Theory of Bolshevism* (Allen & Unwin, 1920)

Sale, Kirkpatrick. *The Conquest of Paradise* (Knopf, 1990)

Salisbury, Neil. *Manitou and Providence* (Oxford, 1982)

Salisbury, Richard. *Anti-Imperialism and International Competition in Central America, 1920-1929* (Scholarly Resources, 1989)

Saxton, Alexander. *The Rise and Fall of the White Republics* (Verso, 1990)

Schaller, Michael. *The American Occupation of Japan* (Oxford, 1985)

Schmidt, Hans. *The United States Occupation of Haiti, 1915-1934* (Rutgers, 1971)

Schweinitz, Karl de. *The Rise & Fall of British India* (Methuen, 1983)

Schoenbaum, David. *Hitler's Social Revolution* (Doubleday, 1966)

Schoultz, Lars. *Human Rights and United States Policy toward Latin America* (Princeton, 1981)

—*National Security and United States Policy toward Latin America* (Princeton, 1987)

Schwarz, Benjamin. *American Counterinsurgency Doctrine and El Salvador* (RAND, 1991)

Sexton, Patricia Cayo. *The War on Labor and the Left* (Westview, 1991)

Shanin, Teodor. *Russia as a 'Developing Society'* (Yale, 1985)

Simpson, Christopher. *Blowback* (Weidenfeld & Nicolson, 1988)

Skidmore, Thomas. *The Politics of Military Rule in Brazil* (Oxford, 1988)

Sklar, Holly. *Washington's War on Nicaragua* (South End, 1988)

Slim, T-Bone. *Juice is Stranger than Friction* (Kerr, 1992)

Smith, Adam. *The Wealth of Nations* (Chicago, 1976; first edition, 1776)

Smith, Joseph. *Unequal Giants* (Pittsburgh, 1991)

Smith, Stephen. *Industrial Policy in Developing Countries* (Economic Policy Institute, 1992)

Smith, Wayne. *The Closest of Enemies* (Norton, 1987)

Solomon, William, and Robert McChesney, eds. *New Perspectives in U.S. Communication History* (Minnesota, 1993)

South Commission. *The Challenge to the South* (Oxford, 1990)

Stannard, David. *American Holocaust* (Oxford, 1992)

Stavrianos, L. S. *Global Rift* (Morrow, 1981)

Stivers, William. *Supremacy and Oil* (Cornell, 1982)

—*America's Confrontation with Revolutionary Change in the Middle East* (St. Martin's, 1986)

Taylor, John. *Indonesia's Forgotten War: the Hidden History of East Timor* (Zed, 1991)

Taylor, Maxwell. *Swords and Plowshares* (Norton, 1972)

Thompson, E.P. *The Making of the English Working Class* (Vintage, 1963)

Todorov, Tzvetan. *The Conquest of America* (Harper & Row, 1985)

Tracy, James, ed. *The Political Economy of Merchant Empires* (Cambridge, 1991)

Van Alstyne, R.W. The Rising American Empire (Oxford 1960)

Vickery, Michael. *Cambodia: 1975-1982* (South End, 1984)

Wachtel, Howard. *The Money Mandarins* (M.E. Sharpe, 1990)

Washington Office on Latin America (WOLA). *Clear and Present Dangers: the U.S. Military and the War on Drugs in the Andes* (October 1991)

Watkins, Kevin. *Fixing the Rules* (Catholic Institute of International Relations, London, 1992)

Wilentz, Amy. *The Rainy Season* (Simon & Schuster, 1989)

Wilkins, Thurman. *Cherokee Tragedy* (Oklahoma, 1986)

Williams, Robert. *Export Agriculture and the Crisis in Central America* (North Carolina, 1986)

Wolpin, Miles. *Military Aid and Counterrevolution in the Third World* (Lexington Books, 1972)

Wood, Bryce. *The Dismantling of the Good Neighbor Policy* (Texas, 1985)

Yergin, Daniel. *The Prize* (Simon & Schuster, 1991)

Young, Alfred, ed. *The American Revolution* (Northern Illinois, 1976)

Zeman, Z.A.B. *The Making and Breaking of Communist Europe* (Blackwell, 1991)

Zwick, Jim, ed. *Mark Twain's Weapons of Satire: Anti-Imperialist Writings on the Philippine-American War* (Syracuse, 1992)

Index

A

Abrams, Elliott, 91, 208
Acheson, Dean, 44, 45, 72
Adams, John, 25
Adams, John Quincy, 24, 143, 228-29, 245
Advertising, 225, 226-27
Africa: economic decline of, 55; G-7 policy in, 30; U.S. policy in, 29, 30, 43. *See also* European conquest; Imperial powers' economic doctrines; Slavery; Third World; *specific countries*
African Americans. *See* Blacks; Racism; Slavery
Agee, Philip, 163
al-Ahram, 116
Albert, Michael, 271
Allen, Max, 223
Allende, Salvador, 36, 189-91
Allman, T.D., 255
Altgeld, John, 284
Amalgamated Association of Iron and Steel Workers (AAISW), 282-83
American Enterprise Institute, 112
Amsden, Alice, 101, 103
And Still the Waters Run (Debo), 231
Anderson, Roger, 63
Andrés Pérez, Carlos, 171
Andrews, Kenneth, 6
Angola, 29, 72, 92-93, 150
Appeal to Reason, 285-86
Arab League, 42-43
Arab-Israeli conflict, 38-39, 49, 135, 254, 267
Arafat, Yasser, 267
Arévalo, Juan José, 174
Argentina, 177, 187
Arias, Oscar, 179

Aristide, Jean-Bertrand, 197-98, 206, 208, 209-11, 213, 215, 216-17, 218
Arnold, General Henry (Hap), 161
Aronson, Bernard, 217
Arruda, José de A., 14-15
Asahi Shimbun, 127-28
Asia: economic growth in, 101-2; effects of European conquest on, 5, 8-9; Japanese aggression in, 239-40, 241-42, 243, 248; Japanese influence in, 55, 101, 240, 250; U.S. policy in, 35, 37, 40, 43, 240. *See also* Indochina; Third World; Vietnam War; *specific countries*
Asiaweek, 130
Asian Development Bank, 257
Austin, Stephen, 27
Australia, 55, 135-36, 152
Avril, Prosper, 209

B

Bailey, Thomas, 22
Baker, James, 105, 142, 189, 253
Balaguer, Joaquín, 198
Ball, George, 125
Bangladesh, 12, 62
Barbie, Klaus, 242
Baring, Sir Evelyn (Lord Cromer), 19
Barkin, David, 188, 189
Barruel, Father, 177
Bartel, Richard, 104
Batista, Fulgencio, 145
Bazin, Marc, 209, 210, 218
Beecher, Henry Ward, 285
Bekken, Jon, 285
Bemis, Samuel Flagg, 28

About South End Press

South End Press is a nonprofit, collectively run book publisher with more than 200 titles in print. Since our founding in 1977, we have tried to meet the needs of readers who are exploring, or are already committed to, the politics of radical social change. Our goal is to publish books that encourage critical thinking and constructive action on the key political, cultural, social, economic, and ecological issues shaping life in the United States and in the world. In this way, we hope to give expression to a wide diversity of democratic social movements and to provide an alternative to the products of corporate publishing.

Through the Institute for Social and Cultural Change, South End Press works with other political media projects—Z Magazine; Speakout, a speakers' bureau; and Alternative Radio—to expand access to information and critical analysis.

To order books, please send a check or money order to: South End Press, 7 Brookline Street, #1, Cambridge, MA 02139-4146. To order by credit card, call 1-800-533-8478. Please include $3.50 for postage and handling for the first book and 50 cents for each additional book. Write or e-mail southend@southendpress.org for a free catalog, or visit our web site: http://www.southendpress.org.

Related Titles

Rogue States: The Rule of Force in World Affairs
Noam Chomsky

Propaganda and the Public Mind: Conversations with Noam Chomsky
Noam Chomsky and David Barsamian

Fateful Triangle: The United States, Israel, and the Palestinians
South End Press Classics Edition
Noam Chomsky

Powers and Prospects: Reflections on Human Nature and the Social Order
Noam Chomksy

On Power and Ideology: The Managua Lectures
Noam Chomsky